DDC

Learning
WordPerfect 6.0
for IBM & Compatibles

IRIS BLANC

DDC *Publishing*

TABLE OF CONTENTS

a

b

INTRODUCTION

LEARNING WORDPERFECT 6.0 THROUGH APPLICATIONS AND EXERCISES will enable you to learn how to use WordPerfect, version 6.0 for DOS word processing software on an IBM PC or compatible computer. Each lesson this book will explain WordPerfect concepts, provide numerous exercises to apply those concepts, and illustrate the necessary keystrokes or mouse actions to complete the applications. Summary exercises are provided to challenge and reinforce the concepts you have learned. Proper formatting of various documents will be presented and reviewed.

After completing the 135 exercises in this book, you will be able to use WordPerfect 6.0 software with ease.

HOW TO USE THIS BOOK

Each exercise contains four parts:
- Notes - explain the WordPerfect concept being introduced.
- Exercise Directions - tell how to complete the exercise.
- Exercises - apply the concept that was introduced.
- Keystrokes/Mouse Procedures - outline the keys or mouse actions to use to complete the exercise.

The keystrokes and mouse actions are provided only when a new concept is introduced. Therefore, if you forget the keystroke/mouse procedures for completing a task, you can use the Help Feature, or you can use the book's keystroke index to refer you the page where the keystroke/mouse procedures are located. Many features in WordPerfect 6.0 (DOS) will look familiar to experienced WordPerfect users. For those users who are upgraders to 6.0 and are comfortable with keystrokes of previous versions 5.1, "Quick keys" will also be provided to make an easy transition to WordPerfect 6.0. In addition, Wordperfect 6.0 screens and icons are provided when necessary to clarify mouse actions or references to WordPerfect 6.0 screen areas.

To test your knowledge of the lesson concepts, you may complete the two summary exercises at the end of each lesson. Final versions of exercises can be found in the Teachers' Guide or on the data/solutions disk, which can be purchased from the Publisher. Because of the variety of printers that are available, your line and page endings may vary with the exercises illustrated throughout the book.

The following appendices are included:

Appendix A: WordPerfect Clipart Graphics and WP Special Characters
Appendix B: Proofreaders' Marks
Appendix C: QUICK REFERENCE to WordPerfect Keystrokes
Appendix D: Index of WordPerfect Functions

LOG OF EXERCISES

LESSON 1: INTRODUCTORY BASICS

1 —
2 —

LESSON 2: CREATING AND PRINTING DOCUMENTS

3 TRY
4 TRYAGAIN
5 DIVE
6 LETTER
7 GOODJOB
8 BLOCK
9 PERSONAL
10 TRYAGAIN, BLOCK, DIVE

SUMMARY A OPEN
SUMMARY B REGRETS

LESSON 3: EDITING DOCUMENTS

11 TRY
12 GOODJOB
13 TRYAGAIN
14 DIVE
15 LETTER
16 TRYAGAIN
17 BLOCK

SUMMARY A REGRETS
SUMMARY B OPEN

LESSON 4: FORMATTING AND EDITING

18 RSVP
19 CONGRATS
20 COMPANY
21 GLOBAL
22 MEMO
23 MEMONEWS
24 DIVE
25 MEMO
26 FOOD
27 MEMONEWS

SUMMARY A INVEST
SUMMARY B BUSNEWS

LESSON 5: ADDITIONAL FORMATTING AND EDITING

28 BULLETIN
29 OCR
30 PERSONAL
31 OCRHANG
32 MEMONEWS
33 BULLETIN
34 DIVE

35 MEMO
36 RESUME

SUMMARY A RESUME
SUMMARY B BATS

LESSON 6: ADDITIONAL FORMATTING AND EDITING

37 TOURS
38 PICNIC
39 PAPER
40 MEMONEWS
41 BULLETIN
42 OCR
43 CARS
44 COLONY
45 CAREER
46 BULLETS

SUMMARY A RESUME
SUMMARY B PRACTICE

LESSON 7: MULTIPLE-PAGE DOCUMENTS

47 NYC
48 PREVIEW
49 DIVE
50 SCORPION
51 COMPUTER
52 VOYAGE
53 USA
54 UPNDOWN
55 PREVIEW
56 USA

SUMMARY A CHOICES
SUMMARY B NUWORLD

LESSON 8: MERGE

57 INVITE.FF
58 INVITE.DF
59 INVITE.FI
60 DUE.FF
61 DUE.DF
62 DUE.FI
63 BUY.FF/BUY.DF/BUY.FI
64 SHOW.FF/SHOW.DF/SHOW.FI
65 MISTAKE.FF/MISTAKE.DF/MISTAKE.FI
66 MISENV/MISLABEL

SUMMARY A TRAVEL
SUMMARY B STOCK.FF/STOCK.DF/
STOCK.FI/STOCKLAB

DIRECTORY OF DOCUMENTS

f

DIRECTORY OF DOCUMENT FORMATS

ACKNOWLEDGEMENTS

TO MY FAMILY:
    ALAN, PAMELA, JAIME AND MOM
Thank you for your continued patience, support, inspiration and love.

ACKNOWLEDGEMENTS:
    Managing Editor:
    Kathy Berkemeyer
    DDC Publishing
    Chicago, IL

    Technical Editor:
    Christine Mahone

    Design and Layout:
    Irwin Bag
    Irwin Bag Associates
    Bethel, Conn.

LESSON 1

Introductory Basics

Exercises 1-2

- The Keyboard

- The WordPerfect 6.0 Screens

- The Ribbon and Button Bars

- Using the Mouse

- Selecting Menu Items

- Exiting Wordperfect

- Getting Help

LESSON 1 / EXERCISES 1-2
INTRODUCTORY BASICS

- The Keyboard
- The WordPerfect 6.0 Screens
- The Ribbon and Button Bars
- Using the Mouse
- Selecting Menu Items
- Exiting WordPerfect
- Getting Help

THE KEYBOARD; THE WORDPERFECT 6.0 SCREENS; THE RIBBON AND BUTTON BARS; USING THE MOUSE; SELECTING MENU ITEMS; EXITING WORDPERFECT

NOTES:

The Keyboard

- In addition to the alphanumeric **keys** found on most typewriters, computers contain additional keys:

  FUNCTION KEYS (F1 through F10 or F12, depending on your keyboard) perform special functions and are located across the top of an enhanced keyboard or on the side of a regular keyboard. (An enhanced keyboard has 12 function keys while a regular keyboard has 10.)

  MODIFIER KEYS (Shift, Alt, and Ctrl) are used in conjunction with other keys to select certain commands. To use a modifier key (Shift, Alt or Ctrl) with a function key, you must hold down the modifier key and tap the function key.

  NUMERIC KEYS allow you to enter numbers quickly when the "Num Lock" key (located above the 7/Home key) is pressed. When "Num

  Lock" is OFF the arrow keys and other application keys found on the numbers (Home, PgUp, End, PgDn) are activated.

  ESCAPE (Esc) KEY is used to cancel some commands and undelete text (to be covered in a later lesson).

  ENTER KEYS (there are two of them on most keyboards) are used to bring the cursor to the next line or may be used to complete a command.

  ARROW KEYS are used to move the cursor (the blinking marker that indicates where the next character to be keyed will appear) through the text in the direction indicated by the arrow.

  PRINT SCREEN KEY allows you to make a quick printout of whatever appears on-screen.

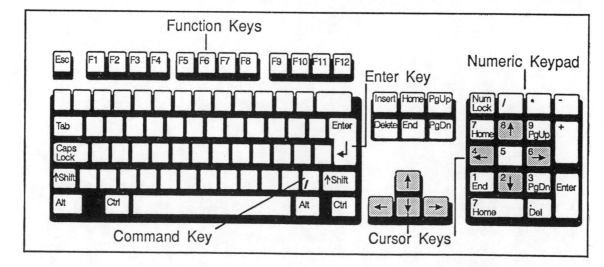

The WordPerfect Screens

- When WordPerfect 6.0 is accessed, the screen display appears in either "Text Mode", "Graphics Mode" or "Page Mode" view. The screen illustrated below left is in "Text Mode" view while the screen Illustrated below right is in "Graphics Mode" view. The differences between Text Mode and Graphics Mode will be explained in Exercise 2. For this exercise, however, you should be in "Text Mode." If your display is different from the one illustrated on the bottom left, press **Alt + V**, **T** to change to "Text Mode."

Note the following screen parts:

The **main menu bar**, located at the top of the WP screen, contains a group of selections that allows you to perform most WordPerfect tasks. Within each main menu item, there are numerous submenu commands which are listed in a "pull-down" menu. You can hide or display the menu bar.

The **cursor** is the blinking marker that appears in the upper left hand corner of the screen. It indicates where the next character to be keyed will appear.

The **status line** displays information about your document:

Type style and
Point size – displays the type style and point size of the current font when a new file is opened.

or–

Filename – displays the current directory and file name of the file on which you are working.

Doc 1 – displays the number of the document that you are currently using.

Pg 1 – displays the page number on which you are currently working.

Ln 1" – displays the vertical position of the cursor in inches as measured from the top of the page.

Pos 1" – displays the horizontal position of the cursor in inches from the left edge of the page.

- The status line will sometimes display messages and warnings.

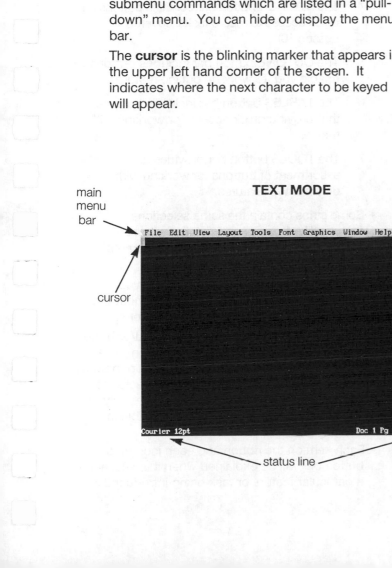

TEXT MODE

main menu bar

cursor

status line

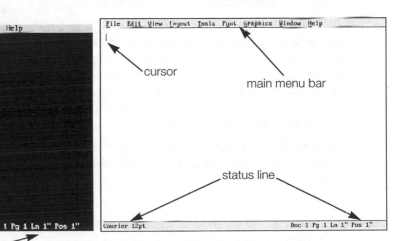

GRAPHICS MODE

cursor

main menu bar

status line

continued . . .

Lesson 1 / Exercise 1

The Ribbon and Button Bars

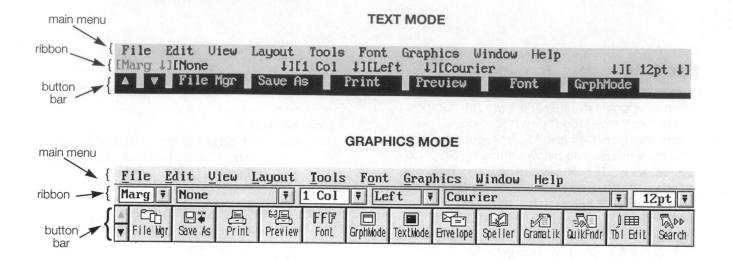

- Your screen might also display a **Ribbon** and/or a **Button bar** which appears below the main menu bar. Note the illustrations above. The first illustration is in Text mode, while the second is in Graphics mode. You must use your mouse to access items on the ribbon and button bars.

- The **ribbon** contains items that will affect the appearance and layout of text on a page. Note the arrows on the ribbon. When you click on one of the arrows next to a selection with your mouse, a "list box" of menu choices will drop down.

- The **button** bar contains icons (symbols or graphic images that represent a command or function in Graphics mode and blocked words in Text mode) that will execute functions. If you have a mouse, you may use the ribbon or button bar item as a possible shortcut to execute a command.

- The "default" button bar, referred to as "WPMAIN," appears when you access WordPerfect (shown above). The arrows that appear at the left of the first button (⌖ - Graphics Mode; ▌ - Text Mode) move your button bar back and forth to display buttons that will not fit on-screen.

- There are a total of seven different strips of buttons, each relating to a different WordPerfect task:

  1. WPMAIN is the default button bar.

  2. The FONTS button bar contains selections which will affect the appearance of your document.

3. The LAYOUT button bar contains selections used for formatting such as line, page and document formatting. It also includes alignment options, headers, footers and footnote selections.

4. The MACROS button bar contains buttons for quick access to macro tasks (covered in Lesson 10).

5. The OUTLINE button bar includes buttons to enable you to work on outline features.

6. The TABLES button bar includes buttons that provide quick access for working with tables.

7. The TOOLS button bar provides an assortment of buttons for working with different WP features.

- Some strips contain the same selections — features like Speller and Print that are used frequently. Changing from one button bar to another will be covered in a later lesson.

- WordPerfect allows you to customize your button bar with the features you use most often by adding and/or rearranging the buttons.

- You can hide or display the ribbon and/or button bar to make more room on your screen. The button bar may be positioned at the top, bottom, left or right of your screen. You can decide to display the picture and text, the picture only or the text only. Pictures will only be visible in Graphics mode.

- Each item on the ribbon and each icon on the button bar will be explained when it is relevant to a particular feature or task being introduced.

Using the Mouse

- When the **mouse** is moved on the tabletop, a corresponding movement of the mouse pointer (▌ - Text Mode; ▷ - Graphics Mode) will occur. The mouse pointer will not move if the mouse is lifted up and placed back on the tabletop.

- The following mouse terminology and their corresponding actions are described below and will be used throughout the book:

point   – move the mouse (on the tabletop) so the mouse pointer points to a specific item.

click   – quickly press and release the mouse button.

NOTE: Use the LEFT mouse button unless otherwise instructed.

double click   – press the mouse button twice in rapid succession.

drag   – press and hold down the mouse button while moving the mouse.

Selecting Menu Items

- You may use either the keyboard or the mouse or a combination of both to select menu items. "Quick keys" (many of which were used in previous versions of WordPerfect) may also be used to accomplish tasks. To issue a command, you can either:

  - use the mouse to point to a menu item and click once.

  - press Alt + highlighted letter to choose a menu and make a selection.

  - click on a button in the button bar.

  - use "quick keys."

- Procedures for completing a task will be illustrated as follows throughout the text:

  Mouse actions are illustrated on the left, keyboard commands are illustrated on the right and "quick keys" are illustrated below the heading. You may use whatever method you find most convenient.

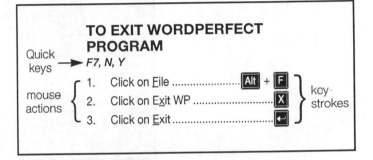

- Once a main menu item is accessed, a **"pull-down"** menu appears listing additional commands. Note the pull-down menu that appears when "File" is accessed:

Pull-down menu

- To access commands from the pull-down menu, you can either:
  - use the mouse to point to the item and click once, or
  - press the highlighted letter, or
  - use the keystrokes shown to the right of word commands (many of which are the same as those used in version 5.1).

continued . . .

Lesson 1 / Exercise 1

Exiting WordPerfect

- To **exit** the WordPerfect program, select "**E**xit WP..." from the "**F**ile" main menu bar.

```
File Edit View Layout Tools Font Graphics Window Help
 New
 Open...            Shft+F10
 Retrieve...
 Close
 Save              Ctrl+F12
 Save As...         F10

 File Manager...    F5
 Master Document   Alt+F5  ▶
 Compare Documents Alt+F5  ▶
 Summary...

 Setup             Shft+F1 ▶

 Print/Fax...       Shft+F7
 Print Preview...   Shft+F7

 Go to Shell...     Ctrl+F1
 Exit...            F7
 Exit WP...         Home,F7    ◀────────  Exit WP

Courier 12pt                          Doc 1 Pg 1 Ln 1" Pos 1"
```

EXERCISE DIRECTIONS:

NOTE: If you do not have a mouse, skip step 1 and use the keystrokes indicated.

1. Roll the mouse on the tabletop (or the mousepad) up, down, left, right.

2. Point to "File" and click once (or press Alt + F) to select this menu item.

   • note the selections on the "drop-down" File menu.

3. Click once off the menu (or press ESCape) to close the "File" option.

4. Point to "Edit" and click once (or press Alt + E) to select this menu item.

   • note the selections on the "drop-down" Edit menu.

5. Click once off the menu (or press ESCAPE) to close the "Edit" option.

6. Select the "View" menu item. Note the drop-down selections.

   <u>If your ribbon and button bar are not displayed:</u>

   • Select Ribbon
   • Select Button bar

7. Close the View option.

8. Select the "Layout" menu item. Note the drop-down selections. Close the Layout option.

9. Select each remaining main menu item. Note the drop-down selections of each. To close an option, click once off the menu or click another option or press ESCape.

10. Select View.

11. Select Button Bar Setup; select Options.

12. Select Bottom. Click on OK.

13. Return button bar to top of screen.

14. Select "File." (Click on "File" or press Alt + F)

15. Select Exit WP.

16. Select Exit.

NOTE: Mouse action procedures are indicated on the left; keyboard procedures are indicated on the right; "quick keys" (if any) are indicated below title. You may use either the mouse or the keystrokes or a combination of both.

TO SELECT A MENU ITEM

1. Click on menu item..... `Alt` + highlighted letter
2. Click on sub-menu item...............highlighted letter

TO CLOSE A MENU

Click off the menu .... `Esc`, `Esc`

TO DISPLAY RIBBON/ BUTTON BAR

Ribbon

1. Click on View .... `Alt` + `V`
2. Click on Ribbon .... `R`

Button Bar

1. Click on View .... `Alt` + `V`
2. Click on Button Bar..................... `B`

NOTE: To hide ribbon/button bar, repeat procedure.

TO CHANGE LOCATION/ STYLE OF BUTTON BAR

1. Click on View .... `Alt` + `V`
2. Click on Button Bar Setup............ `S`
3. Click on Options .... `O`
4. a. Click on a desired position:

   Top .... `T`
   Bottom........................... `B`
   Left side........................ `L`
   Right side...................... `R`

   b. Click on desired style:

   Picture and Text*............ `P`
   Picture Only*.................... `O`
   Text Only .... `X`

   *NOTE: Not available in Text mode.

5. Click on OK .... `↵`

TO EXIT WORDPERFECT PROGRAM

F7, N, Y

1. Click on File .... `Alt` + `F`
2. Click on Exit WP .... `X`
3. Click on Exit................................. `↵`

CHANGING "VIEW" MODES; SELECTING MENU ITEMS; GETTING HELP

NOTES:

Text Mode vs. Graphics Mode vs. Page Mode

- As indicated in Exercise 1, WordPerfect 6.0 gives you the option of displaying your screen in three different view modes. In **Text Mode**, characters appear monospaced. This mode allows you to edit faster than the other modes. In **Graphics Mode**, your screen imitates a WYSIWYG ("What You See is What You Get") environment. In this mode, italics and graphics will be visible on the screen. **Page Mode** allows you to view your entire page so that you can see headers, footers, footnotes, etc.

- The WordPerfect screen will appear differently depending on the view mode you select. For example, menu items show a red character in Text Mode and an underlined character in Graphics Mode; italicized words appear in yellow in Text Mode and actually appear italicized in Graphics Mode. The screen cursor appears as a horizontal line that sits <u>below</u> a character in Text Mode and as a vertical bar which is positioned between characters in Graphics Mode. The vertical cursor is called an "insertion point." The mouse pointer appears as a red rectangle in Text Mode and as an arrow in Graphics Mode. You may use any mode to edit your document. You will find it easier to use graphics mode when working with graphics.

- The documents and screen illustrations in this text will be illustrated in *Graphics Mode. You will, however, be directed to change modes for particular exercises.*

Selecting Menu Items

- In Exercise 1, you selected main menu bar items. Once selected, each main menu item provided a "pull-down" submenu.

- Note the pull-down menu which appears when View is accessed:

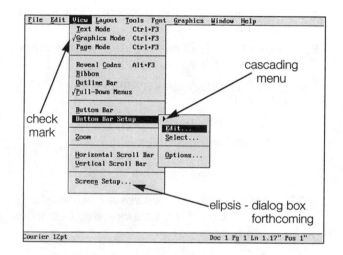

- Some options are dimmed, while others appear black. Dimmed options are not available for selection at this time while black options are.

- A check mark next to a pull-down item means that the option is currently selected.

- An item followed by an arrow opens a "cascading" menu with additional choices.

- An item followed by an ellipsis (...) indicates that a dialog box will be forthcoming.

- A dialog box requires you to provide additional information to complete a task.

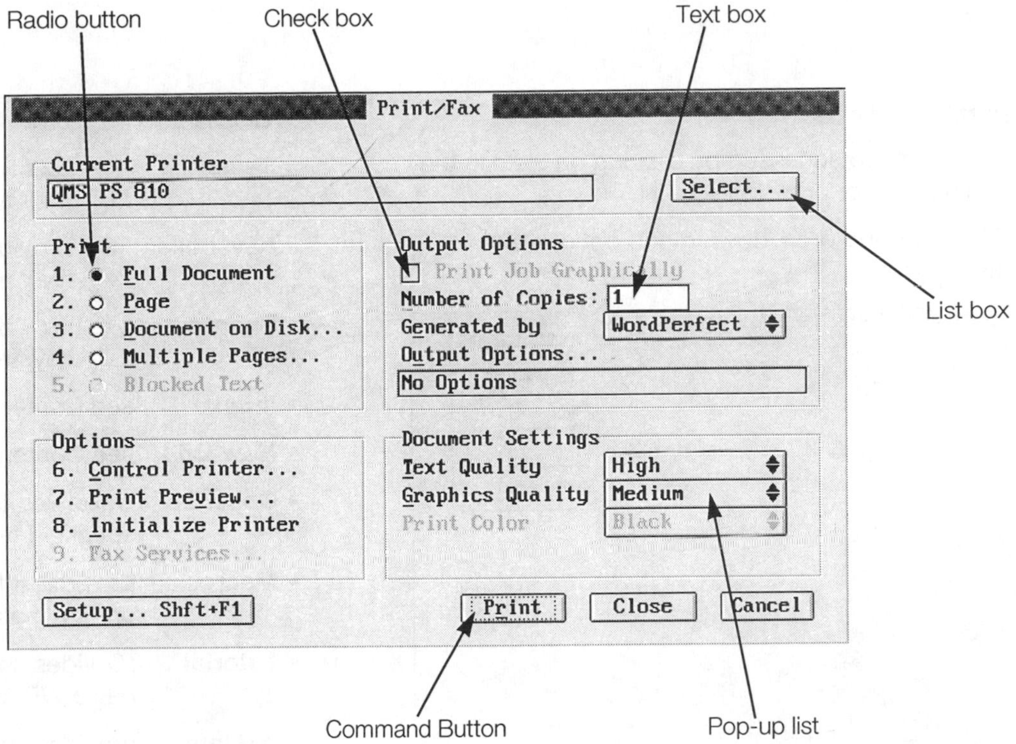

Radio button   Check box   Text box

```
                          Print/Fax
 ┌────────────────────────────────────────────────────────────┐
 │ ┌Current Printer─────────────────────────┐   ┌────────────┐ │
 │ │QMS PS 810                              │   │ Select...  │ │
 │ └────────────────────────────────────────┘   └────────────┘ │
 │ ┌Print──────────────────┐ ┌Output Options─────────────────┐ │
 │ │ 1. ● Full Document    │ │ ☐ Print Job Graphically       │ │
 │ │ 2. ○ Page             │ │ Number of Copies: 1           │ │
 │ │ 3. ○ Document on Disk...│ │ Generated by    WordPerfect ▲▼│ │
 │ │ 4. ○ Multiple Pages...│ │ Output Options...             │ │
 │ │ 5. ○ Blocked Text     │ │ No Options                    │ │
 │ └───────────────────────┘ └───────────────────────────────┘ │
 │ ┌Options────────────────┐ ┌Document Settings──────────────┐ │
 │ │ 6. Control Printer... │ │ Text Quality    High       ▲▼ │ │
 │ │ 7. Print Preview...   │ │ Graphics Quality Medium    ▲▼ │ │
 │ │ 8. Initialize Printer │ │ Print Color      Black     ▲▼ │ │
 │ │ 9. Fax Services...    │ │                               │ │
 │ └───────────────────────┘ └───────────────────────────────┘ │
 │ ┌Setup... Shft+F1┐        ┌Print┐ ┌Close┐ ┌Cancel┐          │
 │ └────────────────┘        └─────┘ └─────┘ └──────┘          │
 └────────────────────────────────────────────────────────────┘
```

List box

Command Button   Pop-up list

- Note the dialog box above which appears after "Print" is selected from the File main menu

- A dialog box contains different ways to ask you for information:

    Text box is a location where you key in information.

    The *Command button* performs an action when you click on your choice. The button is pre-selected and is indicated by a different color (in Text Mode) or by a dotted line around the button (in Graphics Mode). Notice "Print" is the pre-selected action in the illustration above.

    The *Pop-up list* is marked with an up/down arrow (in Text Mode) or triangle (in Graphics Mode). By clicking on the pop-up list arrow, a short list of options appear. Choose one of the choices on the list.

    The *Radio buttons* are round buttons (in Graphics Mode) or parentheses (in Text Mode) used to select or deselect options.

Check box is the small square box or bracket where options may be selected or deselected. mark in the box indicates the option is selected.

The *List box* is indicated by three dots following an option or by a single triangle or down arrow. Once the triangle/arrow is clicked, a list of selections will appear. To see selections at the bottom of the list, you may click on the scroll arrows which appear at the top and bottom of the list box.

To move around a dialog box, you can use the tab key, or use the mouse to click on the item.

To access a selected item, you can:

- press the highlighted letter of the item
- click on the item
- type the number next to the item

continued . . .

Getting Help

- **Help** may be accessed by clicking on <u>H</u>elp in the main menu or pressing Alt + H.

  The following drop-down menu options will assist you:

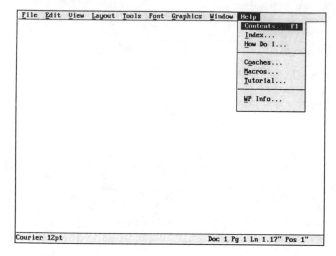

- **Contents**   includes additional help options:

  Index — lists help topics in alphabetical order.

  How Do I — provides instructions for performing tasks.

  Glossary — provides meanings and terms.

  Template — lists function keys and their actions.

  Keystrokes — provides keystrokes and their actions.

  Short-cut keys – provides shortcut keystrokes to access tasks.

- **Index**   see Contents above.

- **How Do I**   see Contents above.

- **Coaches**   walks you through procedures for specified tasks.

- **Macros**   provides information about on-line macros.

- **Tutorial**   provides short exercises to teach basic WP tasks.

- **WP Info**   provides system status information.

To exit Help, click on Cancel or press Escape.

When you have completed the work session, you may **exit** the WordPerfect program. If text is on the screen, WordPerfect will ask if you wish to save your work. Saving a file will be covered in Lesson 2.

EXERCISE DIRECTIONS:

1. Select View from the main menu.

2. Change your display view to Graphics Mode. If it is already displayed, change your view to Text Mode.

   • note the underlined menu item display.
   • note change of screen cursor.
   • note change of mouse pointer.

3. Select View from the main menu.

4. Display the ribbon and the button bar. If they are already displayed, skip to step 5.

   • note the check mark next to each after they have been selected.

5. Hide the ribbon.

6. Select Edit from the main menu.

   • note the gray selections.

7. Select File from the main menu.

8. Select Print/Fax..

   • note the dialog box selections. Use the tab key to move around the dialog box.
   • Click on Full Document.
   • Click on Page.
   • Click on Number of Copies. Type "3."

9. Exit the print dialog box (click on Cancel or press Esc).

10. Select Help from the main menu.

11. Select Contents.

12. Select Template (double click to access).

13. Exit Help.

14. Select File.

15. Exit WordPerfect (Select "Exit WP...")

TO CHANGE "VIEW" MODE

1. Click on View .... Alt + V
2. Click on

   Text Mode............................... T
   or
   Graphics Mode .... G
   or
   Page Mode .... A

TO GET HELP
F1

1. Click on Help.................... Alt + H
2. Click on a help option:

   Contents... C
   Index... I
   How Do I... .... H
   Coaches................................. O
   Macros.................................... M
   Tutorial................................... T
   WP Info... .... W

3. To exit Help items:
   Click on Cancel .... Esc

LESSON 2 / EXERCISES 3-10
CREATING AND PRINTING DOCUMENTS

- Defaults
- Creating a NEW Document
- Customizing the Button Bar
- Cursor/Insertion Point Movements
- Using the Scroll Bars
- Previewing a Document
- Creating a Business Letter

- Creating a Personal Business Letter
- Using the Date Feature
- Printing
  - a document on screen
  - a saved document
  - using File Manager

- Using File Manager
- Saving a Document
- Closing a Document
- Exiting WordPerfect

DEFAULTS; SAVING A NEW DOCUMENT

NOTES:

Default Settings

- Default or initial settings are preset conditions within the program. For example, margins are preset at 1" on the left and right. (WordPerfect assumes you are working on a standard 8.5" x 11" sheet of paper.) The line (Ln) and position (Pos) indicators on the status line are defaulted to inches. When the cursor (or insertion point) is at the left margin, the "Pos" indicator displays 1", indicating a 1" left margin. The "Ln" indicator displays 1", indicating a 1" top margin. (Margin changes will be covered in Lesson 5.)

- Settings such as margins, tabs, line spacing, type style, type size and text alignment are automatically set by the WordPerfect program. (Changing default settings will be covered in later lessons.)

- Line spacing is set for single space; tabs are set .5" apart, type style is set to Courier, type size is set to 12 point and text alignment is set to Left. The ribbon displays text alignment, type style and point size settings:

- Defaults may be changed at any time and as many times as desired throughout a document. Defaults may be changed to affect all documents or individual documents. (Changing defaults will be covered in a later lesson.)

- As you type, the "Pos" indicator on the bottom right of the screen will change. As text advances to another line, the "Ln" indicator will also change. The "Pos" indicator shows where you are horizontally on the page while the "Ln" indicator shows where you are vertically on a page.

- As text is typed, it will automatically advance to the next line. This is called **"word wrap."** It is only necessary to use the ENTER key at the end of a short line or to begin a new paragraph.

- The backspace key may be used to correct immediate errors to the left of the cursor.

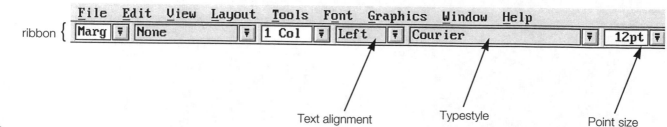

ribbon {

File   Edit   View   Layout   Tools   Font   Graphics   Window   Help

| Marg ▼ | None | ▼ | 1 Col ▼ | Left ▼ | Courier | ▼ | 12pt ▼ |

Text alignment   Typestyle   Point size

Saving a New Document

- When you **save** a document as a new file, you must be aware of where the document is being saved. A disk is like a file cabinet. If you wish to save your file in a particular "drawer" in the cabinet, you must specify the "directory." When saving a file, you must indicate the drive letter where your disk resides and/or directory on the disk where you want your document to be saved. You must also assign a name to the file. For example: **C:\WP60\try** will save your file in drive C (hard drive), directory WP60, under the filename "try." (A colon separates drives from directories and filenames; a backslash (\) separates directories from subdirectories and filenames.)

- A filename may contain a maximum of eight characters and may have an optional extension of one to three characters. The file extension may be used to further identify your document. The filename and extension are separated by a period. Example: **travel.bos**

- Filenames are not case sensitive; they may be typed in either upper or lower case.

- When you save a document for the first time, the dialog box below.

- After saving your document, you can keep the document on the screen and continue working, or you can clear the screen by selecting "Close" from the File menu.

- After saving your document for the first time, you can save the document again by selecting "Save" from the File menu. (See keystrokes for SAVE and CONTINUE.) This is a convenient way to update your file and continue working. Save often to prevent losing data. Documents may also be saved using the "Save As" command. This command is generally used when you want to save your document under a different filename or in a different drive/directory. Save As will be covered further in Exercise 31.

- You do not always have to save your document. By selecting "Close" from the File main menu bar, you will exit your document without saving it and return to a clear window where you can create another document. IF YOU MAKE A MISTAKE AND WOULD LIKE TO BEGIN AGAIN, FOLLOW KEYSTROKES ON PAGE 15 "**TO CLEAR WITHOUT SAVING.**"

SAVE DOCUMENT DIALOG BOX

```
============ Save Document 1 ============

  Filename: [                                        ]

  Format:    [ WordPerfect 6.0                    ↓]

  Setup... Shft+F1    Code Page... F9    (Document has been modified)

  File List... F5   QuickList... F6   Password... F8    OK    Cancel
```

continued . . .

EXERCISE DIRECTIONS:

1. Select Text Mode view.
2. Display the Ribbon.

   • note the default settings for alignment (Left), for type style (Courier) and for type size (12 point).
3. Begin the exercise at the top of your screen (Ln 1").
4. Keyboard the paragraphs on the right, allowing the text to "word wrap" to the next line. Press the return key twice to begin a new paragraph.
5. Correct only immediate errors by using the backspace key.
6. Save the exercise; name it **TRY**.
7. Clear your screen.

As you type, notice the "Pos" indicator on your status line change as the position of your cursor (insertion point) changes.

The wraparound feature allows the operator to decide on line endings, making the use of the return unnecessary except at the end of a paragraph or short line. Each file is saved on a disk or hard drive for recall. Documents must be given a name for identification.

TO SAVE AND CONTINUE
Ctrl + F12

1. Click on File ....`Alt` + `F`
2. Click on Save.................................`S`
3. Type document name.*
4. Click on OK.................................`←`

*If saving on a "disk," indicate the drive where the disk resides before keying the document name. Example: a:try. If saving on a hard drive, it is only necessary to key the document name.

TO SAVE AND CLEAR SCREEN
F7, Y, N

1. Click on File ....`Alt` + `F`
2. Click on Close.................................`C`
3. Click on Yes.................................`Y`
4. Type document name.
5. Click on OK.................................`←`

TO SAVE AND EXIT WORDPERFECT
F7, Y, Y

1. Click on File ....`Alt` + `F`
2. Click on Exit WP... ....`X`
3. Type document name.
4. Click on Save and Exit ....`←`

TO CLEAR WITHOUT SAVING

1. Click on File ....`Alt` + `F`
2. Click on Close.................................`C`
3. Click on No ....`N`

15

TABS; CUSTOMIZING THE BUTTON BAR

NOTES:

- Tab stops are preset .5" apart. Each time the tab key is pressed, the cursor will advance 1/2 inch. Therefore, when the cursor is at the left margin (1") and the tab key is pressed once, the **"Pos"** indicator will show 1.5".

- Defaults may be changed at any time and as many times as desired throughout a document. Thus, if you wanted to tab .8" instead of .5", this could be done. (Changing defaults will be covered in a later lesson.)

- As noted in Exercise 1, the button bar is an on-screen display of icons or pictures that represent commonly used features. Using the button bar icons, you can quickly access commands. The WPMAIN button bar is illustrated below.

- The arrow keys to the left of the buttons may be used to see more or previous selections.

- There are seven different strips of buttons, each related to a particular group of tasks. Since button bars are meant to quickly access tasks, changing from one strip to another can actually be inconvenient and time consuming. As noted earlier, WordPerfect allows you to customize button bars with commonly used tasks. You can add, delete or move buttons to make most-often used buttons more accessible.

- In this exercise, you will change from one button bar to another. Then, you will customize a button bar by adding buttons, then deleting them to restore the WPMAIN to its original grouping. When you become more familiar with other WP tasks, you can create a button bar that suits your needs.

File	Edit	View	Layout	Tools	Font	Graphics	Window	Help

| Marg ▼ | None ▼ | 1 Col ▼ | Left ▼ | Courier ▼ | 12pt ▼ |

WP Main Button Bar: File Mgr | Save As | Print | Preview | Font | GrphMode | TextMode | Envelope | Speller | Gramatik | QuikFndr | Tbl Edit | Search

EXERCISE DIRECTIONS:

1. Start with a clear screen.

2. Display the WPMAIN button bar.

3. Select Graphics Mode view.

4. Change to TOOLS button bar.

5. Return to the WPMAIN button bar.

6. Create a custom button bar with the following tasks in the order listed: GRPHMODE, TEXTMODE, SAVE AS, PREVIEW, DATE TEXT, SPELLER.

7. Select Text Mode view from the button bar.

8. Select Text Mode view from the button bar.

9. Begin the exercise at the top of your screen (1").

10. Keyboard the paragraphs on the right, allowing the text to "word wrap" to the next line. Press the ENTER key twice to begin a new paragraph and <u>press the tab key once to indent the paragraph</u>.

11. Correct only immediate errors by using the backspace key.

12. Select Graphics Mode view from the button bar.

13. Save the exercise using the Save As on the button bar; name it **TRYAGAIN**.

14. Clear your screen.

15. Return the WPMAIN button bar to its original group in the order listed: FILE MGR, SAVE AS, PRINT, PREVIEW, FONT, GRPHMODE, TEXTMODE, ENVELOPE, SPELLER, GRAMATIK, QUIKFNDR, TBL EDIT, SEARCH.

TAB
→ WordPerfect is simple to use since you can begin typing as soon as you enter the program. ↓2x

TAB
→ The way text will lay out or "format" on a page is set by the WordPerfect program. For example, margins are set for 1" on the left and 1" in on the right; line spacing is set for single space; tabs are set to advance the cursor 1/2 inch each time the tab key is pressed. Formats may be changed at any time and as many times throughout the document.

TO TAB
Press Tab .... `Tab`

TO CHANGE BUTTON BARS
1. Click on View .... `Alt` + `V`
2. Click on Button Bar Setup............. `S`
3. Click on Select .... `S`
4. Double click on desired button bar .... `↵`

TO CREATE A CUSTOM BUTTON BAR
1. Click on View ....`Alt` + `V`
2. Click on Button Bar Setup............. `S`
3. Click on Select .... `S`
4. Click on Create .... `C`
5. Type name of new button bar.

NOTE: Button bar name can consist of up to 8 characters.

6. Click on OK.......................... `↵`
7. Click on Add Menu Item .... `E`
8. Click on desired main menu bar item, then click on pull-down menu bar item for which you want to create buttons.
9. Repeat step 8 for each button to be added.
10. Click on OK twice............... `↵`, `↵`

TO MOVE BUTTONS
(in priority order)
1. Click on View .... `Alt` + `V`
2. Click on Button Bar Setup........... `S`
3. Click on Edit......................... `E`

4. Click on button to be moved.
5. Click on Move .... `M`
6. Click on button where you want selected button to be moved TO.
7. Click on Paste............................. `P`
8. Click on OK.................................. `↵`

TO DELETE BUTTONS
(from a strip)
1. Click on View .... `Alt` + `V`
2. Click on Button Bar Setup............. `S`
3. Click on button to be deleted.
4. Click on Delete......................... `D`
5. Click on OK.................................. `↵`

17

SAVING AND EXITING A DOCUMENT; CURSOR / INSERTION POINT MOVEMENTS; "SCROLLING" A DOCUMENT

NOTES:

- This exercise will give you more practice typing text that wraps, using the tab key, and saving a document. Be sure to keyboard it exactly as shown since it will be used in a later exercise for additional editing practice.

- After keyboarding this and the next few exercises, you will practice moving the cursor through the document. This is essential when you are ready to correct errors.

Cursor/Insertion Point Movements

- You may move the cursor/ insertion point using the keyboard or the mouse:

  Keyboard: Press the arrow key in the direction you wish the cursor/insertion point to move. You may use the arrow keys located on the numeric keypad or (depending on your keyboard) the separate arrow keys located to the left of the keypad. You can "express" move the cursor/insertion point from one point on the document to another using special key combinations (see keystrokes on next page).

  Mouse: Move the mouse pointer to where you want to place the cursor/ insertion point. Then, click the LEFT mouse button.

- The cursor/insertion point will only move through text, spaces or codes. The cursor/insertion point stops moving when the end or beginning of your document is reached.

Scrolling a Document

- To move the cursor to a part of the document that does not appear on screen, you can "scroll" your document by pressing and holding the up/down or left/right arrows on the keyboard or using "scroll bars." To display scroll bars, you must access them from View on the main menu. Note the screen below with scroll bars displayed:

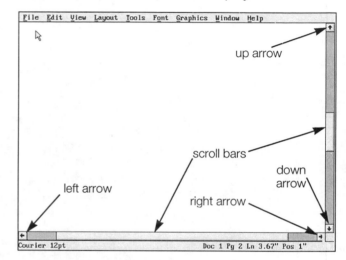

- Once they are visible, click on the up/down arrow on the vertical scroll bar or left/right arrow on the horizontal scroll bar until the desired text is visible on the screen. The horizontal scroll bar is rarely needed.

EXERCISE DIRECTIONS:

1. Start with a clear screen.
2. Display the button bar.
3. Display the Vertical and Horizontal Scroll bars.
4. Select Graphics Mode view from the button bar.
5. Begin the exercise at the top of your screen (1").
6. Keyboard the exercise on next page exactly as shown.
7. Press the ENTER key twice between paragraphs and press the tab key once to indent the first line of the paragraphs indicated.
8. Correct only immediate errors by using the backspace key.

9. After you complete the exercise, move the cursor/insertion point through the document as follows:
   - one line up/down
   - one character right/left
   - previous word
   - end of screen
   - beginning of line
   - end of line
10. Use the horizontal and vertical scroll arrows to scroll your page up and down.
11. Save the exercise using Save As on the button bar; name it **DIVE**.
12. Clear your screen.

DIVING VACATIONS
DIVING IN THE CAYMAN ISLANDS

Do you want to see sharks, barracudas and huge stingrays? Do you want to see gentle angels, too?

The Cayman Islands were discovered by Christopher Columbus in late 1503. The Cayman Islands are located just south of Cuba. The Caymans are the home to only about 125,000 year-around residents. However, they welcome approximately 200,000 visitors each year. Each year more and more visitors arrive. Most visitors come with colorful masks and flippers in their luggage ready to go scuba diving.

Because of the magnificence of the coral reef, scuba diving has become to the Cayman Islands what safaris are to Kenya. If you go into a bookstore, you can buy diving gear.

Now, you are ready to jump in!

Recommendations for Hotel/Diving Accommodations:

Sunset House, Post Office Box 4791, George Towne, Grand Cayman; (800) 854-4767.

Coconut Harbour, Post Office Box 2086, George Towne, Grand Cayman;
(809) 949-7468.

Seeing a shark is frightening at first; they seem to come out of nowhere and then return to nowhere. But as soon as the creature disappears, you will swim after it. You will just want to keep this beautiful, graceful fish in view as long as you can.

TO DISPLAY SCROLL BAR

1. Click on View .... `Alt` + `V`
2. Click on Horizontal
   Scroll Bar .... `H`

   or

   Click on Vertical
   Scroll Bar .... `V`

   Once displayed:

   Click on up/down or left right arrows until desired text is in view or click and drag the scroll box up/down to express move the window.

TO EXPRESS CURSOR/INSERTION POINT MOVEMENTS WITHIN A DOCUMENT

TO MOVE:	PRESS:
One Char. left	`←`
One Char. right	`→`
One line up	`↑`
One line down	`↓`
Previous word	`F2` + `←`
Next word	`F2` + `→`

Top of screen	`Home` + `↑`
Bottom of screen	`Home` + `↓`
Beginning of document	`Home`, `Home`, `↑`
End of document	`Home`, `O`
Top of page	`F2` + `Home`, `↑`
Bottom of page	`F2` + `Home`, `↓`
Beginning of line	`Home` + `←`
End of line	`End`
Top of previous page	`PgUp`
Top of next page	`PgDn`

CREATING A BUSINESS LETTER; PREVIEWING A DOCUMENT

NOTES:

- There are a variety of letter styles for business and personal use.

- The parts of a business letter and the vertical spacing of letter parts are the same regardless of the style used.

- A business letter is comprised of eight parts: 1. **date** 2. **inside address** (to whom and where the letter is going) 3. **salutation** 4. **body** 5. **closing** 6. **signature line** 7. **title line** 8. **reference initials** (the first set of initials belongs to the person who wrote the letter; the second set of initials belongs to the person who typed the letter).

- Whenever you see "yo" as part of the reference initials in an exercise, substitute "your own" initials.

- The letter style illustrated in this exercise is a "modified block" business letter, since the date, closing, signature and title lines begin at the center point of the paper (4.5"). Most business letters are printed on letterhead paper.

- In the inside address, there are two spaces between the state abbreviation and the zip code.

- A letter generally begins 15 lines down from the top of a page or 2.5" in WordPerfect. (There are 6 vertical lines to one inch.) If the letter is long, it may begin 12 lines down or 2" from the top. If the letter is short, it may begin beyond 2.5".

- Margins and the size of the characters (type size) may also be adjusted to accommodate longer or shorter correspondence. Changing margins and type size will be covered in a later lesson.

- To see how your letter will format or appear on a page, WordPerfect allows you to preview your work. You may preview your work by clicking on "Preview" in the button bar or by selecting "Print Preview" from the File main menu.

EXERCISE DIRECTIONS:

1. Start with a clear screen.
2. Display the WPMAIN button bar.
3. Display the vertical and horizontal scroll bars.
4. Select Graphics Mode view from the button bar.
5. Keyboard the letter on the right as directed.
6. Use the default margins and tabs.
7. With your cursor at the top of the screen (1"), press the return key 9 times to begin the date on line (Ln) 2.5".
8. Press the tab key 7 times to begin the date and closing at position (Pos) 4.5" on the page.
9. Press the ENTER key between parts of the letter as directed in the exercise.
10. Correct only immediate errors by using the backspace key.
11. After completing the exercise, use the scroll bar to scroll your page up.
12. Preview your work.
13. Save the exercise using Save As on the button bar; name it **LETTER**.
14. Clear your screen.

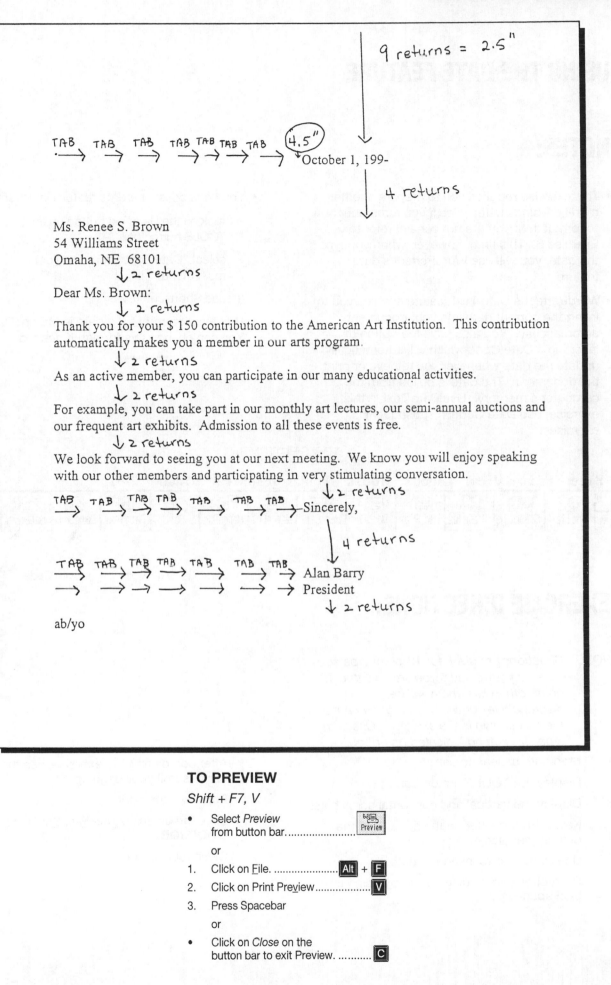

9 returns = 2.5"

TAB TAB TAB TAB TAB TAB TAB (4.5")
October 1, 199-

4 returns

Ms. Renee S. Brown
54 Williams Street
Omaha, NE 68101

↓ 2 returns

Dear Ms. Brown:

↓ 2 returns

Thank you for your $ 150 contribution to the American Art Institution. This contribution automatically makes you a member in our arts program.

↓ 2 returns

As an active member, you can participate in our many educational activities.

↓ 2 returns

For example, you can take part in our monthly art lectures, our semi-annual auctions and our frequent art exhibits. Admission to all these events is free.

↓ 2 returns

We look forward to seeing you at our next meeting. We know you will enjoy speaking with our other members and participating in very stimulating conversation.

↓ 2 returns

TAB TAB TAB TAB TAB TAB TAB Sincerely,

↓ 4 returns

TAB TAB TAB TAB TAB TAB TAB Alan Barry
President

↓ 2 returns

ab/yo

TO PREVIEW

Shift + F7, V

- Select *Preview* from button bar........................ Preview

  or

1. Click on File. .... Alt + F
2. Click on Print Preview.................. V
3. Press Spacebar

   or

- Click on *Close* on the button bar to exit Preview. C

USING THE DATE FEATURE

NOTES:

- This exercise requires you to prepare another modified-block letter. See if you remember how to format it. If you are not certain, refer to Exercise 6. This time, however, when you type the date, you will use WordPerfect's date feature.

- WordPerfect's Date Text feature enables you to insert the current date into your document automatically. You also have the option of inserting a Date Code which will automatically update the date whenever you retrieve or print the document. The date is pulled from the computer's memory. Use Date Text in this exercise; use Date Code in subsequent exercises.

- You can access the date feature in several ways:
  - click on the DateText button on the TOOLS button bar.
  - select "Date Text" from the Tools main menu.
  - use Short-cut keys.

- The default format for a date is Month, Day, Year. You can change this format, if desired.

TOOLS BUTTON BAR

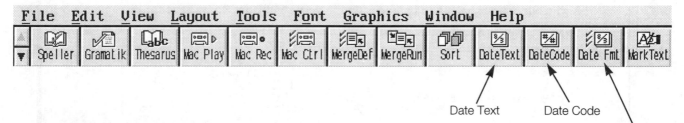

Date Text   Date Code

Date Format

EXERCISE DIRECTIONS:

NOTE: Directions are given for 12-point type size. Be sure your default type size is set to 12 point; otherwise, there will be discrepancies between your document and the one shown in the exercise. Check the type size setting indicated on ribbon.

1. Start with a clear screen.
2. Display the TOOLS button bar.
3. Display the vertical and horizontal scroll bars.
4. Keyboard the letter on the right. Use the default margins.
5. Use Date Text to insert the date.
6. Correct only immediate errors by using the backspace key.

7. After completing the exercise, use the scroll bar to scroll your page up.
8. Preview your work.
9. Save the exercise (use File, Save); name it **GOODJOB**.
10. Clear your screen.

Today's date) Use the date
feature

Mr. Wallace Redfield
23 Main Street
Staten Island, NY   10312

Dear Mr. Redfield:

You are to be commended for an outstanding job as convention
chair. The computer convention held last week was the best I
attended.

The choices you made for lecturers were excellent. Every seminar
I attended was interesting.

Congratulations on a great job.

Sincerely,

Adam Howard
President

ah/yo

TO INSERT CURRENT DATE
Shift + F5, T

- Click on *Date Text* in
  TOOLS button bar .... [DateText]
  or
1. Click on Tools. .... [Alt] + [T]
2. Click on Date .... [D]
3. Click on Text................................ [T]

TO INSERT DATE CODE
Shift + F5, C

- Click on *Date Code* in
  TOOLS button bar .... [DateCode]
  or
1. Click on Tools. .... [Alt] + [T]
2. Click on Date .... [D]
3. Click on Date Code..................... [C]

TO CHANGE DATE FORMAT

- Click on *Date Fmt* in
  TOOLS button bar .... [Date Fmt]
  or
1. Click on Tools. .... [Alt] + [T]
2. Click on Date .... [D]
3. Click on Format... .... [F]
4. Click on desired format
5. Click on OK................................ [↵]

PRINTING A DOCUMENT

NOTES:

- The letter style in this exercise is called "block" or "full block." This style is very popular because all parts of the letter begin at the left margin and there is no need to tab the date and closing. The spacing between letter parts in this style is the same as the modified-block letter.

- WordPerfect allows you to print <u>part</u> or <u>all</u> of a document that is in the screen window. You can print a page of the document, the full document, selected pages of a document, or one or more blocks of text within the document. A document may also be printed from the disk, without retrieving it to the screen.

- Check to see that the printer is turned on and paper is loaded.

- There are several ways to print:

  - click on the print button on the MAIN button bar.

  - select "Print/Fax" from the <u>F</u>ile main menu.

  - use Short-cut keys.

- After accessing print, a dialog box will appear asking you to indicate whether you wish to print the full document (more than one page), a page, the document on disk or multiple pages. You may also indicate the number of copies you desire to be printed. Note the print dialog box to the right.

PRINT/FAX DIALOG BOX

```
┌──────────────────────────────────────────────┐
│                  Print/Fax                     │
│ ┌─Current Printer──────────────────────────┐   │
│ │ QMS PS 810                     │ Select...│  │
│ │                                └──────────┘  │
│ ┌─Print──────────────┐ ┌─Output Options───────┐│
│ │ 1. ● Full Document │ │ ☐ Print Job Graphically││
│ │ 2. ○ Page          │ │ Number of Copies: 1   ││
│ │ 3. ○ Document on Disk...│ Generated by │WordPerfect ⬍│
│ │ 4. ○ Multiple Pages...│ Output Options...    ││
│ │ 5.   Blocked Text  │ │ No Options            ││
│ └────────────────────┘ └──────────────────────┘│
│ ┌─Options────────────┐ ┌─Document Settings────┐│
│ │ 6. Control Printer...│ Text Quality  │High ⬍│││
│ │ 7. Print Preview...│ │ Graphics Quality│Medium ⬍││
│ │ 8. Initialize Printer│ Print Color  │Black ⬍│││
│ │ 9. Fax Services... │ └──────────────────────┘│
│ └────────────────────┘                          │
│ ┌Setup... Shft+F1┐        ┌Print┐┌Close┐┌Cancel┐│
│ └────────────────┘        └─────┘└─────┘└──────┘│
└──────────────────────────────────────────────┘
```

- You can cancel an individual print job or all print jobs while they are printing.

- Pressing the "Caps Lock" key once will enable you to type ALL CAPITAL LETTERS without pressing the shift key. Only letters are changed by "Caps Lock." When the "Caps Lock" key is "ON," the "Pos" indicator will change to an all caps "POS." Pressing the "Caps Lock" key again will turn caps lock "OFF" and end the upper-case mode. If you forget to press the caps lock key to create upper case mode, you can change lower case text to upper case after keyboarding. Case conversion will be covered in Exercise 16.

- In this exercise, you will create a letter and print "a page." In subsequent exercises, you will print multiple copies of a page.

EXERCISE DIRECTIONS:

1. Start with a clear screen.
2. Display the WPMAIN button bar.
3. Select Text Mode view.
4. Keyboard the letter on the right.
5. Use the default margins.
6. Begin the date on line (Ln) 2.5". <u>Use the Date Text feature to insert today's date.</u>
7. Press the ENTER key between parts of the letter as directed in the exercise.
8. Correct only immediate errors by using the backspace key.
9. Preview your work.
10. Print one copy of the (page) exercise by selecting "Print" on the button bar.
11. Save the exercise; name it **BLOCK**.
12. Clear your screen.

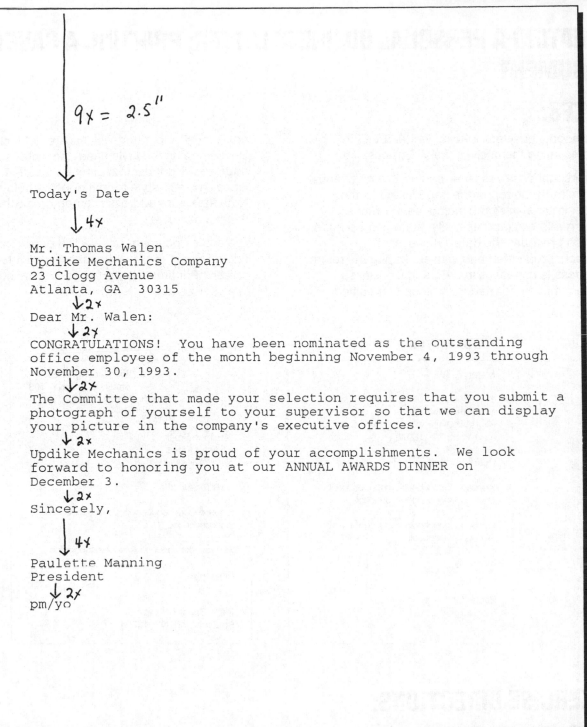

$9x = 2.5''$

Today's Date

↓4x

Mr. Thomas Walen
Updike Mechanics Company
23 Clogg Avenue
Atlanta, GA 30315

↓2x

Dear Mr. Walen:

↓2x

CONGRATULATIONS! You have been nominated as the outstanding office employee of the month beginning November 4, 1993 through November 30, 1993.

↓2x

The Committee that made your selection requires that you submit a photograph of yourself to your supervisor so that we can display your picture in the company's executive offices.

↓2x

Updike Mechanics is proud of your accomplishments. We look forward to honoring you at our ANNUAL AWARDS DINNER on December 3.

↓2x

Sincerely,

↓4x

Paulette Manning
President

↓2x

pm/yo

TO CAPITALIZE

1. Press CAPS LOCK key

NOTE: "Pos" changes to "POS" on status line.

2. Type text.

3. Press CAPS LOCK key to end upper case.

TO PRINT

Document on Screen (Page)
Shift + F7, P, R

1. Click on *Print* in
   MAIN button bar .... [Print]

   or

   Click on *File* .... [Alt] + [F]

2. Click on *Print/Fax...* .... [P]

3. Click on *Page* .... [P]

4. Click on *Print* .... [↵]

TO CANCEL PRINT JOB

Shift + F7, C, C

1. Click on *Print* in
   MAIN button bar .... [Print]

   or

   Click on *File* .... [Alt] + [F]

   Click on *Print/Fax...* .... [P]

2. Click on *Control Printer...* .... [C]

3. Click on *Cancel Job* .... [C]

4. Click on *Yes* .... [Y]
   to cancel highlighted job.

CREATING A PERSONAL BUSINESS LETTER; PRINTING A SAVED DOCUMENT

NOTES:

- A personal business letter is written by individuals representing themselves, not a business firm.

- A personal business letter begins 2.5" or 15 lines down from the top of the page (same as the other letter styles) and includes the writer's return address (address, city, state and zip code) which precedes the date. However, if personalized letterhead is used, keying the return address is unnecessary. Personal business letters may be formatted in block or modified

block style. Operator's initials are not included. Depending on the style used, the writer's return address will appear in a different location on the letter. A block-style format appears below left. Note the return address is typed below the writer's name.

- The entire document or selected pages may be printed from the disk without bringing it to the screen. Printing selected pages will be covered in a later lesson.

BLOCK STYLE

```
March 7, 199-


Mr. John Smith
54 Astor Place
New York, NY  10078

Dear Mr. Smith:


xxxxxxxxxxxxxxxxxxxxxxxxxxxxxx
xxxxxxxxxxxxxxxxxxxxxxxxxxx.


xxxxxxxxxxxxxxxxxxxxxxxxxxxxxx
xxxxxxxxxxxxxxx.

Sincerely,


Paula Zahn
657 Nehring Street
```

MODIFIED-BLOCK STYLE

```
                        657 Nehring Street
                        Staten Island, NY  10324
                        March 7, 199-

Mr. John Smith
54 Astor Place
New York, NY  10078

Dear Mr. Smith:


xxxxxxxxxxxxxxxxxxxxxxxxxxxxxxxxx
xxxxxxxxxxxx.


xxxxxxxxxxxxxxxxxxxxxxxxx xxxxxxx xxx.

Sincerely,


Paula Zahn
Staten Island, NY  10324
```

EXERCISE DIRECTIONS:

NOTE: This exercise assumes you know the name of the document you wish to print.

1. Start with a clear screen.
2. Display the button bar.
3. Display the Vertical and Horizontal Scroll bars.
4. Select Text Mode view.
5. Keyboard the personal business letter on the next page in modified block style as shown.
6. Use the default margins and tabs.
7. Begin the date on Ln 2".
8. Press the tab key 7 times to begin the <u>date</u> and <u>closing</u> at position (Pos) 4.5" on the page.
9. Press the ENTER key between parts of the letter as directed in the exercise.
10. Correct only immediate errors by using the backspace key.
11. After completing the exercise, use the scroll bars to scroll your page up.
12. Save the exercise; name it **PERSONAL**.
13. Clear your screen.
14. Print one copy of LETTER which you saved in Exercise 6.
15. Print one copy of PERSONAL which you just saved in this exercise.

636 Jay Boulevard West
Chaska, MN 55318
Date Code

Ms. Anita Price, Vice President
Milton Investment Counselors
One Pratt Circle
Baltimore, MD 21202

Dear Ms. Price:

Please consider me an applicant for the position of Financial
Advisor that was advertised in the Sunday edition of *The Herald*.

As my enclosed resume will show, I have been working for Sutton
Investment Group for the past six years. I am particularly proud
of several accomplishments:

In 1989, I helped to organize $1.5 million zero-coupon bond
offering for the French Treasury.

In 1990, my group handled $120 million municipal bond offering
for New York City.

In 1991, I helped to underwrite $200 million offering for a
foreign company.

I am confident that my past experience will be an asset to your
organization. If you would like to meet with me for an
interview, I can be reached at the number indicated on my resume.

                              Sincerely,

                              Lawrence Schneider

enclosure

TO PRINT
A Saved Document
(Document on Disk)
Shift + F7 D

1. Click on *Print* in
   MAIN button bar. .... [Print]

   or

   Click on *File*. .... [Alt] + [F]

   Click on *Print*. .... [P]

2. Click on *Document*
   on Disk. .... [D]

3. Type document name.

NOTE: *It may be necessary to
   indicate the drive and/or
   directory where file is located
   when typing document name.
   Example: A: LETTER*

4. Click on OK twice. .... [←], [←]

5. Click on P̲rint. .... [←]

PRINTING A DOCUMENT; USING FILE MANAGER

NOTES:

- Exercise 9 assumed you knew the name of the document you wished to print. However, sometimes you might be unsure of the document name. Then it becomes necessary to view the contents of your disk. File Manager allows you to view the contents of your disk (your file cabinet) or a specific directory (a drawer in the cabinet).

- WordPerfect allows you to print from the FILE MANAGER screen, but you also have other options within the screen. Those options will be covered in later lessons.

- The FILE MANAGER screen provides other information to the user. An illustration of this screen appears on the right. Note the following:

  - the top of the screen includes the directory name, the current date, and the time of day. The bottom of the screen displays the space available and the used space on disk.

  - all files appear in alphabetical order.

  - next to each filename, the size of the file (indicated in bytes, which is equivalent to characters), and the date and time the file was last saved appears.

- You may print any file from the directory even though you might be working on another document at the time.

- If you wish to print more than one file at a time, you can "mark" them. Marking files enables you to print several files using only one print command.

- You may print a copy of the FILE MANAGER screen if you desire a hard copy list of your files (Print List).

EXERCISE DIRECTIONS:

1. Start with a clear screen.
2. Display the WP MAIN button bar.
3. Select Graphics Mode view from the button bar.
4. Assuming you forgot the name of the document you wish to print, access FILE MANAGER.
5. Using the arrow keys, highlight the document, **TRYAGAIN**.
6. Print one copy.
7. Mark the files **BLOCK** and **DIVE**.
8. Print one copy of each.

Current directory

Current date

Current time

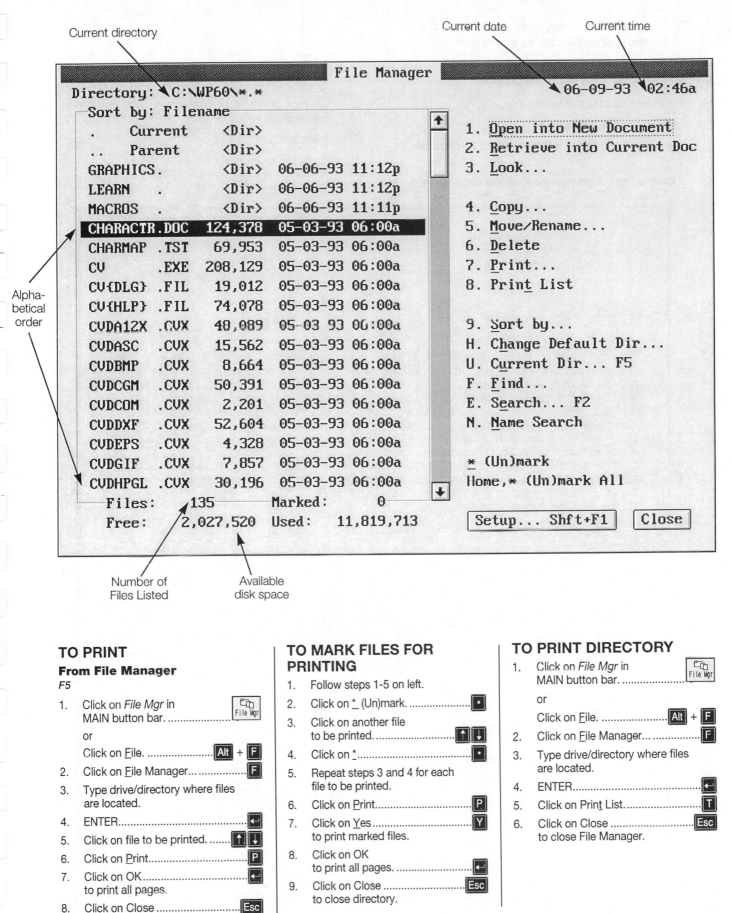

```
                         File Manager
Directory: C:\WP60\*.*                          06-09-93  02:46a
 Sort by: Filename
  .      Current      <Dir>              1. Open into New Document
  ..     Parent       <Dir>              2. Retrieve into Current Doc
  GRAPHICS.           <Dir> 06-06-93 11:12p   3. Look...
  LEARN   .           <Dir> 06-06-93 11:12p
  MACROS  .           <Dir> 06-06-93 11:11p   4. Copy...
  CHARACTR.DOC   124,378  05-03-93 06:00a      5. Move/Rename...
  CHARMAP .TST    69,953  05-03-93 06:00a      6. Delete
  CV      .EXE   208,129  05-03-93 06:00a      7. Print...
  CV{DLG} .FIL    19,012  05-03-93 06:00a      8. Print List
  CV{HLP} .FIL    74,078  05-03-93 06:00a
  CVDA12X .CVX    48,089  05-03-93 06:00a      9. Sort by...
  CVDASC  .CVX    15,562  05-03-93 06:00a      H. Change Default Dir...
  CVDBMP  .CVX     8,664  05-03-93 06:00a      U. Current Dir... F5
  CVDCGM  .CVX    50,391  05-03-93 06:00a      F. Find...
  CVDCOM  .CVX     2,201  05-03-93 06:00a      E. Search... F2
  CVDDXF  .CVX    52,604  05-03-93 06:00a      N. Name Search
  CVDEPS  .CVX     4,328  05-03-93 06:00a
  CVDGIF  .CVX     7,857  05-03-93 06:00a      * (Un)mark
  CVDHPGL .CVX    30,196  05-03-93 06:00a      Home,* (Un)mark All
  Files:     135        Marked:       0
  Free:  2,027,520  Used:   11,819,713    Setup... Shft+F1    Close
```

Alphabetical order

Number of Files Listed

Available disk space

TO PRINT

From File Manager

F5

1. Click on *File Mgr* in MAIN button bar. .... [File Mgr]

   or

   Click on *File.* .... [Alt] + [F]

2. Click on *File Manager*... .... [F]

3. Type drive/directory where files are located.

4. ENTER... [←]

5. Click on file to be printed. .... [↑][↓]

6. Click on *Print*................................. [P]

7. Click on OK...................................... [←]
   to print all pages.

8. Click on Close .... [Esc]
   to close File Manager.

TO MARK FILES FOR PRINTING

1. Follow steps 1-5 on left.

2. Click on *_ (Un)mark. .... [*]

3. Click on another file to be printed......................... [↑][↓]

4. Click on *...................................... [*]

5. Repeat steps 3 and 4 for each file to be printed.

6. Click on *Print*................................ [P]

7. Click on *Yes*................................ [Y]
   to print marked files.

8. Click on OK
   to print all pages. .... [←]

9. Click on Close .... [Esc]
   to close directory.

TO PRINT DIRECTORY

1. Click on *File Mgr* in MAIN button bar. .... [File Mgr]

   or

   Click on *File.* .... [Alt] + [F]

2. Click on *File Manager*... .... [F]

3. Type drive/directory where files are located.

4. ENTER... [←]

5. Click on Print List....................... [T]

6. Click on Close .... [Esc]
   to close File Manager.

Lesson 2 / Summary Exercise A

NOTE: You may work in any view, and display the button and scroll bars as you desire.

EXERCISE DIRECTIONS:

1. Start with a clear screen.

2. Use the default margins.

3. Keyboard the letter below in **modified-block** style.

4. Use the Date Text feature to insert today's date.

5. Correct only immediate errors by using the backspace key.

6. Print one copy.

7. Save the exercise; name it **OPEN**.

8. Clear your screen.

```
Today's date  Mr. Martin Quincy  641 Lexington Avenue  New York,
NY  10022  Dear Mr. Quincy:  We are pleased to announce the
opening of a new subsidiary of our company.  We specialize in
selling, training and service of portable personal computers.
¶This may be hard to believe, but we carry portable personal
computers that can do everything a conventional desktop can.  Our
portables can run all of the same applications as your company's
conventional PCs.  With the purchase of a computer, we will train
two employees in your firm on how to use an application of your
choice. ¶For a free demonstration, call us at 212-456-9876 any
business day from 9:00 a.m. to 5:00 p.m.  Sincerely,  Theresa
Mann  President  tm/yo
```

NOTE: You may work in any view, and display the button and scroll bars as you desire.

EXERCISE DIRECTIONS:

1. Start with a clear screen.

2. Use the default margins.

3. Keyboard the letter below in block (full block) style.

4. Use the Date Code feature to insert today's date.

5. Correct only immediate errors by using the backspace key.

6. Print one copy.

7. Save the exercise; name it **REGRETS**.

8. Clear your screen.

Today's date Ms. Kristin Paulo 765 Rand Road Palatine, IL 60074 Dear Ms. Paulo: Thank you for your inquiry regarding employment with our firm. ¶We have reviewed your qualifications with several members of our firm. We regret to report that we do not have an appropriate vacancy at this time. ¶We will retain your resume in our files in the event that an opening occurs in your field. ¶Your interest in our organization is very much appreciated. We hope to be able to offer you a position at another time. Very truly yours, Carol B. Giles PERSONNEL MANAGER cbg/yo

LESSON 3 / EXERCISES 11-17
EDITING DOCUMENTS

- Opening a Saved Document
- Inserting Text
- Typing Over Text
- Using Undo
- Selecting/Highlighting Text
- Deleting Text
- Undeleting Text
- Updating
- Using Convert Case

OPENING A DOCUMENT; INSERTING / TYPING OVER TEXT

NOTES:

Opening a Document

- Before a file can be revised or edited, it must be opened from the disk and placed on the screen.

- A document is revised when corrections need to be made. **Proofreader's marks** are markings on a document that indicate errors to be corrected. These markings are often abbreviated in the form of symbols. As each proofreader's mark is introduced in an exercise, it is explained and illustrated. A summary list of all proofreader's symbols and their meanings appears in Appendix B. Documents containing proofreader's symbols are often referred to as a "rough-draft" copy. After all revisions are made, the completed document is referred to as a "final copy."

- A document may be opened using Alt + F, O or Shift + F10. If the document name is not known, the document may be opened through File Manager (F5). Note Open Document dialog box below:

- Clicking on the arrow next to the text box lists the last four opened documents.

  Double click on one of the listed documents to open it.

- Opening from File Manager will be covered in the next exercise.

OPEN DOCUMENT DIALOG BOX

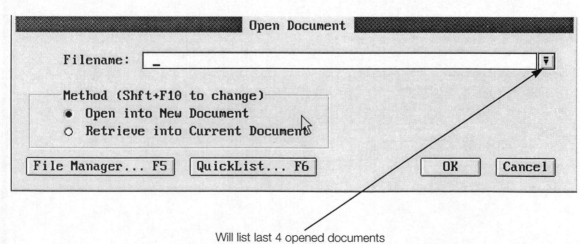

Will list last 4 opened documents

Inserting/Typing Over Text

- To make corrections, use the cursor keys to move to the point of correction or use the mouse to click at the point of correction.

- Text is inserted immediately before the cursor or insertion point. When typing inserted text, the existing text moves to the right. When inserting a word, the space following the word must also be inserted.

- Another way to edit text is to "type over" the existing text with new text. To put WordPerfect in "Typeover" mode, you must press the "Ins" key once. In this mode, existing text does not move to the right; it is typed over.

- Text is automatically adjusted after insertions have been made.

- When a file is retrieved and revisions are made, the revised or updated version must be resaved or "replaced." When a document is resaved, the old version is replaced with the new version. WordPerfect allows you to update your document with or without confirmation. If you select "save" from the File menu, your document will be saved without confirmation and you can continue working; if you "close" your file or "exit," WordPerfect will ask if you wish to save your changes.

- Use Text Mode view for editing.

- To create a new paragraph, place the cursor <u>on the first character</u> (or the insertion point to the left of the first character) of the new paragraph and press the ENTER key twice.

- The proofreader's mark for insertion is: ∧

- The proofreader's mark for a new paragraph is: ¶

EXERCISE DIRECTIONS:

1. Start with a clear screen.
2. Display the WPMAIN button bar.
3. Select Text Mode view from the button bar.
4. Open **TRY**.
5. Make the indicated insertions.
6. Use the "typeover" mode to insert the word "determine" over "decide on" in the second paragraph.
7. Print one copy (see Exercise 8).
8. Close your file; save the changes.

continued . . .

As you type, ^you will notice the "Pos" indicator on your status
line change as the position of your cursor (insertion
point) changes.

The ^" wraparound ^" feature allows the ^computer operator to ~~decide on~~ determine
line endings, making the use of the return unnecessary
except at the end of a paragraph or short line. ¶ Each
file is saved on a disk or hard drive for recall.
Documents must be given a name for identification.

data

or number

key

TO OPEN AN EXISTING DOCUMENT
Shift + F10

1. Click on File ....`Alt` + `F`
2. Click on Open ....`O`
3. Type document name to be retrieved (it may be necessary to preface the document name with the drive/directory where files are located).
4. Click on OK.................................`↵`

TO INSERT TEXT

1. Use cursor arrow keys to place cursor or insertion point one character to the left of where text is to be inserted.

or

Place mouse pointer one character to the left of where text is to be inserted and click once.

2. Type text.

TO TYPEOVER

1. Place cursor where text is to be overwritten.
2. Press "Ins" key. ....`Ins`
3. Type text.
4. Press "Ins" ....`Ins` key to exit TYPEOVER mode.

TO SAVE CHANGES
(without confirmation).
Ctrl + F12

1. Click on File ....`Alt` + `F`
2. Click on Save.............................`S`

TO CLOSE (clear screen) and SAVE CHANGES
(with confirmation).
F7, Y, N

1. Click on File ....`Alt` + `F`
2. Click on Close.............................`C`
3. Click on Yes.................................`Y`

OPENING A DOCUMENT FROM FILE MANAGER; INSERTING TEXT; USING UNDO

NOTES:

- A document may be opened from the File Manager screen if you forget the file name. If you are not certain whether the document you want opened is the right one, you may "Look" at your document before opening it. You can choose to "Look" at your document while you are in File Manager. Note the option in the dialog box below:

- To insert "Computer Associates" in this exercise, place cursor/insertion point at the end of the first line (Mr. Wallace Redfield); press the ENTER key once, then type the insertion.

Using Undo

- WordPerfect allows you to "undo" the last change you made to the document. If you make a change you want to undo, you must select "Undo" from the Edit main menu *immediately*.

- The proofreader's mark for changing upper case to lower case is: / or l.c.

FILE MANAGER DIALOG BOX

```
                         File Manager
Directory:  C:\WP60\*.*                        06-09-93  02:46a
Sort by: Filename
.     Current    <Dir>                    1. Open into New Document
..    Parent     <Dir>                    2. Retrieve into Current Doc
GRAPHICS.        <Dir>  06-06-93 11:12p   3. Look...
LEARN   .        <Dir>  06-06-93 11:12p
MACROS  .        <Dir>  06-06-93 11:11p   4. Copy...
CHARACTR.DOC  124,378   05-03-93 06:00a   5. Move/Rename...
CHARMAP .TST   69,953   05-03-93 06:00a   6. Delete
CV      .EXE  208,129   05-03-93 06:00a   7. Print...
CV{DLG} .FIL   19,012   05-03-93 06:00a   8. Print List
CV{HLP} .FIL   74,078   05-03-93 06:00a
CVDA12X .CVX   48,089   05-03-93 06:00a   9. Sort by...
CVDASC  .CVX   15,562   05-03-93 06:00a   H. Change Default Dir...
CVDBMP  .CVX    8,664   05-03-93 06:00a   U. Current Dir... F5
CVDCGM  .CVX   50,391   05-03-93 06:00a   F. Find...
CVDCOM  .CVX    2,201   05-03-93 06:00a   E. Search... F2
CVDDXF  .CVX   52,604   05-03-93 06:00a   N. Name Search
CVDEPS  .CVX    4,328   05-03-93 06:00a
CVDGIF  .CVX    7,857   05-03-93 06:00a   * (Un)mark
CVDHPGL .CVX   30,196   05-03-93 06:00a   Home,* (Un)mark All
   Files:   135      Marked:     0
   Free:  2,027,520 Used:  11,819,713   Setup... Shft+F1   Close
```

Look at document

EXERCISE DIRECTIONS:

1. Start with a clear screen.

2. Select Text Mode view.

3. "Look" at GOODJOB in the File Manager directory.

4. Open **GOODJOB.**

5. Make the indicated insertions.

6. Use "typeover" mode to change the upper case letters to lower case where you see the proofreader's mark /.

7. After typing the initials, (ah/yo) use Undo. Retype them in ALL CAPS.

8. After typing the initials in ALL CAPS, use Undo.

9. Preview your document.

10. Print one copy.

11. Close your file; save the changes.

Today's date

(Computer Associates)

Mr. Wallace Redfield
23 Main Street
Staten Island, NY 10312

Dear Mr. Redfield:

As a result of your efforts,

You are to be commended for an outstanding job as convention chair. The computer convention held last week was the best I attended. *(person)*

(have) *(in a long while)*

(guest)

The choices you made for lecturers were excellent. Every seminar I attended was interesting. *(and informative)*

Congratulations on a great job.

(Again,)

Sincerely,

Adam Howard
President

ah/yo

TO OPEN
(From File Manager)
Shift + F10, F5, ENTER

1. Click on File .... `Alt` + `F`
2. Click on Open .... `O`
3. Click in File Manager box .... `F5`
4. Type drive and/or directory where files are located.
5. Click on OK .... `⏎`

6. Click on file to be opened .... `↑` `↓`
7. Click on Open .... `O`

TO UNDO (an action)
Ctrl + Z

1. Click on Edit .... `Alt` + `E`
2. Click on Undo. .... `U`

OPENING A DOCUMENT; INSERTING TEXT

NOTES:

- This exercise will enable you to insert text from the top of the page and create a modified block letter. To insert the date, press the return key enough times to bring the "Ln" indicator to 2.5"; then press the tab enough times to bring the "Pos" indicator to 4.5". You are now ready to type the date. Remember to use WordPerfect's date feature.

- After typing the date, you will continue inserting the inside address and salutation. Text will adjust as you continue creating the letter.

EXERCISE DIRECTIONS:

1.	Start with a clear screen.
2.	Select Text Mode view.
3.	Open **TRYAGAIN**.
4.	Use Date Text to insert today's date.
5.	Make the indicated insertions. Follow the formatting for a modified-block letter illustrated in Exercise 6.
6.	Use "typeover" mode to insert the word "start" over "begin" in the second paragraph.
7.	Print one copy.
8.	Close your file; save the changes.

Today's date

Insert {

Ms. Donna Applegate
Consultants Unlimited, Inc.
45 East 45 Street
New York, NY 10022

Dear Ms. Applegate:

In response to your inquiry about software programs, I have outlined below some of the merits of WordPerfect.

WordPerfect is simple to use since you can ~~begin~~ **Start** typing as soon as you enter the program. *(when you begin typing)*

The way text will lay out or "format" on a page is set by the WordPerfect program. For example, margins are set for 1" on the left and 1" on the right; line spacing is set for single space; tabs are set to advance the cursor 1/2 inch each time the tab key is pressed. Formats may be changed at any time and as many times throughout the document. *(automatically)*

(as desired)

Yours truly,

Jerry O'brien
Sales Manager

Insert {

JO/yo

OPENING A DOCUMENT; SELECTING TEXT; DELETING TEXT; UNDELETING TEXT

NOTES:

Deleting text

- Procedures for deleting text vary depending on what is being deleted: a character, previous character, word, line, paragraph, page, remainder of page, or blank line.

- The proofreader's mark for deletion is ✗.

- The proofreader's mark for closing up space is ◡ .

- Use the backspace key to delete characters and close up spaces to the left of the cursor/insertion point.

- To **delete a character or a space** after text is typed, place the cursor (in Text Mode) on the character or space to be deleted, or place the insertion point (in Graphics Mode or Page Mode) immediately to the left of the character or space to be deleted, then press the "Del" key.

Selecting text

- **To delete a block of text** (words, sentences and paragraphs), you must first highlight or "select" the text to be deleted. Text may be "selected" in several ways:

  - by clicking and dragging the mouse over desired text. This is the fastest way to highlight text.

  - by placing the cursor on the first character in the text to be deleted, pressing Alt+F4 (or Alt+E, B) and using the arrow keys to highlight desired text. This procedure is referred to as "block" highlight . To quickly highlight a sentence after block has been accessed (Alt + F4), press the end punctuation in the sentence (period, question mark, exclamation point). The highlighting will continue until it encounters the first occurrence of that mark. To quickly highlight a paragraph, turn on "block" and press ENTER. Highlighting will continue until it encounters a hard return.

  - by selecting "Select" from the Edit menu and choosing Sentence, Paragraph or Page.

- Once the desired text to be deleted has been selected, press the Del key.

- There is an "express" method to delete a word, the remainder of a line, and the remainder of a page without highlighting the text. Note keystroke procedures outlined.

- **To combine two paragraphs into one**, you must delete hard returns that separate the paragraphs. Either highlight the blank space that separates the paragraphs or place the cursor at the end of the paragraph after the period and depress the "Del" key twice, or as many times as necessary to bring the paragraphs together. Sometimes you must adjust the spacing between sentences by inserting two spaces.

- To **delete a tab**, place the cursor at the left margin (to the left of the indent) and press the "Del" key once.

- Note each deletion in the exercise and use the proper keystroke procedure outlined to accomplish it.

Undeleting text

- Text may be restored after it has been deleted. Your cursor/insertion point should be in the location you wish the text to be restored when accessing this task. WordPerfect remembers your last three deletions and allows you to restore them.

EXERCISE DIRECTIONS:

1. Start with a clear screen.
2. Select Text Mode view.
3. Access File Manager.
4. "Look" at each document until you find the document that contains information about the Cayman Islands; then, open that file.
5. Using the procedures indicated, make the deletions shown in the exercise.
6. After deleting the last paragraph (remainder of page), undelete it.
7. Use the mouse to highlight the last paragraph.
8. Delete it again.
9. Print one copy.
10. Close your file; save the changes.

continued . . .

REMAINDER OF LINE ▶ ~~DIVING VACATIONS~~
DIVING IN THE CAYMAN ISLANDS

CHAR/WORD
WORD
Do you want to see sharks, barracudas and ~~huge~~ stingrays? Do you want to see ~~gentle~~ angels, too?

CHAR/
WORD
WORD/CHAR
WORD
The Cayman Islands were discovered by Christopher Columbus in ~~late~~ 1503. The Cayman Islands are located ~~just~~ south of Cuba. The Caymans are ~~the~~ home to only about 25,000 year-around residents. However, they welcome ~~approximately~~ 200,000 visitors

BLOCK-
HIGHLIGHT
SENTENCE ▶
each year. ~~Each year, more and more visitors arrive.~~ Most visitors come with ~~colorful~~ masks and flippers in their luggage ~~ready to go scuba diving.~~ ◀ REMAINDER OF LINE

BLOCK-
HIGHLIGHT
PARAGRAPH
~~Because of the magnificence of the coral reef, scuba diving has become to the Cayman Islands what safaris are to Kenya. If you go into a bookstore, you can buy diving gear.~~

Now, you are ready to jump in.

WORDS
~~Recommendations for~~ Hotel/Diving Accommodations:

PART OF
WORD/CHAR
Sunset House, ~~Post Office~~ Box 4791, George Towne, Grand Cayman; (800) 854-4767.

PART OF
WORD/CHAR
Coconut Harbour, ~~Post Office~~ Box 2086, George Towne, Grand Cayman; (809) 949-7468.

REMAINDER
OF PAGE
~~Seeing a shark is frightening at first; they seem to come out of nowhere and then return to nowhere. But as soon as the creature disappears, you will swim after it. You will just want to keep this beautiful, graceful fish in view as long as you can.~~

TO SELECT TEXT

With mouse

1. Position insertion point at beginning of text to be selected.

2. Hold down left mouse button and drag over text to select.

3. Release left mouse button.

With keyboard
Alt + F4, arrow keys

1. Position cursor in text to be selected.

2. Click on Edit......................`Alt` + `E`

3. Click on Select............................`S`

4. Specify amount of text to select:

   Sentence.......................................`S`

   Paragraph ....`P`

   Page...`A`

TO DELETE

A character

1. Place cursor on character or space to be deleted.

   or

   Place insertion point immediately to the left of character or space to be deleted.

2. Press **Del**ete key. ....`Del`

A word

1. Place cursor anywhere on word to be deleted.

   or

   Place insertion point immediately to the left of character or space to be deleted.

2. Press Crtl + Backspace.....................
   ....`Ctrl` + `Backspace`

Remainder of line

1. Place cursor anywhere on word to be deleted.

   or

   Place insertion point immediately to the left of character or space to be deleted.

2. Press Ctrl + End............`Ctrl` + `End`

Remainder of page

1. Place cursor on first character to be deleted.

   or

   Place insertion point immediately to the left of character or space to be deleted.

2. Press Ctrl+PgDn...........`Ctrl` + `PgDn`

3. Press Y...`Y`
   to confirm deletion.

Using block highlight
Alt + F4

1. Place cursor on first character to be deleted.

   or

   Place insertion point immediately to the left of character or space to be deleted.

2. Select Edit.........................`Alt` + `E`

3. Select Block.................................`B`

4. Choose an express highlight option:.......................press:

   - one character right...................`→`

   - one word right ....`Space`

   - one line down.......................`↓`

   - a sentence.....................................
     ....punctuation mark

   - a paragraph.............................`↵`

5. Press **Del**ete or Backspace key......`Del` or `Backspace`

Using mouse highlight

1. Place cursor on first character to be deleted.

   or

   Place insertion point immediately to the left of character or space to be deleted.

2. Click and drag mouse over text to be deleted.

3. Press **Del**ete or Backspace key......`Del` or `Backspace`

TO UNDELETE
Escape, R or P

1. Click on Edit......................`Alt` + `E`

2. Click on Undelete ....`N`

   Select option:

3. Click on Restore ....`R`

   to restore last deletion.

   or

   • Click on Previous Deletion.......`P`
     until desired deletion appears.

   • Click on Restore ....`R`

OPENING A DOCUMENT; DELETING TEXT

NOTES:

- To bring the date and closing to the left margin (making this letter block style), place the cursor/insertion point at the left margin on the same line as the date and press the **Del**ete key several times until the date moves to the margin. Or, you may use the mouse to highlight the blank space to the left of the date and press the **Del**ete key. Do the same to bring the closing to the left margin.

EXERCISE DIRECTIONS:

1. Start with a clear screen.
2. Select the Text Mode view.
3. Access File Manager.
4. Open **LETTER**.
5. Using the mouse to highlight text blocks, make the indicated deletions. Place the cursor/insertion point appropriately and use the Delete key to make character/space deletions.
6. Preview your work.
7. Print one copy.
8. Close the file; save the changes.

October 1, 199-

Ms. Renee S. Brown
54 Williams Street
Omaha, NE 68101

Dear Ms. Brown:

Thank you for your $ 150 contribution to the American Art Institution. This contribution ~~automatically~~ makes you a member in our arts program.

As an active member, you can participate in our many ~~educational~~ activities.

For example, you can take part in ~~our~~ monthly art lectures, ~~our~~ semi-annual auctions and ~~our~~ frequent art exhibits. Admission to ~~all these~~ events is free.

We look forward to seeing you at our next meeting. ~~We know you will enjoy speaking with our other members and participating in very stimulating conversation.~~

Sincerely,

Alan Barry
President

ab/yo

OPENING A DOCUMENT; DELETING TEXT; UNDO VS. UNDELETE; CONVERT CASE

NOTES:

- In Exercise 12, you learned to use UNDO, and in Exercise 14, you learned to use UNDELETE. Note the distinction:

  Use UNDO to reverse the last change or action made to the document. You may use UNDO to restore text after it has been deleted, *but you must use this command immediately after you delete the text.*

  Use UNDELETE to restore the most recent deletion or up to three previous deletions. For example, if you delete a sentence and then insert a word, you would use UNDELETE to restore the sentence. If you use UNDO, you would remove the inserted word.

- WordPerfect's Convert Case feature allows you to change an existing block of text to all upper or lower case, or lower case with initial caps.

- The proofreaders' mark for capitalization is: ≡

EXERCISE DIRECTIONS:

1. Start with a clear screen.
2. Select the Text Mode view.
3. Open **TRYAGAIN.**
4. Using the mouse to highlight text blocks, make the indicated deletions. Place the cursor/insertion point appropriately and use the Delete key to make character/space deletions.
5. Convert all occurrences of the word WordPerfect to upper case.
6. After all deletions are made, restore or "undelete" the last deletion (*"at any time and as many times"*).
7. Convert the last sentence to upper case.
8. UNDO the last change.
9. Print one copy.
10. Close the file; save the changes.

January 10, 199-

Ms. Donna Applegate
Consultants Unlimited, Inc.
45 East 45 Street
New York, NY 10022

Dear Ms. Applegate:

In response to your inquiry about software programs, I have outlined below some of the merits of WordPerfect.

WordPerfect is simple to use, since you can start typing as soon as you enter the program.

The way text will ~~lay out or~~ format ~~on a page~~ when you begin typing is automatically set by the WordPerfect program. For example, margins are automatically set for 1" on the left and 1" ~~in~~ on the right; line spacing is set for single space; tabs are set to advance the cursor 1/2 inch each time the tab key is depressed.

Formats may be changed ~~at any time and as many times~~ as desired throughout the document.

Yours truly,

Jerry O'brien
Sales Manager

jo/yo

TO CONVERT CASE
Shift + F3, then step 4

1. Select/highlight text to be converted.
2. Click on Edit......................`Alt` + `E`
3. Click on Convert...........................`V`
4. Click on a convert option:

   Uppercase.......................`U`

   Lowercase.......................`L`

   Initial Caps.......................`I`

OPENING A DOCUMENT; INSERTING AND DELETING TEXT; INSERTING A HARD SPACE

NOTES:

- Moving the date and closing to 4.5" (the center of the paper) will make this a modified-block letter. To do this, place the cursor on the first letter of the date (or position the insertion point to the left of the first letter.) Then press the tab key as many times as necessary to bring the test to 4.5".

- To prevent two or more words from splitting during "word wrap" a **hard space** can be inserted between the words. This is particularly necessary when keyboarding first and last names, dates, equations and time.

- The proofreaders' mark for moving text right is ⌐
  or ⊢→

- The proofreaders' mark for inserting a hard space is △

EXERCISE DIRECTIONS:

1. Start with a clear screen.

2. Select the Text Mode view.

3. Open **BLOCK**.

4. Make the indicated revisions; insert a hard space where you see the △ symbol.

5. After all revisions are made, UNDELETE the last deleted sentence.

6. Convert ANNUAL AWARDS DINNER to lower case with initial caps.

7. UNDO this last change.

8. Print one copy.

9. Close your file; save the changes.

Today's Date $\longrightarrow$ 4.5" (tab 7 times)

T.
Mr. Thomas Walen
Updike Mechanics Company
23 Clogg Avenue
Atlanta, GA 30315

Dear Mr. Walen:

, Mr. Walen

CONGRATULATIONS! You have been nominated as the outstanding office employee
of the month beginning NovemberΔ4,Δ1993 through NovemberΔ30,Δ1993. ¶ We made your
selection based on the recommendations of your supervisors.

Selection The Committee that made your selection requires that you submit a photograph of
                                                                          to
yourself to your supervisor so that we can display your picture in the company's executive
offices.

Immediate   , Mr. Quinn.   will then   throughout

Updike Mechanics is proud of your accomplishments. We look forward to honoring you
at our ANNUAL AWARDS DINNER on DecemberΔ3.

Sincerely, $\longrightarrow$ 4.5" (tab 7 times)

Paulette Manning
President

pm/yo

Restore the last delete.

TO INSERT A HARD SPACE

1. Type first word.
2. Press Home +
    SPACEBAR................. [Home] + [Space]
3. Type next word.

NOTES: You may work in any view, and display the button and scroll bars as you desire.

EXERCISE DIRECTIONS:

1. Start with a clear screen.
2. Open **REGRETS** from File Manager.
3. Make the indicated revisions.

4. Convert PERSONNEL MANAGER to lower case with inital caps.
5. Print one copy.
6. Close your file; save the changes.

Today's date)———————————→

Ms. Kristin ~~Turner~~ Paulo
765 Rand ~~Road~~ Avenue
Palatine, IL 60074

Dear Ms. Paulo:

→ Thank you for your recent inquiry regarding employment with ~~our firm.~~ Quartz Industries, Inc.

→ We have reviewed your qualifications with ~~several members of our firm.~~ the various Quartz-affiliated companies and We regret to report that we do not have an appropriate vacancy ~~at this time.~~

(We ~~will~~ are, however, taking the liberty of retain(ing) your resume in our active files in the event ~~that an~~ of future opening(s) ~~occurs~~ in your field.

→ Your interest in our organization is very much appreciated, and We hope to be able to offer you a position at ~~another time.~~ a later date. sincerely

Very truly yours,

Carol B. Giles
~~PERSONNEL MANAGER~~

cbg:yo

NOTES: You may work in any view, and display the button and scroll bars as you desire.

EXERCISE DIRECTIONS:

1. Start with a clear screen.
2. Open **OPEN** from File Manager.
3. **Change the letter style to block.**
4. Make the indicated revisions.
5. Insert a hard space between times and phone numbers.
6. Print one copy.
7. Close your file; save the changes.

(Arnco Industries, Inc.)   January 22, 199-

T.

Mr. Martin Quincy, President
641 Lexington Avenue
New York, NY 10022

Dear Mr. Quincy:

We are pleased to announce the opening of a new subsidary of our company, We COMPUSELLTRAIN. specialize in ~~selling~~, training and ~~service~~ of portable personal computers.
Service   sales

~~This may be hard to believe, but~~ we carry a full line of portable personal computers that can do (All of) everything a conventional desktop can. Our portables can run ~~all of~~ the same applications (computers) as your company's conventional PCs. With the purchase of a computer, we will train two employees on your firm on ~~how to~~ use an application of your choice.

(The) (of)

~~For a free demonstration, call us at 212-456-9876 any business day from 9:00 a.m. to 5:00 p.m.~~

A | The rep for your area is Ms. Sally Hansen. She will phone you to discuss your possible needs.

Very truly yours   The graphics
~~Sincerely,~~   capabilities are
                          outstanding.

Theresa Mann
President

tm:yo

Restore the deleted paragraph.

LESSON 4 / EXERCISES 18-27
FORMATTING AND EDITING

- Text Alignments
- Centering Page Top to Bottom
- Justification: Left, Center, Right, Full

- Spell Check
- Creating a Memorandum
- Emphasizing Text: Bold, Underline, Double Underline, Italics, Outline, Shadow

- Romoving Emphasis Styles
- Using the Repeat Key

TEXT ALIGNMENT: CENTER; CENTER PAGE FROM TOP TO BOTTOM (HORIZONTAL AND VERTICAL CENTERING)

NOTES:

- WordPerfect provides a convenient method of centering individual lines of text. By using a special code or clicking on the Center button on the LAYOUT button bar text can be horizontally centered between margins, on a tab or in a column. You may center before or after typing text.

- Text may also be centered vertically on a page (center page from top to bottom). If there are returns before or after the centered text,

WordPerfect will include them in the vertical centering. Therefore, if you plan to vertically center text, be sure to start the text at the top of your screen.

- This exercise will give you practice centering text horizontally and vertically.

The proofreader's mark for centering is: ⊐⊏

EXERCISE DIRECTIONS:

1. Select Graphics Mode view.
2. Display LAYOUT button bar (Alt + V, S, S, LAYOUT).
3. Begin the exercise at the top of a clear screen.
4. Use the default margins.
5. Center the page from top to bottom (vertically center).
6. Create the announcement on the right as indicated.
7. Preview your work.
8. Print one copy.
9. Save the exercise; name it **RSVP.**

Celebrate

↓2×

On The Hudson

↓3×

This New Year's Eve, there is no more elegant, more beautiful spot than the Hudson River Cafe. Dance with the Statue of Liberty in view to the sounds of our live band and DJ.

↓2×

Enjoy a six-course Hudson Valley feast and a spectacular dessert to be remembered as the last memory of the year.

↓3×

NEW YEAR'S EVE DINNER DANCE

↓3×

Call for reservations 212-876-9888. Our courteous staff will be glad to assist you at any time. We are located at Four World Financial Center.

↓2×

HUDSON RIVER CLUB

TO CENTER

Before typing

1. Place cursor/insertion point at beginning of line to be centered.

2. Press Shift + F6 .... `Shift`+`F6`

   or

- Click on *Center*
  in LAYOUT button bar. .... `Center`

3. Type text.

4. Press ENTER .... `↵`
   to return to left margin.

After typing

1. Select/highlight text to be centered.

2. Press Shift + F6................`Shift`+`F6`

   or

- Click on *Center*
  in LAYOUT button bar. ....`Center`

TO CENTER PAGE TOP TO BOTTOM (Vertically Center)

Shift + F8, P, C

NOTE: The text will not appear centered on the screen, but will appear centered on the page in preview mode and will print with text centered vertically.

1. Place cursor at beginning of page to be centered.

2. Click on Layout .... `Alt`+`L`

3. Click on Page.............................. `P`

4. Click in Center
   Current Page box.................... `C`

5. Click on OK.............................. `↵`

6. Click on Close............................ `↵`

53

TEXT ALIGNMENT: FLUSH RIGHT; CENTER PAGE FROM TOP TO BOTTOM

NOTES:

- Flush right is a feature that aligns individual lines or parts of a line of text at the right margin. You may flush right before or after typing text by using a special code or clicking on the Flush Rgt button on the LAYOUT button bar.

- Right alignment is particularly useful when typing dates, creating invitations or business headings.

EXERCISE DIRECTIONS:

1. Select Graphics Mode view.
2. Display the LAYOUT button bar (Alt + V, S, S, LAYOUT).
3. Begin the exercise at the top of a clear screen.
4. Use the default margins.
5. Center the page from top to bottom.
6. Center and right align text as indicated.
7. Print one copy.
8. Save the exercise; name it **CONGRATS.**

MORITZ & CHASE
↓2x
Is Pleased to Announce that the following Associates will become members of the firm on
↓2x
January 1, 1994
↓2x

DENVER   Steven M. Jones

NEW YORK   Arthur J. Williams

SAN FRANCISCO   Roberta W. Asher
                                          Donna Newman

WASHINGTON, D.C.   Pamela T. Blanco

and that the following Of Counsel will become members of the firm on
↓2x
January 1, 1994
↓2x

LONDON   Raymond T. Sedgewick

LOS ANGELES   Angela Tsacoumis
                                          Roberto Vasquez

TO FLUSH RIGHT
Before typing
1. Place cursor/insertion point at beginning of line to flush right.
2. Press Alt + F6 .... `Alt` + `F6`
   or
• Click on *Flush Rgt* in LAYOUT button bar. .... `FlushRgt`
3. Type text.
4. Press ENTER. .... `⏎`
   to return to left margin.

After typing
1. Select/highlight text to flush right.
2. Press Alt + F6. .... `Alt` + `F6`
   or
• Click on *Flush Rgt* in LAYOUT button bar. .... `FlushRgt`

TEXT ALIGNMENT: JUSTIFICATION

NOTES:

- Justification allows you to align all text that follows the justification code until another justification code is entered. WordPerfect provides four kinds of alignment options:

Left	– all lines are even at the left margin but are ragged at the right margin.
Center	– all lines are centered between the margins.
Right	– all lines are ragged at the left margin and are even at the right margin.
Full	– all lines are even at the left and right margins.

- Note example of each alignment option on next page.

- Justification should be used to affect blocks of text, not individual lines.

- Justification may be changed before or after typing text.

  Caution: when you change justification to existing text, all text following the code will change. Do not be alarmed. Insert another justification code to restore your text as desired.

- By default, WordPerfect applies *left* justification to your text. Note the "Left" justification setting which appears on the Ribbon.

- Justification may be set on the ribbon, through the menus, or by clicking the JustLeft, JustCntr, JustRght, or JustFull on the LAYOUT button bar.

- Full justification will not display on the screen in Text Mode, but may be seen in Graphics Mode or in Print Preview.

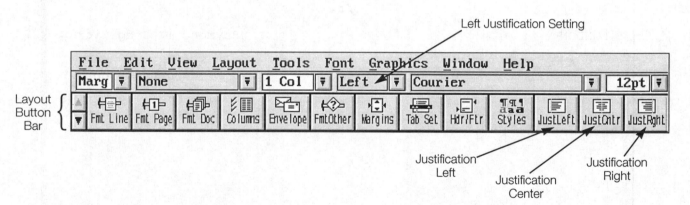

EXERCISE DIRECTIONS:

1. Select Graphics Mode view.

2. Display the LAYOUT button bar (Alt + V, S, S, LAYOUT)

3. Begin the exercise at the top of a clear screen.

4. Center the page top to bottom.

5. Type each section of text on the right, changing the justification alignment appropriately.

6. Print one copy.

7. Convert the last block of text from upper case to lower case with initial capitals.

8. Preview your document.

9. Save the exercise; name it **COMPANY.**

Janet Reed is our consultant who can advise you about software companies and their products that can best meet the needs of those in the accounting and personal finance areas. In addition, she can evaluate your general office work flow and recommend hardware configurations and software to best serve your needs. Below is a brief list of software companies and the products they produce.

↓ 3x

ACCOUNTING & PERSONAL FINANCE
SOFTWARE COMPANIES
Astrix
Absolute Solutions
Check Mark Software
Computer Associates
Softview
Teleware
TimeSlips Corporation

↓ 3x

BUSINESS & PRESENTATION
SOFTWARE COMPANIES
ACIUS
AISB
Aldus
Aston-Tate
CE Software
Fox Software
Microsoft
PowerUP!
Satori

↓ 3x

CALL 1-800-205-9831
ANY BUSINESS DAY
FOR INFORMATION
ABOUT
THE ABOVE COMPANIES
AND THEIR PRODUCTS

TO JUSTIFY

Shift + F8 L, J

1. Place cursor at beginning of text to receive justification change (*before typing text*).

   or

- Select/highlight text to receive justification change (*after typing text*).

2. Click on Layout .... `Alt` + `L`

3. Click on Justification .... `J`

4. Click on a justification option:

   Left .... `L`

   Center .... `C`

   Right .... `R`

   Full .... `F`

or

1. Place cursor at beginning of text to receive justification change (*before typing text*).

   or

- Select/highlight text to receive justification change (*after typing text*).

2. Click on a justification button on the LAYOUT button bar:

   JustLeft .... `JustLeft`

   JustCntr .... `JustCntr`

   JustRght .... `JustRght`

   JustFull .... `JustFull`

or

1. Place cursor at beginning of text to receive justification change (*before typing text*).

   or

- Select/highlight text to receive justification change (*after typing text*).

2. Click on justification arrow on the ribbon.

3. Double click on a justification option:

   Left

   Center

   Right

   Full

TEXT ALIGNMENT; USING SPELL CHECK

NOTES:

- The WordPerfect spelling feature will check the spelling of your document and look for double words, words containing numbers and irregular capitalization. A word, page or entire document may be checked for spelling errors. The speller compares the words in your document with the words in the WordPerfect dictionary. When a misspelled word is found, spell check offers possible spelling choices so you can replace the

error. Spell check may be accessed through the menus or by clicking on the Speller button in the MAIN and TOOLS button bars.

- Special words may be added to the supplementary dictionary.

- Spell check does not find errors in word usage. Finding usage errors will be covered when Grammatik is introduced in Exercise 38.

EXERCISE DIRECTIONS:

1. Select Text Mode view.
2. Display the LAYOUT button bar.
3. Keyboard the letter on the right exactly as shown including the circled misspelled words. Align text flush right where indicated. Use full justification for paragraph text.

4. Display the TOOLS/or WPMAIN button bar.
5 After completing the exercise, spell check the page by clicking on Speller in the button bar.
6. Preview your document.
7. Print one copy.
8. Save the file; name it **GLOBAL**.

TO SPELL CHECK
Alt + F1, S, then step 5

1. • To check a **word**, select/highlight the word.
   • To check a **page,** position cursor anywhere on the page.
   • To check a **document,** position cursor anywhere in the document.
   • To check a **document from the cursor positon,** position cursor where spell check is to begin.
2. Click on *Speller* in TOOLS or WPMAIN button bar. .... [Speller] then skip to step 5.
   or
   • Click on Tools .... [Alt] + [T]

3. Click on Writing Tools.................. [W]
4. Click on Speller .... [S]
5. Click on a spell check option:
   Word .... [W]
   Page... [P]
   Document .... [D]
   From Cursor .... [F]
6. If an error is found, click on one or more options:
   • Skip Once .... [O] to ignore selected word and continue
   • Skip in this Document.............. [S] to ignore all occurrences of word in document.
   • Add to Dictionary .... [T] to add word to WP dictionary.

- Edit Word .... [W] to make changes to word not found in WP dictionary.
- Ignore Numbers .... [I] to ignore numbers while spell checking.
- Replace Word .... [R] to replace word with suggested spelling.
   or
- highlight correct spelling from list of suggestions.
- press ENTER........................... [↵]

7. Click on Cancel........................... [↵]
   or
   To cancel a spell check:
   Click on Cancel .... [Esc]

THE GLOBAL TRAVEL GROUP
485 Madison Avenue
New York, NY 10034

PHONE: (212) 234-4566
FAX: (212) 345-9877

Today' Date

Mr. Astrit Ibrosi
45 Lake View Drive
Huntington, NY 11543

Dear Mr. Ibrosi:

Ms. Packer in our office has (refered) your letter to me. You had
asked her to provide you with a list of hotels in the San Francisco
area that have a business center which offers laptop rentals, fax
services, and teleconferencing capabilities.

Since I am the representative for the San Francisco area, I have
compiled a list of hotels that offer the services you requested.
They appear below:

                    Regency Central
                     Surry Hotel
                    Fairmont Hotel
                 Renaissance Center
                    Marriott Mark
                     Grand Hyatt

When you are ready to make your reservations, please call our
office. If you have any other travel needs, call GLOBAL. Our
(expereinced) staff will give you prompt and (courtous) service and
will answer all your travel questions.

Sincerely,

Marietta Dunn
Travel Representative

md/yo

CREATING A MEMORANDUM; TEXT ALIGNMENT; USING SPELL CHECK

NOTES:

- The "memo" is a written communication within a company. Companies create memos on blank paper or on letterhead. Some use preprinted forms, while others create the memo form.

- A memo should begin 1" from the top of the page, which is the top of your screen. The word "MEMORANDUM" may be centered as illustrated or it may be omitted, if desired.

- Memorandums are usually prepared with all parts beginning at the left margin.

- "Re" (in reference to) is often used in place of the word "Subject" in the memorandum heading.

- Memorandums are generally not centered vertically.

- Double space between each part of the memorandum heading; the body of the memo begins a triple space below the subject line.

- If copies are to be sent to others, a copy notation may be indicated as the last item on a page.

EXERCISE DIRECTIONS:

1. Select Text Mode view.
2. Display the LAYOUT button bar.
3. Keyboard the memorandum on the right, centering text where indicated. Use full justification on paragraph text.
4. Display the TOOLS button bar.
5. After completing the exercise, spell check the page.
6. Preview your document.
7. Print one copy.
8. Save the exercise; name it **MEMO.**

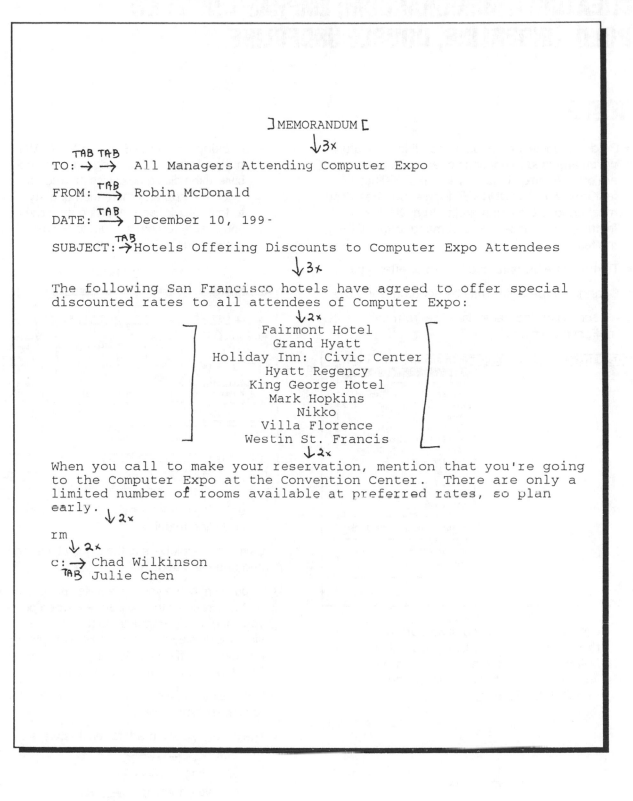

]MEMORANDUM [
                    ↓3x
TAB TAB
TO: → →   All Managers Attending Computer Expo

FROM: TAB→ Robin McDonald

DATE: TAB→ December 10, 199-

SUBJECT: TAB→Hotels Offering Discounts to Computer Expo Attendees
                    ↓3x

The following San Francisco hotels have agreed to offer special
discounted rates to all attendees of Computer Expo:
                    ↓2x
                Fairmont Hotel
                Grand Hyatt
        Holiday Inn: Civic Center
                Hyatt Regency
            King George Hotel
                Mark Hopkins
                    Nikko
                Villa Florence
            Westin St. Francis
                    ↓2x
When you call to make your reservation, mention that you're going
to the Computer Expo at the Convention Center. There are only a
limited number of rooms available at preferred rates, so plan
early. ↓2x

rm
    ↓2x
c: → Chad Wilkinson
  TAB Julie Chen

CREATING A MEMORANDUM; EMPHASIZING TEXT: BOLD, UNDERLINE, DOUBLE UNDERLINE

NOTES:

• Bold, underline, and double underline are features which are used to enhance or emphasize text and are often referred to as "type styles." These features work as "ON/OFF" toggle switches. You must choose the command to turn ON the feature; then choose the command to turn OFF the feature.

• Text may be emphasized before or after typing.

• Changing type styles may be accomplished by:

  – accessing the particular style from the Font main menu.

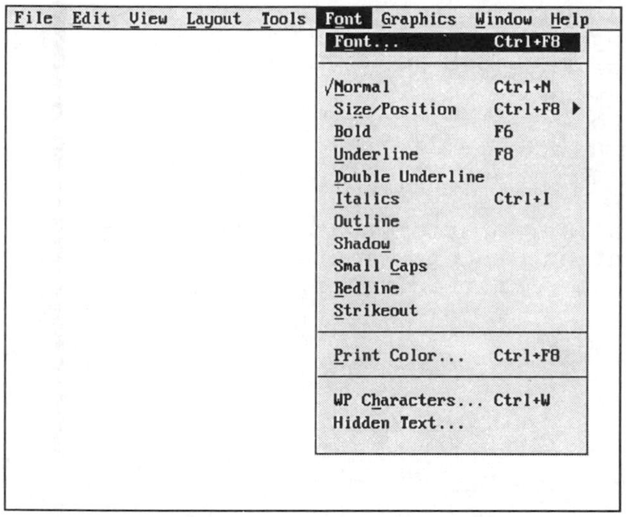

  – clicking on the desired style button in the FONTS button bar illustrated below. After bolding desired, text, you must return to "Normal" mode to turn OFF the feature.

  – clicking on FONTS in the WPMAIN button bar and selecting the desired style in the dialog box. Use this method if you are applying more than one style to text. Again, after applying the styles you desire, you must return to "Normal" mode to turn OFF the feature.

FONT DIALOG BOX

Normal Mode

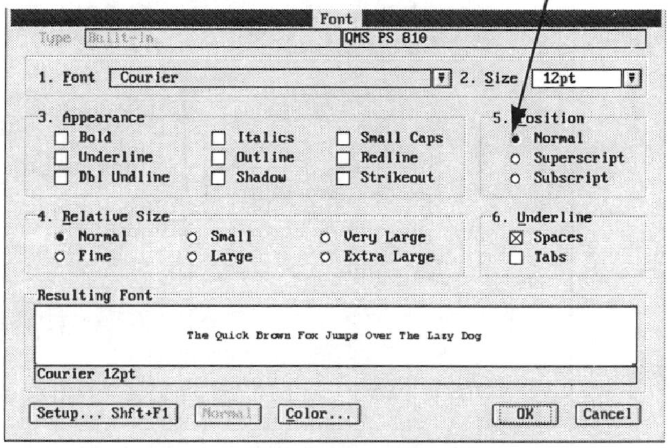

  – using "quick" keys for bold and underline features.

• Using the quick keys is the simplist way to bold and underline text.

• If you wish to see your type style changes appear on the screen as they will appear when printed, you should use Graphics Mode view. Text mode view will display the changes by highlighting each change in a different color. If you preview while in Text Mode, the styles will be visible.

• In this exercise, you may use any method desired to change type styles.

• The proofreader's mark for each style is:

  bold: ⁓⁓⁓ 
  underline: _____
  double underline: ═══

Normal Mode

Fonts Button Bar

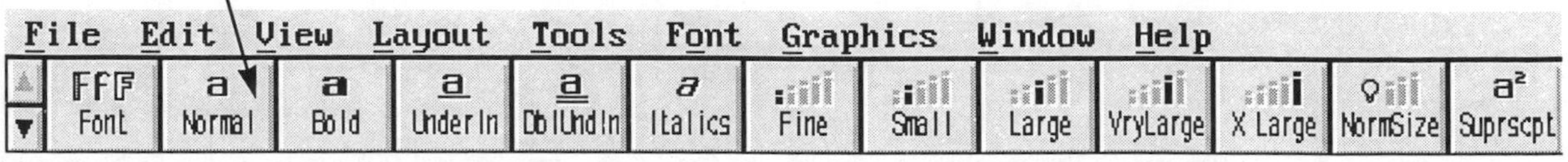

EXERCISE DIRECTIONS:

1. Select Graphics Mode view.

2. Display the MAIN button bar.

3. Start with a clear screen.

4. Keyboard the memorandum on the next page, bolding, underlining and double underlining where indicated.

5. Spell check.

6. Preview your document.

7. Print one copy.

8. Save the exercise; name it **MEMONEWS.**

continued . . .

MEMORANDUM

TO: The Staff

FROM: Sarah Walesk

DATE: December 9, 199-

RE: Computer Expo

I strongly urge you to attend this year's Computer Expo. In four
days, you'll pick up all the latest computer news and discover
new ways to put your computer to work -- in the office, in the
lab, in the studio, in the classroom, or in your home.

Here are some of the events you can look forward to:

Keynote Sessions. These sessions will feature luminaries from
the computer world who will offer you insights from industry.
Application Workshops. Join a series of two-hour learning
sessions which will provide guidelines, tips and "how-to's" on
popular software packages.
Programmer/Developer Forums. Veteran and novice computer users
will brainstorm so you can learn about innovative advances and
techniques.

If you are interested in attending, see Derek Brennan. He will
pre-register anyone from our company who wishes to attend. This
will save you long lines at the show.

sw

TO BOLD

Before typing

F6, type text, F6

1. Click on F<u>o</u>nt.....................`Alt` + `O`
2. Click on <u>B</u>old...............................`B`
3. Type text.
4. Repeat steps 1 and 2 to turn OFF feature.

    or

    • Click on *Font button* in FONTS button bar...............`FFF Font`

    • Click on *Bold button*.............`a Bold`

    • Type text
    • Click on *Normal button* ....`a Normal`

After typing

select text, F6

1. Select/highlight text to be bolded.
2. Click on F<u>o</u>nt.....................`Alt` + `O`

    Click on <u>B</u>old...............................`B`

    or

    • Click on *Font button* in FONTS button bar...........`FFF Font`

    • Click on *Bold button*.............`a Bold`

TO UNDERLINE/DOUBLE UNDERLINE

Before typing

F8, type text, F8 (for underline only)

1. Click on F<u>o</u>nt.....................`Alt` + `O`
2. Click on <u>U</u>nderline.........................`U`

    or

    Click on <u>D</u>ouble Underline.............`D`
3. Type text.
4. Repeat steps 1 and 2 to turn OFF feature.

    or

    • Click on *Font button* in FONTS button bar...............`FFF Font`

    • Click on *Underln* or *DblUndln* button...................`a Underln` or `a DblUndln`

    • Type text.
    • Click on *Normal button*...............................`a Normal`

After typing

select text, F8 (for underline only)

1. Select/highlight text to be underlined.
2. Click on F<u>o</u>nt.....................`Alt` + `O`

    Click on <u>U</u>nderline.........................`U`

    or

    Click on <u>D</u>ouble Underline............`D`

    or

    • Click on *Font button* in FONTS button bar..........`FFF Font`

    • Click on *Underln* or *DblUndln* button...................`a Underln` or `a DblUndln`

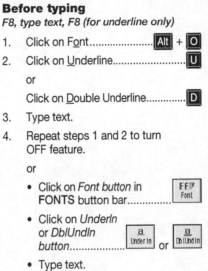

EMPHASIZING TEXT: BOLD, UNDERLINE, DOUBLE UNDERLINE

EXERCISE DIRECTIONS:

1. Select Graphics Mode view.
2. Display FONTS button bar.
3. Start with a clear screen.
4. Open **DIVE.**
5. Make the indicated revisions, bolding and underlining where shown.
6. In addition to bolding, double underline DIVING IN THE CAYMAN ISLANDS.
7. Preview your document.
8. Print one copy.
9. Close your file; save the changes.

double underline
and bold

DIVING IN THE CAYMAN ISLANDS → center

and angel fish

Do you want to see sharks, barracudas ~~and~~ stingrays? ~~Do you want to see angels, too?~~

The Cayman Islands were discovered by Christopher Columbus in 1503. ~~The Cayman Islands~~ and are located south of Cuba. The Caymans are home to ~~only~~ about 25,000 year-around residents. However, they welcome 200,000 visitors each year. Most visitors come with masks and flippers in their luggage. ~~Now, you are ready to jump in!~~

Hotel/Diving Accommodations:

Sunset House, PO Box 479, George Town, Grand Cayman; (800) 854-4767.

Coconut Harbour, PO Box 2086, George Town, Grand Cayman; (809) 949-7468.

Red Sail Sports, PO Box 1588, George Town, Grand Cayman; (809) 979-7965.

Cayman Diving Lodge, PO Box 11, East End, Grand Cayman; (809) 947-7555.

Anchorage View, PO Box 2123, Grand Cayman; (809) 947-4209.

EMPHASIZING TEXT: ITALICS, OUTLINE, SHADOW, SMALL CAPS

NOTES:

- In addition to bold, underline and double underline, WordPerfect provides other emphasis styles. These include italics, outline, shadow and small caps. Note examples of each:

  italics
  outline
  shadow
  SMALL CAPS

- Like the other styles, these may be applied before or after typing text. They may be accessed using the same methods previously presented for the other styles (see Exercise 24).

- You must use Graphics Mode view to see the type styles as they will appear when printed.

Text Mode view will display the changes by highlighting each in a different color.

However, if you preview your document while in Text Mode, the styles will be visible.

- If your printer does not support italics, the printed copy will appear underlined. Some type styles will not apply to certain type faces. For example, if you use outline or shadow on Courier, it simply appears bolded.

- To insert and center the line, "Sir Francis Drake," place the cursor at the end of the previous line, and press the return key. Since the hotels were centered as a block, the center format will apply to the newly inserted line.

EXERCISE DIRECTIONS:

1. Select Graphics Mode view.
2. Display the FONTS button bar.
3. Start with a clear screen.
4. Open **MEMO**.
5. Make the indicated revisions.
6. Preview your document.
7. Print one copy.
8. Close your file; save the changes.

TO SET ITALICS
Before typing
Ctrl + I, type text, Ctrl + I
1. Click on Font.................. Alt + O
2. Click on Italics.................. I
3. Type text.
4. Repeat steps 1 and 2 to turn OFF.
   or
   - Click on *Font button* in FONT button bar.............. [FFF Font]
   - Click on *Italics button*.......... [a Italics]
   - Type text.
   - Click on *Normal button*........ [a Normal]

After typing
select text, Ctrl + I
1. Select/highlight text to be italicized.
2. Click on Font.................. Alt + O
   Click on Italics.................. I

or
- Click on *Font button* in FONT button bar.............. [FFF Font]
- Click on *Italics button*.......... [a Italics]

TO USE OUTLINE/ SHADOW/SMALL CAPS
Before typing
1. Click on Font.................. Alt + O
2. Click on Outline.................. T
   or
   Click on Shadow.................. W
   or
   Click on Small Caps.............. C
3. Type text.
4. Repeat steps 1 and 2 to turn OFF.
   or
   - Click on *Font button* in FONT button bar.............. [FFF Font]

- Click on *Outline, Shadow or SmallCap button* ...... [Outline], [Shadow] or [SmallCap]
- Type text.
- Click on *Normal button*........ [a Normal]

After typing
1. Select/highlight text to be underlined.
2. Click on Font.................. Alt + O
   Click on Outline.................. T
   or
   Click on Shadow.................. W
   or
   Click on Small Caps.............. C
   or
   - Click on *Font button* in FONT button bar.............. [FFF Font]
   - Click on *Outline, Shadow or SmallCap button*...... [Outline], [Shadow] or [SmallCap]

MEMORANDUM } set to shadow

TO: ~~All~~ Managers Attending Computer Expo

FROM: Robin McDonald

DATE: December 10, 199-

SUBJECT: Hotels Offering Discounts to Computer Expo Attendees

The following San Francisco hotels have agreed to offer special discounted rates to all attendees of Computer Expo:

Fairmont Hotel
Grand Hyatt
Holiday Inn: Civic Center
Hyatt Regency
King George Hotel
~~Mark Hopkins~~
Sir Francis Drake → Nikko
Villa Florence
Westin St. Francis

} set to small caps

When you ~~call to~~ make your reservation, mention that you're ~~going to~~ (attending) the Computer Expo at the Convention Center. ~~There are only~~ a limited number of rooms available at preferred rates, so plan early.

All hotels listed in bold above are within 20 minutes of the Convention Center.

set to italics

rm

c: Chad Wilkinson
    Julie Chen

TEXT ALIGNMENT; EMPHASIZING TEXT

NOTES:

- •. Remember, if you are aligning blocks of text, use justification alignments.

EXERCISE DIRECTIONS:

1. Select Graphics Mode view.
2. Display the FONTS button bar.
3. Start with a clear screen.
4. Format the menu on the right, applying alignments and type styles as indicated.
5. Center the page top to bottom.
6. Preview your document.
7. Print one copy.
8. Save the file; name it **FOOD.**

The Sherwood Forest Inn

↓2x

125 Pine Hill Road
Arlington, VA 22207
703-987-4443

↓2x

BREAKFAST MENU

↓3x

BEVERAGES

↓2x

Herbal Tea...*$1.00*
Coffee...*$2.00*
Cappuccino...*$2.50*

↓3x

FRUITS

↓2x

Berry Refresher...*$3.00*
Sparkling Citrus Blend...*$3.00*
Baked Apples...*$3.50*

↓3x

GRAINS

↓2x

Fruity Oatmeal...*$3.50*
Bran Muffins...*$3.00*
Whole Wheat Zucchini Bread...*$3.00*
Four-Grain Pancakes...*$5.00*

↓3x

EGGS

↓2x

Baked Eggs with Creamed Spinach...*$6.50*
Poached Eggs with Hollandaise Sauce...*$6.00*
Scrambled Eggs...*$2.50*
Sweet Pepper and Onion Frittata...*$6.50*

↓4x

David Zeiss, Proprietor

REMOVING EMPHASIS STYLES; USING THE REPEAT KEY

NOTES:

Removing Emphasis Styles

- If you decide you would like to remove the emphasis style you applied to text, select/highlight the text where style is to be removed, and repeat the procedure used to apply the style. You can also remove emphasis styles by deleting the codes that were inserted when the styles were applied. Deleting codes will be covered in Lesson 31.

Using the Repeat Key

- The Repeat Key can save you time if you need to keyboard repetitive keystrokes. For example, the horizontal double line in this exercise may be created by using the Repeat function and the equal key. The repetition number is defaulted for 8 but can be changed at any time.

- This exercise requires that you remove some of the styles you entered earlier and to insert a horizontal double line after the subject line using the Repeat key.

- Repeat may be accessed by selecting "Repeat" from the Edit in the main menu.

EXERCISE DIRECTIONS:

1. Select any view mode.
2. Start with a clear screen.
3. Open **MEMONEWS** from File Manager directory.
4. Make the indicated revisions.
5. Preview your document.
6. Print one copy.
7. Close your file; save the changes.

MEMORANDUM

delete double underline

Delete bold

TO: The Staff

FROM: Sarah Walesk

DATE: December 9, 199-

RE: Computer Expo

Create a horizontal line using the equal key

↓2x

↓2x

wi I strongly urge you to attend this year's Computer Expo. In four days, you'll pick up all the latest computer news and discover new ways to put your computer to work -- in the office, in the lab, in the studio, in the classroom, or in your home.

Here are some of the events you can look forward to:

Keynote Sessions. These sessions will feature luminaries from the computer world who will offer you insights from industry.
Application Workshops. Join a series of two-hour learning sessions which will provide guidelines, tips and "how-to's" on popular software packages.
Programmer/Developer Forums. Veteran and novice computer users will brainstorm so you can learn about innovative advances and techniques.

Delete underline If you are interested in attending, see Derek Brennan. He will pre-register anyone from our company who wishes to attend. This will save you long lines at the show.

sw

Restore the lasted deleted sentence

TO REMOVE STYLE

1. Select/highlight text to return to normal.
2. Click on F<u>o</u>nt .... `Alt` + `O`
3. Click on style to be removed.

TO SET REPEAT VALUE

Ctrl + R

1. Position cursor/insertion point where repeat value will begin.

2. Click on <u>E</u>dit .... `Alt` + `E`
3. Click on <u>R</u>epeat .... `R`
4. Type count number.
5. ENTER, ENTER .... `↵` , `↵`
6. Click on <u>E</u>dit .... `Alt` + `E`
7. Click on <u>R</u>epeat .... `R`
8. Type character or code to be repeated

EXERCISE DIRECTIONS:

1. Create the announcement below, centering, underscoring, double underscoring, bolding, using italics, and flush right where indicated.

2. Use any desired symbol to create the horizontal lines.

3. Center the page from top to bottom.

4. Spell check the document.

5. Preview your document

6. Print one copy.

7. Save the exercise; name it **INVEST.**

March 27, 199-

40,000,000 Shares

DACEENE

Quality Municipal Fund, Inc.

Common Stock

++

Price $12 Per Share

++

Copies of the Prospectus may be obtained from such
of the Underwriters as may legally offer these
securities in compliance with the securities laws of the
respective states.

ALEX, CROWN & SONS   LIDDER, PEABODY & CO.

ADVESTIN, INC.   THE ROBINSON-JEFFREY COMPANY

THE CHICAGO CORPORATION   FERRIS, QUAKER WATS & CO.

SOUTHEAST SECURITIES, INC.   RIDER INVESTMENTS, INC.

HUNTINGTON SECURITIES CORPORATION

EXERCISE DIRECTIONS:

1. Create the memorandum below, centering, underscoring, bolding and using italics where indicated.

2. Center, bold and double underline the word MEMORANDUM at the top of the document.

3. Spell check the document.

4. Preview your document.

5. Print one copy.

6. Save the exercise; name it **BUSNEWS**.

TO: Caroline Herrara//FROM: Adam Varnet//SUBJECT: <u>Business News and Updates</u> Article//DATE: Today's//At our meeting on Friday, you indicated that you wanted me to provide you with suggestions of companies that you could write a feature story about in next month's issue of <u>Business News and Updates</u>.

I have done some research and found that the following companies are either announcing a new product, acquiring assets of another company, announcing a merger with another company, or announcing a new patent. You might want to do some preliminary interviews with their executives (I have listed the person to contact in italics) to learn more details and make a final determination as to which one would provide the best information for a feature article.

<u>**Abbott Laboratories**</u>
Located in Abbott Park, IL, this company makes hospital products and signed a long-term supply agreement with a foreign company. Contact: *George Richards*

<u>**Bank One Corp**</u>
Located in Columbus, OH, this company will acquire a commercial banking company in Springfield, IL. Contact: *Thomas Quinn*

<u>**Comshare, Inc.**</u>
Located in Ann Arbor, MI, this company purchased the assets and business of a Texas corporation. Contact: *Pamela Sutton*

<u>**Mesa Limited**</u>
Located in Amarillo, TX, this natural gas company agreed to sell part of its oil and gas interests to a Houston corporation. Contact: *Juan Perez*

You have done an outstanding job as feature editor, and I always look forward to receiving my copy. If you need any additional information, let me know.

yo

LESSON 5 / EXERCISES 28-36
ADDITIONAL FORMATTING AND EDITING

- Creating a One-Page Report
- Changing Line Spacing
- Setting Margins
- Creating a Personal Business Letter

- Indenting / Double Indenting Text
- Hanging Indents
- Revealing Codes
- Moving Text (Cut and Paste)

- Copying Text (Copy and Paste)
- Saving With a New Filename (Save As)
- Creating a Resume

CREATING A ONE-PAGE REPORT; CHANGING LINE SPACING; INDENTING TEXT

NOTES:

- A report or manuscript generally begins 2" from the top of the page and is prepared in double space. The title of a report is centered and keyed in all caps. A quadruple space follows the title.

- Reports are double spaced. Tab each new paragraph once.

- Margins will vary depending on how the report will be bound. For an unbound report, use margins of 1" on the left and right (the default).

Line Spacing

- A line spacing change affects text beginning with the paragraph in which the cursor was placed. If your line spacing is set for double space, **two returns will result in four blank lines.**

- Line spacing may be accessed by selecting "Line" from the Layout main menu or pressing Shift + F8. The dialog box shown below will appear.

- Note that the default is set to single space. By clicking in the line spacing box, you may change spacing as desired or you may click on the list arrows to set spacing in small increments.

LINE FORMAT DIALOG BOX

File   Edit   View   Layout   Tools   Font   Graphics   Window   Help

```
                          Line Format

1. Tab Set...    Rel: -1",-0.5",+0",+0.5",+1",+1.5",+2",...

2. Justification                    Hyphenation
   • Left                           6. ☐ Hyphenation
   ○ Center
   ○ Right                          7. Hyphenation Zone
   ○ Full                              Left:  10 %
   ○ Full, All Lines                   Right: 4  %

3. Line Spacing: 1.0  ⬍            8. Line Height
                                       • Auto
4. Line Numbering... Off               ○ Fixed:

5. Paragraph Borders...              [ OK ]  [ Cancel ]
```

Line Spacing

Courier 12pt   Doc 2 Pg 1 Ln 1" Pos 1"

Indenting Text

- WordPerfect's <u>left</u> indent feature moves a complete paragraph one tab stop to the right and sets a temporary left margin for the paragraph. The <u>double indent</u> feature allows you to simultaneously indent paragraph text one tab stop from the left and right margin.

- Paragraphs may be indented <u>before</u> or <u>after</u> text is typed.

- Since text is indented to a tab setting, accessing the indent feature once will indent text .5" to the right; accessing it twice will indent text 1", etc. The same is true for the double indent feature: accessing it once will indent text .5" on the left and right; accessing it twice will indent it 1" from the left and right margin, etc.

- The indent mode is ended by a hard return.

- The proofreader's symbol for indenting is: ⌉(right)
⌊ (left)

EXERCISE DIRECTIONS:

1. Select Text Mode view.

2. Start with a clear screen.

3. Use the default margins (1" on the left and right).

4. Keyboard the report on the next page. Start the title on Ln 2". Use the asterisk (*) before and after the heading.

5. Double space the first and last paragraphs; double indent and single space the middle paragraphs.

6. Spell check the document.

7. Preview your document.

8. Print one copy.

9. Save the exercise; name it **BULLETIN.**

continued . . .

******ELECTRONIC BULLETIN BOARDS******

↓ 4x

TAB → Thousands of people across the nation are using computer bulletin boards. Through their computer, they spend hours on line "talking" with other users, "discussing" topics ranging from zoology, finding information about taxes or taxis, completing graduate courses to even exchanging wedding vows. Some productive uses of bulletin boards are: Return 2x

Change line spacing

Double indent (1")

1"

A system set up by a hospital in West Virginia offers detailed answers to medical questions for people who don't want to travel great distances necessary to see a doctor.

A system created by a retired guidance counselor in Atlanta provides current information on scholarships and loans.

A system operated by a car expert in Las Vegas lists thousands of collectors' cars.

TAB → Besides the fee of subscribing to a bulletin board, the cost of "talking" on your computer is the same as talking on your phone, since phone lines are used for data transmission.

TAB → All you need to connect a bulletin board is a computer and a modem connected to a telephone line. While most bulletin boards are free, some of the largest are professional operations that charge a fee.

TO CHANGE LINE SPACING
Shift + F8 L S

1. Place cursor/insertion within the paragraph where line spacing change will begin.
2. Click Layout. .... **Alt** + **L**
3. Click on Line .... **L**
4. Click on Line Spacing .... **S**
5. Type desired spacing:

   Examples:

   1.5 = one and one-half space

   2 = double space

   3 = triple space
6. Click on OK .... **⏎**

TO LEFT INDENT
F4

1. Click on Layout .... **Alt** + **L**
2. Click on Alignment. .... **A**
3. Click on Indent (->) .... **I**

NOTE: Repeat steps 1-3 until desired indentation is achieved.

4. Type paragraph.
5. ENTER .... **⏎**
   to end indent mode.

TO DOUBLE INDENT
Shift + F4

1. Click on Layout. .... **Alt** + **L**
2. Click on Alignment. .... **A**
3. Click on Double Indent (-> <-) .... **D**

NOTE: Repeat steps 1-3 until desired indentation is achieved.

4. Type paragraph.
5. ENTER .... **⏎**
   to end indent mode.

CREATING A ONE-PAGE REPORT; CHANGING LINE SPACING; CHANGING MARGINS; INDENTING TEXT

NOTES:

- WordPerfect measures margins in inches.

- The default margins are: 1" left, 1" right, 1" top and 1" bottom.

- A left/right margin change affects text beginning with the paragraph in which the cursor is placed. To change margins for the entire document, place the cursor/insertion point at the beginning, or within the first paragraph, of the text to receive the margin change.

- Each margin is measured from the edge of the page. Since text is centered between existing left/right margins, change left/right margins before centering the title of a report.

- Margins may be accessed by selecting "Margins" from the Layout main menu or pressing Shift + F8. The following dialog box will appear after accessing margins:

- By clicking in each margin box, you may change margins as desired.

- It is only necessary to change top and bottom margins if additional vertical space is needed on the page. Most documents, however, should have at least a 1" top margin (the default).

- To indent numbered items (enumerations) as shown in the exercise, tab once, type the number, then (left) indent the paragraph text.

- To quickly bring the cursor/insertion point to the "home" position, (the top left of the page) press the home key once; then press the up arrow key once.

MARGIN FORMAT DIALOG BOX

```
┌──────────────── Margin Format ────────────────┐
│ ┌─Document Margins────────────────────────┐    │
│ │ 1. Left Margin:            [1"        ]  │    │
│ │ 2. Right Margin:           [1"        ]  │    │
│ │                                          │    │
│ │ 3. Top Margin:             [1"        ]  │    │
│ │ 4. Bottom Margin:          [1"        ]  │    │
│ └──────────────────────────────────────────┘   │
│ ┌─Paragraph Margins───────────────────────┐    │
│ │ 5. Left Margin Adjustment:  [0"       ]  │    │
│ │ 6. Right Margin Adjustment: [0"       ]  │    │
│ │                                          │    │
│ │ 7. First Line Indent:       [0"       ]  │    │
│ │ 8. Paragraph Spacing:       [1.0    ][↕] │    │
│ └──────────────────────────────────────────┘   │
│              [  OK  ]   [Cancel]                │
└────────────────────────────────────────────────┘
```

EXERCISE DIRECTIONS:

1. Select Text Mode view.

2. Start with a clear screen.

3. Set 1.5" left and right margins, and a .5" bottom margin.

4. Keyboard the report on the right. Start the title on Ln 2".

5. Double space the first two paragraphs; single space and double indent numbered paragraphs.

6. Center, bold, underline and italicize where indicated.

7. Spell check the document.

8. Preview your document.

9. Print one copy.

10. Save the exercise; name it **OCR**.

<u>OPTICAL CHARACTER RECOGNITION AT WORK</u>

↓ 4x

Set double space →

Optical Character Recognition, or **OCR**, converts paper documents to digital format. Therefore, it is possible to have an **OCR** device *read* text and have it appear on the computer's screen, without rekeying copy. Some **OCR** units have the ability to recognize a wide variety of fonts, reproduce tabs, text centering, and other formatting. Most **OCR** units process pages three or four times faster than the average typist's 70 words per minute.

Here are some interesting ways in which companies use Optical Character Recognition to ease their work loads:

double indent

TAB → 1. A Boston service bureau recently scanned and republished a client's large medical catalog, a project that would have been too time consuming to undertake.

TAB → 2. A New York-based newspaper plans to create data files of their back issues, many of which were published in 1845.

TAB → 3. A Maryland company needed to transfer files from an aging word processing system to a newer one. It discovered that printing the files from the old system and then scanning them into the new system was less expensive.

TO MOVE CURSOR HOME

Press HOME, ↑ .... [Home] , [↑]

TO SET MARGINS
(Left/Right, Top/Bottom)
Shift + F8

1. Place cursor/insertion point within the paragraph where margin change will begin.
2. Click on Layout .... [Alt] + [L]
3. Click on Margins .... [M]

4. Click on desired margin setting:
   Left Margin .... [L]
   Right Margin .... [R]
   Top Margin .... [T]
   Bottom Margin................. [B]
5. Type desired margin.
6. Click on OK............................... [↵]

CHANGING MARGINS; HANGING INDENTS

NOTES:

- When all the lines in a paragraph are indented *except* the first line, a "hanging indent" is created.

- A hanging indented paragraph appears below. Note the effect:

    This paragraph is an example of a "hanging indent." Note that all the lines in the paragraph are indented except the first line. This can be an effective way to emphasize paragraph text.

- To create a hanging indent, place cursor/insertion where the hanging indent is to begin. Then, select "Alignment" from the Layout main menu. Select "Hanging Indent" from the drop-down menu:

- The "Back Tab" selection may be used to move the cursor back to the previous tab setting. This has the same effect as the "Hanging Indent" feature. This selection also enables you to move the cursor left of the left margin to the previous tab setting. The cursor/insertion point and the subsequent text on the line will move.

EXERCISE DIRECTIONS:

1. Select Text Mode view.
2. Start with a clear screen.
3. Open **PERSONAL**.
4. Set 1.5" left and right margins at the third paragraph.
5. Create hanging indents on the three paragraphs as indicated.
6. Reset 1" left and right margins at the last paragraph.
7. Make the indicated revisions.
8. Preview your document.
9. Print one copy.
10. Close the file; save the changes.

636 Jay Boulevard West
Chaska, MN 55318
Date Code

Ms. Anita Price, Vice President
Milton Investment Counselors
One Pratt Circle
Baltimore, MD 21202

Dear Ms. Price:

Please consider me an applicant for the position of Financial
Advisor that was advertised in the Sunday edition of *The Herald*.

As my enclosed resume will show, I have been working for Sutton
Investment Group for the past six years. I am particularly proud
of several accomplishments: *while employed at Sutton*

Change margins 1.5" L/R

In 1989, I helped to organize $1.5 million zero-coupon bond
offering for the French Treasury.

Create hanging ¶s

In 1990, my group handled $120 million municipal bond offering
for New York City.

In 1991, I helped to underwrite $200 million offering for a
foreign company.

Change Margins 1" L/R

I am confident that my past experience will be an asset to your
organization. If you would like to meet with me for an
interview, I can be reached at ~~the number indicated on my resume~~.
405-422-6059

              Sincerely,

              Lawrence Schneider

enclosure

TO CREATE A HANGING INDENT/BACK TAB
Shift + Tab

1. Position cursor/insertion point where hanging indent/back tab will begin.
2. Click on Layout .... Alt + L
3. Click Alignment .... A
4. Click on:

   Back Tab....................................... B

   or

   Hanging Indent .... H

AUTO CODE PLACEMENT; REVEAL CODES; FIRST LINE INDENTS; SAVE AS

NOTES:

Auto Code Placement

- As a document is created in WordPerfect, codes are inserted that determine the document's appearance. These codes are not displayed on the screen but can be revealed when necessary. Certain codes need to be at the top of the screen; other codes need to be at the beginning of the paragraph. WordPerfect's auto code placement feature places codes where they belong, even if your cursor is at a different place when you insert the code. For example, if you insert a "center page top to bottom" code in the middle of your document, WordPerfect automatically places the code at the top of your document.

- To change auto code placement, select Setup/Environment from the File main menu.

- By default, the auto code placement feature is ON. When it is turned OFF, codes remain where they are inserted.

Reveal Codes

- When the "reveal codes" feature is selected, a "tab rule" is displayed by reversing the normal display of the screen. The codes that were inserted when you typed the document appear within the text below the tab rule. An example of this screen and its symbols appears below.

- The reveal codes feature may be accessed by selecting "Reveal Codes" from View in the main menu or by pressing Alt + F3. To exit reveal codes, repeat the procedure.

- The reveal codes feature is very useful when editing a document. The top and bottom parts of the document, OCR, appear in the illustration below with the codes displayed.

- To delete a code, move the cursor/insertion point so that it sits on that code which appears before the word or sentence; then, press the DELete key.

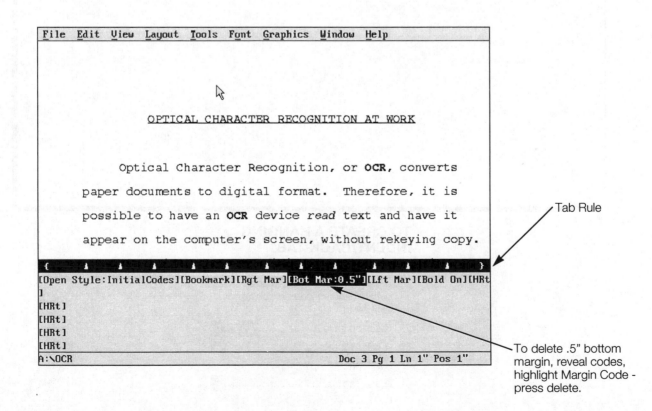

Tab Rule

To delete .5" bottom margin, reveal codes, highlight Margin Code - press delete.

First Line Indents

- The first line indent feature allows you to set the amount of space each paragraph indents. If you wanted to indent each paragraph 1.5" from the left margin, you could set it using this feature. This would eliminate the need of having to use the tab key or set a tab stop. You can change the first line indent amount throughout the document. This feature can be set in the Margin Format Dialog Box.

Save As

- "Save As" allows you to resave a document under a new file name or in a different location. When a document is saved under a new file name, the original document remains intact.

```
┌────────────────────────────────────┐
│▓▓▓▓▓▓▓▓▓  Margin Format  ▓▓▓▓▓▓▓▓▓▓│
├────────────────────────────────────┤
│ ┌─Document Margins─────────────────┐│
│ │ 1. Left Margin:        [1"     ] ││
│ │ 2. Right Margin:       [1"     ] ││
│ │                                  ││
│ │ 3. Top Margin:         [1"     ] ││
│ │ 4. Bottom Margin:      [1"     ] ││
│ └──────────────────────────────────┘│
│ ┌─Paragraph Margins────────────────┐│
│ │ 5. Left Margin Adjustment:  [0"] ││
│ │ 6. Right Margin Adjustment: [0"] ││
│ │                                  ││
│ │ 7. First Line Indent:  [0"     ] ││
│ │ 8. Paragraph Spacing:  [1.0  ]⊟  ││
│ └──────────────────────────────────┘│
│              [ OK ]  [Cancel]        │
└────────────────────────────────────┘
```

EXERCISE DIRECTIONS:

1. Select Text Mode view.

2. Display the scroll bars.

3. Start with a clear screen.

4. Open **OCR.**

5. Position your cursor/insertion point at the top of the screen.

6. Reveal your codes.

7. Delete the bottom margin code [Bot Mar:05"].

8. Scroll the page up (use the down scroll arrow) so your cursor is positioned one line above the first single-spaced paragraph.

9. Delete the Left/Right indent code [Lft/Rgt Indent] and the numbers in each single spaced paragraph. Do not delete the tab code.

10. Insert a hanging indent code at the beginning of each single-spaced paragraph as shown.

11. Exit Reveal Codes.

12. Preview your document.

13. Print one copy.

14. Save As **OCRHANG.**

15. Change each hanging indented paragraph to a first line indent of 1.5".

NOTE: Reveal your codes and delete the hanging indent codes. Then reset the first line indent amount.

16. Save As **OCRINDENT.**

17. Close the file.

continued . . .

<u>OPTICAL CHARACTER RECOGNITION AT WORK</u>

Optical Character Recognition, or **OCR**, converts paper documents to digital format. Therefore, it is possible to have an **OCR** device *read* text and have it appear on the computer's screen, without rekeying copy. Some **OCR** units have the ability to recognize a wide variety of fonts, reproduce tabs, text centering, and other formatting. Most **OCR** units process pages three or four times faster than the average typist's 70 words per minute.

Here are some interesting ways in which companies use Optical Character Recognition to ease their work loads:

A Boston service bureau recently scanned and republished a client's large medical catalog, a project that would have been too time consuming to undertake.

A New York-based newspaper plans to create data files of their back issues, many of which were published in 1845.

A Maryland company needed to transfer files from an aging word processing system to a newer one. It discovered that printing the files from the old system and then scanning them into the new system was less expensive.

TO REVEAL CODES
(and Delete)
Alt + F3

1. Click on View .... `Alt` + `V`
2. Click on Reveal Codes .... `C`
3. Place cursor/insertion point on code to be deleted.
4. Press DELete .... `Del`
5. Repeat steps 1 & 2 to exit reveal codes

   or

- Press Alt + F3. .... `Alt` + `F3`

TO SAVE AS
F10

1. Click on File .... `Alt` + `F`
2. Click on Save As .... `A`
3. Type new file name.
4. Click on OK.............................. `↵`

TO SET FIRST LINE INDENT

1. Click on Layout .... `Alt` + `L`
2. Click on Margins .... `M`
3. Click on First Line Indent .... `F`
4. Type the indent amount (in inches from the left margin).
5. Click on OK.............................. `↵`

MOVING TEXT; CHANGING MARGINS

NOTES:

- The move feature allows you to move a block of text, a sentence, a paragraph, a page, or a column to another location in the same document or to another document. (Moving text to another document will be covered in a later lesson.) Moving text is also known as a "cut and paste" procedure. WordPerfect provides several methods to move text. The "cut and paste" and "drag and drop" methods are the most convenient. Use any method you find easier.

- Whatever method you choose, you must first select/highlight the text you wish to move.

Cut and Paste

- Once text has been highlighted, select "Cut and Paste" from the Edit main menu bar. When text is "cut," it temporarily disappears from the screen to a temporary storage area in the computer's memory. The following message in the status area will then display: "Move cursor; press Enter to retrieve."

- To reinsert or "paste" text (retrieve it from the clipboard to the screen), move the cursor/insertion point to the *immediate left* of where the text is to be reinserted (use the arrow keys or click once to get to the reinsert location), and press Enter.

Drag and Drop

- Using this feature, you can select/highlight the text to be moved, "drag" it from its current location, and "drop" it into its new location. After selecting the text, position the pointer anywhere in the selection, click and hold down the mouse button as you drag the highlighted text to the new location. (A shadowed box appears in graphics mode.) Then, release the mouse button.

- When moving a word or sentence, be sure to move the space following the word or sentence. To insure that the spaces following a sentence or a paragraph are also moved, you may use the procedure for "a Sentence/Paragraph/Page" shown in the keystrokes on page 89.

- If text was not reinserted at the correct point, you can "Undo" (Alt + E, U or Ctrl + Z) to "uninsert" the text and retry the "pasting" procedure. It is sometimes necessary to insert or delete spaces, returns, or tabs after completing the move.

- This exercise requires that you move the middle paragraphs as indicated, indent the middle paragraphs, and insert and indent a new paragraph.

- If you indent the text and then move the indented paragraph, be sure the indent code to the left of the text is moved along with the paragraph. To insure that it is, reveal your codes and check to see that your cursor is sitting on the indent code before you move the paragraph.

- The proofreader's mark for moving is or

EXERCISE DIRECTIONS:

1. Select Graphics Mode view.
2. Display the scroll bars.
3. Start with a clear screen.
4. Open **MEMONEWS** from File Manager directory.
5. Set left and right margins to 1.5" below the horizontal line.
6. Make the indicated revisions.

7. Move the "RE" line above the DATE line using the "drag and drop" method.

NOTE: If you do not have a mouse, use another move method.

8. Move the remaining paragraphs as directed using any move method desired.
9. Preview your document.
10. Print one copy.
11. Close your file; save the changes.

MEMORANDUM

TO: The Staff

FROM: Sarah Walesk

move DATE: December 9, 199-

RE: Computer Expo

(Change margins to 1.5" on left and right)

===

I strongly urge you to attend this year's Computer Expo. In four days, you will pick up the latest computer news and discover new ways to put your computer to work -- in the office, in the lab, in the studio, in the classroom, or in your home.

Here are some of the events you can look forward to:

move .5"

Keynote Sessions. These sessions will feature luminaries from the computer world who will offer you insights from industry,

Application Workshops. Join a series of two-hour learning sessions which will provide guidelines, tips and "how-to's" on popular software packages.

Programmer/Developer Forums. Veteran and novice computer users will brainstorm so you can learn about innovative advances and techniques.

.5"

If you are interested in attending, see Derek Brennan. He will pre-register anyone from our company who wishes to attend. This will save you long lines at the show.

sw

Insert

Special Interest Group Meetings. These sessions will include Education Workshops for teachers, resources and recommendations for the home office worker, and ways to fully utilize your computer in a law office. *.5"*

.5"

TO MOVE
Highlight text, Ctrl + F4, 1, move cursor, ENTER

Using "Cut and Paste"

1. Highlight/select text to be moved (cut). ..... `Alt` + `F4`, `→` `←` `↑` `↓`
2. Click on Edit....................... `Alt` + `E`
3. Click on Cut and Paste .... `E`
4. Position cursor/insertion point where text is to be reinserted.
5. ENTER.. `↵`

Using "Drag and Drop"

1. Highlight/select text to be moved.
2. Position mouse pointer on selected text.
3. Click and hold mouse button.
   (A shadowed box appears in graphics mode.)
4. Drag text to new location.
5. Release mouse button.

A sentence/ paragraph/page

1. Position cursor on first character of text to be moved.
2. Press Ctrl + F4 .... `Ctrl` + `F4`
3. Select:
   Sentence.......................... `S`
   or-Paragraph .... `R`
   or-Page.......................... `A`
4. Click on Cut and Paste............... `E`
5. Place cursor where text is to be reinserted.
6. ENTER................................. `↵`

MOVING TEXT; CHANGING MARGINS

NOTES:

- In this exercise you will move indented paragraphs. Reveal your codes and be sure your cursor is sitting on the indent code when you move the paragraph.

- The proofreader's mark for inserting a space is: #̭

EXERCISE DIRECTIONS:

1. Select Text Mode view.
2. Display the scroll bars.
3. Start with a clear screen.
4. Open **BULLETIN.**
5. Move the paragraphs as directed using any method desired.
6. Full justify paragraph text.
7. Print one copy.
8. Close your file; save the changes.

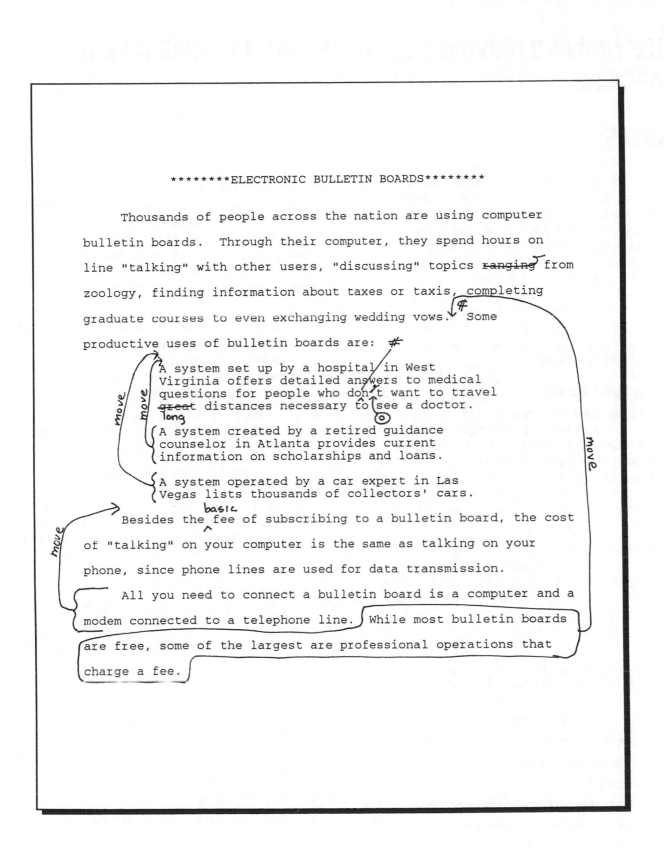

********ELECTRONIC BULLETIN BOARDS********

Thousands of people across the nation are using computer bulletin boards. Through their computer, they spend hours on line "talking" with other users, "discussing" topics ~~ranging~~ from zoology, finding information about taxes or taxis, completing graduate courses to even exchanging wedding vows. Some productive uses of bulletin boards are:

A system set up by a hospital in West Virginia offers detailed answers to medical questions for people who don't want to travel ~~great~~ long distances necessary to see a doctor.

A system created by a retired guidance counselor in Atlanta provides current information on scholarships and loans.

A system operated by a car expert in Las Vegas lists thousands of collectors' cars.

Besides the basic fee of subscribing to a bulletin board, the cost of "talking" on your computer is the same as talking on your phone, since phone lines are used for data transmission.

All you need to connect a bulletin board is a computer and a modem connected to a telephone line. While most bulletin boards are free, some of the largest are professional operations that charge a fee.

move   move   move   move

COPYING AND MOVING TEXT; CHANGING LINE SPACING AND MARGINS

NOTES:

- The copy feature allows you to leave text in its original location while placing it in a different location in the same document or another document (copying text to another document will be covered in a later lesson). Remember, the move feature removes the text from its original location and places it elsewhere. Copying text is also known as a "Copy and Paste" procedure. WordPerfect provides several methods to copy text. The "copy and paste" and "drag and copy" methods are most convenient. Use any method you find to be easier.

Copy and Paste

- The procedure for copying text is similar to moving. Once text has been highlighted, select "Copy and Paste" from the Edit main menu bar. When text is "copied" it will remain on the screen while a copy of it is placed temporarily in the computer's memory. The message in the status area will then display: "Move cursor; press Enter to retrieve."

- To reinsert or "paste" a copy of the text, move the cursor/insertion point to the *immediate left* of where the text is to be reinserted (use the arrow keys or click once to get to the reinsert location), and press Enter.

Drag and Copy

- Using this feature, you can select/highlight the text to be copied, click anywhere in the selection, *press the Ctrl key while dragging text to a new location*, (a black shadowed box appears in Graphics Mode) and "drop" a copy into its new location by releasing the mouse button.

- To insure that the spaces following a sentence or a paragraph are also copied, you may use the procedure for copying "a Sentence/Paragraph/Page" shown in the keystrokes on the next page.

- Like move, if text was not copied properly, you can "Undo" (Alt + E, U or Ctrl + Z) to delete the copied text immediately after pasting it.

- In this exercise be sure that the bold code is moved/copied along with the hotel information. To insure that you do, reveal your codes and check to see that your cursor is sitting on the bold code before you move/copy the paragraph.

EXERCISE DIRECTIONS:

1. Select Text Mode view.
2. Display the scroll bars.
3. Start with a clear screen.
4. Open **DIVE.**
5. Set the left and right margins to 1.5".
6. Insert paragraphs as indicated.
7. Double space paragraph text; single space hotel information.
8. Copy and move hotel information as directed.
9. Preview your document.
10. Print one copy.
11. Close the file; save the changes.

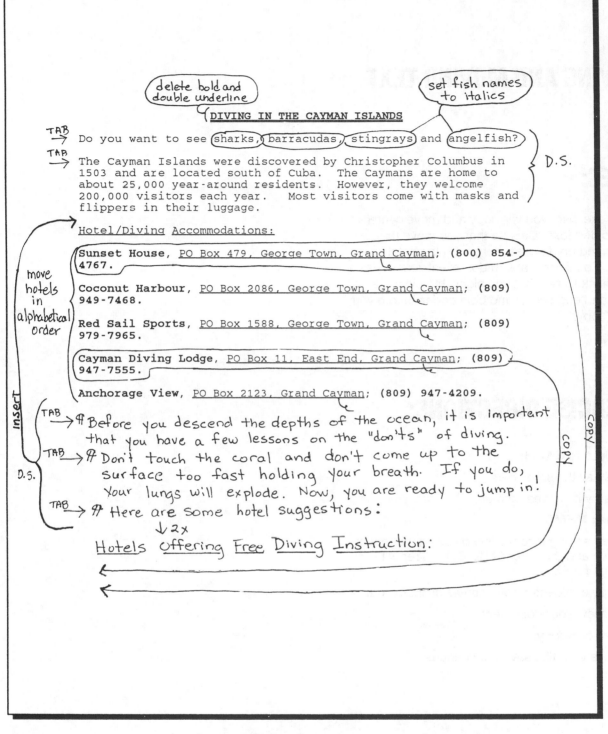

delete bold and double underline

set fish names to italics

DIVING IN THE CAYMAN ISLANDS

TAB → Do you want to see (sharks, barracudas, stingrays) and (angelfish?)

TAB → The Cayman Islands were discovered by Christopher Columbus in 1503 and are located south of Cuba. The Caymans are home to about 25,000 year-around residents. However, they welcome 200,000 visitors each year. Most visitors come with masks and flippers in their luggage. } D.S.

Hotel/Diving Accommodations:

move hotels in alphabetical order

insert

Sunset House, PO Box 479, George Town, Grand Cayman; (800) 854-4767.

Coconut Harbour, PO Box 2086, George Town, Grand Cayman; (809) 949-7468.

Red Sail Sports, PO Box 1588, George Town, Grand Cayman; (809) 979-7965.

Cayman Diving Lodge, PO Box 11, East End, Grand Cayman; (809) 947-7555.

Anchorage View, PO Box 2123, Grand Cayman; (809) 947-4209.

TAB → ¶ Before you descend the depths of the ocean, it is important that you have a few lessons on the "don'ts" of diving.

D.S. TAB → ¶ Don't touch the coral and don't come up to the surface too fast holding your breath. If you do, your lungs will explode. Now, you are ready to jump in!

TAB → ¶ Here are some hotel suggestions:

↓ 2x

Hotels Offering Free Diving Instruction:

copy

TO COPY

Highlight text, Ctrl + F4, 2, move cursor, ENTER

1. Highlight/select text to be copied..... Alt + F4 , → ← ↑ ↓
2. Click on Edit...................... Alt + E
3. Click on Copy and Paste............. Y
4. Position cursor/insertion point where text is to be reinserted.
5. ENTER.. ←

Using "Drag and Copy"

1. Highlight/select text to be copied.
2. Position mouse pointer on selected text.
3. Press and hold **CTRL** <u>while</u> clicking and holding left mouse button. (A black shadowed box appears in graphics mode.)
4. Drag text to new location.
5. Release mouse button.

A sentence / paragraph / page

1. Position cursor on first character of text to be copied.
2. Press Ctrl + F4 .... Ctrl + F4
3. Select:
   Sentence........................... S
   or- Paragraph .... R
   or-Page........................... A
4. Select Copy and Paste............... Y
5. Place cursor where text is to be reinserted.
6. ENTER.. ←

COPYING AND MOVING TEXT

NOTES:

- In this exercise, you will copy and move centered and bolded text. Be sure that you move the center and bold codes along with the hotel name. To insure that you do, reveal your codes and check to see that you highlight/select the begin and end center and bold codes before you move/copy.

EXERCISE DIRECTIONS:

1. Select Text Mode view.
2. Display the scroll bars.
3. Start with a clear screen.
4. Open **MEMO.**
5. Create the horizontal line by using the repeat value and the asterisk (*). Set the repeat value for 65.
6. Copy and center hotel names as indicated.
7. Preview your document.
8. Print one copy.
9. Close your file; save the changes.

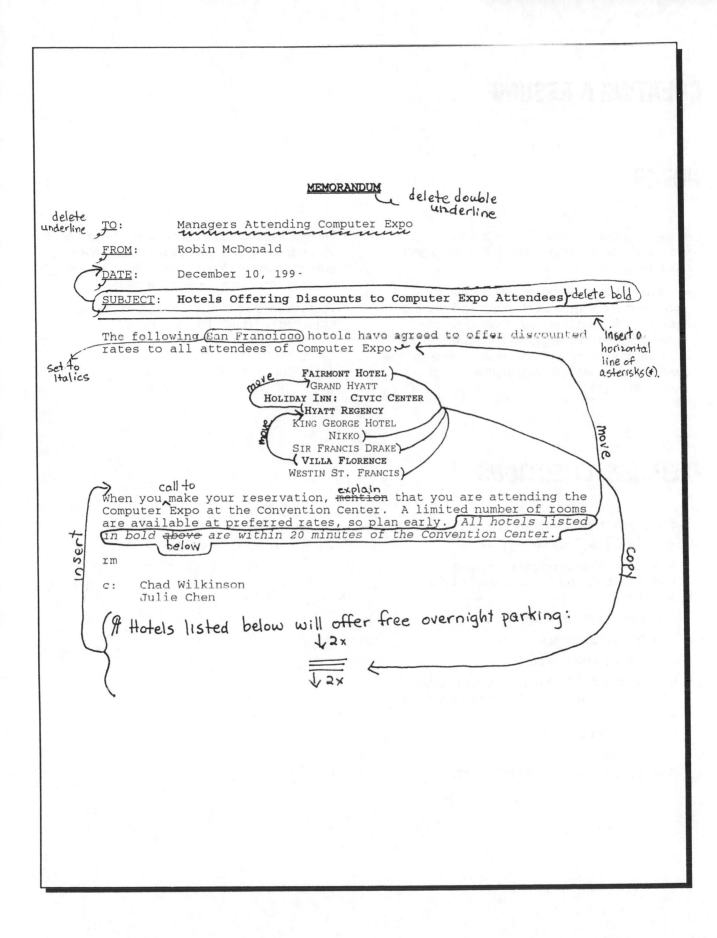

MEMORANDUM   *delete double underline*

delete underline

TO: Managers Attending Computer Expo

FROM: Robin McDonald

DATE: December 10, 199-

SUBJECT: **Hotels Offering Discounts to Computer Expo Attendees**   *delete bold*

The following (San Francisco) hotels have agreed to offer discounted rates to all attendees of Computer Expo.

Set to Italics

Insert a horizontal line of asterisks (*).

move
        FAIRMONT HOTEL
        GRAND HYATT
HOLIDAY INN: CIVIC CENTER
        HYATT REGENCY
        KING GEORGE HOTEL
        NIKKO
        SIR FRANCIS DRAKE
        VILLA FLORENCE
        WESTIN ST. FRANCIS

move

move

copy

call to
When you make your reservation, ~~mention~~ *explain* that you are attending the Computer Expo at the Convention Center. A limited number of rooms are available at preferred rates, so plan early. *All hotels listed in bold ~~above~~ below are within 20 minutes of the Convention Center.*

Insert

rm

c: Chad Wilkinson
     Julie Chen

¶ Hotels listed below will offer free overnight parking:

↓2x

↓2x

CREATING A RESUME

NOTES:

- A resume is a document which lists your experience, skills and abilities. It is used to gain employment.

- A resume is usually enclosed with a letter of application and sent to an employer. It forms the basis of getting the interview. Since a resume leaves a prospective employer with an impression of you, it should highlight your most positive qualities and be attractively formatted.

- Resume formats vary depending on the extent of your education and work experience. Unless education and work experience are extensive, resumes should not exceed one page.

- Your education and work experience should be listed beginning with the most recent.

EXERCISE DIRECTIONS:

1. Select any desired view mode.
2. Start with a clear screen.
3. Format the resume on the right using underline, bold and italics as shown in the exercise.
4. Begin the exercise on Ln 1".
5. Use the default margins.
6. Spell check the document.
7. Move high school information below college information. (The most recent education must be listed first.)
8. Preview your document.
9. Print one copy.
10. Save the exercise; name it **RESUME.**

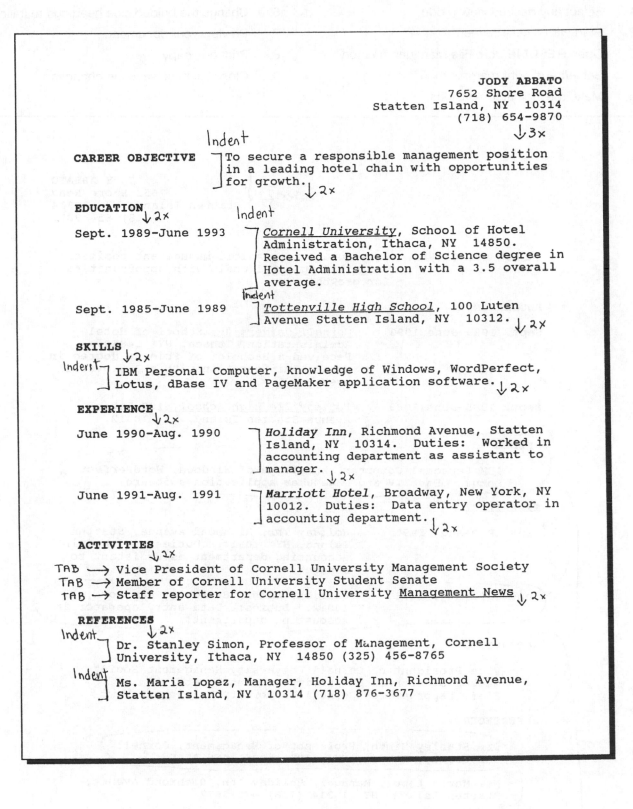

JODY ABBATO
7652 Shore Road
Statten Island, NY 10314
(718) 654-9870
↓3x

Indent

CAREER OBJECTIVE ⌐To secure a responsible management position
in a leading hotel chain with opportunities
for growth. ↓2x

EDUCATION ↓2x   Indent

Sept. 1989-June 1993 ⌐_Cornell University_, School of Hotel
Administration, Ithaca, NY 14850.
Received a Bachelor of Science degree in
Hotel Administration with a 3.5 overall
average.
Indent
Sept. 1985-June 1989 ⌐_Tottenville High School_, 100 Luten
Avenue Statten Island, NY 10312. ↓2x

SKILLS ↓2x

Indent⌐IBM Personal Computer, knowledge of Windows, WordPerfect,
Lotus, dBase IV and PageMaker application software. ↓2x

EXPERIENCE ↓2x

June 1990-Aug. 1990 ⌐_Holiday Inn_, Richmond Avenue, Statten
Island, NY 10314. Duties: Worked in
accounting department as assistant to
manager. ↓2x

June 1991-Aug. 1991 ⌐_Marriott Hotel_, Broadway, New York, NY
10012. Duties: Data entry operator in
accounting department. ↓2x

ACTIVITIES ↓2x

TAB ⟶ Vice President of Cornell University Management Society
TAB ⟶ Member of Cornell University Student Senate
TAB ⟶ Staff reporter for Cornell University _Management News_ ↓2x

REFERENCES ↓2x

Indent⌐Dr. Stanley Simon, Professor of Management, Cornell
University, Ithaca, NY 14850 (325) 456-8765

Indent⌐Ms. Maria Lopez, Manager, Holiday Inn, Richmond Avenue,
Statten Island, NY 10314 (718) 876-3677

EXERCISE DIRECTIONS:

1. Select any desired view mode.
2. Start with a clear screen.
3. Open **RESUME** from File Manager directory.
4. Set left and right margins to .5"
5. Make the indicated revisions.

6. Change the bolded side headings to italics.
7. Preview your document.
8. Print one copy.
9. Close your file; save the changes.

Center ←
```
                                            JODY ABBATO
                                          7652 Shore Road
                                     Statten Island, NY  10314
                                          (718) 654-9870
```

CAREER OBJECTIVE   To secure a responsible management position
                        in a leading hotel chain with opportunities
                        for growth.

EDUCATION

Sept. 1989-June 1993   *Cornell University*, School of Hotel
                        Administration, Ithaca, NY 14850.
                        Received a Bachelor of Science degree in
                        Hotel Administration with a 3.5 overall
                        average.

Sept. 1985-June 1989   *Tottenville High School*, 100 Luten
                        Avenue Statten Island, NY 10312.

SKILLS

        IBM Personal Computer, knowledge of Windows, WordPerfect,
        Lotus, dBase IV and PageMaker application software.

EXPERIENCE

June 1990-Aug. 1990   *Holiday Inn*, Richmond Avenue, Statten
                        Island, NY 10314. Duties: Worked in
                        accounting department as assistant to
                        manager.

June 1991-Aug. 1991   *Marriott Hotel*, Broadway, New York, NY
                        10012. Duties: Data entry operator in
                        accounting department.

ACTIVITIES

        Vice President of Cornell University Management Society
        Member of Cornell University Student Senate
        Staff reporter for Cornell University Management News

REFERENCES

        Dr. Stanley Simon, Professor of Management, Cornell
        University, Ithaca, NY 14850 (325) 456-8765

        Ms. Maria Lopez, Manager, Holiday Inn, Richmond Avenue,
        Statten Island, NY 10314 (718) 876-3677

HOBBIES
TAB → Skiing, Reading, Tennis

EXERCISE DIRECTIONS:

1. Select any desired view mode.

2. Start with a clear screen.

3. Create a one-page report from the text below.

4. Set left and right margins to .5".

5. Single space and double indent bolded bat species and their descriptions.

6. Spell check the exercise.

7. Print one copy.

8. Save the exercise; name it **BATS.**

BATS¶Do bats get in your hair? Do vampire bats exist? How blind is a bat? These are questions you might ask yourself if you were ever near a cave, an attic or another sheltered place. ¶A bat is the only mammal that can fly. They usually stay in dark places, tend to live in colonies, come out only at night, and hang upside down when they are resting. As night approaches, they head for their feeding grounds. Bats have an excellent sense of smell and hearing and depend on these senses to navigate and find food at night. Bats eat large numbers of insects and are, therefore, valuable to people. ¶The following is a description of several bat species: ¶**Vampire Bats.** These mammals feed on the blood of other animals and live in Central and South America. Vampire bats swallow about 1 tablespoon of blood a day. They leave their victims with a small wound which heals quickly, but these bats can carry rabies. **¶Brown Bats.** They live in the United States in buildings and caves and have a wingspan of about 12 inches. **¶Free-Tailed Bats.** These brown bats have a wingspan of up to 12 inches, live in colonies, mostly in caves in Southern United States and Mexico. **¶Red Bats.** With a wingspan of 12 inches, these bats live alone in trees and fly south every winter. The male has bright red, white-tipped fur, while the female has a grayish red fur. ¶Now, to answer the questions asked earlier: Bats do not get tangled in people's hair. Bats tend to be frightened of people and will fly away. Bats are not blind. All species of bats can see, but they see very poorly, especially at night. But, vampire bats DO exist; they are one of several kinds of bat species which have been described here.

LESSON 6 / EXERCISES 37-46
ADDITIONAL FORMATTING AND EDITING

- Using Thesaurus
- Using Grammar Check (Grammatik)
- Document Information
- Searching and Replacing Text/Codes
- Hyphenating Text
- Outlining

THESAURUS; DOCUMENT INFORMATION

NOTES:

Thesaurus

- The thesaurus feature lists synonyms and antonyms of a desired word and also indicates the word's part of speech.

- Thesaurus may be accessed by selecting Writing Tools from the Tools main menu bar or clicking on the "Thesarus" button on the TOOLS button bar.

- Once you access thesaurus, a drop down menu will appear giving you several options:

Look Up	- will allow you to look up words marked with bullets (headwords).
View	- move to the on-screen document to edit the page.
Clear Column	- will allow you to clear a column once it is filled.
History	- will allow you to see a list of words you have already examined.
Replace	- will replace a word in your document with a word highlighted in the thesaurus list.

- It is sometimes necessary to edit the new word in your document so that it fits properly in the sentence (example: singular/plural).

THESAURUS DIALOG BOX

100

Document Information

- The document information feature provides you with a statistics summary of your document. It will list the number of characters, words, lines, sentences, paragraphs and pages in your document. In addition, it will indicate the average word length, average words per sentence, maximum words per sentence and document size. This is a particularly useful feature if you are required to submit a report with a specified word or page count.

- Document information may be accessed within the Writing Tools submenu.

EXERCISE DIRECTIONS:

1. Select Text Mode view.
2. Start with a clear screen.
3. Use the default margins.
4. Begin the exercise on Ln 1.5".
5. Keyboard the letter on the next page as indicated.
6. Full justify only the indented paragraphs.
7. Using the thesaurus feature, substitute the words marked in the brackets. Be sure the tense of the new word is the same as the one it replaces.
8. Use the date feature to insert today's date.
9. Preview your document.
10. Access document information to determine the total number of words in this document.
11. Print one copy.
12. Save the exercise; name it **TOURS.**

continued . . .

Today's date   ← 1.5"

Ms. Christine Sabbio
876 North LaSalle Street
Chicago, IL 60601

add "ing" to replacement word

Dear Ms. Sabbio:

You called last week ⟨inquiring⟩ about horseback riding tours in the United States, particularly the eastern half of the country with English-style riding.

Since I have been unable to ⟨reach⟩ you by phone, I am outlining in this letter some information about riding tours that I think will interest you.

.5"

(double indent and full justify)

EQUITABLE TOURS - This company offers riding tours of two to eight days and is located in Woodstock, Vermont. The cost ranges from $579 for four days to $1,229 for eight. They will arrange itineraries in Northern California and in Arizona.

EQUESTRIAN RIDES - This company offers riding tours from inn to inn through the Sugarbush, Vermont area between the Green Mountains and Lake Champlain. There are five-day rides at $795 and six-day rides for $960.

.5"

HOOFBEATS INTERNATIONAL - This company is located in New Jersey and offers instruction. They will arrange riding tours in upstate New York where participants may ⟨mix⟩ lessons with trail rides and stay at the farm or a nearby inn. The ⟨cost⟩ varies according to the program.

While there are many other riding tours available, I have outlined what I believe to be the best three. If you ⟨desire⟩ more information about riding tours, please call me.

Sincerely,

Paula Badar
Travel Agent

pb/yo

TO USE THESAURUS

Alt + F1

1. Place cursor/insertion point on word to be looked up.
2. Click on Tools .... `Alt` + `T`
3. Click on Writing Tools................... `W`
4. Click on Thesaurus .... `T`
5. Select a thesaurus option:

   to replace word

   • Highlight word to replace word in document.

   • Click on Replace...................... `R`

or

to display "headword" synonyms

• Highlight word

• ENTER .... `↵`

or

to view list already examined

• Click on History........................ `H`
  to display synonyms for a word not listed

• Click on Look Up .... `L`

• Type word.

• ENTER .... `↵`

TO GET DOCUMENT INFORMATION

1. Place cursor/insertion point anywhere in document.
2. Click on Tools .... `Alt` + `T`
3. Click on Writing Tools................. `W`
4. Click on Document Information .... `D`
5. Click on OK................................. `↵`
   to close dialog box.

GRAMMAR CHECK (GRAMMATIK); THESAURUS; DOCUMENT INFORMATION

NOTES:

- GRAMMATIK is WordPerfect's grammar check feature that will check your document for proper usage and mechanics errors. Style errors such as cliches, jargon or wordiness will not be detected.

- Grammatik checks your document from the cursor position.

- If you desire, Grammatik will check spelling errors and usage errors simultaneously.

- Grammatik checks for errors based on the writing style you are using. The default writing style is set to "General-Standard Formality" but the following other options are available:

Business Letter	Memo	Report
Technical	Documentation	Proposal
Journalism	Advertising	Fiction

- When you select a writing style, WordPerfect applies different grammar rules to detect different kinds of writing errors.

- Grammatik may be accessed by selecting Writing Styles from the Tools main menu bar or clicking on the "Gramatik" button on the TOOLS BUTTON BAR.

- Once Grammatik is accessed, select "Interactive" to tell WordPerfect to begin proofing. It will stop at each problem and wait for your response. When Grammatik detects an error, the following menu will appear:

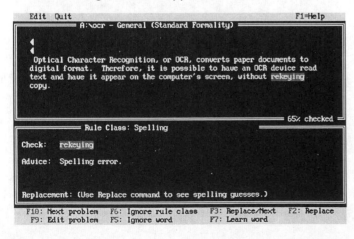

The screen provides you with the following information:

Rule Class	-	indicates the grammar error category to which your error belongs.
Check	-	highlights the detected error.
Advice	-	provides suggestion for correcting error.
Replacements	-	provides suggestions for replacing the error, if a replacement is applicable. If a replacement is not applicable, this option will not display.

- After displaying the error information, you may press the keys indicated to select an action:

F2 Replace	will replace the error with the suggestion indicated.
F3 Replace/ Next	will replace the error with the suggestion and continue scanning the document.
F5 Ignore Word	will ignore the word and continue checking.
F6 Ignore Rule Class	will direct WordPerfect not to apply this grammar rule to the remaining document.
F7 Learn Word	will add the selected word to the user dictionary.
F9 Edit Problem	will allow you edit the problem as you desire.
F10 Next Problem	will ignore the suggestion and continue scanning the document.

- To quit Grammatik, press Escape or click on Quit and follow prompts.

EXERCISE DIRECTIONS:

1.   Select Text Mode view.

2.   Start with a clear screen.

3.   Use the default margins.

4.   Begin the exercise at the top of your screen.

5.   Keyboard the memo on the next page exactly as shown including the circled misspelled words and usage errors. Insert a hard space where you see the symbol △.

6.   Using the thesaurus feature, substitute the words marked in brackets.

7.   Use Grammatik to grammar and spell check the document. Accept WordPerfect's suggestions for correcting grammar and spelling errors.

8.   Insert a hard space between names, dates and times.

9.   Access document information to determine the total number of words in this document.

10. Preview your document.

11. Save the exercise; name it **PICNIC.**

continued . . .

TO: STAFF

FROM: JANET GARCIA

RE: ANNUAL COMPANY PICNIC

DATE: TODAY'S

This year, our picnic will be Saturday, May△8 at Fairview Meadow
Country Club. Fairview is a newly (referbished) facility that
offers tennis courts, ball fields and excellent outdoor cooking
and dining (accomodations.)

                    WHAT YOU NEED TO KNOW

        The swimming pool will be (available) to us
        exclusively between noon and 3:30△p.m. The
        Club has beach chairs, but you must bring
        your own towels.

(double
indent)   The company will provide all food, but
        Mr.△Thomas and Mr.△Gordon (requests) that you
        bring your own drinks.

        Employees are welcome to bring (there)
        children, so bring the family.

If you plan to attend, or if you have any other questions, call
Joan Saunders at (extention)△104, by Thursday, May△6.

jg/yo

TO GRAMMAR CHECK

Alt + F1, G, I

1. Position cursor at the beginning of document.
2. Click on Tools .... `Alt` + `T`
3. Click on Writing Tools .... `W`
4. Click on Grammatik .... `G`
5. Press I .... `I`
    to begin an "Interactive check."
6. When error is highlighted, press an action function key:

F10 (Next Problem)...................... `F10`
to ignore suggestion continue

F6 (Ignore Rule Class)
*to not apply rule to
remaining document*.................... `F6`

F3 (Replace/Next) .... `F3`
to replace and continue

F2 (Replace)............................... `F2`
*to replace error with
suggestion.*

F9 (Edit)
to edit as desired .... `F9`

To Quit Grammatik

7. • Press Escape .... `Esc`
    • Type Y....................................... `Y`
    • Press Q .... `Q`

GRAMMAR CHECK; THESAURUS; DOCUMENT INFORMATION

NOTES:

- In this exercise, you will direct WordPerfect to check your document for errors based on an "Advertising" writing style. If you do not change the writing style from the default General-Standard Formality," Grammatik will flag the first sentence in this exercise as a "fragment." Fragments are acceptable when writing advertising text to make a statement and draw attention. They are not acceptable in formal business writing.

- To change writing styles, access Grammmatik, then press Alt + P to open the "Preferences" menu. Select "Advertising" from the "Writing Style" submenu.

EXERCISE DIRECTIONS:

1. Select Graphics Mode View.
2. Start with a clear screen.
3. Set left and right margins to 1.5".
4. Set first line indent to 1.5"
5. Keyboard the advertisement on the right exactly as shown including the circled misspelled words and usage errors.
6. Use center justification for the centered items.
7. Using the thesaurus feature, substitute the words marked in brackets.
8. Change writing style to "Advertising."
9. Using Grammatik, grammar and spell check the document. Accept WordPerfect's suggestions for correcting grammar and spelling errors and make the necessary changes to correct them.
10. Center the exercise vertically (center page top to bottom).
11. Preview your document.
12. Access document information to determine the total number of words in this document.
13. Save the exercise; name it **PAPER.**

WATERSHED PAPER

Papers that perform. Consistently. Time after time. Thats what you can always expect when you specify WATERSHEDS premium text, cover and writing finishes. And now you can see how brillintly our papers perform with a variety of inks thanks to our new *Think Ink Guide.*

This invaluable tool features more than 400 visual references to help you make accurate color choices. And get the results you expect. You'll find printed examples of black, metallic and solid colors in halftones, line art and screen tints on every one of our four leading lines of paper:

ENVIRONMENT
CLASSIC LINEN
CREST LINEN
RAIN DROP

Discover for yourself how **WATERSHED PAPER** can be combined with a myriad of inks to expand your creativity.

For you're copy of our new *Think Ink Guide,* just *call* the representives listed on the enclosed brochure and ask for your guide.

TO CHANGE WRITING STYLE
Alt + F1, G, Alt + P, W

1. Position cursor at the beginning of document.
2. Click on Tools .... `Alt` + `T`
3. Click on Writing Tools.................. `W`
4. Click on Grammatik .... `G`
5. Click on Preferences.......... `Alt` + `P`
6. Click on Writing Style................... `W`
7. Highlight writing option.up/ down arrow keys
8. ENTER... `↵`

To check document, go to step 5 on page 124.

SEARCHING TEXT

NOTES:

- The **search** feature will scan your document and search for occurrences of specified text or codes. Once the desired text or code is found, it can be edited or replaced.

- "Search" can be selected from the Edit main menu. Once selected, the following dialog box appears:

SEARCH DIALOG BOX

```
┌─────────────────────Search──────────────────────┐
│                                                  │
│  Search For: [                                ]  │
│                                                  │
│  □ Backward Search       □ Find Whole Words Only │
│  □ Case Sensitive Search □ Extended Search (Hdrs, Ftrs, etc.) │
│                                                  │
│  [Codes... F5] [Specific Codes... Shft+F5]  [Search F2] [Cancel] │
└──────────────────────────────────────────────────┘
```

- After entering the text or code to be searched in the Search For entry field, you can click in one of the four check boxes to specify the kind of search you desire.

  Backward Search will search from the end of your document. Otherwise, WordPerfect searches in a forward direction (from the cursor to the end of the document).

Case Sensitive will search for text exactly in the case it was typed: lower or upper case.

Find Whole Word Only will search for whole words only.

For example, if you selected this option in searching for the word "the," WordPerfect would not flag words in which "the" was a part of the word, like "**the**se," "**the**saurus," "**the**sis," etc.

Extended Search will search for words, phrases or codes in headers and footers and other places not in document window.

- To search for a code, click on the "Codes" (F5) dialog box. To search for a code that requires specific numbers or information, like a margin code, click on "Specific Codes" dialog box. (To find a "Left Margin" code [LftMar], you would need to specify the actual amount of the left margin.)

- In this exercise, you will search for the words shown in brackets. The search feature will quickly place the cursor on those words so you can edit them, using the thesaurus feature.

EXERCISE DIRECTIONS:

1. Select Text Mode view.
2. Start with a clear screen.
3. Open **MEMONEWS.**
4. Full justify the indented paragraphs.
5. Search for each word marked in brackets to quickly place cursor on them. Then, using the thesaurus feature, substitute the words marked in brackets. Be sure the tense of the new word is the same as the one it replaces.
6. Preview your document.
7. Access document information to determine the number of sentences in this document.
8. Close the file; save the changes.

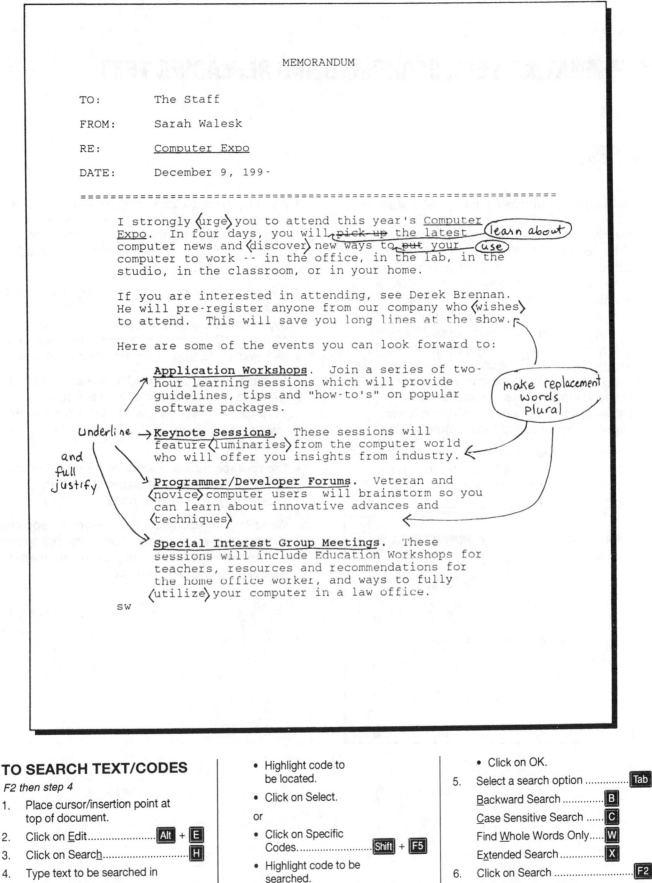

MEMORANDUM

TO: The Staff

FROM: Sarah Walesk

RE: <u>Computer Expo</u>

DATE: December 9, 199-

==

I strongly (urge) you to attend this year's <u>Computer Expo</u>. In four days, you will pick-up the latest ~~(learn about)~~ computer news and (discover) new ways to put your (use) computer to work -- in the office, in the lab, in the studio, in the classroom, or in your home.

If you are interested in attending, see Derek Brennan. He will pre-register anyone from our company who (wishes) to attend. This will save you long lines at the show.

Here are some of the events you can look forward to:

[handwritten note: make replacement words plural]

<u>Application Workshops</u>. Join a series of two-hour learning sessions which will provide guidelines, tips and "how-to's" on popular software packages.

[handwritten: Underline] → <u>Keynote Sessions</u>. These sessions will feature (luminaries) from the computer world who will offer you insights from industry.

[handwritten: and full justify]

<u>Programmer/Developer Forums</u>. Veteran and (novice) computer users will brainstorm so you can learn about innovative advances and (techniques).

<u>Special Interest Group Meetings</u>. These sessions will include Education Workshops for teachers, resources and recommendations for the home office worker, and ways to fully (utilize) your computer in a law office.

sw

TO SEARCH TEXT/CODES

F2 then step 4

1. Place cursor/insertion point at top of document.
2. Click on E̲dit .... `Alt` + `E`
3. Click on Searc̲h .... `H`
4. Type text to be searched in "Search For" box.

   or

   • Click on Codes. .... `F5`

• Highlight code to be located.

• Click on Select.

or

• Click on Specific Codes. .... `Shift` + `F5`

• Highlight code to be searched.

• Click on Select.

• Type additional code information.

• Click on OK.

5. Select a search option .... `Tab`

   B̲ackward Search .... `B`

   C̲ase Sensitive Search ...... `C`

   Find W̲hole Words Only..... `W`

   E̲xtended Search .... `X`

6. Click on Search .... `F2`

7. Press F2 to search for each occurrence.

HYPHENATING TEXT; SEARCHING AND REPLACING TEXT

NOTES:

- Hyphenation produces a tighter right margin. If text is full justified and hyphenated, the sentences will have smaller gaps between words. By default, WordPerfect's hyphenation feature is set to Off. In the Off position, WordPerfect will wrap any word that extends beyond the right margin. When hyphenation is "On," a word that starts before the left edge of the "hyphenation zone" and extends beyond the right edge of the zone, will be hyphenated. To change the width of the space a word must span before hyphenation divides it, you may change the "hyphenation zone." Increase the percentage of the zone to hyphenate fewer words; decrease to hyphenate more words.

- Hyphenation may be accessed by selecting "Line" from the Layout main menu. The following dialog box appears:

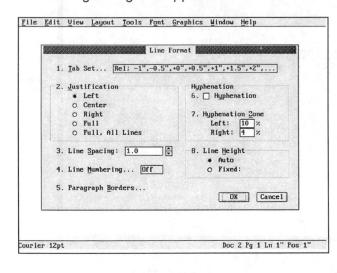

- If you type a word containing a hyphen, such as sister-in-law or self-control, and you wish to keep the words together even if it spans the hyphenation zone, type the word with a "hard hyphen" (HOME + -).

- If you wish to be prompted for every hyphenation situation, you must change the default hyphenation Environment setting from "Never" to "Always." Changing settings may be accessed by selecting "Setup" from the File main menu.

- As explained in Exercise 40, the **search** feature will scan your document and search for occurrences of text or codes. Once the desired text or code is found, it can be edited or replaced.

- The **replace** feature searches for occurrences of text or codes and replaces them with another word, phrase or code.

  WordPerfect gives you the option of replacing all occurrences of text or codes (global search and replace) or confirming each replacement (selective search and replace).

- "Replace" can be selected from the Edit main menu. Once selected, the following dialog box appears. (Note its similarity to the Search Dialog Box.)

SEARCH AND REPLACE DIALOG BOX

```
▒▒▒▒▒▒▒▒▒▒ Search and Replace ▒▒▒▒▒▒▒▒▒▒

 Search For:   _____

 Replace With: <Nothing>_____

   □ Confirm Replacement      □ Find Whole Words Only
   □ Backward Search          □ Extended Search (Hdrs, Ftrs, etc.)
   □ Case Sensitive Search    □ Limit Number of Matches:

   [ Codes... F5 ] [ Specific Codes... Shft+F5 ]    [ Replace F2 ] [ Cancel ]
```

- After entering the text or code to be searched in the "Search For" entry field and the text or code to be replaced in the "Replace With" entry field, you can click in one of the six check boxes to specify the kind of search you desire.

  Confirm Replacement will stop each time an occurrence is found and ask you to confirm replacement.

  Backward Search will search from the end of your document. Otherwise, WordPerfect searches in a forward direction (from the cursor to the end of the document).

Case Sensitive will search for text exactly in the case it was typed: lower or upper case.

Find Whole Word Only will search for whole words only.

For example, if you selected this option in searching for the word "the," WordPerfect would not flag words in which "the" was a part of the word, like "**the**se," "**the**saurus," "**the**sis," etc.

Extended Search will search for words, phrases or codes in headers and footers and other places not in document window.

Limited Number of Matches - limits the number of times a word, code or phrase can be replaced.

- To search and replace a code, click on "Codes" to open the dialog box. To search and replace a code that requires specific numbers or information, like a margin code, click on "Specific Codes" to open the dialog box.

EXERCISE DIRECTIONS:

1. Select Text Mode view.
2. Start with a clear screen.
3. Open **BULLETIN**.
4. Left align (justify) the first and last paragraphs.
5. Hyphenate the indented paragraphs.
6. Change the hyphenation zone to 8%.
7. Using the thesaurus feature, replace words marked in brackets.
8. Search for the word "bulletin" and replace with "BULLETIN."
9. Preview your document.
10. Print one copy.
11. Close the file; save the changes.

continued . . .

Search for "bulletin"
and replace with "BULLETIN"

********ELECTRONIC BULLETIN BOARDS********

Thousands of people across the nation are using computer bulletin boards. Through their computer, they spend hours on line "talking" with other users, "discussing" topics from zoology, finding information about taxes or taxis, completing graduate courses to even exchanging wedding vows. While most bulletin boards are free, some of the largest are professional operations that (charge) a fee.   *left align (justify)*

Some (productive) uses of bulletin boards are:

A system operated by a car expert in Las Vegas lists thousands of collectors' cars.

A system (created) by a retired guidance counselor in Atlanta provides current information on scholarships and loans.   *hyphenate*

A system set up by a hospital in West Virginia offers detailed answers to medical questions for people who do not want to travel long distances necessary to see a doctor.

All you need to (connect) a bulletin board is a computer and a modem connected to a telephone line.

Besides the basic fee of subscribing to a bulletin board, the cost of "talking" on your computer is the same as talking on your phone, since phone lines are used for data transmission.   *left align (justify)*

TO HYPHENATE

Shift + F8, L

1. Position cursor where hyphenation is to begin.
2. Click on Layout .... Alt + L
3. Click on Line L
4. Click in Hyphenation check box. .... Y
5. Click on OK .... ↵

To change hyphenation zone

1. Follow steps 1-4 above.
2. Click on Hyphenation Zone .... Z
3. Type a new left percentage
4. ENTER .... ↵
5. Type a new right percentage
6. Click on OK .... ↵

TO SEARCH AND REPLACE

Alt + F2

1. Place cursor/insertion point at top of document.
2. Click on Edit .... Alt + E
3. Click on Replace L
4. Type text to be searched in "Search For" box.
5. ENTER .... ↵
6. Type text to be replaced IN "Replace With" box.
7. ENTER .... ↵

   or

   • Click on Codes F5
   • Highlight code to be searched.
   • Click on Select.
   • Click on Codes.
   • Highlight code to be replaced.
   • Click on Select.

   or

   • Click on Specific Codes .... Shift + F5
   • Highlight code to be searched.
   • Click on Select.
   • Type additional code information.
   • Highlight code to be replaced.
   • Type additional code information.
   • Click on Select.

8. Select a search option:

   Confirm Replacement .... F
   Backward Search .... B
   Case Sensitive Search C
   Find Whole Words Only ..... W
   Extended Search X
   Limit Number of Matches .. L

9. Click on Replace F2
10. Press F2 to search and replace each occurrence.

115

HYPHENATING TEXT; SEARCHING AND REPLACING TEXT

NOTES:

- In this exercise, you will search for a bolded "OCR" and replace it with an unbolded "Optical Character Recognition." When entering the search word, be sure to enter the [Bold On] code and the [Bold Off] code as part of that word.

- To edit the indented paragraphs, delete the numbers, reveal your codes and delete the tab codes. Then, enter another double indent code to indent the paragraphs 1" from the left and right margins.

EXERCISE DIRECTIONS:

1. Select Text Mode view.

2. Start with a clear screen.

3. Open **OCR.**

4. Delete returns at the top of your page so the document begins at 1".

5. Full justify the document.

6. Set the left hyphenation zone to 6%; hyphenate the document.

7. Edit the indented paragraphs by deleting the numbers and the tab codes. Enter another double indent code to indent the paragraphs 1" from the left and right margins.

8. Using thesaurus, substitute the words marked in brackets.

9. Search for the word **"OCR"** and replace with "Optical Character Recognition," except for the first occurence of the word.

10. Preview your document.

11. Print one copy.

12. Close the file; save the changes.

full justify document

<u>OPTICAL CHARACTER RECOGNITION AT WORK</u>

Search for OCR and replace with Optical Character Recognition (except for first occurrence)

Optical Character Recognition, or **OCR**, converts paper documents to digital format. Therefore, it is possible to have an **OCR** device *read* text and have it appear on the computer's screen, without rekeying copy. Some **OCR** units have the ability to recognize a wide variety of fonts, reproduce tabs, text centering, and other formatting.   Most **OCR** units process pages three or four times faster than the average typist's 70 words per minute.

Here are some interesting ways in which companies use Optical Character Recognition to ease their work loads:

1. A Boston service bureau recently scanned and republished a client's large medical catalog, a project that would have been too time consuming to undertake.

2. A New York-based newspaper plans to create data files of their back issues, many of which were published in 1845.

3. A Maryland company needed to transfer files from an aging word processing system to a newer one. It discovered that printing the files from the old system and then scanning them into the new system was less expensive.

insert

¶ At the supermarket checkout stand a laser beam "reads" the bar code on an item and gives the information—— item, price, etc.,—— to the cash register.

1"

1"

OUTLINING

NOTES:

- An outline is used to organize information about a subject for the purpose of making a speech or writing a report. There are two types of outlines: a **topic outline** and a **sentence outline**. A topic outline summarizes the main and subtopics in short phrases while a sentence outline uses complete sentences for each.

- Outlines will include several levels of information.

- To access the outline feature to create a simple outline, select "Outline" from the Tools main menu bar. The following cascading menu will appear:

```
File  Edit  View  Layout  Tools  Font  Graphics  Window  Help
                           Writing Tools...  Alt+F1

                           Macro                    ▶
                           Outline                  ▶
                           Merge          Outline Options...
                           Sort...
                           Date           Begin New Outline...
                                          Outline Style...
                           Index          End Outline
                           Table of Conte
                           List           Next Level          Tab
                           Cross-Referenc Previous Level      Shft+Tab
                           Table of Autho Change to Outline Level  Ctrl+T
                           Generate...
                                          Hide Family
                           Math           Show Family
                           Spreadsheet    Hide Body Text

                           Hypertext...   Move Family
                           Sound Clip     Copy Family
                                          Cut Family
                                          Paste

Courier 12pt                              Doc 2 Pg 1 Ln 1" Pos 1"
```

- After selecting "Begin New Outline...," another menu will appear indicating the outline styles available to you:

EXERCISE DIRECTIONS:

1. Select Text Mode view.
2. Start with a clear screen.
3. Set 1.5" left and right margins.
4. Center the heading on Ln 2".

```
File  Edit  View  Layout  Tools  Font  Graphics  Window  Help
                        Outline Style List
List Styles from: ● Document   ○ Personal Library   ○ Shared Library

  Name         Type       Description
  Bullets      ▶Outline   ● ○ ─ ▪ ✱ + · x
  Headings     ▶Outline   Document Headings
  Legal        ▶Outline   1  1.1  1.1.1  etc.
  Legal 2      ▶Outline   1  1.01  1.01.01  etc.
  Numbers      ▶Outline   Paragraph Numbers Only (No Level Styles)
  Outline      ▶Outline   I. A. 1. a. (1) (a) i) a)
  Paragraph    ▶Outline   1. a. i. (1) (a) (i) 1) a)


  1. Select    3. Edit...   5. Copy...    7. Save...   9. Mark
  2. Create... 4. Delete... 6. Options... 8. Retrieve... N. Name Search
              ▶ Denotes library style              [Close]

Courier 12pt                              Doc 2 Pg 1 Ln 1" Pos 1"
```

- The outline feature may also be used for numbered paragraphs and bulleted lists. For now, we will concentrate on the "outline" style. The other styles will be covered in later exercises.

- The "Outline" style will produce an outline with levels like the illustration in the exercise and will insert outline characters automatically at the appropriate outline levels.

- When you complete your outline, you must select "End Outline" from the Outline cascading menu.

- An outline generally begins 2" from the top of the page and has a centered heading. A triple space follows the heading. The outline feature is then accessed.

- The tab key is used to advance to a lower level (from III. to A or from B to 1). If you make an error by advancing too far to the next level, press **Shift + Tab** to move backward through the levels (from A to III. or from 1 to B).

5. Using the outline feature and the "outline" format, create the topic outline on the right.
6. Spell check the exercise.
7. Preview your document.
8. Print one copy.
9. Save the exercise; name it **CARS.**

PURCHASING VS. NOT PURCHASING A CAR

↓3ˣ

I.   Reasons for Purchasing a Car

↓2ˣ

   A.   Convenience
   B.   Prestige

↓2ˣ

II. Reasons for Not Purchasing a Car

↓2ˣ

   A.   Inconvenience
      1.   Expense of gasoline
      2.   Crowded roads
      3.   Parking problems
         a.   Expensive parking garages
         b.   Increasing tows
   B.   Hazards
      1.   Possibility of accidents
      2.   Unpredictable weather
   C.   Bad Financial Investment
      1.   High taxes
      2.   High interest rates
   D.   Continuing Costs
      1.   Fuel
      2.   Maintenance
         a.   Brakes
         b.   Oil
         c.   Filter
         d.   Tuneup
            (1) Points
            (2) Plugs
            (3) Timing

TO OUTLINE
Ctrl + F5

1. Place cursor where outline is to begin.
2. Click on Tools .... Alt + T
3. Click on Outline .... O
4. Click on Begin New Outline .... B
5. Highlight an outline style in the Style List Dialog box

NOTE: Select "Outline" for this exercise.

6. ENTER .... ↵

NOTE: The first outline level will display.

7. Type text for first level.
8. ENTER .... ↵
9. Press TAB .... Tab
(or Press Shift + Tab to return to previous level).

10. Type text for next level.
11. ENTER .... ↵
• To type text for next level, repeat steps 7-8.
• To return to previous level, press Shift + Tab

to end outline

12. Click on Tools .... Alt + T
13. Click on Outline .... O
14. Click on End Outline .... E

119

OUTLINING

NOTES:

- In this exercise, you will prepare a sentence outline. The sentence outline is more difficult to write, but it has an important advantage: many of the sentences can be used within your report.

EXERCISE DIRECTIONS:

1. Select Text Mode view.
2. Start with a clear screen.
3. Use the default margins.
4. Begin the exercise on Ln 2".
5. Using the outline feature and the "outline" format, create the sentence outline on the right.
6. Spell check the exercise.
7. Preview your document.
8. Print one copy.
9. Save the exercise; name it **COLONY.**

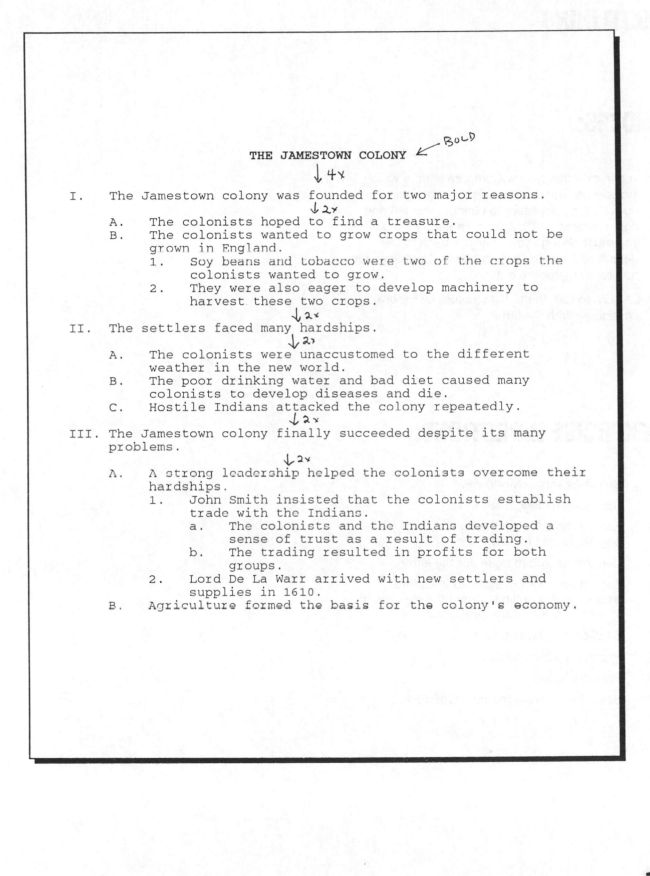

THE JAMESTOWN COLONY ← BOLD

↓ 4x

I.   The Jamestown colony was founded for two major reasons.

↓ 2x

    A.   The colonists hoped to find a treasure.

    B.   The colonists wanted to grow crops that could not be grown in England.

        1.   Soy beans and tobacco were two of the crops the colonists wanted to grow.

        2.   They were also eager to develop machinery to harvest these two crops.

↓ 2x

II. The settlers faced many hardships.

↓ 2x

    A.   The colonists were unaccustomed to the different weather in the new world.

    B.   The poor drinking water and bad diet caused many colonists to develop diseases and die.

    C.   Hostile Indians attacked the colony repeatedly.

↓ 2x

III. The Jamestown colony finally succeeded despite its many problems.

↓ 2x

    A.   A strong leadership helped the colonists overcome their hardships.

        1.   John Smith insisted that the colonists establish trade with the Indians.

            a.   The colonists and the Indians developed a sense of trust as a result of trading.

            b.   The trading resulted in profits for both groups.

        2.   Lord De La Warr arrived with new settlers and supplies in 1610.

    B.   Agriculture formed the basis for the colony's economy.

OUTLINING

NOTES:

- In this exercise, you will prepare a letter which includes an outline. In order to center the outline, it is necessary to change your left and right margins to 2". After completing the outline, you must change your margins back to the default of 1" on the left and right. Double space before and after the outline.

- Be sure to turn the outline feature off before continuing with the letter.

EXERCISE DIRECTIONS:

1. Select Graphics Mode view.
2. Start with a clear screen.
3. Format the letter on the right in block style beginning on Ln 1.5".
4. Use the default margins for the letter.
5. Set left and right margins to 2" before beginning the outline. Reset the margins to 1" for the remainder of the letter.
6. Spell check the exercise.
7. Preview your document.
8. Print one copy.
9. Save the exercise; name it **CAREER.**

Today's date ⟵ 1.5"

Mr. Ronald Mangano, Assistant Principal
New Dorp High School
465 New Dorp Lane
Staten Island, NY 10306

Dear Mr. Mangano:

(italics) I would once again like to make a presentation to your classes on *Choosing and Planning a Career*. A brief outline of my planned talk appears below:

Set 2" left/right margins →

    I.   **CHOOSING AND PLANNING A CAREER** ⟩— bold
        ↓2×
        A.   Discovering the World of Work
        B.   Investigating Career Fields
            1.   Medicine
            2.   Business
                a.   Marketing
                b.   Brokerage
                c.   Computer-related
                    (1) Technician
                    (2) Programmer
                    (3) Data Entry Operator
            3.   Teaching
            4.   Engineering
             ↓2×
    II.   **GETTING A JOB** ⟩—— bold
        ↓2×
        A.   Being Interviewed
            1.   How to dress
            2.   What to say
        B.   Writing a Resume
           ↓2×

Set 1" left and right margins →

While I may not have enough time to include all the material in my presentation, the outline will give you an overview of my topic. I look forward to addressing your classes on March 31.

Sincerely,

Janice Waller
Recruitment Representative

jw/yo

BULLETED LISTS; PARAGRAPH NUMBERING

NOTES:

- A bullet is a round dot or symbol which is used to highlight points of information or itemize a list that does not need to be in any particular order.

- Symbol bullets enable you to create interesting bullets other than the typical round dot.

- Through WordPerfect's outline feature, you can insert bullets automatically to create a bulleted list for each paragraph you type. You can also select from a variety of "bullet" symbols.

- The outline feature also allows you to create numbered paragraphs for items that *do* need to be in a particular order.

EXERCISE DIRECTIONS:

1. Select Text Mode view.
2. Start with a clear screen.
3. Set left and right margins to 1.5".
4. Begin the exercise on Ln 2".
5. Format the exercise as shown on the right using the outline feature to create the bullets and numbered list. Use a bullet other than the round dot.
6. Spell check the exercise.
7. Preview your document.
8. Print one copy.
9. Save the exercise; name it **JOB.**

THE IMPORTANCE OF A RESUME

A resume is used to get you to see potential employers and to organize the important facts about you in a written document. It should contain brief but sufficient information to tell a prospective employer:

☺ What you can do.
☺ What is your level or education.
☺ What you have done.
☺ What you know.
☺ What kind of job you want.

Your resume should accomplish several objectives:

1. It will serve as your introduction.
2. It will save time for both the employer and applicant.
3. It will serve as a focus for, and improve, your personal interview. When you have outlined your outstanding qualities, you will find it easier to discuss them at an interview.
4. It will provide the employer with a visual reminder of what you said at the interview.

So, when you begin your preparation, proofread it carefully. Remember, your resume is a representation of yourself. It makes the first and last impression of who you are.

TO CREATE A BULLETED OR NUMBERED LIST
Ctrl + F5

1. Place cursor where bulleted or numbered list is to begin.
2. Click on Tools .... Alt + T
3. Click on Outline .... O
4. Click on Begin New Outline... .... B
5. Highlight an outline style in Outline Style List Dialog box:

Bullets

or

Numbers

6. ENTER............................. ↵
NOTE: The first bullet or number will display.
7. Type first paragraph.
8. ENTER............................. ↵
9. Type next paragraph.
10. ENTER............................. ↵
11. Repeat steps 7-8 for remaining paragraphs.
to end bullets/numbered list
12. Click on Tools .... Alt + T
13 Click on Outline .... O
14. Click on End Outline... .... E

TO CREATE BULLET STYLES

1. Click on Tools .... Alt + T
2. Click on Outline........................... O
3. Click on Outline Style................... O
4. Highlight Bullets .
5. Click on Edit............................ E
6. Click on Numbers .... U
7. Click on List Bullets................... F5
8. Highlight desired bullet style.
9. Enter............................... ↵
10. Click on OK............................. ↵
11. Click on Close........................... ↵ **125**

EXERCISE DIRECTIONS:

1. Open **RESUME**.
2. Make the indicated revisions.
3. Underline side headings.
4. Hyphenate the document.
5. Search for "Statten" and replace with "Staten."
6. Using the thesaurus feature, substitute the words makred in brackets.
7. Preview your document.
8. Print one copy.
9. Close the file; save the changes.

JODY ABBATO
7652 Shore Road
Statten Island, NY 10314
(718) 654-9870

CAREER OBJECTIVE   To ⟨secure⟩ a responsible management position in a leading hotel chain with opportunities for ⟨growth.⟩

EDUCATION

Sept. 1989-June 1993   _Cornell University_, School of Hotel Administration, Ithaca, NY 14850. Received a Bachelor of Science degree in Hotel Administration with a 3.5 overall average.

Sept. 1985-June 1989   _Tottenville High School_, 100 Luten Avenue Statten Island, NY 10312.

EXPERIENCE

June 1991-Aug. 1991   _Marriott Hotel_, Broadway, New York, NY 10012. Duties: Data entry operator in accounting department.

June 1990-Aug. 1990   _Holiday Inn_, Richmond Avenue, Statten Island, NY 10314. Duties: Worked in accounting department as assistant to manager.

HOBBIES

Skiing, Reading, Tennis

ACTIVITIES

Vice President of Cornell University Management Society
Member of Cornell University Student Senate
Staff reporter for Cornell University Management News

SKILLS

IBM Personal Computer, knowledge of Windows, WordPerfect, Lotus, dBase IV and PageMaker application software.

REFERENCES

Ms. Maria Lopez, Manager, Holiday Inn, Richmond Avenue, Statten Island, NY 10314 (718) 876-3677

Dr. Stanley Simon, Professor of Management, Cornell University, Ithaca, NY 14850 (325) 456-8765

EXERCISE DIRECTIONS:

1. Create the letter below, in any style, inserting the outline indicated. Reset margins, as desired, before and after creating the outline so that the outline appears indented on the left and right.

2. Begin the exercise on Ln 1.5".

3. Hyphenate your document.

4. Print one copy.

5. Save the exercise; name it **PRACTICE.**

Today's date Mr. Raymond Mangano 645 Avenue of Americas New York, NY 10010 ¶Dear Mr. Mangano:¶In response to your inquiry, WordPerfect <u>does</u> contain an outline feature. ¶Each outline level is marked with a different character type which is specific to that level. Roman numerals are displayed for each Level 1 outline. Level 2 entries are marked with an uppercase letter, Level 3 entries are marked with an Arabic number, etc. Note the sample topic outline below:¶

I.   WHAT IS A FLOOD A. Its Extent B. Its Effects 1. Bad effects a. Destroys property and homes b. Carries off topsoil c. Causes injuries and deaths 2. Good effects a. Creates fertile regions b. Transports soil c. Causes injuries and deaths 2. Good effects a. Creates fertile regions
b. Transports soil (1) Nile Valley (2) Mississippi Valley
II. KINDS OF FLOODS A. River Floods B. Seacoast Floods
1. Causes 2. Great Floods¶

I think the above illustration should clarify outline levels. If you have any further questions, call me or check WordPerfect's reference manual. ¶Yours truly, Crystal Williams Marketing Directory cw/yo

LESSON 7 / EXERCISES 47-56
MULTIPLE - PAGE DOCUMENTS

- Creating a Two-Page Letter
- Creating a Multiple-Page Report
- Footnoting/Endnoting
- Printing Multiple Copies
- Searching and Replacing
- Using Bookmarks/ QuickMarks
- Using Headers/Footers/Page Numbers
- Widow/Orphan Protection
- Using Superscripts/ Subscripts
- Moving Text from One Page to Another
- Using GO TO

MULTIPLE-PAGE DOCUMENTS: A TWO-PAGE LETTER

NOTES:

- WordPerfect assumes you are working on a page measuring 8 1/2" wide x 11" long. Since WordPerfect uses a default 1" top and bottom margin, there are exactly 9" of vertical space on a standard page for entering text.

- The "Ln" indicator shows how far you are from the top of the page. Therefore, when you enter text beyond 9.83" (the last line of the 9 inches), WordPerfect automatically inserts a dashed horizontal line across the screen to indicate the end of one page and the start of another. When WordPerfect ends the page, this is referred to as a "soft page break." Once the cursor is below the horizontal line, you will note that the "Pg" indicator on the status line displays "Pg 2."

- If you wish to end the page before 9.83," you can do so by entering a "hard page break." A hard page break is indicated by a double horizontal line.

- You can delete a hard page break; text that appeared below the hard page break will flow on to the previous page, as room allows.

- A multiple-page letter requires a heading on the second and succeeding pages. The heading should begin at 1" and include the name of the addressee (to whom the letter is going), the page number, and the date.

- In this exercise, allow WordPerfect to insert page breaks for you.

- WordPerfect allows you to specify how much of the document you wish to print: the current page, selected pages, document on disk, selected text or the full document. Note dialog box with these options:

```
                                    Print/Fax
 Current Printer
 QMS PS 810                                          Select...

 Print                          Output Options
 1. • Full Document             ☐ Print Job Graphically
 2. O Page                      Number of Copies: 1
 3. O Document on Disk...       Generated by      WordPerfect  ⬦
 4. O Multiple Pages...         Output Options...
 5.   Blocked Text              No Options

 Options                        Document Settings
 6. Control Printer...          Text Quality      High      ⬦
 7. Print Preview...            Graphics Quality  Medium    ⬦
 8. Initialize Printer          Print Color       Black     ⬦
 9. Fax Services...

 Setup... Shft+F1                    Print   Close   Cancel
```

- When printing all pages in a multiple page document, you must indicate that you are printing a "Full Document," not a "Page." Therefore, after accessing the print command, select Full Document as your print option. Your cursor may be on any page in the document when directing WordPerfect to print the "full document."

EXERCISE DIRECTIONS:

1. Select Text Mode view.
2. Start with a clear screen.
3. Format the letter on the right in block style.
4. Begin the exercise on Ln 2.5".
5. Use the outline bullet feature to create the bullets on the first page.
6. Include the second-page heading immediately after WordPerfect inserts the page break.

7. Use the outline paragraph feature to create the numbered paragraphs on the second page.
8. Spell check the exercise.
9. Print one copy of the full document.
10. Print one copy of page two.
11. Save the exercise; name it **NYC.**

continued . . .

2.5"

Today's date

Mr. Brendon Basler
54 West Brook Lane
Fort Worth, TX 76102-1349

Dear Mr. Basler:

I am so glad to hear that you might be moving to Manhattan. You
asked me to write and tell you what it is like living in
Manhattan. Since I have been a New Yorker for most of my life
and love every minute of it, I will describe to you what it might
be like for you to live here.

begin bullet outline

- If you move to an apartment in Manhattan with a view, you
  might see the Empire State Building, the Metropolitan Life
  Tower, the Chrysler Building or even the Citicorp Center.
  Depending on where your apartment is located, you might even
  see the twin towers of the World Trade Center. The Brooklyn
  and Manhattan Bridges are off to the east and on a clear day
  you can see the Hudson River.

- Traffic in New York, as well as waiting in long lines at the
  post office and the movie theaters, can be very frustrating.
  However, after you have lived here for a short while, you
  will know the best times to avoid long lines.

- It is absolutely unnecessary and <u>very</u> expensive to own a car
  in Manhattan. The bus and subway system are excellent ways
  to travel within the City.

- There is always something to do here. If you love the
  opera, ballet, theater, museums, art galleries, and eating
  foods from all over the world, then New York is the place
  for you.

end bullet outline

Before you actually make the move, I suggest that you come here
for an extended visit. Not everyone loves it here.

You mentioned that you would be visiting some time next month. I
have listed on the next page some of the hotels (and their phone
numbers) you might want to consider staying in while you are
visiting. I have included those that would be in walking

Mr. Brendon Basler
Page 2
Today's date

distance to your meeting locations. And, while you are attending
your meetings, your family can take advantage of some of the
sights and shopping near your hotel. I have called the hotels to
be certain they can accommodate you and your family. They all
seem to have availability at the time you are planning to visit.

begin → paragraph outline

1. **Plaza Hotel** - located at 59th Street and Central Park South
   at the foot of Central Park. 1-800-228-3000.

2. **The Pierre Hotel** - located at 61st Street and Fifth Avenue
   across the street from Central Park. 1-800-332-3442.

3. **The Drake Swissotel** - located at 56th Street and Park
   Avenue. 212-421-0900.

end → paragraph outline

Of course, you realize that there are many other hotel options
available to you. If these are not satisfactory, let me know and
I will call you with other recommendations.

Good luck with your decision. When you get to New York, I will
show you some of the sights and sounds of the City. Hopefully,
you will then be able to decide whether or not New York City is
the place for you.

Sincerely,

Pamela Davis

pd/yo

TO PRINT A MULTIPLE-PAGE DOCUMENT
Shift + F7, F

1. Click on File .... `Alt` + `F`
2. Click on Print/Fax .... `P`
3. Click on Full Document.............. `F`
4. Click on Print.................... `R` or `↵`

TO PRINT SELECTED PAGES
Shift + F7, M

1. Click on File .... `Alt` + `F`
2. Click on Print/Fax .... `P`
3. Click on Multiple Pages .... `M`
4. Click on Page/Label Range.......... `P`
5. Type selected page(s) using the following formats:

   3-9 = pages 3, 4, 5, 6, 7, 8 and 9

   3,6 = pages 3 and 6

   3-5,9 = pages 3, 4, 5, and 9

-9 = all pages before and including 9

9- = all pages after and including 9

AND/OR Odd/Even Pages:

- Click on Odd/Even Pages `O`
- Select:

   Both .... `B`

   Odd............................ `O`

   Even.......................... `E`

- Click on OK .... `↵`
6. Click on Print.................. `R` or `↵`

MULTIPLE-PAGE DOCUMENTS: CREATING A TWO-PAGE LETTER WITH SPECIAL NOTATIONS; PRINTING MULTIPLE COPIES; USING BOOKMARKS

NOTES:

- Some letters may include special parts in addition to those you have learned thus far. The letter in this exercise contains four special letter parts: a mailing notation, a subject line, an enclosure and a copy notation.

- When a letter is sent by a *special mail service* such as EXPRESS MAIL, REGISTERED MAIL, CERTIFIED MAIL or BY HAND (via a messenger service), it is necessary to include an appropriate notation on the letter. This notation is placed two lines below the date. The name of mail service is usually typed in all caps.

- The *subject* identifies or summarizes the body of the letter. It is typed a double space below the salutation. Two returns follow it. The subject line may be typed at the left margin or centered in modified-block style. The word "Subject" may be typed in all caps or in upper and lower case. Sometimes, "Re" (in reference to) is used instead of "Subject."

- An *enclosure* or attachment notation is used to indicate that something else besides the letter is included in the envelope. The enclosure or attachment notation is keyed one or two lines below the reference initials and may be typed in several ways (the number indicates how many items are enclosed in the envelope):

ENC.	Enclosure	Enclosures (2)
Enc.	Encls.	Attachment
Encl.	Encls (2)	Attachments (2)

- If copies of the document are to be sent to others, *a copy notation* is typed two lines below the enclosure/attachment notation (or the reference initials if there is no enclosure/ attachment). A copy notation may be typed in several ways:

Copy to:	c:
Copy to	pc: (photocopy)

- The *Bookmark* feature allows you to quickly return to a desired location in a document. This is a convenient feature if, for example, you are editing a large document and have to leave your work for a time. A bookmark keeps your place. When you return to work, you can open your file, "find the bookmark" in your document and quickly return to the place you had marked. Or, you might not have all the information needed to complete your document when you begin. Setting bookmarks will enable you to return to those sections of the document which need more development or information inserted.

- You can have several bookmarks in a single document; however, the name of each bookmark must be distinctive for easy identification. The bookmark name can be the first line of the paragraph or a one-word or character name.

- Your cursor may be anywhere in the document when you start a search for a bookmark.

- Access the Bookmark feature by selecting Edit from the main menu bar.

- In this exercise you will set several bookmarks as you create your document, find them when you have completed your document and insert additional information at each bookmark location.

EXERCISE DIRECTIONS:

1. Select Text Mode view.

2. Start with a clear screen.

3. Format the letter on the next page in block style.

4. Begin the exercise on Ln 2.5".

5. Double indent the paragraphs 1" on the left and right.

6. Set bookmarks where indicated; name the first one **1stINDENT,** the second, **2ndINDENT** and the third, **copyto.**

7. Insert a hard-page break where indicated and include the second-page heading.

8. Spell check the exercise.

9. Save the exercise; name it **PREVIEW.**

10. Find the first bookmark, **1stINDENT.** Insert the following sentence at the bookmark location:

    Furthermore, they have captured the objects on film so true to life that anyone watching them is captivated.

11. Find the second bookmark, **2ndINDENT.** Insert the following as the third indented paragraph:

    I will institute a program which will make schools throughout the country aware of their vocational potential.

12. Find the third bookmark, **copyto.** Insert a copy notation also to *Tien Lee*.

13. Print three copies of page 1 and one copy of page 2.

14. Close your file; save the changes.

continued . . .

Today's date

REGISTERED MAIL
    DS
Ms. Elizabeth DeKan
Broward College
576 Southfield Road
Marietta, GA 30068
    DS
Dear Ms. DeKan:
    DS
Subject: Educational Films for High Schools and Colleges
    DS
Thank you for your interest in the films that we have available
for high school and college students. We are pleased to send you
the enclosed flyer which describes the films in detail. Also
enclosed is a summary of those films that have recently been
added to our collection since the publication of the flyer.

There have been many positive reactions to our films. Just three
weeks ago, a group of educators, editors and vocational experts
were invited to view the films at the annual EDUCATORS' CON-
FERENCE. Here are some of their comments:

We will be sure to send the films in time for you to preview
them. Please be sure to list the date on which you wish to
preview the film.

Mr. William R. Bondlow, Jr., president of the National Vocational
Center in Washington, D.C. and editor-in-chief of Science
Careers, said,

      I like the films very much. They are in-
      novative and a great benefit to all those
      interested in the earth sciences as a profes-
      sional career.

(Create bookmark)

Ms. Andra Burke, a leading expert presently assigned to the
United States Interior Department, praised the films by saying
that,

TO PRINT MULTIPLE COPIES:
Shift + F7, N

1. Click on File .... `Alt` + `F`
2. Click on Print/Fax .... `P`
3. Click on Number of Copies .... `N`
4. Type desired number of copies to print

5. Click on a print option:

    Full Document .... `F`

    Page.................................. `P`

    Document on Disk............ `D`

    Multiple Pages.................. `M`

6. Click on Print..................... `R` or `↵`

TO INSERT HARD PAGE BREAK

1. Place cursor where new page is to begin.
2. Press **Ctrl + Enter** .... `Ctrl` + `↵`

continued . . .

Ms. Elizabeth DeKan
Page 2
Today's date

I" They are a major educational advance in career placement, which will serve as a source I"
of motivation for all future geologists.

(Create bookmark)
A member of the National Education Center, Dr. Lawrence Pilgrim,
also liked the films and said,

These are just some of the reactions we have had to our films.
We know you will have a similar reaction.

We would very much like to send you the films that you would like
during the summer session. You can use the summer to review
them. It is important that your request be received quickly
since the demand for the films is great, particularly during the
summer sessions at colleges and universities throughout the
country.

Cordially,

William DeVane
Executive Vice President
Marketing Department

wd/yo
   DS
Enclosures (2)
   DS
Copy to Robert R. Redford
        Nancy Jackson

(Create bookmark)

TO DELETE HARD PAGE BREAK

1. Place cursor immediately after hard page break line.

2. Press **Backspace** .... `Backspace`

   OR

   • Reveal Codes .... `Alt` + `F3`

   • Place cursor on hard page break code (HPg).

   • Press Delete .... `Del`

TO SET A BOOKMARK
Shift + F12

1. Place cursor where you want bookmark.

2. Click on Edit .... `Alt` | `E`

3. Click on Bookmark .... `K`

4. Click on Create .... `C`

NOTE: Bookmark Name box contains either text following the cursor or is empty for you to enter a desired name.

5. ENTER .... `↵`
   to accept text as bookmark name

   OR

   type new bookmark name .... *name*

6. Click on OK .... `↵`

TO FIND A BOOKMARK
Shift + F12

1. Click on Edit .... `Alt` + `E`

2. Click on Bookmark .... `K`

3. Highlight name of bookmark you want to find.

4. Click on Find .... `F`

135

MULTIPLE-PAGE DOCUMENTS: A TWO-PAGE LETTER; USING QUICKMARKS

NOTES:

- Bookmarks are used when you want to return to more than one location in a single document. However, if you need to use one only bookmark in a document, you can set a "QuickMark." A "QuickMark" is a generic bookmark. WordPerfect allows you to have only one QuickMark in a document. If you place a second QuickMark, the first one will be deleted. Because only one QuickMark may be inserted in a document, it does not need to be named.

- WordPerfect automatically places a QuickMark at the cursor location whenever you save a document. You may, however, turn this option off.

- QuickMark can be accessed within the Bookmark option which is found in Edit on the main menu bar.

- In this exercise, you will open the document DIVE, create a modified-block letter from the text, set a QuickMark, and use "Save As" to save it under a new file name.

EXERCISE DIRECTIONS:

1. Select Text Mode view.

2. Start with a clear screen.

3. Open **DIVE.**

4. Create a two-page, modified-block style letter from the document on the right. (Check to see that your left and right margins are set to 1.5".)

5. Begin the exercise on Ln 2.5".

6. Single space the text. (Reveal codes and delete the double space code.)

7. Use the Case Convert feature to change the subject line from all caps to upper and lower case.

8. Set a QuickMark at the beginning of the third paragraph.

9. Make the remaining revisions.

10. Spell check the exercise.

11. Print one copy.

12. Find the QuickMark. Insert the following *new paragraph* at the quickmark location:

    Some hotels do not have a beach. Instead, they have a cliff from which you can make entry into the ocean. When the sun sets, you can see the incredible sights down below.

13. Save the document as a new file (Save As); name it **DIVING.**

Insert {
Mr. Kenyatta Belcher
80 Avenue P
Cambridge, MA 02138

Today's date

Dear Ken:

] Subject: ~~DIVING IN THE CAYMAN ISLANDS~~ [

Do you want to see *sharks, barracudas, stingrays* and *angelfish*?

The Cayman Islands were discovered by Christopher Columbus in 1503 and are located south of Cuba. The Caymans are home to about 25,000 year-around residents. However, they welcome 200,000 visitors each year. Most visitors come with masks and flippers in their luggage.

SS

Set a QuickMark

Before you descend the depths of the ocean, it is important that you have a few lessons on the "don'ts" of diving.

Don't touch the coral and don't come up to the surface too fast holding your breath. If you do, your lungs will explode. Now, you are ready to jump in!

Here are some hotel suggestions:

Hotel/Diving Accommodations:

.5"
Anchorage View, PO Box 2123, Grand Cayman; **(809) 947-4209.**
Cayman Diving Lodge, PO Box 11, East End, Grand Cayman; **(809) 947-7555.**
Coconut Harbour, PO Box 2086, George Town, Grand Cayman; **(809) 949-7468.**
Red Sail Sports, PO Box 1588, George Town, Grand Cayman; **(809) 979-7965.**
Sunset House, PO Box 479, George Town, Grand Cayman; **(800) 854-4767.**
.5"

Hotels Offering Free Diving Instruction

.5"
Cayman Diving Lodge, PO Box 11, East End, Grand Cayman; **(809) 947-7555.**
Sunset House, PO Box 479, George Town, Grand Cayman; **(800) 854-4767.**
.5"

I am enclosing a brochure which will give you more details about the Cayman Islands. If you have any additional questions, please feel free to call me at any time.

Yours truly,

jr/yo
enclosure

John Rogers
Travel Agent

TO SET A QUICKMARK
Shift + F12

1. Place cursor/insertion point where you want quickmark placed.
2. Click on Edit .... Alt + E
3. Click on Bookmark .... K
4. Click on QuickMark .... Q

TO FIND QUICKMARK

1. Click on Edit .... Alt + E
2. Click on Bookmark .... K
3. Click on Find QuickMark I

TO TURN OFF QUICKMARK ON SAVE

1. Click on Edit .... Alt + E
2. Click on Bookmark .... K
3. Click on "Set QuickMark in Document on Save" .... S to deselect this option.
4. Click on OK .... ↵

MULTIPLE-PAGE DOCUMENTS: FOOTNOTES

NOTES:

- A **footnote** is used in a document to give information about the source of quoted material.

  The information includes: the author's name, the publication, the date of the publication and the page number from which the quote was taken.

- A footnote is usually printed at the bottom of a page, but may be printed immediately below the last line of text. A **separator line** separates footnote text from the regular text on the page.

- A **reference number** appears immediately after the quote in the text, and a corresponding footnote number or symbol appears at the bottom of the page.

- WordPerfect's footnote feature automatically inserts the reference number after the quote, inserts the separator line, numbers the footnote, and formats your page so that the footnote appears on the same page as the reference number.

- The footnote does not display on the screen in Text and Graphics Modes, but may be seen using Print Preview. You can see the footnote in your document if you are using Page Mode.

- The Footnote feature can be accessed from Layout on the main menu bar or by clicking on the *Foot Cr* button on the LAYOUT button bar.

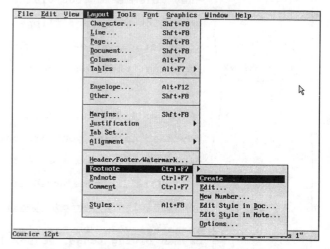

- In this exercise, you will create a report with footnotes, and include a QuickMark.

LAYOUT BUTTON BAR

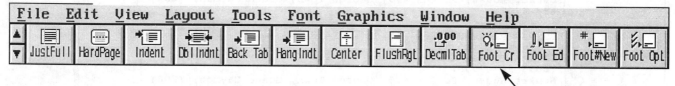

Footnote create

EXERCISE DIRECTIONS:

1. Select Page Mode view.
2. Start with a clear screen.
3. Create the report on the right in double space.
4. Use the default margins.
5. Begin the exercise on Ln 2".
6. Type until you reach each reference number; use the footnote feature to insert the reference number and the footnote text.
7. Set a QuickMark at the end of the second paragraph.

8. Spell check the exercise.
9. Find the QuickMark. Insert the following sentences at the QuickMark location:

   It belongs to a class of animals called <u>arachnids</u>, the same family that spiders, mites and ticks also belong. Scorpions live in warm countries in most parts of the world.

10. Print one copy.
11. Save the exercise; name it **SCORPION**.

THE SCORPION  2"

What is the first thing you think of when you hear the word "scorpion?" Most people think of "sting," "unsightly insect" or "poisonous."

The scorpion is a small animal with a dangerous poisonous stinger in its tail. The scorpion is <u>not</u> an insect. Scorpions eat large insects and spiders, and are most active at night. "Scorpions capture and hold their prey with their pedipalps, which have teeth. They then stab the prey with their stingers."[1]

The scorpion's stinger is a curved organ in the end of its tail. Two glands at the base give out a poison that flows from two pores. "Of the more than forty species of scorpions found in the United States, only two are considered to be harmful to people."[2] While a scorpion's sting is painful, it does not usually cause death.

(handwritten: Create Quickmark)

REFERENCE NUMBERS

SEPARATOR LINE

_____

[1]Gottfried, et. al, <u>Biology</u>, (New Jersey: Prentice-Hall, Inc. 1983), p. 461.

[2]<u>Ibid</u>., p. 461.

FOOTNOTES

TO FOOTNOTE
Ctrl + F7

1. Type to the reference number
   or
   place cursor at the location of the first reference number.
2. Click on Layout .... `Alt` + `L`
3. Click on Footnote .... `F`
4. Click on Create .... `C`

NOTE: A blank window appears with automatically assigned reference number.

5. Type footnote text.
6. Press F7 (Exit) .... `F7`
   to return to document.
7. Repeat steps 1-6 for each footnote.
   or
1. Follow step 1 above.
2. Click on *Foot Cr* button on LAYOUT button bar .... `Foot Cr`
3. Follow steps 5-7 above.

MULTIPLE PAGE DOCUMENTS:
ENDNOTES; EDITING A FOOTNOTE / ENDNOTE

NOTES:

- An **Endnote** contains the same information as a footnote, but is printed at the end of a document or on a separate page and differs in format. Compare the endnotes on the right with the footnotes in the previous exercise.

- It is possible to have both footnotes and endnotes in the same document.

- Like footnotes, endnotes do not display on the screen in Text and Graphics Modes, but you may see them when you preview the document. You can view the endnote in Page Mode.

- If you need to make a correction to the footnote/endnote, you must return to the footnote window to edit the note. When you edit, add, or delete footnotes or endnotes, WordPerfect renumbers and reformats them accordingly.

- The Endnote feature can be accessed from Layout on the main menu bar, or by clicking on the *End Cr* button the LAYOUT button bar.

- In this exercise, you will create a report with endnotes appearing on a separate page.

LAYOUT BUTTON BAR

Endnote create

EXERCISE DIRECTIONS:

1. Select Text Mode View.

2. Start with a clear screen.

3. Create the report on the right in double space.

4. Use the default margins.

5. Begin the exercise on Ln 2".

6. Type until you reach each reference number; use the endnote feature to insert the reference number and the endnote text.

7. Place the endnotes on a separate page.

8. Spell check the exercise.

9. Edit endnote number 1. Change the page number to 4.

10. Preview your document.

11. Print one copy.

12. Save the exercise; name it **COMPUTER**.

<u>COMPUTERS</u> **AND** <u>TERMINALS</u>

"A computer is an electronic or mechanical device used to perform high speed arithmetic and logical operations."[1] A computer system is composed of a computer (or computers) together with a peripheral equipment such as scanners, printers and terminals. A terminal is an electronic device used by a person to send or receive information from a computer system."[2]

A terminal usually consists of a keyboard connected to a television monitor and/or a printer.

1.David Chandler, <u>Dialing for Data</u>, (New York: Random House 1994), p. 5.

2.<u>Ibid</u>., p. 6.

TO ENDNOTE

1. Type to the reference number
   or
   place cursor at the location of the first reference number.
2. Click on Layout................. Alt + L
3. Click on Endnote .... E
4. Click on Create C

NOTE: A blank window appears with an automatically assigned reference number.

5. Type endnote text.
6. Press F7 (Exit)............................ F7
   to return to document.
7. Repeat steps 1-6 for each endnote.

TO PLACE ENDNOTES ON SEPARATE PAGE

8. Press PgDn
   to place cursor at end of text.
9. Press Ctrl + Enter
10. Click on Layout................. Alt + L
11. Click on Endnote .... E
12. Click on Placement...................... P
13. Click on No .... N

NOTE: In Text Mode, Endnote Placement Code appears followed by hard page break.

TO EDIT FOOTNOTE/ ENDNOTE

1. Click on Layout................. Alt + L
2. Click on Endnote .... E
3. Click on Edit................................ E
4. Type footnote/endnote number to edit.
5. Click on OK................................ ↵
6. Make desired correction.
7. Press F7..................................... F7
   to return to document
   or
1. Follow step 1 above.
2. Click on End Cr button on LAYOUT button bar............ End Cr
3. Follow steps 4-5 above.

MULTIPLE-PAGE DOCUMENTS: CREATING HEADERS, FOOTERS AND PAGE NUMBERS

NOTES:

- A **header** is the text (such as a chapter title, a date, or a company name) which prints at the *top* of every page or every page or every other page, while a **footer** is the same text which prints at the *bottom* of every page or every other page.

- After typing the desired header or footer once, WordPerfect's header/footer feature will automatically insert it on every page or on specific pages of your document.

- The header will print just below the top margin; the footer will print just above the bottom margin. However, the header/footer printing line may be changed, if desired. You may also adjust the spacing below a header or above a footer.

- You can create several header A's and B's and Footer A's and B's in a document, but you can have only two headers and two footers active on any given page.

- Page numbers must be included on multiple-page documents. You may include page numbers as part of the header or footer text.

- Since headers, footers and page numbers usually appear on the second and succeeding pages of a report, you must suppress them on the first page. Note the keystroke procedures to suppress text indicated on page 145.

- Headers, footers and page numbers do not display on the screen in Text and Graphics Modes, but may be seen using Print Preview. However, you can see the header, footer, and page number in Page Mode.

- If you plan to insert a header on the left side of your pages, insert page numbers on the top right side or bottom of your pages. Be sure that your header/footer text does not overlap or appear too close to the page number.

- Headers, footers and page numbers may be inserted after the document is typed.

- If you need to edit the header, you can return to the header window and make desired change.

- The Header/Footer/Watermark feature can be accessed from the Layout main menu bar or by clicking on the *Hdr/Ftr* button on the LAYOUT BUTTON BAR. (Watermarks will be covered in a later lesson.)

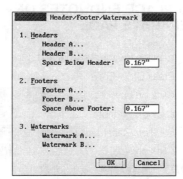

LAYOUT BUTTON BAR

Header/Footer

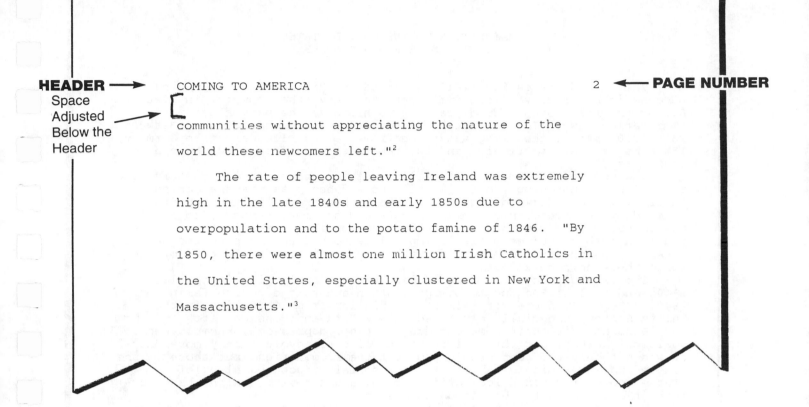

HEADER ⟶ COMING TO AMERICA   2 ⟵ **PAGE NUMBER**
Space
Adjusted
Below the   communities without appreciating the nature of the
Header
                world these newcomers left."[2]

                    The rate of people leaving Ireland was extremely

                high in the late 1840s and early 1850s due to

                overpopulation and to the potato famine of 1846. "By

                1850, there were almost one million Irish Catholics in

                the United States, especially clustered in New York and

                Massachusetts."[3]

EXERCISE DIRECTIONS:

1. Select Page Mode view.

2. Start with a clear screen.

3. Create the report on the next page in double space.

    NOTE: Set the same margins in the footnote window as used for the body text.

4. Begin the exercise on Ln 2".

5. Set 1.5" left and right margins.

6. Create the header DIFFICULTIES COMING TO AMERICA. Include a right-aligned page number as part of the header. **Suppress the header/page number on the first page.**

7. Set the space below the header to 0.21"

8. Spell check the exercise.

9. Preview your document.

10. Edit the header. Delete DIFFICULTIES from the title.

11. Print one copy.

12. Save the exercise; name it **VOYAGE.**

    NOTE: While the exercise is shown in single space, you are to use double space. Your printed document wili result in three pages, and footnotes will appear on the same pages as reference numbers.

IMMIGRATION TO THE UNITED STATES
IN THE NINETEENTH CENTURY

The United States is sometimes called the "Nation of Immigrants" because it has received more immigrants than any other country in history. During the first one hundred years of US history, the nation had no immigration laws. Immigration began to climb during the 1830s. "Between 1830-1840, 44% of the immigrants came from Ireland, 30% came from Germany, 15% came from Great Britain, and the remainder came from other European countries."[1]

The movement to America of millions of immigrants in the century after the 1820s was not simply a flight of impoverished peasants abandoning underdeveloped, backward regions for the riches and unlimited opportunities offered by the American economy. People did not move randomly to America but emanated from very specific regions at specific times in the nineteenth and twentieth centuries. "It is impossible to understand even the nature of American immigrant communities without appreciating the nature of the world these newcomers left."[2]

The rate of people leaving Ireland was extremely high in the late 1840s and early 1850s due to overpopulation and to the potato famine of 1846. "By 1850, there were almost one million Irish Catholics in the United States, especially clustered in New York and Massachusetts."[3]

Germans left their homeland due to severe depression, unemployment, political unrest, and the failure of the liberal revolutionary movement. It was not only the poor people who left their countries, but those in the middle and lower-middle levels of their social structures also left. "Those too poor could seldom afford to go, and the very wealthy had too much of a stake in the homelands to depart."[4]

Many immigrants came to America as a result of the lure of new land, in part, the result of the attraction of the frontier. America was in a very real sense the last frontier--a land of diverse peoples that, even under the worst conditions, maintained a way of life that permitted more freedom of belief and action than was held abroad. "While this perception was not entirely based in reality, it was the conviction that was often held in Europe and that became part of the ever-present American Dream."[5]

---

[1]Lewis Paul Todd and Merle Curti, Rise of the American Nation (New York: Harcourt Brace Jovanovich, Inc., 1972), p. 297.

[2]Bodner, John, The Transplanted (Bloomington: Indiana University Press, 1985), p. 54.

[3]E. Allen Richardson, Strangers in This Land (New York: The Pilgrim Press, 1988), p. 6.

[4]Ibid., p. 13.

[5]Ibid., p. 72.

TO CREATE HEADERS/FOOTERS
Shift + F8

1. Place cursor on first page where you want new header/footer to appear.

2. Click on Layout .... Alt + L

3. Click on Header/ Footer/Watermark .... H

4. Click on Headers or Footers .... H or F

NOTE: *To adjust space between header/footer and document text, click on "Space Below Header/Footer" and type amount of space.*

5. Click on Header A or Header B .... A or B

6. Click on where header/footer will occur:

   a. All Pages .... A
   b. Even Pages V
   c. Odd Pages .... O

7. Click on Create C

8. Type header/footer text.

To add a page number:

a. Position cursor where number will appear.

b. Click on Layout .... Alt + L

c. Click on Page........................... P

d. Click on Page Numbering........ N

e. Click on Insert Formatted Page Number.. I

To suppress header/footer on first page:

f. Click on Suppress.................... U
   • Click on Suppress All............ S

g. Click on OK .... ↵

9. Press F7 .... F7
   to return to document.

or

1. Follow step 1 above.

2. Click on *Hdr/Ftr* button on LAYOUT button bar .... [Hdr/Ftr]

3. Follow steps 5-10 above.

TO EDIT HEADER/FOOTER
Shift + F8

1. Place cursor on first page where you want change to occur.

2. Follow steps 2-5 above.

3. Click on Edit................................ E

4. Edit header/footer text.

5. Press F7 to return to document................. F7

MULTIPLE PAGE DOCUMENTS: CREATING HEADERS, FOOTERS AND PAGE NUMBERS; WIDOW / ORPHAN PROTECTION

NOTES:

• Sometimes after a multiple-page document is created, you may discover that the last line of a paragraph is printed by itself at the top of a page. This is called a **widow** line. Or, you may discover that the first line of a paragraph appears by itself on the last line of the page. This is called an **orphan** line. Widow and orphan lines should be avoided. WordPerfect contains a "widow/orphan line" protection feature to eliminate widows and orphans in a document.

• The widow/orphan protection feature can be accessed by selecting Other from the Layout main menu bar or by clicking on *FmtOther* button on the LAYOUT Button Bar.

• When page numbers are not part of the header/footer text, you have more placement options. Page numbers may be inserted at the top or bottom left, center or right. WordPerfect provides five different numbering styles:

Numbers:	1, 2, 3, 4, 5, etc.
Lower Letters:	a, b, c, d, e, f, etc.
Upper Letters:	A, B, C, D, E, F, etc.
Lower Roman:	i, ii, iii, iv, v, etc.
Upper Roman:	I, II, III, IV, V, etc.

• In this exercise, you will prepare a report with footnotes and a header, and page numbers that are not part of the header text (to be positioned at the bottom center of second and succeeding pages). Remember to suppress headers and page numbers on the first page.

LAYOUT BUTTON BAR

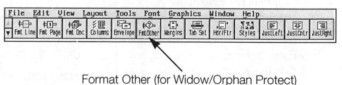

Format Other (for Widow/Orphan Protect)

• When a quotation is longer than two sentences, it is single spaced and indented. In this exercise, you will indent the quoted material as directed.

Other Format

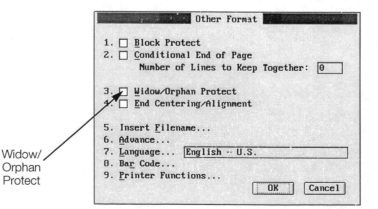

Widow/Orphan Protect

EXERCISE DIRECTIONS:

1. Select Page Mode view.

2. Start with a clear screen.

3. Create the report on the next page in double space.

NOTE: Set the same margins in the footnote window as used for the body text.

4. Begin the exercise on Ln 2".

5. Set 1.5" left and right margins for the *document*.

6. Turn widow/orphan protection ON.

7. Double indent and single space the quoted text as indicated.

8. Create the header, BUILDING THE UNITED STATES OF AMERICA.

NOTE: Set the same margins in the header window as used in the body text.

9. Include an Upper Roman page number on the bottom center of the second and succeeding pages.

10. Spell check the exercise.

11. Edit the header to read, BUILDING THE U. S. A.

12. Preview your document.

13. Print one copy.

14. Save the exercise; name it **USA.**

NOTE: While the exercise is shown in single space, you are to use double space. Your printed document will result in three pages, and footnotes will appear on the same pages as reference numbers.

continued . . .

IMMIGRATION'S IMPACT IN THE UNITED STATES

The opportunity to directly transfer a skill into the American economy was great for newcomers prior to the 1880s. "Coal-mining and steel-producing companies in the East, railroads, gold- and silver-mining interests in the West, and textile mills in New England all sought a variety of ethnic groups as potential sources of inexpensive labor."[1] Because immigrants were eager to work, they contributed to the wealth of the growing nation. During the 1830s, American textile mills welcomed hand-loom weavers from England and North Ireland whose jobs had been displaced by power looms. It was this migration that established the fine-cotton-goods trade of Philadelphia. "Nearly the entire English silk industry migrated to America after the Civil War, when high American tariffs allowed the industry to prosper on this side of the Atlantic."[2]

Whether immigrants were recruited directly for their abilities or followed existing networks into unskilled jobs, they inevitably moved within groups of friends and relatives and worked and lived in clusters.

As the Industrial Revolution progressed, immigrants were enticed to come to the United States through the mills and factories who sent representatives overseas to secure cheap labor. An example was the Amoskeag Manufacturing Company, located along the banks of the Merrimack River in Manchester, New Hampshire. In the 1870s, the Amoskeag Company recruited women from Scotland who were expert gingham weavers. Agreements were set specifying a fixed period of time during which employees would guarantee to work for the company.[3]

In the 1820s, Irish immigrants did most of the hard work in building the canals in the United States. In fact, Irish immigrants played a large role in building the Erie Canal. American contractors encouraged Irish immigrants to come to the United States to work on the roads, canals, and railroads, and manufacturers lured them into the new mills and factories.

"Most German immigrants settled in the middle western states of Ohio, Indiana, Illinois, Wisconsin and Missouri."[4] With encouragement to move west from the Homestead Act of 1862, which offered public land free to immigrants who intended to become citizens, German immigrants comprised a large portion of the pioneers moving west. "They were masterful farmers and they built prosperous farms."[5]

---

[1]E. Allen Richardson, Strangers in This Land (New York: The Pilgrim Press, 1988), p. 67

[2]John Bodnar, The Transplanted (Bloomington: Indiana University Press, 1985), p. 54

[3]Ibid., p. 72.

[4]David A. Gerber, The Making of An American Pluralism (Chicago: University of Illinois, 1989), p. 124.

[5]Bodnar, op. cit., p. 86.

TO INSERT PAGE NUMBERS
Shift + F8

1. Place cursor at beginning of document or page.
2. Click on Layout .... `Alt` + `L`
3. Click on Page.............................. `P`
4. Click on Page Numbering............. `N`
5. Click on Page Number Position.... `P`
6. Click on a page number position option:

   Top Left .... `F`
   Top Center.......................... `E`
   Top Right............................ `I`
   Alternating, Top .... `T`
   Bottom Left........................ `L`
   Bottom Center................. `C`
   Bottom Right .... `R`
   Alternating, Bottom .... `B`
   None .... `N`

TO CHANGE NUMBERING METHOD

7. Click on Page Number................. `N`
8. Click on Numbering Method......... `M`
9. Select a numbering method option:

   Numbers .... `N`
   Lower Letters.................... `E`
   Upper Letters.................... `L`
   Lower Roman .... `O`
   Upper Roman .... `R`
10. Click on OK............................... `↵`
    until you return to document.

TO SET WIDOW/ORPHAN PROTECTION
Shift + F8, 7

1. Place cursor where you want protection to begin.
2. Click on Layout................. `Alt` + `L`
3. Click on Other.............................. `O`
4. Click on Widow/Orphan Protect... `W`
5. Click on OK.................................. `↵`

   OR

1. Follow step 1 above.
2. Click *FmtOther* on the LAYOUT button bar ....
3. Follow steps 4-5 above.

MULTIPLE-PAGE DOCUMENTS: CREATING HEADERS, FOOTERS AND PAGE NUMBERS; USING SUPERSCRIPTS AND SUBSCRIPTS

NOTES:

- **Superscripts** are characters that are printed a half-line above the normal typing line; **subscripts** are characters that are printed a half-line below the normal typing line.

- Superscripts and subscripts are commonly used in mathematical and scientific formulas, and footnotes.

- WordPerfect's footnote feature automatically creates the superscript when footnoting. In order to raise or lower a character for any other purpose, it is necessary to use the superscript/subscript feature.

- Superscripts/subscripts do not display as a raised or lowered character on the screen in Text Mode. (They can be seen in Text Mode using Print Preview.) However, they will display properly in Graphics and Page Modes.

- When using superscripts/subscripts with single-spaced text, the raised and lowered characters will sometimes interfere with the lines above or below.

- Superscripts/subscripts may be accessed through the Size/Position option on the Font main menu bar or by clicking the Font button on the WPMAIN or FONTS button bars.

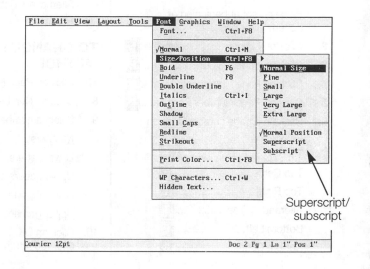

Superscript/subscript

WPMAIN BUTTON BAR

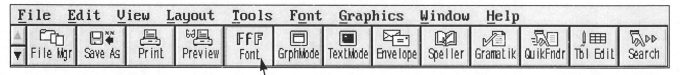

Font

EXERCISE DIRECTIONS:

1. Select Page Mode view.
2. Start with a clear screen.
3. Create the report on the right in double space.
4. Begin the exercise on Ln 2".
5. Since this report will be left bound, set a 2" left margin.
6. Full justify the document.
7. Include a page number at the top right of second and succeeding pages.
8. Include a bold, italics, and centered footer that reads, SUPERSCRIPT/SUBSCRIPT on the second and succeeding pages. (Be sure to suppress footer and page number on the first page.)
9. Turn widow/orphan protection ON.
10. Spell check the exercise.
11. Preview your document.
12. Save the exercise; name it **UPNDOWN**.

USING SUPERSCRIPTS AND SUBSCRIPTS
IN ALGEBRA AND CHEMISTRY

Superscripts and subscripts are commonly used in mathematical equations and scientific formulas. In algebra, superscripts are primarily used, while in science, subscripts are primarily used. Let's look at a few examples.

Multiplication in Algebra - **Superscripts**

Multiplication in algebra is usually demonstrated by writing two or more expressions together without a multiplication symbol. Example: a x b is written *ab*. Sometimes you may see a formula that is written ab^4. The little, raised number is called the **exponent**. It indicates the number of times a quantity is multiplied by itself. Therefore, a x a is written a^2. This is called the square of a. It means that "a" is multiplied by itself. If you wanted to multiply a x a x a, the formula would be written a^3. This is called the cube of "a". If you wanted to multiply a x a x a x a, the formula would be written as a^4. A typical formula used to multiply an expression consisting of two or more terms by a single term or expression would look like this: $(5b^2c+2d)(3bd)$.

Chemical Compounds in Chemistry - **Subscripts**

In chemistry, chemical compounds have common names and are also represented by a formula. Many of the common names of chemical compounds are so familiar to us, yet the compound name sounds so scientific. For example, water is a chemical compound with which we are probably the most familiar. Its common name is "water" and it is represented by the formula H_2O. Laughing gas is another common name of a chemical compound. Its compound name is nitrous oxide and is represented by the formula N_2O. Baking soda, or sodium bicarbonate, is represented by the formula $NaHCO_3$. A compound which is not as familiar is ammonium hydroxide. However, when we look at the common name, it really is one we might have used: ammonia water. It is represented by the formula NH_4OH. Since you probably have used some of the compounds mentioned, you may be a chemist and not even know it!

TO SUPERSCRIPT/ SUBSCRIPT
Ctrl + F8, P

1. Place cursor where superscript/subscript is to be inserted.
2. Click on Font..................... Alt + O
3. Click on Size/Position.................. Z
4. Click on Superscript or Subscript........................... P or B
5. Type text to be super/subscripted.
6. Press Right Arrow key .... →
   to revert to Normal text.

MULTIPLE PAGE DOCUMENTS:
MOVING TEXT FROM ONE PAGE TO ANOTHER; USING "GO TO"

NOTES:

- The procedure for moving blocks of text from one page to another is the same as moving blocks of text on the same page. However, if text is to be moved from one page to another, the "go to" feature may be used to quickly advance to the page where the text is to be reinserted. "Go to" may be accessed from Edit on the main menu bar or by pressing Ctrl + Home.

- "Go To" may be used at any time to advance to another page.

- If a hard page break was inserted, delete the break, then move the text. WordPerfect will then insert a soft page break. If the soft page break is not in a satisfactory location, insert a hard page break in a desired location.

- After moving the paragraph in this exercise, it may be necessary to move the second-page heading appropriately.

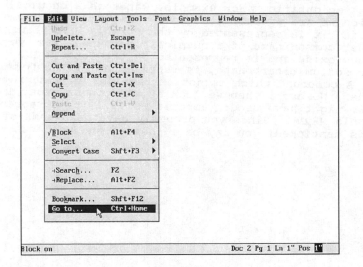

EXERCISE DIRECTIONS:

1. Select Graphics Mode view.
2. Start with a clear screen.
3. Open **PREVIEW.**
4. Make the indicated revisions.
5. Using the thesaurus, replace the words marked in brackets. Be sure replacement words maintain the same tense/endings as original words.
6. Print one copy.
7. Close the file; save the changes.

continued . . .

← ———————————————————— Today's date

REGISTERED MAIL

Ms. Elizabeth DeKan
Broward College
576 Southfield Road
Marietta, GA 30068

Dear Ms. DeKan:

<u>Subject</u>: Educational Films for High Schools and Colleges

Thank you for your interest in the films that we have available
for high school and college students. We are pleased to send you
the enclosed flyer which describes the films in detail. Also
enclosed is a ⟨summary⟩ of those films that have recently been
added to our collection since the publication of the flyer.

There have been many positive reactions to our films. Just three
weeks ago, a group of educators, editors and vocational experts
were invited to view the films at the annual EDUCATOR'S CON-
FERENCE. Here are some of their comments:

MOVE TO NEXT PAGE

(A) We will be sure to send the films in time for you to preview
them. Please be sure to list the date on which you wish to
preview the film.

INSERT

(B) Mr. William R. Bondlow, Jr., president of the National Vocational
Center in Washington, D.C. and editor-in-chief of <u>Science Care-
ers</u>, said,

        I like the films very much. They are in-
        novative and a great benefit to all those
        interested in the earth sciences as a profes-
        sional career. Furthermore, they have cap-
        tured the objects on film so true to life
        that anyone watching them is captivated.

(C) Ms. Andra Burke, a ⟨leading⟩ expert presently assigned to the
United States Interior Department, praised the films by saying
that,

move to next page

TO MOVE TEXT USING "GO TO"

1. Highlight/select text to be moved (cut).
2. Click on Edit......................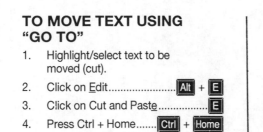 Alt + E
3. Click on Cut and Past<u>e</u>................ E
4. Press Ctrl + Home....... Ctrl + Home

5. Type page number where text is to be reinserted.
6. ENTER.. ⏎
7. Place cursor where text is to be reinserted.
8. ENTER.. ⏎

Ms. Elizabeth DeKan
Page 2
Today's date

Insert
Ⓒ

They are a major educational advance in career placement, which will serve as a source
of motivation for all future geologists.

MOVE
TO
Previous
page

A member of the National Education Center, Dr. Lawrence Pilgrim,
also liked the films and said,

Ⓑ

I will institute a program which will make
schools throughout the country aware of their
vocational potential.

These are just some of the ⟨reactions⟩ we have had to our films.
We know you will have a similar reaction.

Insert
Ⓐ

We would very much like to send you the films that you would like
during the summer session. ~~You can use the summer to review~~
~~them.~~ It is important that your request be received ⟨quickly⟩
since the demand for the films is great, particularly during the
summer sessions~~, at colleges and universities throughout the~~
~~country.~~

Cordially,

William DeVane
Executive Vice President
Marketing Department

wd/yo
Enclosures (2)

Copy to   Robert R. Redford
           Nancy Jackson
           Tien Lee

TO GO TO

1. Click on Edit .... `Alt` + `E`
2. Click on Go To .... `Ctrl` + `Home`
3. Type page number to "go to."
4. ENTER .... `↵`
    or
    - Press Ctrl + Home
    - Follow steps 3-4 above.

MULTIPLE PAGE DOCUMENTS:
MOVING TEXT FROM ONE PAGE TO ANOTHER; USING "GO TO"

NOTES:

- Moving paragraphs in this exercise will not affect footnote placement. WordPerfect will automatically readjust footnote placement.

- To change page numbers from Upper Roman to Arabic Numbers (1,2,3, etc.) you can delete the page number method code (Pg Num Meth) and reinsert a new one.

EXERCISE DIRECTIONS:

1. Select Page Mode view.
2. Start with a clear screen.
3. Open **USA**.
4. Make the indicated revisions.
5. Full justify the document.
6. Turn hyphenation ON (Shift + F8, L, Y).
7. Using the thesaurus, replace the words marked in brackets. Be sure replacement words maintain the same tense/endings as original words.
8. Change page number method from Upper Roman to Arabic Numbers.
9. Print one copy.
10. Close the file; save the changes.

full justify and hyphenate entire document

IMMIGRATION'S IMPACT IN THE UNITED STATES)-bold

The opportunity to directly transfer a skill into the American economy was great for newcomers prior to the 1880s. *Single space and indent quote* → "Coal-mining and steel-producing companies in the East, railroads, gold- and silver-mining interests in the West, and textile mills in New England all sought a variety of ethnic groups as potential sources of inexpensive labor."[1] Because immigrants were eager to work, they contributed to the wealth of the growing nation. During the 1830s, American textile mills ⟨welcomed⟩ hand-loom weavers from England and North Ireland whose jobs had been displaced by power looms. It was this migration that ⟨established⟩ the fine-cotton-goods trade of Philadelphia. "Nearly the entire English silk industry migrated to America after the Civil War, when high American tariffs allowed the industry to prosper on this side of the Atlantic."[2]

Insert (A) → Whether immigrants were recruited directly for their abilities or followed existing networks into

---

[1] E. Allen Richardson, <u>Strangers in This Land</u> (New York: The Pilgrim Press, 1988), p. 67

[2] John Bodnar, <u>The Transplanted</u> (Bloomington: Indiana University Press, 1985), p. 54

continued . . .

BUILDING THE U. S. A.

unskilled jobs, they inevitably moved within ⟨groups⟩ of

friends and relatives and worked and lived in clusters.

As the Industrial Revolution progressed,
immigrants were enticed to come to the United
States through the mills and factories who
sent representatives overseas to secure cheap
labor. An example was the Amoskeag
Manufacturing Company, located along the
banks of the Merrimack River in Manchester,
New Hampshire. In the 1870s, the Amoskeag
Company recruited women from Scotland who
were expert gingham weavers. Agreements were
set specifying a fixed period of time during
which employees would guarantee to work for
the company.[3]

(handwritten: move to page 1)

(A) In the 1820s, Irish immigrants did most of the

hard work in building the canals in the United States.

In fact, Irish immigrants played a large role in

building the Erie Canal. American contractors

encouraged Irish immigrants to come to the United

States to work on the roads, canals, and railroads, and

manufacturers ⟨lured⟩ them into the new mills and

factories.

"Most German immigrants settled in the middle

western states of Ohio, Indiana, Illinois, Wisconsin

and Missouri."[4] With encouragement to move west from

the Homestead Act of 1862, which offered public land

free to immigrants who intended to become citizens,

---

[3]*Ibid*., p. 72.

[4]David A. Gerber, <u>The Making of An American
Pluralism</u> (Chicago: University of Illinois, 1989), p.
124.

(handwritten: (II) — change to Arabic numbers)

BUILDING THE U. S. A.

German immigrants ⟨comprised⟩ a large portion of the pioneers moving west. "They were masterful farmers and they built prosperous farms."[5]

---

[5]Bodnar, op. cit., p. 86.

Ⓘ — change to Arabic numbers

EXERCISE DIRECTIONS:

1. Use any desired view mode.

2. Create a two-page letter <u>in any style</u> from the text below. Include a proper heading for the second page.

3. Use the default margins.

4. Send the letter SPECIAL DELIVERY and include an appropriate subject line.

5. To format the numbered items:

   a. set your left margin to 1.5".

   b. use the outline feature to create the numbered paragraphs.

   c. when you have completed typing the numbered items, turn off the outline feature, and reset your left margin to 1".

6. Turn hyphenation ON.

7. Spell check the exercise.

8. Print one copy.

9. Save the exercise; name it **CHOICES**.

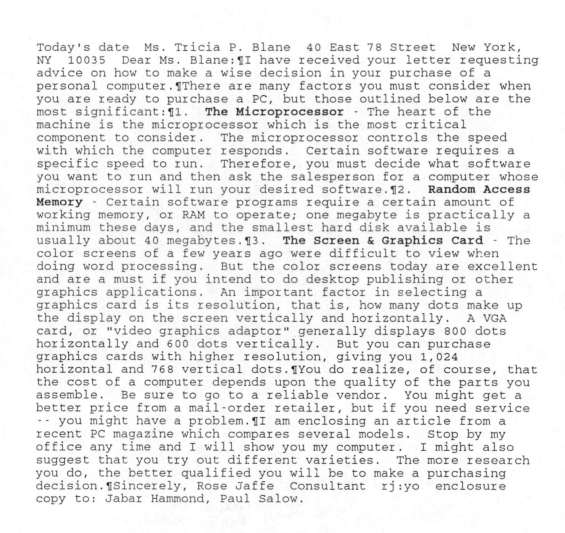

Today's date Ms. Tricia P. Blane 40 East 78 Street New York, NY 10035 Dear Ms. Blane:¶I have received your letter requesting advice on how to make a wise decision in your purchase of a personal computer.¶There are many factors you must consider when you are ready to purchase a PC, but those outlined below are the most significant:¶1. **The Microprocessor** - The heart of the machine is the microprocessor which is the most critical component to consider. The microprocessor controls the speed with which the computer responds. Certain software requires a specific speed to run. Therefore, you must decide what software you want to run and then ask the salesperson for a computer whose microprocessor will run your desired software.¶2. **Random Access Memory** - Certain software programs require a certain amount of working memory, or RAM to operate; one megabyte is practically a minimum these days, and the smallest hard disk available is usually about 40 megabytes.¶3. **The Screen & Graphics Card** - The color screens of a few years ago were difficult to view when doing word processing. But the color screens today are excellent and are a must if you intend to do desktop publishing or other graphics applications. An important factor in selecting a graphics card is its resolution, that is, how many dots make up the display on the screen vertically and horizontally. A VGA card, or "video graphics adaptor" generally displays 800 dots horizontally and 600 dots vertically. But you can purchase graphics cards with higher resolution, giving you 1,024 horizontal and 768 vertical dots.¶You do realize, of course, that the cost of a computer depends upon the quality of the parts you assemble. Be sure to go to a reliable vendor. You might get a better price from a mail-order retailer, but if you need service -- you might have a problem.¶I am enclosing an article from a recent PC magazine which compares several models. Stop by my office any time and I will show you my computer. I might also suggest that you try out different varieties. The more research you do, the better qualified you will be to make a purchasing decision.¶Sincerely, Rose Jaffe Consultant rj:yo enclosure copy to: Jabar Hammond, Paul Salow.

EXERCISE DIRECTIONS:

1. Use any desired view mode.
2. Create the report below.
3. Set a 1.5" left margin for the *document*.
4. Include a bold, right-aligned header, **LABOR IN COLONIAL AMERICA**, and a page number on the second and succeeding pages. You may place the page number where desired.
5. Full justify the document.
6. Turn widow/orphan protection ON.
7. Spell check the exercise.
8. Print one copy.
9. Save the exercise; name it **NUWORLD**.

LABOR IN COLONIAL AMERICA¶Labor was a key issue in colonial America. The American labor force consisted of indentured servants, redemptioners from Europe, slaves from Africa and the colonists themselves.¶Indentured servants were the first source of foreign labor to arrive in the new world. Scores came from England between 1698 and 1700. "Out of 3,257 people who left for America, 918 of them were on their way to Maryland, a major port of indentured servants and redemptioners."[1]¶The new world offered much to the Europeans. Most European laborers desired the political and economic freedoms of America. The British capitalists offered those who wanted to come to America, but could not afford it, the opportunity to do so by having them agree to surrender a portion of their life to work as a laborer in return for having those expenses paid. This was the beginning of indentured servants.¶Why were people so willing to enter into a life of servitude in a new country? Conditions in Europe during this period were poor. Political and economic problems existed. People were lured to the new world by its promise for religious freedom and an opportunity for a better life.¶The colonists realized that in the development of a new country, labor is the most important element of production. They recognized the importance of a good labor supply. Because the supply of good white servants infrequently met the demand, more than half of all persons who came to America, south of England, were servants.¶The contract of servitude was simple. Europeans who were unable to pay their own passage across the Atlantic become bond servants for a period of years to some colonial master who paid for them. "It was a legal contract by which the servant bound himself to serve the master in such employments as the master might assign for a given length of time usually in a specified plantation."[2] The contract included other clauses. A more skilled worker might collect wages and also be excluded from field labor. Education was included in a child's indenture. "Four years for each adult was the average time of servitude. Children usually worked until they were 21."[3]¶ Servitude was cruel; it subjected large numbers of people to a hard, laborious, and dangerous way of life. Many who came found the work too difficult; they were not ready for this type of life. "In the first few years, it killed fifty or seventy-five out of every hundred."[4]

---

[1]Emerson Smith, Colonists in Bondage, (New York: Holt Rinehart and Winston, Inc., 1975), p. 308.

[2]Ibid., p. 45.

[3]Ibid., p. 47.

[4]Percy Brackson and John Falcon, History of Agriculture in Northern United States, (New York: Alfred A. Knopf, Inc., 1974), p. 117.

LESSON 8 / EXERCISES 57-66
MERGING DOCUMENTS

- **Creating the Form File**
- **Creating the Data (Text) File**
- **Defining Conditions for Merge**
- **Creating the Data (Table) File**
- **Preparing Envelopes/ Labels**

MERGE: CREATING THE "FORM" FILE

NOTES:

- WordPerfect's merge feature allows you to mass produce letters, envelopes, mailing labels and other documents so they appear to be personalized.

- To send the same letter or other documents to many different people, you need only type the document once and type the name and address list once. WordPerfect will merge and print the letter with each individual name and address, making it appear as though each letter was personally typed.

- A "form" file (the form letter) is combined with a data file (the names and addresses of those that will receive the letters) to produce a "merged" document. The same data file may then be used to produce the envelopes and/or labels, thus making it unnecessary to type the name and address list a second time.

- The **form file** contains information that does not change. All formatting (margins, spacing, etc.), graphics and paper size information should be included in the form file. Codes are inserted where variable information will be placed. (Variable information contains text that **will** change from letter to letter.) In a typical letter, the variable information includes the inside address and the salutation.

- Variable information must be identified. Each piece of variable information is called a **field**. Each field is referenced either by number or name. In this exercise, the fields will be referenced by name. If you don't name your fields, WordPerfect will number them for you.

MERGED DOCUMENT

FORM FILE

```
Today's date

FIELD(TITLE) FIELD(FIRST) FIELD(LAST)
FIELD(ADDRESS)
FIELD(CITY), FIELD(STATE)  FIELD(ZIP)

Dear FIELD(TITLE) FIELD(LAST):

You are cordially invited to attend our
annual spring fashion show.  The show
will take place at the Plaza Hotel in
New York City Friday evening, June 22 at
7:30 p.m.  Refreshments will be served.

We appreciate your contributions and
continued support of the Fashion
Institute. We know you will see several
outstanding collections at the showing.
Please let me know if you plan to attend
by calling my office any day between
9:00 a.m. and 5:00 p.m.

We are looking forward to your attending
this special event.

Sincerely,


Thomas Mann
President
Fashion Institute
```

+

DATA FILE

```
Mr. ENDFIELD
Peter ENDFIELD
Ringler ENDFIELD
23 Preston Avenue ENFIELD
NY ENFIELD
BellemoreENFIELD
11010ENFIELD
ENDRECORD
-----------------------------------
Mr. ENFIELD
FredENFIELD
LeBostENFIELD
98-67 Kew Gardens RoadENFIELD
Forest HIllsENFIELD
11432ENFIELD
ENDRECORD
-----------------------------------
Ms.ENFIELD
MaryENFIELD
McCleanENFIELD
765 Belmill RoadENFIELD
RoslynENFIELD
NYENFIELD
11577ENFIELD
ENDRECORD
-----------------------------------
MS.ENFIELD
LorraineENFIELD
OelserENFIELD
1275ENFIELD
NEW YORKENFIELD
10028ENFIELD
ENDRECORD
```

=

```
Today's date

Mr. Fred LeBost
98-67 Kew Gardens Road
Forest Hills, NY  11432
```

```
Today's date

Ms. Mary McClean
765 Belmill Road
Roslyn, NY  11577
```

```
Today's date

Mr. Peter Ringler
23 Preston Avenue
Bellemore, NY  11010
```

```
Today's date

Ms. Lorraine Oelser
1275 Broadway
New York, NY  10028

Dear Ms. Oelser:

You are cordially invited to attend our
annual spring fashion show.  The show
will take place at the Plaza Hotel in
New York City Friday evening, June 22 at
7:30 p.m.  Refreshments will be served.

We appreciate your contributions and
continued support of the Fashion
Institute. We know you will see several
outstanding collections at the showing.
Please let me know if you plan to attend
by calling my office any day between
9:00 a.m. and 5:00 p.m.

We are looking forward to your attending
this special event.

Sincerely,


Thomas Mann
President
Fashion Institute
```

- In the exercise on page 188, the inside address and salutation are divided into fields, with each field given a name. The illustration indicates how fields display on the screen after the codes are entered in WordPerfect. Each field is named for what will eventually be inserted into that location. The first field is named "title," the second is named "first," the third field is named "last," the fourth field is named "address," the fifth field is named "city," the sixth field is named "state," and the seventh field is named "zip."

- As you enter each field, space between the fields as you would want the spacing to appear when text is inserted in the letter.

- The same field name can be inserted in the letter as many times as desired. Note that **FIELD**(TITLE) and **FIELD**(LAST) are used twice since the letter contains two occurrences of someone's title and last name.

- When you complete the "form" file, print one copy to use as reference for preparing the data file. The data file must contain the same fields as the form file. Otherwise, the final document will not merge properly.

- After the form file is created, it must be saved.

- To access the merge feature, select "Merge" from the Tools main menu bar.

```
 File  Edit  View  Layout  Tools  Font  Graphics  Window  Help
                          Writing Tools...  Alt+F1

                          Macro                    ▶
                          Outline          Ctrl+F5 ▶
                          Merge            Shft+F9 ▶
                          Sort...          Ctrl+F9
                          Date             Shft+F5 ▶

                          Index            Alt+F5  ▶
                          Table of Contents Alt+F5 ▶
                          List             Alt+F5  ▶
                          Cross-Reference  Alt+F5  ▶
                          Table of Authorities    ▶
                          Generate...      Alt+F5

                          Math             Alt+F7  ▶
                          Spreadsheet      Alt+F7  ▶

                          Hypertext...     Alt+F5
                          Sound Clip       Ctrl+F7 ▶

 Courier 12pt                        Doc 1 Pg 1 Ln 1" Pos 1"
```

- Follow the keystrokes noted on the next page to complete the procedure.

- In this exercise, you will create a "form" letter file.

EXERCISE DIRECTIONS:

1. Select Text Mode view.
2. Start with a clear screen.
3. Create the "form" letter as shown on the next page.
4. Use the default margins.
5. Begin the exercise on Ln 2.5".
6. Spell check the exercise.
7. Print one copy. (Keep your printout for reference to create the next exercise.)
8. Save the exercise; name it **INVITE.FF**

continued . . .

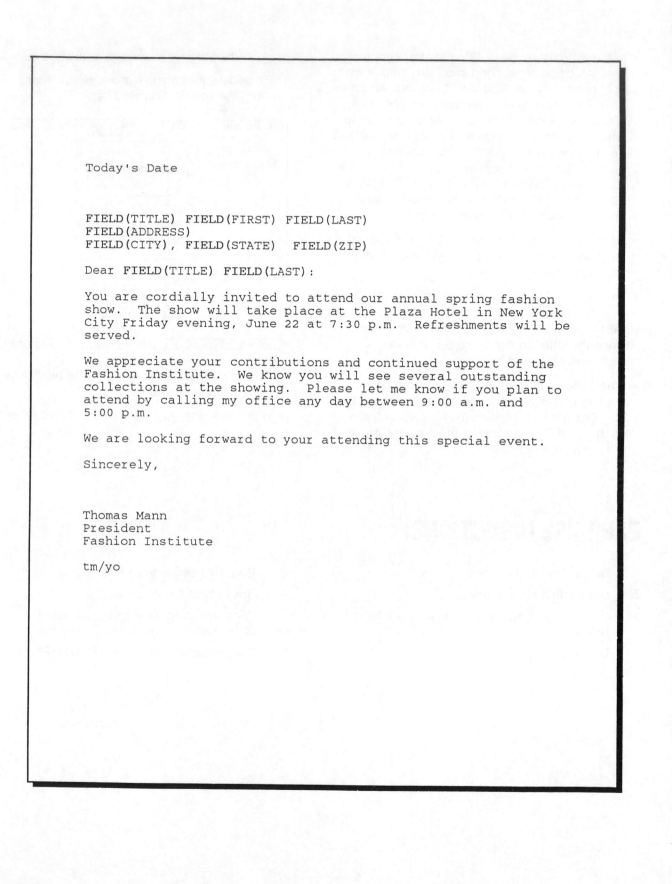

```
Today's Date


FIELD(TITLE) FIELD(FIRST) FIELD(LAST)
FIELD(ADDRESS)
FIELD(CITY), FIELD(STATE)  FIELD(ZIP)

Dear FIELD(TITLE) FIELD(LAST):

You are cordially invited to attend our annual spring fashion
show.  The show will take place at the Plaza Hotel in New York
City Friday evening, June 22 at 7:30 p.m.  Refreshments will be
served.

We appreciate your contributions and continued support of the
Fashion Institute.  We know you will see several outstanding
collections at the showing.  Please let me know if you plan to
attend by calling my office any day between 9:00 a.m. and
5:00 p.m.

We are looking forward to your attending this special event.

Sincerely,


Thomas Mann
President
Fashion Institute

tm/yo
```

TO CREATE A "FORM" FILE
Shift + F9

1. Open a new document.
2. Click on <u>T</u>ools .... `Alt` + `T`
3. Click on M<u>e</u>rge .... `E`
4. Click on <u>D</u>efine .... `D`
5. Click on <u>F</u>orm .... `F`
6. Click on OK .... `↵`

7. Type to first field location.
8. Press Shift + F9 .... `Shift` + `F9`
9. Click on <u>F</u>ield .... `F`
10. Type name of first field (TITLE, for example) in Parameter Entry dialog box.
11. Click on OK .... `↵`
12. Repeat steps 7-9 for each field.

13. Type remainder of document.

NOTE: SAVE THIS FILE AS USUAL.

TIP: USE THE EXTENSION .FF (as noted in the exercise directions) TO DESIGNATE THIS FILE AS THE "FORM FILE."

MERGE: CREATING THE "DATA" (TEXT) FILE

NOTES:

- In this exercise, you will create the "Data" (Text) File. The data file contains the inside addresses and salutations of those people who will be receiving the letter you created in the form file.

- A data file may contain many **records.** A record is a collection of related information. In this exercise, for example, a record is the inside address and salutation of one person. The information in each record is divided into "fields." **The fields used in the form file MUST match the information used in the data file.**

- Note the illustration below of one record in a data file as it appears on the screen. Note, too, that the information for each field matches the fields used in the form file (shown in the illustration below). Since the comma used after the city was inserted in the form file, it should not be entered again in the data file. Otherwise, two commas will result when the documents are merged.

DATA FILE   **FORM FILE**

Mr.**ENDFIELD**
John**ENDFIELD**
Smith**ENDFIELD**
405 West End Avenue**ENDFIELD**
New York**ENDFIELD**
NY**ENDFIELD**
10087**ENDFIELD**
ENDRECORD

```
Today's Date

FIELD(TITLE) FIELD(FIRST) FIELD(LAST)
FIELD(ADDRESS)
FIELD(CITY), FIELD(STATE) FIELD(ZIP)

Dear FIELD(TITLE) FIELD(LAST):

You are cordially invited to attend
our annual spring fashion show. The
show will take place at the Plaza
Hotel in New York City Friday evening,
June 22 at 7:30 p.m.  Refreshments
will be served.

We appreciate your contributions and
continueed support of the Fashion
Institute. We know you will see
several outstanding collections at the
showing.  Please let me know if you
plan to attend by calling my office
any day between 9:00 a.m. and 5:00
```

- When you created the form file, you named each field (Title, First, Last, etc.)   Since the fields used in the form file must match the information used in the data file, it is also a good idea to name the fields in your data file.   WordPerfect allows you to do this. Before you enter the actual names, addresses, etc., in your data file, you create a "field name list," listing all the fields you used in your data file. This will act as a "prompt" for you when entering the data text. Note the illustration below of the field list which displays at the top of the screen after you create the field name list.

- After the data file is created, it must be saved.

- To create the data file, you must access the merge feature by selecting "Merge" from the Tools main menu bar. Follow the keystrokes noted on the next page to complete the procedure.

- In this exercise, you will create a data file. In the next exercise, you will merge the data file with the form file.

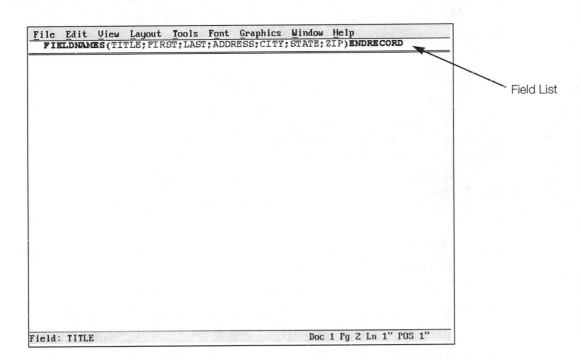

Field List

EXERCISE DIRECTIONS:

1. Select Text Mode view.

2. Start with a clear screen.

3. Create a data file as illustrated on the next page.

   NOTE: As you enter the information in each record, refer to the field list at the top of your screen to be sure information in the data file matches the fields in the form file.

4. Use the default margins.

5. Begin the exercise on Ln 1" (at the top of your screen).

6. Save the exercise; name it **INVITE.DF**

continued . . .

```
FIELDNAMES(TITLE;FIRST;LAST;ADDRESS;CITY;STATE;ZIP)ENDRECORD
============================================================
Mr.ENDFIELD
PeterENDFIELD
RinglerENDFIELD
23 Preston AvenueENDFIELD
BellemoreENDFIELD
NYENDFIELD
11010ENDFIELD
ENDRECORD
============================================================
Mr.ENDFIELD
FredENDFIELD
LeBostENDFIELD
98-67 Kew Gardens RoadENDFIELD
Forest HillsENDFIELD
NYENDFIELD
11432ENDFIELD
ENDRECORD
============================================================
Ms.ENDFIELD
MaryENDFIELD
McCleanENDFIELD
765 Belmill RoadENDFIELD
RoslynENDFIELD
NYENDFIELD
11577ENDFIELD
ENDRECORD
============================================================
Ms.ENDFIELD
LorraineENDFIELD
OelserENDFIELD
1275 BroadwayENDFIELD
New YorkENDFIELD
NYENDFIELD
10028ENDFIELD
ENDRECORD
```

TO CREATE THE "DATA" (TEXT) FILE
Shift + F9, 2

To Assign Field Names
1. Position cursor at the top of document.
2. Click on Tools .... `Alt` + `T`
3. Click on Merge .... `E`
4. Click on Define .... `D`
5. Click on Data [Text] .... `D`
6. Click on Field Names .... `N`

7. Type first field name (used in form file).

   Example: TITLE
8. ENTER .... `↵`
9. Repeat steps 7-8 for each field name (used in form file).
10. Click on OK .... `↵`

NOTE: Field names will appear across the top of screen.

To Enter Data:
11. Type *data* for first field ....*data text*
12. Press Shift + F9 .... `Shift` + `F9`
13. Click on End Field .... `F`

14. Repeat steps 12-13 for each field to receive data.
15. After all fields are entered:
    Press Shift + F9 .... `Shift` + `F9`
16. Click on End Record .... `E`

NOTE: This will insert a hard page break.

17. Repeat steps 11-16 for each record.

NOTE: SAVE THIS FILE AS USUAL.

TIP: USE THE EXTENSION .DF (as noted in the exercise directions) to DESIGNATE THIS FILE AS A "DATA FILE."

MERGE: MERGING THE "FORM" AND "DATA" FILES

NOTES:

- Once the form and data files have been created, they may be merged to create a third document.

- The final merged third document will appear as separate pages, each page representing a record. This document may be saved under its own file name. This is particularly helpful if you wish to edit individual documents. For example, a P.S. or special mailing notation might be added to selected letters.

- If the form and data files do not merge properly, check each file to see that the fields used in the form file have information that matches the fields used in the data file.

- After the merge is complete, you have several output options:

Current Document merges to the current document window, showing you the merge on the screen and allowing you to save as a third document.

Unused Document merges to a new document window, showing you the merge on the screen and allowing you to save as a third document.

Printer merges directly to the printer without showing the merge on the screen or allowing you to save on a disk.

File merges to a file you specify without showing the merge on the screen.

NOTE: Saving as a separate file uses up disk space unnecessarily.

- It is possible to merge selected records rather than all the records contained in the data file by "marking" them at the beginning of the merge process.

- To begin the merge process, you can select "Merge" from Tools on the main menu bar. To more quickly begin the merge process you may click on the *MergeRun* button on the TOOLS Button Bar. Follow the keystrokes noted on page 175 to complete the process.

- In this exercise, you will merge the form file with the data file created in the two previous exercises and you will "mark" selected records to be merged.

TOOLS BUTTON BAR

File	Edit	View	Layout	Tools	Font	Graphics	Window	Help

Speller	Gramatik	Thesarus	Mac Play	Mac Rec	Mac Ctrl	MergeDef	MergeRun	Sort	DateText	DateCode	Date Fmt	MarkText

Merge Run

EXERCISE DIRECTIONS:

1. Select Text Mode view.

2. Start with a clear screen.

3. Merge the form file **INVITE.FF** with the data file **INVITE.DF** to an Unused Document.

4. Merge and print only those letters addressed to females.

HINT: *Use the TITLE field to mark selected records.*

5. Save the merged letters under a new document name: **INVITE.FI**

continued . . .

FORM FILE

Today's date

FIELD(TITLE) **FIELD**(FIRST) **FIELD**(LAST)
FIELD(ADDRESS)
FIELD(CITY), **FIELD**(STATE) **FIELD**(ZIP)

Dear **FIELD**(TITLE) **FIELD**(LAST):

You are cordially invited to attend our
annual spring fashion show. The show will
take place at the Plaza Hotel in New York
City Friday evening, June 22 at 7:30 p.m.
Refreshments will be served.

We appreciate your contributions and
continued support of the Fashion Institute.
We know you will see several outstanding
collections at the showing. Please let me
know if you plan to attend by calling my
office any day between 9:00 a.m. and 5:00
p.m.

We are looking forward to your attending
this special event.

Sincerely,

Thomas Mann
President
Fashion Institute

tm/yo

+

DATA FILE

Mr. ENDFIELD
Peter ENDFIELD
Ringler ENDFIELD
23 Preston Avenue ENFIELD
NY ENFIELD
BellemoreENFIELD
11010ENFIELD
ENDRECORD

Mr. ENFIELD
FredENFIELD
LeBostENFIELD
98-67 Kew Gardens RoadENFIELD
Forest HIllsENFIELD
11432ENFIELD
ENDRECORD

Ms.ENFIELD
MaryENFIELD
McCleanENFIELD
765 Belmill RoadENFIELD
RosylnENFIELD
NYENFIELD
11577ENFIELD
ENDRECORD

MS.ENFIELD
LorraineENFIELD
OelserENFIELD
1275ENFIELD
NEW YORKENFIELD
10028ENFIELD

MERGED DOCUMENTS

=

Today's date

Ms. Lorraine Oelser
1275 Broadway
New York, NY 10028

Dear Ms. Oelser:

You are cordially invited to attend our
annual spring fashion show. The show
will take place at the Plaza Hotel in
New York City Friday evening, June 22 at
7:30 p.m. Refreshments will be served.

We appreciate your contributions and
continued support of the Fashion
Institute. We know you will see several
outstanding collections at the showing.
Please let me know if you plan to attend
by calling my office any day between
9:00 a.m. and 5:00 p.m.

We are looking forward to your attending
this special event.

Sincerely,

Thomas Mann
President
Fashion Institute

tm/yo

TO MERGE THE "FORM" AND "DATA" FILES

Ctrl + F9, M then step 4

1. Click on Tools .... `Alt` + `T`
2. Click on Merge .... `E`
3. Click on Run .... `R`

4. Type name of form file ...... *form name*
5. ENTER .... `↵`

6. Type name of data file .... *data name*

To Change Output

- Click on Output .... `O`
- Click on an Output Option:

Current Document .... `C`

Unused Document .... `U`

Printer .... `P`

File .... `F`

- To Merge "selected" Records

  - Click on Data File Options .... `T`
  - Click on Data Record Selection .... `S`

- Click on Mark Records to Include .... `M`
- Highlight field you wish to mark.
- Click on Select .... `↵`

For each record you wish to merge:

- Highlight record ....
- Click on Mark Record .... `M`
- Click on OK .... `↵`

7. Click on Merge .... `M`

   OR

1. Click on *MergeRun* button on the TOOLS button bar .... `MergeRun`
2. Follow steps 4-7 above.

MERGE: CREATING THE "FORM" FILE

NOTES:

- In this exercise, you will create a form file which contains more variables than in the previous exercise. Note that the same field name is assigned to variables that will contain the same information.

EXERCISE DIRECTIONS:

1. Select Text Mode view.
2. Start with a clear screen.
3. Create the "form" letter file as shown on the right.
4. Use the default margins.
5. Begin the exercise on Ln 2.5"
6. Spell check the exercise.
7. Print one copy. (Keep your printout for reference to create the next exercise.)
8. Save the exercise; name it **DUE.FF**

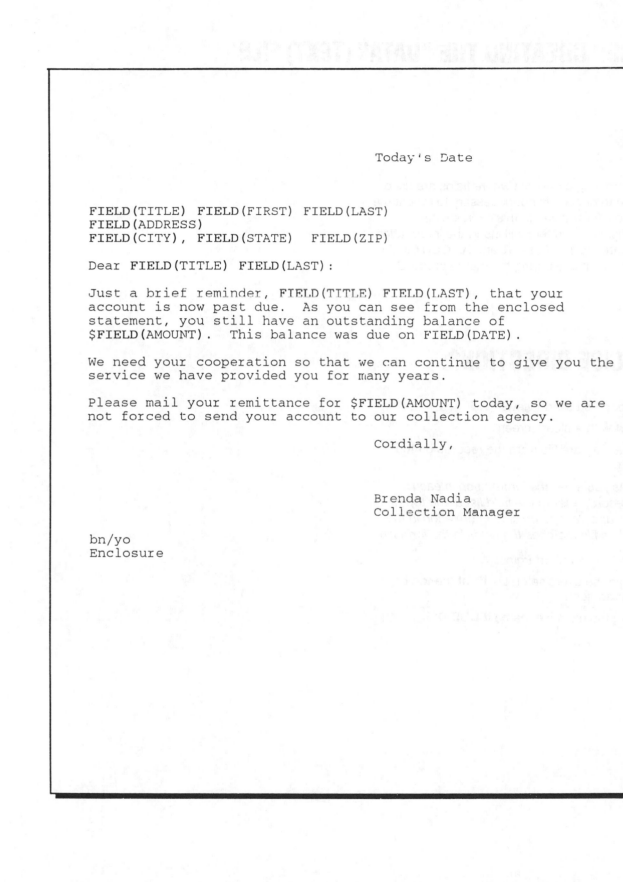

```
                              Today's Date


FIELD(TITLE)  FIELD(FIRST)  FIELD(LAST)
FIELD(ADDRESS)
FIELD(CITY),  FIELD(STATE)   FIELD(ZIP)

Dear FIELD(TITLE)  FIELD(LAST):

Just a brief reminder, FIELD(TITLE) FIELD(LAST), that your
account is now past due.  As you can see from the enclosed
statement, you still have an outstanding balance of
$FIELD(AMOUNT).  This balance was due on FIELD(DATE).

We need your cooperation so that we can continue to give you the
service we have provided you for many years.

Please mail your remittance for $FIELD(AMOUNT) today, so we are
not forced to send your account to our collection agency.

                              Cordially,



                              Brenda Nadia
                              Collection Manager


bn/yo
Enclosure
```

MERGE: CREATING THE "DATA" (TEXT) FILE

NOTES:

• When creating a data file where fields are used more than once, it is not necessary to repeat the variable information. In this exercise, for example, WordPerfect will insert the information that relates to TITLE, LAST and AMOUNT in the appropriate place during the merge process.

EXERCISE DIRECTIONS:

1. Select Text Mode view.
2. Start with a clear screen.
3. Create a data file from the records on the right.

NOTE: As you enter the information in each record, refer to the field list at the top of your screen to be sure information in the data file matches the fields in the form file.

4. Use the default margins.
5. Begin the exercise on Ln 1" (at the top of your screen).
6. Save the exercise; name it **DUE.DF**

```
FIELDNAMES(TITLE;FIRST;LAST;ADDRESS;CITY;STATE;ZIP;AMOUNT;DATE)
ENDRECORD
================================================================
Ms.ENDFIELD
VanessaENDFIELD
JacksonENDFIELD
48 Endor AvenueENDFIELD
BrooklynENDFIELD
NYENDFIELD
11221ENDFIELD
256.98ENDFIELD
March 1ENDFIELD
ENDRECORD
================================================================
Mr.ENDFIELD
KennethENDFIELD
HallENDFIELD
5 Windsor DriveENDFIELD
West Long BranchENDFIELD
NJENDFIELD
07764ENDFIELD
450.50ENDFIELD
March 15ENDFIELD
ENDRECORD
================================================================
Mr.ENDFIELD
GlennENDFIELD
BabbinENDFIELD
187 Beach 147 StreetENDFIELD
QueensENDFIELD
NYENDFIELD
11694ENDFIELD
128.86ENDFIELD
February 28ENDFIELD
ENDRECORD
================================================================
Ms.ENDFIELD
StefanieENDFIELD
EatonENDFIELD
137 Brighton AvenueENDFIELD
Perth AmboyENDFIELD
NJENDFIELD
08861ENDFIELD
612.75ENDFIELD
February 15ENDFIELD
ENDRECORD
================================================================
Ms.ENDFIELD
ShirleyENDFIELD
KeeENDFIELD
876 Ocean ParkwayENDFIELD
BrooklynENDFIELD
NYENDFIELD
11244ENDFIELD
449.08ENDFIELD
April 15ENDFIELD
ENDRECORD
```

MERGE: MERGING THE "FORM" AND "DATA" FILES

NOTES:

- In addition to marking specific data records to merge, WordPerfect allows you to define conditions that data records must meet to be included in the merge. In this exercise, for example, if you wanted to merge only those letters in which individuals owe more than $200, you could direct WordPerfect to select the record only if it meets the condition (or conditions) you define. Or, if you wanted to merge only those letters of individuals who live in New Jersey and owe more than $200, you would set two conditions for your merge.

- **To Define Conditions for the Merge,** select "Data File Options" on the first MergeRun (Ctrl + F9) dialog box:

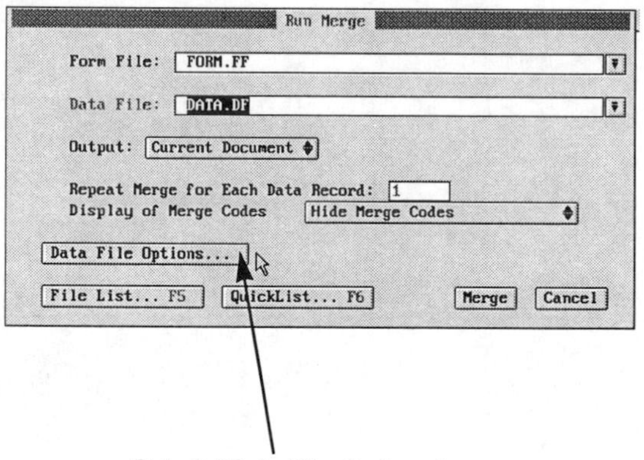

Select "Data File Options"

- After selecting Data File Options, select "Define Conditions" on the second Run Merge dialog box:

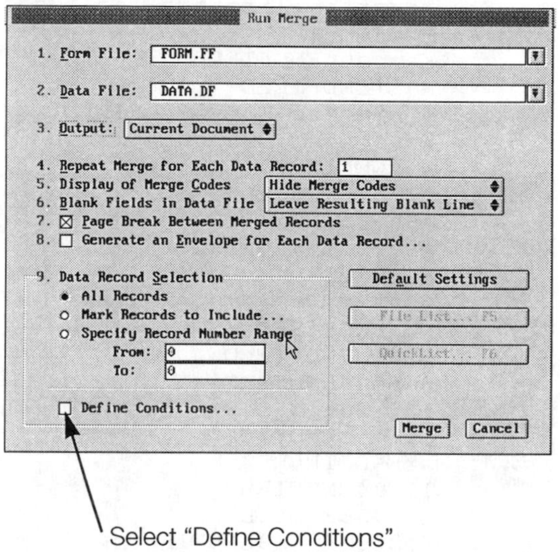

Select "Define Conditions"

• The following "Define Conditions for Record Selection" dialog box will appear which will display a table with four rows, representing conditions, and three columns, representing fields. A record is selected for merge if it meets any one of the conditions you define.

```
File                    Run Merge
        Define Conditions for Record Selection



   Condition 1. [_____]  [_____]  [_____]
   Condition 2. [_____]  [_____]  [_____]
   Condition 3. [_____]  [_____]  [_____]
   Condition 4. [_____]  [_____]  [_____]



 [Example... F4] [Clear All] [Clear Column F0]    [ OK ] [Cancel]
Courier 12pt                    Doc 1 Pg 1 Ln 1" POS 1"
```

The selection criteria can include any of the following:

Criteria	Records that will be Selected	Examples
Single value	All records in which the selected field match the value	NJ
List of values	All records in which the selected field matches one of the values	NJ;NY
Range of values	All data records in which the selected field is within the range of values	NJ-NY
Excluded values	All records in which the selected field does not match value	!NY
Zero or more	All records in which the selected field is a possible match of the wildcard value	New*
One character	All records in which the selected field is a possible match of the wildcard value	1008?

• In this exercise, you will merge the "form" and "data" files you created in previous exercises based on specific criteria.

EXERCISE DIRECTIONS:

1. Select Text Mode view.

2. Start with a clear screen.

3. Merge the form file **DUE.FF** with the data file **DUE.DF** to an Unused Document.

4. Define the following criteria for your merge:

   Merge and print only those letters to individuals who live in *New Jersey* and owe *more than $200*.

HINT: In the STATE field, enter single value NJ; in the AMOUNT field, enter single value >200.

5. Print the full document (one copy of each merged letter).

6. Save the merged letters under a new document name: **DUE.FI**

continued . . .

FORM FILE

Today's Date

FIELD(TITLE) FIELD(FIRST) FIELD(LAST)
FIELD(ADDRESS)
FIELD(CITY), FIELD(STATE)   FIELD(IP)

Dear FIELD(TITLE) FIELD(LAST):

Just a brief reminder, FIELD(TITLE) FIELD(LAST), that your
account is now past due. As you can see from the enclosed
statement, you still have an outstanding balance of
 FIELD(AMOUNT). This balance was due on FIELD(DATE).

We need your cooperation so that we can continue to give you the
service we have provided you for many years.

Please mail your remittance for FIELD(AMOUNT) today, so we are
not forced to send your account to our collection agency.

                    Cordially,

                    Brenda Nadia
                    Collection Manager

bn/yo
Enclosure

DATA FILE

FIELDNAMES(TITLE;FIRST;LAST;ADDRESS;CITY;STATE;ZIP;AMOUNT;DATE)
ENDRECORD
Ms.ENDFIELD
VanessaENDFIELD
JacksonENDFIELD
46 Ender AvenueENDFIELD
BrooklynENDFIELD
NYENDFIELD
11222ENDFIELD
156.98ENDFIELD
March 1ENDFIELD
ENDRECORD
Mr.ENDFIELD
KennethENDFIELD
HallENDFIELD
5 Windsor DriveENDFIELD
West Long BranchENDFIELD
NYENDFIELD
450.35ENDFIELD
March 15ENDFIELD
ENDRECORD
Mr.ENDFIELD
GlennENDFIELD
BabbisENDFIELD
187 Beach 147 StreetENDFIELD
QueensENDFIELD
NYENDFIELD
11694ENDFIELD
128.66ENDFIELD
February 15ENDFIELD
ENDRECORD
Ms.ENDFIELD
StefanieENDFIELD
EatonENDFIELD
137 Brighton AvenueENDFIELD
Perth AmboyENDFIELD
NJENDFIELD
0886lENDFIELD
612.75ENDFIELD
February 15ENDFIELD
ENDRECORD
Mr.ENDFIELD
ShirleyENDFIELD
WeeENDFIELD
876 Ocean ParkwayENDFIELD
BrooklynENDFIELD
NYENDFIELD
11244ENDFIELD
449.08ENDFIELD
April 15ENDFIELD
ENDRECORD

SELECTED MERGED DOCUMENTS

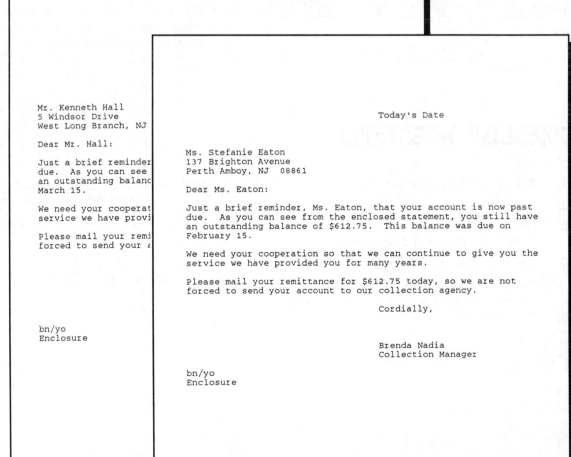

Mr. Kenneth Hall
5 Windsor Drive
West Long Branch, NJ

Dear Mr. Hall:

Just a brief reminder
due. As you can see
an outstanding balanc
March 15.

We need your cooperat
service we have provi

Please mail your remi
forced to send your a

bn/yo
Enclosure

Today's Date

Ms. Stefanie Eaton
137 Brighton Avenue
Perth Amboy, NJ 08861

Dear Ms. Eaton:

Just a brief reminder, Ms. Eaton, that your account is now past
due. As you can see from the enclosed statement, you still have
an outstanding balance of $612.75. This balance was due on
February 15.

We need your cooperation so that we can continue to give you the
service we have provided you for many years.

Please mail your remittance for $612.75 today, so we are not
forced to send your account to our collection agency.

                    Cordially,

                    Brenda Nadia
                    Collection Manager

bn/yo
Enclosure

TO MERGE WITH CONDITIONS

Ctrl + F9, M, then step 4

1. Click on Tools .... `Alt` + `T`
2. Click on Merge.............................. `E`
3. Click on Run................................. `R`
4. Type name of form file ......*form name*
5. ENTER... `↵`
6. Type name of data file.......*data name*

   To Merge with conditions:

   a. Click on Data File Options........... `T`
   b. Click on Data Record Selection... `S`
   c. Click on Define Conditions .... `C`
   d. Press 1 to select first field on which to set a condition. (A list of fields from data file will display.)

e. Highlight field on which you will set a condition. (For this exercise, select STATE.)

f. ENTER

g. Type selection criteria. (For this exercise, type NJ.)

h. ENTER.

i. Press 6 to select another field on which to set a condition. (The list of fields from data file will display again.)

OR

• Press 2 to add another condition to the first field.

j. Highlight field on which you will set a condition. (For this exercise, select AMOUNT.)

k. Type selection criteria. (For this exercise, type >200.)

l. ENTER

m. Repeat steps i-l to select another field to set conditions or to add conditions to a field which has been selected.

7. Click on Merge............................. `M`

   OR

1. Click on *MergeRun* button on the TOOLS button bar........ `MergeRun`

2. Follow steps 4-7 above.

MERGE: CREATING AND MERGING THE "FORM" AND "DATA" (TEXT) FILES

NOTES:

- In the previous two exercises, you divided each individual's name into three fields: TITLE, FIRST, LAST. You could have, however, used one field name (NAME) to represent an entire individual's name. It is only necessary to break down a field if you intend to selectively merge the documents on that field. In the previous exercises, for example, if you break down the name field into three fields, you can then selectively merge letters addressed to females or doctors (TITLE field).

- *Remember, keep the number of (different, not repeat) fields used in the form file consistent with the number of fields used in the data file.* In the exercise on the right, there are eight different field names in the form file. While the address field contains one line in some records and two lines in others (some contain a company name), there are, nonetheless, eight "ENDFIELD" notations for each record in the data file. (Fields can be one or several lines.)

- You can use the keyboard to quickly insert the two most common commands into your data file. Press F9 to insert the ENDFIELD code. Press Shift + F9, 2 to insert the ENDRECORD code.

- In this exercise, you will create and merge the "form" and "data" files based on specific criteria. It is important that you click on "Clear All" in the *Define Conditions...* for Record Selection Table box so that previous settings will not interfere with the new merge.

Clear All

EXERCISE DIRECTIONS:

1. Select Text Mode view.
2. Start with a clear screen.
3. Create the "form" letter file as shown on the right.
4. Use the default margins.
5. Begin the exercise on Ln 2.5".
6. Spell check the exercise.
7. Save the exercise; name it **BUY.FF**
8. Begin a NEW document (start with a clear screen).
9. Create a data file as shown on the right.

NOTE: *As you enter the information in each record, refer to the field list at the top of your screen to be sure information in the data file matches the fields in the form file.*

10. Use the default margins.
11. Begin the exercise on Ln 1".
12. Save the exercise; name it **BUY.DF**
13. Begin a NEW document.
14. Merge the form file with the data file to an Unused Document.
15. Define the following criteria for your merge:

    Merge and print only those letters to companies in *Texas* and *California* (TX;CA).

16. Print the full document (one copy of each merged letter).
17. Save the merged letters under a new document name: **BUY.FI**

Today's date

FIELD(NAME)
FIELD(ADDRESS)
FIELD(CITY), FIELD(ST) FIELD(ZIP)

Dear FIELD(TINAME):

We received your order for FIELD(QUAN) FIELD(SOFTPKG) software
packages. We will process it immediately. To expedite the
order, we are arranging to have the software shipped directly
from our warehouse in your city, FIELD(CITY).

The cost of the software packages totals $FIELD(AMOUNT). We
would appreciate payment as soon as you receive your order.

Thank you, FIELD(TINAME), for your confidence in our company. I
know you will be satisfied with our customer support service.

Sincerely,

Yolanda Reeves
Sales Manager

yr/yo

FORM FILE

+

DATA FILE

```
FIELDNAMES(NAME;ADDRESS;CITY;ST;ZIP;TINAME;QUAN;SOFTPKG;AMOUNT)
ENDRECORD
==============================================================
Mr. Jason LochnerENDFIELD
Computerland Associates
65 Linden BoulevardENDFIELD
HoustonENDFIELD
TXENDFIELD
77069ENDFIELD
Mr. LochnerENDFIELD
twoENDFIELD
Lotus 1-2-3ENDFIELD
810.76ENDFIELD
ENDRECORD
==============================================================
Ms. Rose ZaffaranoENDFIELD
Richmond Tile Company
654 Hammond DriveENDFIELD
Los AngelesENDFIELD
CAENDFIELD
90210ENDFIELD
Ms. ZaffaranoENDFIELD
threeENDFIELD
ExcellENDFIELD
1,221.98ENDFIELD
ENDRECORD
==============================================================
Ms. Valerie VetriENDFIELD
70 Klondike AvenueENDFIELD
ClevelandENDFIELD
OHENDFIELD
44199ENDFIELD
Ms. VetriENDFIELD
fourENDFIELD
PrintShopENDFIELD
235.85ENDFIELD
ENDRECORD
==============================================================
Mr. Deepa LakhaniENDFIELD
Knoll Stationery Supplies
87 Rockhill RoadENDFIELD
San DiegoENDFIELD
CAENDFIELD
88912ENDFIELD
Mr. LakhaniENDFIELD
twoENDFIELD
WordPerfect for WindowsENDFIELD
512.34ENDFIELD
ENDRECORD
==============================================================
Ms. Diane NordquistENDFIELD
43-98 Sela DriveENDFIELD
DallasENDFIELD
TXENDFIELD
76767ENDFIELD
Ms. NordquistENDFIELD
twoENDFIELD
Microsoft WordENDFIELD
555.87ENDFIELD
ENDRECORD
```

MERGE: CREATING AND MERGING THE "FORM" AND "DATA" (TEXT) FILES; PREPARING ENVELOPES

NOTES:

- WordPerfect makes it possible for you to create envelopes while merging a letter or other form file or create envelopes independently using a separate form file. (Creating a separate form file for envelopes and labels will be covered in a later lesson.) During the merge process, an envelope for each data record is created and placed at the end of the merged file.

- After selecting Generating an Envelope for Each Data Record from the Run Merge dialog box, an Envelope Dialog box appears.

  In this dialog box, you must first specify the envelope size you will require. WordPerfect provides two envelope sizes:

  legal size: 9.5" x 4.13"   (default)
  letter size: 8.66" x 4.33"

You must then enter the fields in the Mailing Address section that will be needed for the envelope, that is, just the fields used in the inside address. (You may also include a return address [your address]. However, since most companies use a preprinted return address, this feature would be used for personal correspondence).

- To prepare envelopes for the records in this exercise, for example, you would use NAME, ADDRESS, CITY, ST and ZIP as your inside address fields. Follow the procedures indicated to prepare envelopes while merging.

ENVELOPE DIALOG BOX

Generate an Envelope for
Each Data Record

EXERCISE DIRECTIONS:

1. Select Text Mode view.

2. Start with a clear screen.

3. Create the "form" letter as shown on the next page.

4. Use the default margins.

5. Begin the exercise on Ln 2.5".

6. Spell check the exercise.

7. Save the exercise; name it **SHOW.FF**

8. Begin a NEW document (start with a clear screen).

9. Create a data file as shown on the next page.

   NOTE: As you enter the information in each record, refer to the field list at the top of your screen to be sure information in the data file matches the fields in the form file.

10. Use the default margins.

11. Begin the exercise on Ln 1".

12. Save the exercise; name it **SHOW.DF**

13. Begin a NEW document.

14. Merge the form file with the data file to an Unused Document.

15. Prepare an envelope for each letter generated in the merge.

16. Print the full document (one copy of each merged letter).

    NOTE: If you have a printer with an envelope feeder, insert envelopes and print an envelope for each letter; otherwise, print the envelope text on 8.5" x 11" paper.

17. Save the merged letters (and envelope text) under a new document name: **SHOW.FI**

continued . . .

Today's date

FIELD(NAME)
FIELD(ADDRESS)
FIELD(CITY), FIELD(ST) FIELD(ZIP)

Dear FIELD(TILAST):

As a preferred client of Taks Department Store, we are extending
this invitation to you for our spring fashion show. The evening
of FIELD(DATE) at FIELD(TIME) has been reserved for this private
showing of our spring fashions.

We are confident that you will find our spring collection
refreshing and most exciting.

Please join us for refreshments after the show where you can meet
many of the designers. We look forward to seeing you on FIELD(DATE).

Sincerely,

Amanda Desmond
Collections Department

ad/yo

FORM FILE

+

DATA FILE

```
FIELDNAMES(NAME;ADDRESS;CITY;ST;ZIP;TILAST;DATE;TIME)ENDRECORD
==============================================================
Ms. Claude MontaneENDFIELD
456 Winding Woods WayENDFIELD
ManalapanENDFIELD
NJENDFIELD
07609ENDFIELD
Ms. MontaneENDFIELD
January 18ENDFIELD
6:30 p.m.ENDFIELD
ENDRECORD
==============================================================
Ms. Maria VasquezENDFIELD
1111 Chiffon AvenueENDFIELD
WoodbridgeENDFIELD
NJENDFIELD
00723ENDFIELD
Ms. VasquezENDFIELD
January 20ENDFIELD
8:30 p.m.ENDFIELD
ENDRECORD
==============================================================
Ms. Gladys GraffENDFIELD
23 East 80 StreetENDFIELD
New YorkENDFIELD
NYENDFIELD
10023ENDFIELD
Ms. GraffENDFIELD
January 21ENDFIELD
8:30 p.m.ENDFIELD
ENDRECORD
==============================================================
Ms. Harriet FeiwellENDFIELD
Ragtime Sportswear, Inc.
1248 Seventh AvenueENDFIELD
New YorkENDFIELD
NYENDFIELD
10045ENDFIELD
Ms. FeiwellENDFIELD
January 21ENDFIELD
8:30 p.m.ENDFIELD
ENDRECORD
==============================================================
```

TO CREATE ENVELOPES WHILE MERGING
Ctrl + F9, 1

1. Click on Tools .... `Alt` + `T`
2. Click on Merge............................. `E`
3. Click on Run................................. `R`
4. Type name of form file ......*form name*
5. ENTER... `↵`
6. Type name of data file ....*data file*
7. ENTER... `↵`
8. Click on Data File Options .... `T`
9. Click on Generate an Envelope
   for Each Data Record .... `E`

NOTE: *The following Envelope dialog box will appear:*

10. Select an envelope size from
    Envelope pop-up list (use default).
11. Click on Mailing Address.............. `M`
12. Press Shift+F9................ `Shift` + `F9`
13. Click on Field .... `F`

14. Type first field name of the
    inside address

NOTE: *Check your form letter file for exact field names.*

15. ENTER... `↵`
16. Repeat steps 12-15 for each
    field name in inside address.
17. Press F7
    to exit dialog box. .... `F7`
18. Click on Insert .... `↵`
19. Click on Merge............................. `↵`

MERGE: CREATING THE "FORM" FILE; CREATING THE DATA (TABLE) FILE; MERGING

NOTES:

- In this exercise, you will create a form file from the letter illustrated. However, the data file will be created using a "table" format rather than a "text" format (used in previous exercises).

- The Data Table File makes it easier for you to enter your data in a table rather than as a list. This way, each field is clearly contained in a table "cell" or box.

- Note the illustration on the right of data entered in a data table. Each column is a field and each row is a record. Use the tab key to move from column to column. As you move to each column, the status line will indicate the cell position: A1, B1, etc.

- WordPerfect divides the cell space across a page based on the number of fields to be used. When you enter data into the "cells," it may break in awkward places (see illustration) since space is limited across an 8.5" x 11" page. Allow the text to wrap within the cell; use the enter key only when you intend to begin a new line (after the company name in the address field).

- Follow the keystroke procedures on page 190 to create the data table file. The merge procedure remains the same.

EXERCISE DIRECTIONS:

1. Select Text Mode view.
2. Start with a clear screen.
3. Create the form letter as shown on the right.
4. Use the default margins.
5. Begin the exercise on Ln 2.5"
6. Spell check the exercise.
7. Save the exercise; name it **MISTAKE.FF**
8. Begin a NEW document.
9. Create a data table as shown on the right.
10. Use the default margins.
11. Save the exercise; name it **MISTAKE.DF**
12. Begin a NEW document.
13. Merge the form file with the data file to an Unused Document.
14. Prepare an envelope for each letter generated in the merge.
15. Print the full document (one copy of each merged letter).
16. Save the merged letters under a new document name: **MISTAKE.FI**

Today's date

FIELD(NAME)
FIELD(ADDRESS)
FIELD(CITY), FIELD(ST)   FIELD(ZIP)

Dear FIELD(TINAME):

Thank you for your check No. FIELD(CKNO), in the amount of
$FIELD(AMT). We notice that you erroneously deducted a discount,
even though the discount period has expired.

We know this is an oversight. We are returning your check No.
FIELD(CKNO), and we would appreciate your sending us another
check for $FIELD(NWAMT) to cover the correct amount.

Thank you for your attention to this matter.

Sincerely,

Arnold Zahn
Credit Manager

az/yo

FORM FILE

+

DATA FILE

COLUMNS

	A	B	C	D	E	F	G	H	I
	NAME	ADDRESS	CITY	ST	TINAME	ZIP	CKNO	AMT	NWAMT
1	Mr. Harold Dembo	Holistic, Inc. 654 Sanborn Street	Denver	CO	Mr. Dembo	80202	8768	654.85	682.75
2	Ms. Jennifer Downing	7659 Utica Avenue	San Antonio	TX	Ms. Downing	78202	6543	76.99	109.10
3	Mr. Daniel Davis	Acme Plumbing Supply 90 Plaza Z	Milwaukee	WI	Mr. Davis	53212	7888	333.33	386.86

R O W S

TO CREATE THE "DATA" (TABLE) FILE
Shift + F9, t

1. Place cursor at top of screen.
2. Press Shift + F9............. Shift + F9
3. Select Data (Table)....................... T
4. Select Create a Table with
   Field Names.................................. N
5. Type first field name.
6. ENTER.. ⏎

7. Repeat steps 5-6 for each field name.
8. ENTER twice. .... ⏎ , ⏎

NOTE: Table appears on screen with field names appearing across the top.

9. Enter data for first field beginning in cell A1.

NOTE: Text may break awkwardly. Use the enter key only when you intend to begin a new line.

10. Press TAB................................ Tab
11. Enter data for each remaining field to complete the first row (record).
12. Press TAB................................ Tab
    to insert a new row.
13. Repeat steps 9-12 for each record.

NOTE: SAVE THIS FILE AS USUAL.

TIP: (USE THE EXTENSION DF [as done previously] to DESIGNATE THIS FILE AS A "DATA FILE."

MERGE: CREATING ENVELOPES / LABELS

NOTES:

Envelopes

• In Exercises 64 and 65 you created envelopes while merging. WordPerfect also allows you to create a separate envelope file which may be merged with your data file at any time. The envelope file simply contains the fields to be included in the envelope. Once the envelope file is created and saved, it may be merged with any data file (providing the field names match the names used in the data file).

• The envelope file may be created by accessing Envelope from Layout on the main menu bar.

Mailing Labels

• To create mailing labels, you must specify the label format and define the size and type of the label you intend to use.

• Labels may be accessed through the Page option on the Layout main menu bar. The following dialog box will appear allowing you to select a label format:

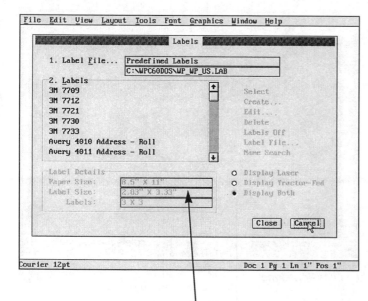

Indicates size of labels you have selected and how they are arranged on the page

• You must know the type of labels you intend to use. Each option indicates the label size and how labels are arranged on a page. If you select "3M 7730" as your label type, the dialog box indicates that the label size is 2.63" x 1" and that the labels are arranged 3 x 10 (three labels across the page and 10 rows down the page).

• Once the label format has been specified, a "blank" label will display on the screen. Enter only the field name merge codes for the inside address (NAME, ADDRESS, CITY, ST, ZIP) on the first blank label, and save it. This is your label file.

• Once a mailing form label file is created and saved, it is merged with a data file. WordPerfect considers the entire sheet of labels as a physical page. To see the labels as they will be arranged when you print, use Page Mode as you type the labels or use Print Preview to view the labels before you print them.

• When you are ready to print, load your printer with the proper size and type of label paper you specified, and print. When you print a single label page, the entire physical page is printed.

• In this exercise, you will prepare an envelope file and a label file for the records in Exercise 65 (MISTAKE). You will merge the envelope file with the data file; then, you will merge the label file with the data file. Follow the keystrokes carefully.

EXERCISE DIRECTIONS:

1. Select Page Mode view.

2. Start with a clear screen.

3. Create an envelope file:
   - Use a legal size envelope size.
   - Use the inside address field names in Exercise 65 MISTAKE):

     NAME
     ADDRESS
     CITY, ST ZIP

4. Save the file; name it **MISENV.**

5. Merge the form envelope file **MISENV** with the data file **MISTAKE.DF.**

6. Print an envelope for each person in the data file (if you have a printer with an envelope feeder; otherwise, print the envelope text on 8.5" x 11" paper).

7. Create a label file:
   - Use "3M 7730" as your label type.
   - Use the inside address field names in Exercise 65 MISTAKE):

     NAME
     ADDRESS
     CITY, ST ZIP

8. Save the file; name it **MISLABEL.**

9. Merge the form label file **MISLABEL** with the data file **MISTAKE.DF**

10. Print one copy of the page (if you have the label type specified, insert a sheet of labels and print).

continued . . .

INSIDE ADDRESS FIELD NAMES

```
FIELD(NAME) ↵
FIELD(ADDRESS) ↵
FIELD(CITY), FIELD(ST)  FIELD(ZIP)
```

MERGED LABEL FILE WITH DATA FILE

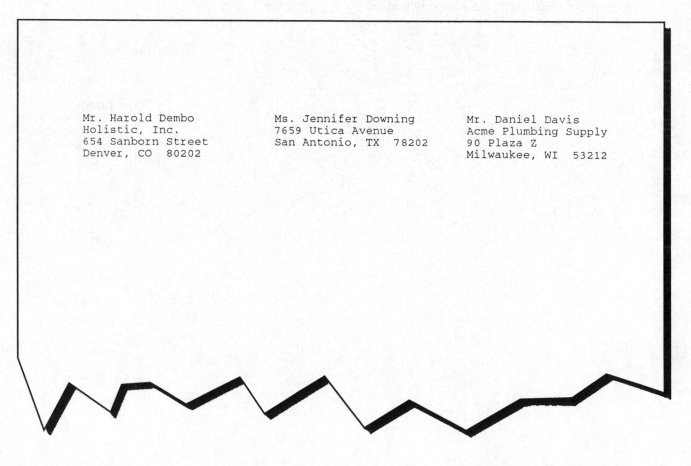

```
Mr. Harold Dembo        Ms. Jennifer Downing     Mr. Daniel Davis
Holistic, Inc.          7659 Utica Avenue        Acme Plumbing Supply
654 Sanborn Street      San Antonio, TX  78202   90 Plaza Z
Denver, CO  80202                                Milwaukee, WI  53212
```

TO CREATE AN ENVELOPE FILE
Alt + F12

1. Click on Layout .... **Alt** + **L**
2. Click on Envelope .... **V**
3. Click on Envelope Size .... **E**
   select an envelope size
   from Envelope pop-up list
   (use default).
4. Click on Mailing Address .... **M**
5. Press Shift+F9 .... **Shift** + **F9**
6. Click on Field .... **F**
7. Type first field name of the
   inside address.

*NOTE: Check your form letter file
for exact field names.*

8. ENTER... **↵**
9. Repeat steps 5-8 for each field
   name in inside address.
10. Press F7
    to exit dialog box. **F7**
11. Click on Insert .... **↵**
12. Click on Yes (to save file)............. **Y**

TO CREATE A LABEL FILE
Shift + F8, P, L

1. Select Page Mode view.
2. Click on Layout .... **Alt** + **L**
3. Click on Page............................. **P**
4. Click on Labels .... **L**
5. Highlight label type................. **↑ ↓**
6. ENTER twice .... **↵** , **↵**

---

*NOTE: If this is the first time you
have selected a label
definition with your printer,
the following printer dialog
box displays. Select a
printing option, if desired;
otherwise, continue with
step 8.*

• Select a printing option:

Location	how labels are fed into your printer
Prompt to Load	specify if you want WordPerfect to prompt you to load paper.
Use Rotated (Landscape) Font	specify if you want to print with landscape fonts
Adjust Text	adjust where text prints on page.

• Click on OK
• Click on Close

7. Press Shift + F9............. **Shift** + **F9**
8. Click on Form............................ **F**
9. Click on Field .... **F**
10. Type first field name of the
    inside address.

---

*NOTE: Check your form letter file
for exact field names.*

11. ENTER... **↵**
12. Repeat steps 8-12 for each field
    name in inside address.
13. Press F7
    to save. **F7**
14. Click on Yes .... **Y**
15. Type label file name.

TO MERGE ENVELOPE OR LABEL FILE with DATA FILE

1. Begin a NEW document.
2. Press Ctrl + F9 .... **Ctrl** + **F9**
3. Click on Merge............................. **M**
4. Type form
   file name: ....*(envelope file name
   ....or label file name)*
5. ENTER... **↵**
6. Type data file name .....*data file name*
7. ENTER... **↵**
8. Click on Merge............................. **↵**

EXERCISE DIRECTIONS:

1. Create a form file and a data file from the information below.

2. Format the form file using any letter style.

3. Create the data file using either a text or table file format (as desired).

NOTE: The data file illustrated below was formatted as a Data Table file.

4. Name the form file: **TRAVEL.FF;** name the data file: **TRAVEL.DF.**

5. Merge the form and data files.

6. Save the merged letters under a new document name: **TRAVEL.FI.**

7. Print one copy of the merged file.

8. Create a label form file using "3M 7730" label type; name it **TRAVLAB.**

9. Merge the label file with the data file.

10. Print one copy of the label page.

FORM FILE

Today's date¶Dear Traveler: Thank you for your inquiry about a cruise to FIELD(PORT). We are enclosing a brochure on FIELD(TITLE) which might be of interest to you if you should decide to sail to FIELD(PORT). There are two sailings scheduled during the FIELD(SEASON) months: FIELD(MONTH1) and FIELD(MONTH2).¶If you would like more information about a vacation of a lifetime, call FIELD(REP), who is one of the representatives in our office who will be delighted to help you. ¶Sincerely, Susan Crawford Travel Agent sc/yo

DATA FILE

NAME	ADDRESS	CITY	ST	ZIP	PORT	TITLE	SEASON	MONTH1	MONTH2	REP
Ms. Beverly Oberlin	65 Court Street	Bangor	ME	04141	Spain	Hidden Treasures	spring	March 27	April 15	Sarah
Mr. Wayne Viscosa	ABC, Incorporated 690 Elbow Drive	Fairfax	VA	23808	Bahamas	Carribbean Coral	summer	June 29	August 1	Patrick
Ms. Edna Hamil	76 Rider Avenue	Redbank	NJ	07728	St. Martin	Breathtaking Voyages	winter	January 15	March 1	Michael

EXERCISE DIRECTIONS:

1. Create a form file and a data file from the information below.

2. Format the form file using any letter style.

3. Create the data file using either a text or table file format (as desired.)

NOTE: The data file illustrated below was formatted as a Data Table file.

4. Name the form file: **STOCK.FF**; name the data file: **STOCK.DF**

5. Merge the form and data files.

6. Define the following criteria for your merge:

Merge and print only those letters to individuals who should have received the *Model III Work Kit* and who live in *Ohio*.

7. Save the merged letters under a new document name: **STOCK.FI.**

8. Print one copy of the merged file.

9. Create a label form file using "3M 7730" label type; name it **STOCKLAB.**

10. Merge the label file with the data file.

11. Print one copy of the label page.

FORM FILE

Today's date¶Thank you for your order dated _____. ¶There are several items on your order that we do not presently have in stock. This includes the _____. ¶We are arranging to have these items shipped directly to you from the _____ in Los Angeles.¶There will be no additional delivery charges from Los Angeles. We will absorb the additional costs incurred. Once again, thank you for your order.¶Sincerely, John Bo Hingh Customer Service jbh/yo

DATA FILE

NAME	ADDRESS	CITY	ST	ZIP	TINAME	DATE	ITEM	COMPANY
Mr. James G. McBride	Valley Home Furnishings 23 Home Street	Dayton	OH	45416	Mr. McBride	January 20	Model III Work Kit	Bell Company
Ms. Gloria Porter	3635 Boyle Avenue	Akron	OH	44315	Ms. Porter	February 2	Model III Work Kit	ABC Manufacturing Company
Mr. Elliot Beverly	Beverly, Rudick and Shane, Inc. 23 Sunset Boulevard	Los Angeles	CA	90052	Mr. Beverly	June 1	Do-It-Yourself Rug	Bell Company
Mr. Jose Torres	26 Meeker Street	Ann Arbor	MI	48109	Mr. Torres	July 10	Leather Kit	P & P Industries, Inc.
Ms. Ronnie Giordano, President	Coop Industries 345 West 49 Street	Cincinnati	OH	45227	Ms. Giordano	July 5	Model III Work Kit	Bell Company

LESSON 9 / EXERCISES 67-74
DOCUMENT ASSEMBLY

- Windowing
- Opening Multiple Document Windows
- Moving/Copying Text from One Document to Another
- Retrieving Text
- Combining Paragraphs
- Appending Text

DOCUMENT ASSEMBLY: WINDOWING; OPENING MULTIPLE DOCUMENTS

NOTES:

- WordPerfect allows you to open and work with up to nine documents at one time. As you open a new document on-screen, the new document replaces the original document. The original document is still there; it has been "overlapped" by the new one. (Each time you open another document, the status line indicates "Doc 1", "Doc 2," "Doc 3", etc.) Working with multiple documents is a convenient feature for moving and/or copying text from one document to another.

- "Windowing" allows you to view those documents on the same screen as you work with them. This may be accomplished in Text, Graphics and Page view modes.

Framing and Maximizing a Window

- When you begin a new document, WordPerfect provides a full-screen or "maximized" window without a frame, ready for you to begin typing. The frame is the border around the document window which you do not see when the window is "maximized." When you add a frame to the document window, you can move, size and close the window using the controls within the frame. To add a frame, select "Frame" from the Window main menu bar or double click on the status line. Note the illustration of a framed maximized window in Graphics Mode:

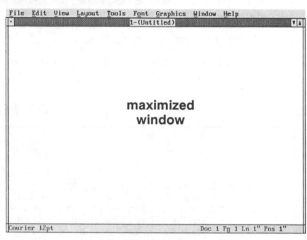

Minimizing a Window

- When you minimize a window, your document is reduced to a small rectangle. This allows you to view several documents at one time. To minimize a window, click on the down arrow (minimize arrow) in the upper right corner of the framed document or select "Minimize" from the Window main menu bar. Note the illustration below of a framed minimized window:

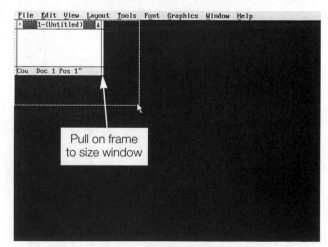

Pull on frame to size window

You can size the window by dragging the left, right or bottom side of the frame to "stretch" or "shrink" the document window.

Multiple Windows (Documents)

- When you have more than one document window open, you can "Cascade" them. Cascaded windows overlap so that the title bar of each window is displayed. Note the illustration below of four documents which have been opened and are cascaded:

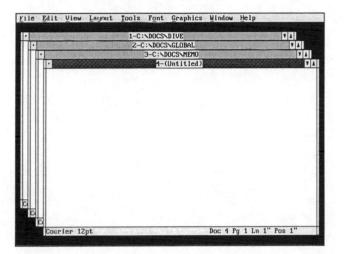

- To cascade a window, select "Cascade" from the Window main menu bar. The "active" document will be the one that is fully displayed. To make a document window active (bringing it to the top), click in the desired window.

- When windows are cascaded, the back document cannot be seen unless you make it active. As you bring the back document forward to make active, note that the status line indicates the "Document number" (the number assigned to it in the order it was opened).

- To view several documents at one time, you can divide the screen or "tile" document windows. Tiled windows are arranged on the screen with no overlapping. Note the illustration below of four documents which have been opened and are tiled:

- To make a tiled window active, click in the window.

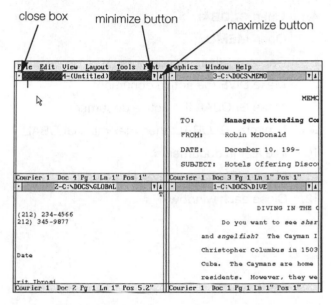

- To close a window, click on the "Close Box" (the dot in the upper left-hand corner of the window frame) or select "Close" from the File main menu bar.

- To enlarge or maximize a document, click on the up arrow (maximize button) in the upper right corner of the framed document.

- You can switch between windows whether or not they are currently displayed by selecting one of the following from the Window main menu or using the keystrokes noted:

Next (Ctrl + Y)	makes the next window active.
Previous	makes the previous window active.
Switch (Shift + F3)	switches between the current active window and the last active window.
Switch to (F3)	lists all current windows and lets you choose one.

continued . . .

EXERCISE DIRECTIONS:

1. Select Graphics Mode view.
2. Open a NEW document.
3. Open **DIVE.**
4. Open **GLOBAL.**
5. Open **MEMO.**
6. Cascade all the documents.
7. Make DIVE the active document.
8. Make GLOBAL the active document.
9. Minimize GLOBAL; then maximize GLOBAL.
10. Tile all the documents.
11. Make MEMO the active document.
12. Close each window.

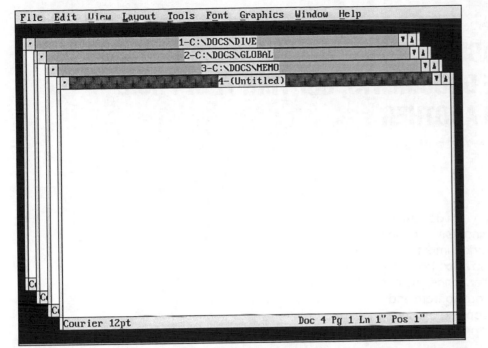

CASCADED

TILED

TO OPEN MULTIPLE DOCUMENTS
Shift + F10

1. Click on File .... Alt + F
2. Click on Open .... O
3. Type file name to be opened.
4. ENTER... ⏎
5. Repeat steps 1-4 for each document to be opened.

NOTE: *The original document has been "overlapped" with the new document. The status line indicates you are in "Doc 2".*

TO SWITCH BETWEEN DOCUMENTS
Shift + F3

Between two documents

1. Click on Window............... Alt + W
2. Click on Switch .... S

Between more than two documents
F3

1. Click on Window............... Alt + W
2. Click on Switch To........................ W
3. Click on document name to be switched to.

TO CASCADE DOCUMENTS

1. Click on Window............... Alt + W
2. Click on Cascade............................ C

TO TILE

1. Click on Window............... Alt + W
2. Click on Tile .... T

DOCUMENT ASSEMBLY:
OPENING MULTIPLE DOCUMENTS; COPYING TEXT FROM
ONE DOCUMENT TO ANOTHER

NOTES:

- The procedure to copy text from one document to another is the same as copying text from one location to another in the same document. Windowing makes it easy to copy text from one document and place it in another, since you can actually see where the text is coming from and where it is going. Reminder: copying text leaves text in its original location and "pastes" a copy of it in the new location.

- In this exercise, you will open several documents, tile them, and copy some text from each to create a new document. This procedure may also be used for moving text from one document to another.

EXERCISE DIRECTIONS:

1. Select Graphics Mode view.

2. Start with a clear screen.

3. Type the letter exactly as shown on the right.

4. Use the default margins; begin the exercise on Ln 2.5".

5. Open **GLOBAL, MEMO** and **DIVE**.

6. Tile all the documents.

7. Display vertical and horizontal scroll bars in each window.

HINT: *Make each window active; then press Alt+V, V; Alt+V, H.*

8. Copy letterhead from GLOBAL to the top of the NEW document. Copy the remaining indicated text in each document into the NEW document. Leave a double space before and after each insert.

NOTE: *The document from which you are copying must be the active document. When you are ready to place the text, the NEW document must be the active document. Follow keystrokes carefully.*

9. Close all documents except the NEW document.

10. Maximize the NEW document window.

11. Change text in small caps to normal.

12. Insert an asterisk after Fairmont Hotel and Grand Hyatt in the second hotel listing.

13. Insert an appropriate page 2 heading in the NEW document.

14. Spell check the NEW document.

15. Close and save the NEW document; name it **HOTELS.**

16. Print one copy of the new document.

HOTELS

Today's date

Mr. Richard Lawrence
45 Penguin Place
Bronx, NY 10466

Dear Mr. Lawrence:

As per your request, I have compiled a list of hotels that should
meet the needs of your scheduled trip to San Francisco.

Since you indicated that you will be attending the Computer Expo
while you are there, I have also listed hotels that offer a
discount to attendees. Those that offer a business center are
indicated with an asterisk.

San Francisco Hotels with a Business Center:

San Francisco Hotels Offering Discounts to Computer Expo
Attendees:

The Cayman Island information is listed below:

Hotels in the Cayman Islands Offering Diving Accommodations:

Hotels in the Cayman Islands Offering Free Diving Instruction:

I am enclosing several brochures which will provide you with
pictures of the hotels listed above and information on the
vacation packages available in the Cayman Islands.

When you have decided upon a hotel, please let me know, and I
will make your complete travel arrangements.

Sincerely,

Marietta Dunn
Travel Representative

md/yo
enclosures

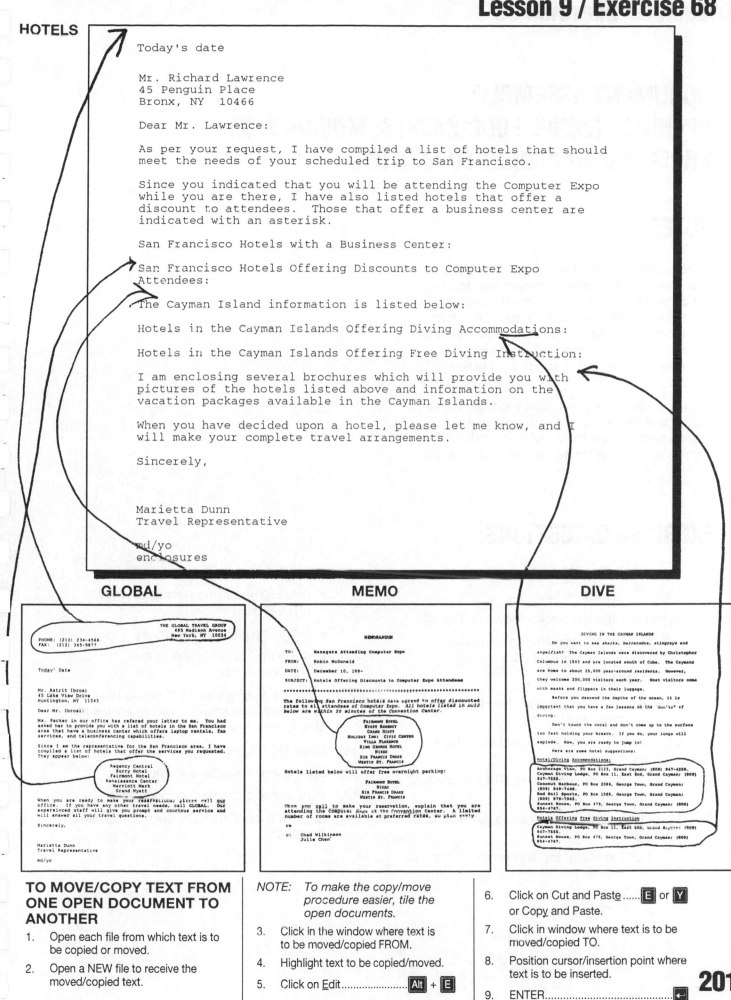

GLOBAL

THE GLOBAL TRAVEL GROUP
485 Madison Avenue
New York, NY 10034

PHONE: (212) 234-4566
FAX: (212) 345-9877

Today' Date

Mr. Astrit Ibrosi
45 Lake View Drive
Huntington, NY 11543

Dear Mr. Ibrosi:

Ms. Packer in our office has refered your letter to me. You had
asked her to provide you with a list of hotels in the San Francisco
area that have a business center which offers laptop rentals, fax
services, and teleconferencing capabilities.

Since I am the representative for the San Francisco area, I have
compiled a list of hotels that offer the services you requested.
They appear below:

Regency Central
Surry Hotel
Fairmont Hotel
Renaissance Center
Marriott Mark
Grand Hyatt

When you are ready to make your reservations, please call our
office. If you have any other travel needs, call GLOBAL. Our
experienced staff will give you prompt and courteous service and
will answer all your travel questions.

Sincerely,

Marietta Dunn
Travel Representative

md/yo

MEMO

MEMORANDUM

TO: Managers Attending Computer Expo
FROM: Robin McDonald
DATE: December 10, 199-
SUBJECT: Hotels Offering Discounts to Computer Expo Attendees

••

The following San Francisco hotels have agreed to offer discounted
rates to all attendees of Computer Expo. All hotels listed in bold
below are within 20 minutes of the Convention Center.

FAIRMONT HOTEL
HYATT REGENCY
GRAND HYATT
HOLIDAY INN: CIVIC CENTER
VILLA FLORENCE
KING GEORGE HOTEL
NIKKO
SIR FRANCIS DRAKE
WESTIN ST. FRANCIS

Hotels listed below will offer free overnight parking:

FAIRMONT HOTEL
NIKKO
SIR FRANCIS DRAKE
WESTIN ST. FRANCIS

When you call to make your reservation, explain that you are
attending the Computer Expo at the Convention Center. A limited
number of rooms are available at preferred rates, so plan early.

rm

c: Chad Wilkinson
    Julie Chen

DIVE

DIVING IN THE CAYMAN ISLANDS

Do you want to see *sharks, barracudas, stingrays* and
angelfish? The Cayman Islands were discovered by Christopher
Columbus in 1503 and are located south of Cuba. The Caymans
are home to about 25,000 year-around residents. However,
they welcome 200,000 visitors each year. Most visitors come
with masks and flippers in their luggage.

Before you descend the depths of the ocean, it is
important that you have a few lessons on the "don'ts" of
diving.

Don't touch the coral and don't come up to the surface
too fast holding your breath. If you do, your lungs will
explode. Now, you are ready to jump in!

Here are some hotel suggestions:

Hotel/Diving Accommodations:

Anchorage View, PO Box 2123, Grand Cayman; (809) 947-4209.
Cayman Diving Lodge, PO Box 11, East End, Grand Cayman; (809)
947-7555.
Coconut Harbour, PO Box 2086, George Town, Grand Cayman;
(809) 949-7468.
Red Sail Sports, PO Box 1588, George Town, Grand Cayman;
(809) 979-7965.
Sunset House, PO Box 479, George Town, Grand Cayman; (800)
854-4767.

Hotels Offering Free Diving Instruction

Cayman Diving Lodge, PO Box 11, East End, Grand Cayman; (809)
947-7555.
Sunset House, PO Box 479, George Town, Grand Cayman; (800)
854-4767.

TO MOVE/COPY TEXT FROM ONE OPEN DOCUMENT TO ANOTHER

1. Open each file from which text is to be copied or moved.

2. Open a NEW file to receive the moved/copied text.

NOTE: To make the copy/move procedure easier, tile the open documents.

3. Click in the window where text is to be moved/copied FROM.

4. Highlight text to be copied/moved.

5. Click on Edit .... Alt + E

6. Click on Cut and Paste ...... E or Y or Copy and Paste.

7. Click in window where text is to be moved/copied TO.

8. Position cursor/insertion point where text is to be inserted.

9. ENTER ....

DOCUMENT ASSEMBLY:
OPENING MULTIPLE DOCUMENTS; MOVING TEXT
FROM ONE DOCUMENT TO ANOTHER

NOTES:

• The procedure to move text from one document to another is the same as moving text from one location to another in the same document. Windowing makes it easier to move text from one document and place it in another. Reminder: moving text "cuts" (removes) text from its original location and "pastes" it in the new location.

• In this exercise, you will open two documents, copy and move text from one document into a document. Follow the keystrokes outlined in the previous exercise for moving and copying text.

EXERCISE DIRECTIONS:

1. Select Graphics Mode view.

2. Start with a clear screen.

3. Type the letter exactly as shown on the right.

4. Set .5" left, right, top and bottom margins; begin the exercise on Ln 2.5".

5. Open **HOTELS.**

6. Tile the documents; stretch the HOTELS window across the screen.

7. Display vertical and horizontal scroll bars in each window.

8. Copy the letterhead from HOTELS to the top of the NEW document.

9. Make the following changes to the HOTEL document:

    • set .5" left, right, top and bottom margins.

    • delete the second-page heading.

    • delete "The Cayman Island information is listed below."

    • delete the enclosure notation.

    • move the indicated text to the NEW document.

10. Copy the closing from HOTELS to the bottom of the NEW document. Type an enclosure notation below the initials.

11. Close HOTELS; save the changes.

12. Spell check the NEW document.

13. Print one copy of the new document.

14. Close and save the NEW document; name it **CAYMAN.**

Today's date

Ms. Edith Kline
298 West End Avenue
New York, NY 10029

Dear Ms. Kline:

The Cayman Islands is an excellent vacation choice. Since you and your husband enjoy scuba diving, you could not have picked a better place to descend the depths of the ocean!

As per your request, I have listed below those hotels in the Cayman Islands that offer diving accommodations and those that offer free diving instruction.

Since these hotels are quite popular, make your reservations early. Let me know when we can help you to arrange your vacation plans.

HOTELS P. 1

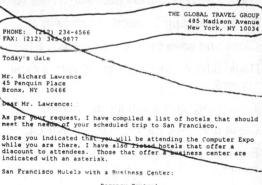

THE GLOBAL TRAVEL GROUP
485 Madison Avenue
New York, NY 10034

PHONE: (212) 234-4566
FAX: (212) 345-9877

Today's date

Mr. Richard Lawrence
45 Penguin Place
Bronx, NY 10466

Dear Mr. Lawrence:

As per your request, I have compiled a list of hotels that should meet the needs of your scheduled trip to San Francisco.

Since you indicated that you will be attending the Computer Expo while you are there, I have also listed hotels that offer a discount to attendees. Those that offer a business center are indicated with an asterisk.

San Francisco Hotels with a Business Center:

Regency Central
Surry Hotel
Fairmont Hotel
Renaissance Center
Marriott Mark
Grand Hyatt

San Francisco Hotels Offering Discounts to Computer Expo Attendees:

Fairmont Hotel*
Hyatt Regency
Grand Hyatt*
Holiday Inn: Civic Center
Villa Florence
King George Hotel
Nikko
Sir Francis Drake
Westin St. Francis

The Cayman Island information is listed below:

HOTELS P. 2

Mr. Richard Lawrence
Page 2
Today's date

Hotels in the Cayman Islands Offering Diving Accommodations:

Anchorage View, PO Box 2123, Grand Cayman; (809) 947-4209.
Cayman Diving Lodge, PO Box 11, East End, Grand Cayman; (809) 947-7555.
Coconut Harbour, PO Box 2086, George Town, Grand Cayman; (809) 949-7468.
Red Sail Sports, PO Box 1588, George Town, Grand Cayman; (809) 979-7965.
Sunset House, PO Box 479, George Town, Grand Cayman; (800) 854-4767.

Hotels in The Cayman Islands Offering Free Diving Instruction:

Cayman Diving Lodge, PO Box 11, East End, Grand Cayman; (809) 947-7555.
Sunset House, PO Box 479, George Town, Grand Cayman; (800) 854-4767.

I am enclosing several brochures which will provide you with pictures of the hotels listed above and information on the vacation packages available in the Cayman Islands.

When you have decided upon a hotel, please let me know, and I will make your complete travel arrangements.

Sincerely,

Marietta Dunn
Travel Representative

md/yo
enclosures

DOCUMENT ASSEMBLY:
RETRIEVING TEXT; COMBINING PARAGRAPHS

NOTES:

* When preparing specific documents, the same wording is often used for many of the paragraphs in those documents. For example, in a Last Will and Testament, many of the paragraphs are standard and are used for all clients. Only those paragraphs that relate to specific items or names are changed, and sometimes relevant information is inserted after the document is created.

* "Standard" text is often referred to as "boilerplate," or "repetitive text."

* Standard or repetitive text may be saved under its own file name and *retrieved* into a document when needed.

* When you "retrieve" a document, the document text is made part of the current document window. This is quite different from "opening" a document.

* When you "open" a document, each new opened document is layered over the previous one. The status line indicates "Doc 2", "Doc 3", etc., numbering each opened document. As noted in Exercise 67, you can switch between open documents (the top document is the active one), cascade or tile them then click in the document window you wish to activate.

* In this exercise, you will create a separate document for each standard paragraph indicated on the right. These paragraphs will be retrieved in future exercises to assemble various documents. The keystrokes for retrieving a document are outlined in the next exercise.

EXERCISE DIRECTIONS:

1. Select Text Mode view.
2. Begin a NEW document (start with a clear screen).
3. Type paragraph 1 exactly as shown.
4. Close and save the file; name it **COL1**.
5. Begin a NEW document (start with a clear screen).
6. Type paragraph 2 exactly as shown.
7. Close and save the file; name **COL2**.
8. Begin a NEW document (start with a clear screen).
9. Type paragraph 3 exactly as shown.
10. Close and save the file; name it **COL3.**
11. Begin a NEW document (start with a clear screen).
12. Type the closing (paragraph 4) exactly as shown.
13. Close and save the file; name it **CLOSING.**
14. Begin a NEW document (start with a clear screen).
15. Type paragraph 5 exactly as shown.
16. Close and save the file; name it **WILL1.**
17. Begin a NEW document (start with a clear screen).
18. Type paragraph 6 exactly as shown.
19. Close and save the file; name it **WILL4.**
20. Begin a NEW document (start with a clear screen).
21. Type paragraph 7 exactly as shown.
22. Close and save the file; name it **REMIT.**
23. Begin a NEW document (start with a clear screen).
24. Type paragraph 8 exactly as shown.
25. Close and save the file; name it **REMIND.**

PARAGRAPH 1

I know this is just an oversight, but your account is now past due. We would appreciate a remittance from you as soon as possible. ↓2x

PARAGRAPH 2

Unless we receive your full payment within five days we will be forced to turn your account over to our collection department. ↓2x

PARAGRAPH 3

Thank you for your attention to this matter. ↓2x

PARAGRAPH 4

Cordially,

↓4x

Carole V. Russo
Manager
↓2x
cvr/

PARAGRAPH 5

I, *, of *, do make, publish and declare this to be my Last Will and Testament, hereby revoking all wills and codicils heretofore made by me. ↓2x

PARAGRAPH 6

IN TESTIMONY WHEREOF, I have to this my Last Will and Testament, subscribed my name and affixed my seal, this * day of *, 199*. ↓2x

_____
     *   (Pos. 4.1")

Signed, sealed, published and declared by the above-named testator, as and for his Last Will and Testament, in our presence, and we at his request, in his presence and in the presence of each other, do hereunto, sign our names and set down our addresses as attesting witnesses, all on this * day of * 199*. ↓2x

_____ residing at _____

_____ residing at _____

_____ residing at _____

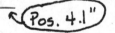

(Pos 3.8") (Pos 5.1") (Pos 7.4")

PARAGRAPH 7

We shall expect your remittance in the amount of * within the next ten days.

PARAGRAPH 8

Our last reminder to you that your account was past due was mailed to you on *.

DOCUMENT ASSEMBLY:
RETRIEVING TEXT; COMBINING PARAGRAPHS

NOTES:

- Unlike "opened" documents, "retrieved" documents are made part of the current document window.

- When paragraphs are retrieved into a new document to be assembled with other paragraphs, you must save the new assembled document under a new file name. In this way, the "retrieved" file will remain intact.

- To retrieve a document, select "Retrieve" from the File main menu bar, or press Shift + F10 and click on "Retrieve into Current Document."

- In this exercise, you will create a new document and retrieve the standard paragraphs (you saved earlier) into it to assemble a collection letter. You will also save the subject line so that you can retrieve it in future collection letters.

EXERCISE DIRECTIONS:

1. Select Text Mode view.
2. Begin a NEW document (start with a clear screen).
3. Create the letter as shown on the right.
4. Use the default margins.
5. Begin the exercise on Ln 2.5"
6. Retrieve the named paragraphs where indicated.

7. Spell check the document.
8. Highlight and save the subject line (Save Block) to a new file; name it **SUBJECT**.
9. Save the assembled document; name it **COLLECT**.
10. Print one copy of the assembled document.

Today's date

Ms. Anita Kane
Haneswear Sports, Inc.
65 Mountain Lane
Wichita, KS 72087

Dear Ms. Kane:

SAVE AS A NEW DOCUMENT

SUBJECT: YOUR OVERDUE ACCOUNT

Retrieve COL1 → ¶You are a valued customer. We would not like to see your credit standing jeoparidized.

Retrieve → COL2 ¶

Retrieve → COL3 ¶

Retrieve → CLOSING ¶

TO RETRIEVE
Shift + F10, click on "Retrieve into Current Document"

1. Place cursor where you want document retrieved.
2. Click on File .... Alt + F
3. Click on Retrieve .... R
4. Type name of document to retrieve.
5. Click on OK .... ⏎

TO SAVE BLOCK
F10

1. Highlight text to be saved.
2. Click on File .... Alt + F
3. Click on Save As .... S
   (Save Block dialog box will appear)
   or
   Click on *Save As* on
   WPMAIN button bar. .... [Save As]
4. Type file name of highlighted text to be saved.
5. Click on OK .... ⏎

DOCUMENT ASSEMBLY:
RETRIEVING TEXT; COMBINING PARAGRAPHS

NOTES:

- In this exercise, you will create a Last Will and Testament by retrieving previously saved standard paragraphs. When you created the standard paragraphs for the Will (in the previous exercise), you inserted an asterisk (*) in locations where variable information would be inserted. To insert the appropriate text at the asterisk locations, use the search feature to quickly locate the asterisk, backspace to delete the asterisk, then insert the appropriate information. You may also use "GoTo" to quickly locate the asterisk.

- A review of search, "GoTo" and setting first line indents is outlined in this exercise.

EXERCISE DIRECTIONS:

1. Select Text Mode view.

2. Begin a NEW document (start with a clear screen).

3. Create the Last Will and Testament indicated to the right.

4. Use the default margins.

5. Begin the exercise on Ln 2".

6. Set a paragraph indent of 2" for FIRST, SECOND and THIRD paragraphs.
   (Shift + F8, M, F)

7. Retrieve the noted paragraphs.

8. Using the search or "Goto" (Ctrl + Home) features, locate each asterisk and insert the appropriate information indicated.

9. Spell check the exercise.

10. Save the assembled document; name it **LASTWILL**.

A Retrieve → WILL1

LAST WILL AND TESTAMENT
OF
JOHN RICHARD ADAMS ↓4x

*=John Richard Adams   * = 105 Oakwood Lane, Goshen, NY

FIRST: I direct all my just debts, the expenses of my last illness and funeral, and the expenses of administering my estate be paid as soon as convenient.

SECOND: I give all my articles of personal, household or domestic use or adornment, including automobile and boats, to my wife, Mary Adams, or, if she does not survive me, to my children Thomas Adams and Betsy Adams, as shall survive me, in shares substantially equal as to value.

THIRD: I give and devise all my residential real property, and all my interest in any policies of insurance thereon, to my wife, Mary Adams, if she survives me or if she does not survive me, to my surviving children, to be held by them jointly.

A Retrieve → WILL4

* = third   * = January   * =1994

* John Richard Adams

TO SET PARAGRAPH MARGINS
Shift + F8, M, F

1. Click on Layout................. `Alt` + `L`
2. Click on Margins .... `M`
3. Click on First Line Indent .... `F`
4. Type indent amount (from left margin).
5. ENTER............................... `↵`
6. Click on OK .... `↵`

TO SEARCH TEXT/CODES
F2 then step 3

1. Place cursor/insertion point at top of document.
2. Click on Edit..................... `Alt` + `E`

3. Click on Search........................... `H`
4. Type text to be located in "Search For" box
   or
   • Click on Codes.
   • Highlight code to be located.
   • Click on Select
   or
   • Click on Specific Codes.
   • Highlight code to be located.
   • Click on Select.
   • Type additional code information.
   • Click on OK.
5. Select a search option:
   Backward Search .... `B`
   Case Sensitive Search................. `C`

   Find Whole Words Only .... `W`
   Extended Search .... `X`
6. Click on Search .... `F2`
7. Press F2 to search for each occurrence.

TO "GOTO"
Ctrl + Home

1. Place cursor before text to be located.
2. Press Ctrl + Home
3. Type character to "go to."
4. Repeat steps 2-3 for each desired "go to."

DOCUMENT ASSEMBLY: APPENDING TEXT

NOTES:

- The append feature allows you to add a block of text to the end of a file which has been saved on a disk. However, if you do not have a specific file to which you want to append the text, WordPerfect will allow you to create a new file.

- The append feature is helpful when you are working on a document and decide that a portion of it may be used in another document or at a later time.

- After appending text to another file, retrieve that file and adjust spacing as needed before printing.

- "Append" may be accessed from the Edit main menu bar.

- In this exercise, you will create another collection letter by retrieving previously saved standard paragraphs. You will include a P. S. notation (indicated in the directions), then append the notation to a document which has been saved on disk.

EXERCISE DIRECTIONS:

1. Select Text Mode view.

2. Start with a clear screen.

3. Create the collection letter as shown on the right.

4. Use the default margins.

5. Begin the exercise on Ln 2.5"

6. Retrieve the noted paragraphs.

7. Include a P. S. notation that reads:

    Please forward your check to our new offices, 50 Harbor Street, Philadelphia, PA 19103.

8. Spell check the exercise.

9. Append the P. S. notation to the document, COLLECT.

10. Save the assembled document; name it **PASTDUE**.

11. Print one copy of PASTDUE and one copy of COLLECT.

Today's date

Mr. Judd Yakov, President
Accessories, Inc.
56 Waverly Place
Rochester, NY 14602

Dear Mr. Yakov:

Retrieve Subject →

We are disappointed that you have not responded to our previous letters in which we reminded you that your account is now more than three months past due.

Retrieve Col2 → ¶

Retrieve COL3 → ¶

Retrieve CLOSING → ¶

TO APPEND TEXT

Ctrl + F4, A

1. Highlight text you want to append.
2. Click on Edit.....................`Alt` + `E`
3. Click on Append ....`A`
4. Click on To File ....`F`
5. Type name of document to which text will be appended.
6. Click on OK...............................`↵`

DOCUMENT ASSEMBLY: APPENDING TEXT

NOTES:

* In this exercise, you will create a single-spaced report. After completing it, you will append the last paragraph to a new file. In a later exercise, you will retrieve the file.

EXERCISE DIRECTIONS:

1. Select Text Mode view.
2. Begin a NEW document (start with a clear screen).
3. Create the report on the right.
4. Use the default margins.
5. Begin the exercise on Ln 2".
6. Reset left and right margins to 1.5" for the numbered paragraphs.
7. Use the Outline paragraph numbering feature to number the paragraphs (Alt + T, O, B).
8. Full justify the numbered paragraphs.
9. Spell check the exercise.
10. Append the warranty paragraph as indicated to a new file; name it **WARRANTY.**
11. Print one copy.
12. Save the exercise; name it **LASER.**

FACTS ABOUT LASTER POINTER HIGHLIGHTER

↓ 3x

The Trinitron Laser Pointer Highlighter is a unique device which allows you to point to relevant drawings, illustrations, or other references when you are conducting a lecture. All you need to do is aim the red laser beam at whatever it is you are referring. Your audience will be immediately focused. Using the Trinitron Laser Pointer is a professional way to conduct a presentation, especially when there is a need to make reference to charts, etc. Here are some facts and safety tips:

1. **POWER**. Use two 9-volt alkaline batteries which are supplied. An AC Adaptor/Charger and a three-hour rechargeable Ni-cad power pack are optional.

2. **SAFETY**. The Trinitron Highlighter laser pointer complies with all electrical and safety regulations covering class III laser products. Staring into the beam should be avoided. *Do not direct the beam toward a person's eye.*

3. **BATTERIES**. The Trinitron Highlighter laser pointer uses two 9-volt alkaline batteries which are installed.

4. **OPERATION**. Slide the on/off safety switch up to turn on the laser pointer. Turn it off after use to prevent accidental use and drainage of batteries. To use the pointer, aim it at the object or area to be highlighted. Turn on the laser by pressing the on/off red bar switch. Releasing the switch turns off the laser.

5. **WARRANTY**. Trinitron warrants this unit will be free of defects in workmanship and materials for a period of one year from the date of purchase. This warranty does not cover damages resulting from accident, misuse or neglect. If your laser pointer fails to operate properly under normal use during the warranty period because of a defect in workmanship or material, Trinitron will repair or replace (at our option) the laser pointer with no cost to you except for shipping.

append to a new file

After using Trinitron once, you will never be able to conduct a lecture or presentation without it!

EXERCISE DIRECTIONS:

1. Begin a NEW document.
2. Create the Press Release shown below.
3. Use the default margins.
4. Begin the exercise on Ln 2".
5. Open LASER.
6. Tile the documents.
7. Copy the first paragraph from LASER

to the NEW document as indicated.

8. Retrieve WARRANTY into the NEW document where shown.
9. Close LASER.
10. Print the assembled document.
11. Close and save the NEW document; name it **PRESS.**

PRESS

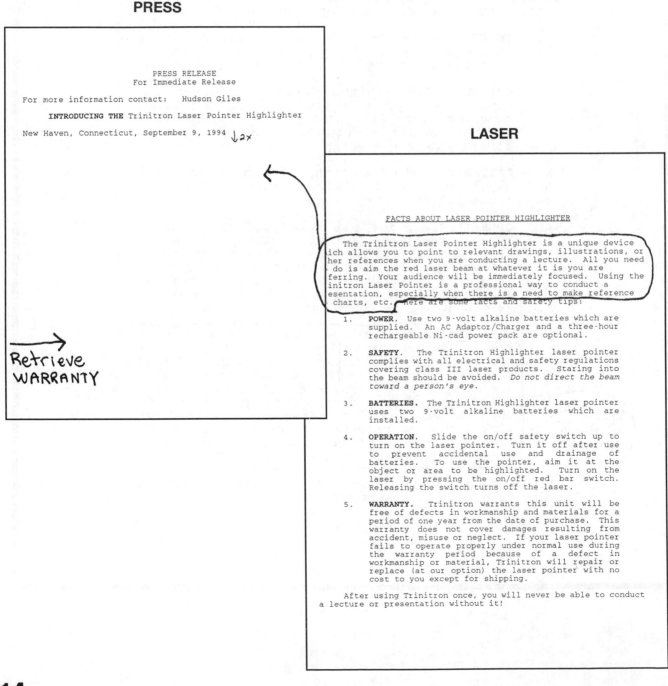

```
                    PRESS RELEASE
                 For Immediate Release
For more information contact:   Hudson Giles
      INTRODUCING THE Trinitron Laser Pointer Highlighter
New Haven, Connecticut, September 9, 1994  ↓2x
```

Retrieve
WARRANTY

LASER

```
              FACTS ABOUT LASER POINTER HIGHLIGHTER

   The Trinitron Laser Pointer Highlighter is a unique device
which allows you to point to relevant drawings, illustrations, or
other references when you are conducting a lecture.  All you need
to do is aim the red laser beam at whatever it is you are
referring.  Your audience will be immediately focused.  Using the
Trinitron Laser Pointer is a professional way to conduct a
presentation, especially when there is a need to make reference
to charts, etc.  Here are some facts and safety tips:

   1.   POWER.  Use two 9-volt alkaline batteries which are
        supplied.  An AC Adaptor/Charger and a three-hour
        rechargeable Ni-cad power pack are optional.

   2.   SAFETY.  The Trinitron Highlighter laser pointer
        complies with all electrical and safety regulations
        covering class III laser products.  Staring into
        the beam should be avoided.  Do not direct the beam
        toward a person's eye.

   3.   BATTERIES.  The Trinitron Highlighter laser pointer
        uses two 9-volt alkaline batteries which are
        installed.

   4.   OPERATION.  Slide the on/off safety switch up to
        turn on the laser pointer.  Turn it off after use
        to prevent accidental use and drainage of
        batteries.  To use the pointer, aim it at the
        object or area to be highlighted.  Turn on the
        laser by pressing the on/off red bar switch.
        Releasing the switch turns off the laser.

   5.   WARRANTY.  Trinitron warrants this unit will be
        free of defects in workmanship and materials for a
        period of one year from the date of purchase.  This
        warranty does not cover damages resulting from
        accident, misuse or neglect.  If your laser pointer
        fails to operate properly under normal use during
        the warranty period because of a defect in
        workmanship or material, Trinitron will repair or
        replace (at our option) the laser pointer with no
        cost to you except for shipping.

   After using Trinitron once, you will never be able to conduct
a lecture or presentation without it!
```

EXERCISE DIRECTIONS:

1. Begin a NEW document.
2. Create the collection letter as shown.
3. Use the default margins.
4. Begin the exercise on Ln 2.5"
5. Open COLLECT.
6. Tile the documents.
7. Copy the inside address and salutation from COLLECT to the NEW document as indicated.

8. Retrieve REMIND where indicated; insert January 4 in place of the asterisk.
9. Retrieve REMIT where indicated; insert $386.98 in place of the asterisk.
10. Retrieve CLOSING where indicated.
11. Print one copy of the assembled document.
12. Close and save the NEW document; name it **REMIND2**.

Today's date

{ Copy inside address and salutation from COLLECT

Retrieve REMIND → ¶

We do value your patronage. The best way to maintain a good working relationship is to have a good credit record. If you have any questions, please feel free to phone me.

Retrieve REMIT → ¶

Retrieve CLOSING →

LESSON 10 / EXERCISES 75-79
MACROS

- Recording a Macro
- Playing a Macro

MACROS: RECORDING "DESCRIPTIVE" MACROS

NOTES:

- A macro is a saved series of commands and keystrokes, which may be "played back" with a single keystroke or mouse click. Macros may be used to record repetitive phrases. When the phrase is needed, it is played back with a single keystroke. Or, a macro may be used to automate a particular task like printing, spell checking, changing margins and/or line spacing. Rather than press many keys to access a task, it is possible to "record" the process and play it back with one keystroke.

- Once a macro is created, it must be named. A "descriptive" macro is one to which you give a descriptive name as you create it. The name may have one to eight characters, like any DOS file. WordPerfect assigns a .WPM file extension to a saved macro file.

- The WordPerfect 6.0 macro language also includes programming commands and operators such as AND, OR, LABEL and CHAR. These commands let you create macros that can evaluate conditional statements that respond to the user. The macro exercises in this text will not cover programming commands. See documentation for macro programming command information.

- Recording a macro may be accessed by selecting "Macro" from the Tools main menu bar or by clicking on "Mac Rec" on the TOOLS button bar.

- Record a macro carefully. When "Recording Macro" is displayed in the lower left of your screen, any key you press will be recorded in the macro.

- In this exercise, you will create several "descriptive" macros. You will "play back" these macros in subsequent exercises.

EXERCISE DIRECTIONS:

1. Select Text Mode view.

2. Start with a clear screen.

3. Create macro #1; name it **PSA**. Insert a hard space (Home + Spacebar) between the words.

4. Clear your screen without saving changes.

5. Create macro #2; name it **CTG**. Insert a hard space between the words.

6. Clear your screen without saving changes.

macro #1:

```
PsA MicroComputerSystems, Inc.
```

macro #2:

```
CompuTechnology Group, Inc.
```

TO RECORD A DESCRIPTIVE MACRO

Ctrl + F10, name macro, record it,
Ctrl + F10

Click on *Mac Rec*
on the TOOLS button bar................. [Mac Rec]
and skip to step 4

or

1. Click on <u>T</u>ools.................. [Alt] + [T]
2. Click on <u>M</u>acro. .... [M]
3. Click <u>R</u>ecord. .... [R]

4. Type macro name.
5. Click on OK ...,,,,,,....................... [←]
6. Type keystrokes to be recorded.

To stop recording macro:

7. Click on <u>T</u>ools.................... [Alt] + [T]
8. Click on <u>M</u>acro .... [M]
9. Click on <u>S</u>top .... [S]

MACROS: PLAYING A "DESCRIPTIVE" MACRO

NOTES:

- Once a macro has been recorded and saved, it can be "played back" into your document whenever desired.

- Macro playback may be accessed by selecting "Macro" from the Tools main menu bar or by clicking on "Mac Play" in the TOOLS button bar.

```
File  Edit  View  Layout  Tools  Font  Graphics  Window  Help
                   Writing Tools...  Alt+F1

                   Macro                    ▶ ┌──────────────────────┐
                   Outline        Ctrl+F5     │Play...      Alt+F10  │
                   Merge          Shft+F9     │Record...    Ctrl+F10 │
                   Sort...        Ctrl+F9     │Control...   Ctrl+PgUp│
                   Date           Shft+F5     └──────────────────────┘

                   Index          Alt+F5  ▶
                   Table of Contents Alt+F5 ▶
                   List           Alt+F5  ▶
                   Cross-Reference Alt+F5 ▶
                   Table of Authorities  ▶
                   Generate...    Alt+F5

                   Math           Alt+F7  ▶
                   Spreadsheet    Alt+F7  ▶

                   Hypertext...   Alt+F5
                   Sound Clip     Ctrl+F7 ▶

Courier 12pt                        Doc 1 Pg 1 Ln 1" POS 1"
```

- In this exercise, you will create a legal letter, and where indicated, recall and play back two macros you created in Exercise 75. You will note that this document contains a "re" line, which is commonly used in legal correspondence. "Re" means "in reference to" or "subject." Two returns are inserted before and after typing the "re" line.

EXERCISE DIRECTIONS:

1. Select Text Mode view.
2. Start with a clear screen.
3. Create the letter on the right.
4. Begin the exercise on Ln 2.5". Use the default margins.
5. Full justify paragraph text.
6. Play back the **PSA** and **CTG** macros wherever they appear in the text.
7. Spell check.
8. Preview your document.
9. Print one copy.
10. Save the exercise; name it **SETTLE.**

Today's date

Thomas Wolfe, Esq.
Wolfe, Escada & Yates
803 Park Avenue
New York, NY 10023

Dear Mr. Wolfe:

Re: **[Macro PSA]** vs.
     ABC Manufacturing Company

I am enclosing a copy of the Bill of Sale that transfers all Gordon's assets to **[Macro PSA]**.

In addition, you asked us to represent **[Macro CTG]** in their $200,000 payment to **[Macro PSA]**. Because of this payment, **[Macro CTG]** became subrogated to the claim made by **[Macro PSA]**, and **[Macro PSA]** cannot settle this matter without the approval of **[Macro CTG]**

[Macro CTG] would also be entitled to recover some portion of any judgment recovered by **[Macro PSA]** in the above action. In order to get a settlement in this matter, we will need to obtain a release of ABC Manufacturing Company by **[Macro CTG]**

Let's discuss this so that we can quickly settle this matter.

Very truly yours,

David Altmann, Esq.

da/yo
enclosure

TO PLAY BACK A MACRO
Alt + F10

1. Position cursor where macro is to be played back.

2. Click on "*Mac Play*" in the TOOLS button bar. .... [Mac Play] then skip to step 5

or

- Click on Tools .... [Alt] + [T]

3. Click on Macro .... [M]

4. Click on Play .... [P]

5. Type name of macro to be played.

6. Click on OK .... [↵]

MACROS: RECORDING "ALT + LETTER" MACROS

NOTES:

- In Exercise 75, you created a descriptive macro in which you assigned the macro a descriptive name. WordPerfect allows you to create an "Alt + Letter" macro in which you assign a one-character name. When you are ready to play it back, you press Alt + the one letter. The *advantage* of this macro type is that it will save you several keystrokes compared to the descriptive macro.

  The *disadvantage* of the Alt + letter macros is that you can create only 26 of them (one for each letter of the alphabet). Also, some Alt + letter combinations activate a menu. For Example, Alt + L activates the Layout menu. If you create an Alt + L macro and then press Alt + L, the macro will execute; the pull-down menu will not. Use the Alt + letter macros for commands that you utilize most frequently.

- The Alt + letter macro is accessed using the same procedure as the descriptive macro. See keystrokes on the right.

- In this exercise, you will create several macros using the Alt + letter combinations. One of the macros will record a repetitive word; the other four will record commands: print previewing, displaying the button bar, changing button bars, and changing margins. When creating the macro to display the button bar, (Alt + V, B) you cannot use Alt + V as the name of your macro since Alt + V activates the View menu.

EXERCISE DIRECTIONS:

1. Select Text Mode view.

2. Start with a clear screen.

3. Create macro #1; name it **T**.

4. Clear your screen.

5. Create macro #2 (displaying the button bar); name it **D**.

6. Clear your screen.

7. Create macro #3: (changing button bars) ; name it **C**.

8. Clear your screen.

9. Create macro #4: (print preview); name it **P**.

10. Clear your screen.

11. Create macro #5: (change margins to 1.5"); name it **M**.

12. Clear your screen.

macro #1:

DocumentTech Publishing Assistant

macro #2:

Alt + V, B

macro #3:

Alt + V, S, S, highlight TOOLS, ENTER

macro #4:

Alt + F, V

macro #5

Shift + F8, M, L, 1.5", ENTER, R, 1.5, ENTER, ENTER

TO RECORD AN "Alt + letter" MACRO
Ctrl + F10, name macro, record it, Ctrl + F10

1. Click on *Mac Rec* on the TOOLS button bar. .... and skip to step 4

   or

   • Click on Tools. .... `Alt` + `T`
2. Click on Macro. .... `M`

3. Click Record. .... `R`
4. Type Alt + letter. `Alt` + `letter`
5. Click on OK .... `↵`
6. Type keystrokes to be recorded.

To stop recording macro:

7. Click on Tools .... `Alt` + `T`
8. Click on Macro .... `M`
9. Click on Stop .... `S`

MACROS: PLAYING "ALT + LETTER" MACROS

NOTES:

- To play back a one-letter macro, you simply press Alt + the letter. Because you need not access the Play Macro dialog box, this method is easier to access than playing the descriptive macro.

- In this exercise, you will create a "News Release," which is a document that is prepared and sent to various newspapers and magazines announcing a new product of a company. Each time the product name appears, you will play back one of the macros you created in the previous exercise.

EXERCISE DIRECTIONS:

1. Select Text Mode view.

2. Start with a clear screen.

3. Play the **D** macro to display the button bar.

    NOTE: If the button bar is already displayed, ignore this step.

4. Play the **C** macro to change to the TOOLS button bar.

5. Create the News Release shown on the right.

6. Begin the exercise on Ln 2". Use the default margins. Use the Date Text feature on the button bar to insert current date (where shown).

7. Play the **T** macro whenever Document**Tech** Pub̲lishing Assistant appears in the text.

8. Spell check.

9. Play the **P** macro to preview the document.

10. Print one copy.

11. Save the exercise; name it **DOCUMENT.**

```
                    PRESS RELEASE
                 For Immediate Release

For more information contact:  Corine Cardoza


     INTRODUCING the DocumentTech Publishing Assistant

Cambridge, Massachusetts, March 7, 199 — USE DATE TEXT FEATURE

The DocumentTech Publishing Assistant is the first in a series of
publishing products that put together three distinct
technologies--digital scanning, laser imaging and xerograph--into
one simplified publishing solution.  The DocumentTech Publishing
Assistant provides high quality, low cost and quick turnaround.
DocumentTech Publishing Assistant eliminates complicated pre-
press operations.  It has a built-in scanner and quickly captures
text, line art and photos, and converts them to digital masters.

Even booklet marking becomes easier.  DocumentTech Publishing
Assistant has a signature booklet feature which will
automatically turn out 11 x 17 or digest size (8.5 x 11) collated
sets ready to be stitched, folded and trimmed.  DocumentTech
Publishing Assistant prints an amazing 135 pages per minute and
has a concurrent input/output capability.  This means that while
you are publishing one job, you'll be scanning, revising and
readying others.  Furthermore, DocumentTech Publishing Assistant
comes in a networked version.

                          ###
```

TO PLAY "Alt + Letter" MACROS

1. Position cursor where macro is to be played back (for repetitive phrases).

2. Press Alt + letter (used when creating macro).

MACROS: RECORDING "INTERACTIVE" MACROS

NOTES:

- An "Interactive" macro is one in which you give the macro input while it is playing back. When you record an interactive macro, a PAUSE code is entered at the point where information will be inserted. When the macro is played back, it will pause for you to type the variable text.

- In this exercise, you will record two macros that contain pauses.

EXERCISE DIRECTIONS:

1. Select Text Mode view.

2. Start with a clear screen.

3. Create macro #1 as shown on the right, inserting a "pause" code where indicated; name it **S.**

4. Clear your screen.

5. Create macro #2 as shown on the right, inserting a "pause" code where indicated; name it **R.**

6. Clear your screen.

7. Play the **D** macro to display the button bar.

NOTE: If the button bar is already displayed, ignore this step.

8. Play the **C** macro to change to the TOOLS button bar.

9. Play the **M** macro to change the left and right margins to 1.5".

10. Create the letter shown below the macros.

11. Begin the exercise on Ln 2.5".

12. Use the Date Text feature on the button bar to insert the current date.

13. Full justify paragraph text.

14. Spell check the exercise.

15. Print one copy.

16. Save the exercise; name it **PAUSE.**

TO RECORD A MACRO WITH A PAUSE

1. Click on *Mac Rec* on the TOOLS button bar. .... [Mac Rec] and skip to step 4

   or

   Click on Tools. .... [Alt] + [T]

2. Click on Macro............................ [M]

3. Click on Record. .... [R]

4. Type Alt + letter.

5. Click on OK.................................. [↵]

6. Type keystrokes to be recorded until you reach place where you wish to pause.

7. Press Ctrl + PgUp......... [Ctrl] + [PgUp]

8. Click on Macro Commands.......... [C]

9. Highlight PAUSE

10. ENTER.. [↵]

11. Continue typing keystrokes to be recorded.

To stop recording macro:

12. Click on Tools .... [Alt] + [T]

13. Click on Macro............................ [M]

14. Click on Stop .... [S]

TO PLAY A MACRO WITH A PAUSE
Alt + F10

1. Place cursor where macro is to be played back.

2. Click on "*Mac Play*" in the TOOLS button bar .... [Mac Play] then skip to step 5

   or

- Click on Tools .... [Alt] + [T]

3. Click on Macro............................ [M]

4. Click on Play .... [P]

5. Type name of macro to be played.

6. ENTER.. [↵]

7. Type desired text when macro pauses.

8. ENTER.. [↵] to continue playback.

MACRO # 1

We shall expect your remittance in the amount of {PAUSE} within the next ten days.

MACRO # 2

Our last reminder to you that your account was past due was mailed to you on {PAUSE}.

Todays date

Mr. Andrew S. Stone
321 Saxony Place
Indianapolis, IN 46204

Dear Mr. Stone:

Your account is now more than thirty days past due. **[Macro R - January 5]**

[Macro S - $288.94]

We do value your patronage. The best way to maintain a good working relationship is to have a good credit record. If you have any questions, please feel free to phone me.

Sincerely,

Taylor Jones
Credit Manager

tj/yo

EXERCISE DIRECTIONS:

1. Create the following macro in italics: name it **TRIN**:

   TriniTron Laser Highlighter

2. Clear your screen.

3. Create the letter below in any style.

4. Play back the macros indicated.

5. Retrieve the document, WARRANTY where indicated. Double indent this paragraph .5" from the margins.

6. Spell check the exercise.

7. Print one copy.

8. Save the exercise; name it **CLIENT**.

[Macro M] Today's date Ms. Rosetta Stone 751 Hamlin Place Old Bridge, NJ 08754 Dear Ms. Stone: ¶I am delighted to learn that you have purchased a **[Macro TRIN]** and that you are enjoying the use of it. I am sorry that you did not receive the warranty card which should have been enclosed with your **[Macro TRIN]**. ¶I do not have any loose warranty cards that I can send you. However, I will state the warranty policy in the paragraph below. ¶**[Retrieve WARRANTY.]** ¶Show this letter with the indicated warranty policy, along with your bill of sale, to your local dealer. He will then repair your **[Macro TRIN]**. ¶If you should have any problems, let me know. I know you will get many years of enjoyment from your **[Macro TRIN]**. Sincerely, Shirley Chen Customer Service sc/yo **[Macro P].**

EXERCISE DIRECTIONS:

1. Create the following macro in italics; name it **AD:**

   RideTheTrack ExerciSer

2. Clear your screen.

3. • Create the following macro to change to double space; name it **DS:**

   Shift + F8, L, S, 2, ENTER, ENTER, ENTER

   • Create the following macro to change to single space; name it **SS:**

   Shift + F8, L, S, 1, ENTER, ENTER, ENTER

4. Clear your screen.

5. Create the advertisement below. Begin on Ln 2".

6. Play back the macros indicated.

7. Spell check the exercise.

8. Save the exercise; name it **WORKOUT.**

[Macro M]

DISCOVER AN EXCITING NEW WAY TO
ACHIEVE WELLNESS OF BODY AND MIND

[Macro DS]

According to medical fitness experts, regular aerobic exercise is essential for achieving all-around wellness. Aerobic exercise helps you prevent illness, feel better physically and mentally, boost your energy level, and increase the years on your life. That's why you need **[Macro AD]**. **[Macro AD]** will provide you with the following benefits:

[Macro SS]

TAB → • Double Indent — you can burn more fat than on other exercisers and burn up to 1,100 calories per hour!

TAB → • you can improve your cardiovascular fitness and lower your overall cholestrol level.

TAB → • you'll feel more mentally alert, relaxed, positive and self-confident.

[Macro DS]

With regular workouts on a **[Macro AD]**, you'll feel wonderful because you're doing something positive for yourself.

Seven out of ten **[Macro AD]** owners use their machines an average of three times per week.

Call your **[Macro AD]** representative today at 1-800-555-4444 to receive a FREE video and brochure.

[Macro AD]

[Macro P]

LESSON 11 / EXERCISES 80-102
COLUMNS / TABLES

- Creating Text Columns
- Creating Tabular Columns
- Creating Tables
- Editing Tables

TEXT COLUMNS: NEWSPAPER-STYLE

NOTES:

- WordPerfect's newspaper-style column feature allows text to flow from one column to another. When the first column is filled with text, additional text will automatically continue to flow into the next column.

- WordPerfect provides two types of newspaper columns. In *regular newspaper columns*, text flows down one column to the bottom of a page then starts again at the top of the next column. In *balanced newspaper columns*, each column is adjusted on the page so that they are equal in length.

- Newspaper-style columns are particularly helpful when creating newsletters, pamphlets, brochures, lists or articles.

- You may select the number of columns you desire for a particular document and/or the distance between columns, sometimes called the **gutter** space. If you do not specify the distance between columns, WordPerfect will do so for you. WordPerfect will automatically calculate columns of equal width; however, the column margins can be set individually to create unequal columns.

- Columns may be created before or after typing text.

- The column feature is accessed by selecting "Columns" from the Layout main menu. The following dialog box will appear:

- Note that you do not need to select a column type since "Newspaper" is the default setting.

- After defining the columns and clicking on OK (thus turning ON the column feature), the word "Col" will appear in the status line. You must turn OFF the column feature when you have completed your columnar document if you plan to continue the document without columns.

- If you desire to include a vertical line between columns, you may select "Column Borders" from the dialog box option.

- Line spacing may also be set on the dialog box (Line Spacing Between Rows).

- To quickly create regular newspaper columns without accessing the dialog box, you can click on the Column button on the ribbon and specify the number of columns you desire.

- Whether you use the ribbon or the dialog box to define columns, be sure to turn the column feature OFF (return to one column on the ribbon) when you no longer want columns.

- You can retrieve text from a file into newspaper-style columns. When retrieving text from a file into columns, be sure your cursor is within the column mode. You can do this by checking to see that the status area contains the word "Col."

- The cursor can be moved from one column to another quickly by pressing Ctrl + Home and the left or right arrow key.

- In this exercise, you will create a two-column report using newspaper-style columns.

column button

File Edit View Layout Tools Font Graphics Window Help
Marg ▼	None ▼	1 Col ▼	Left ▼	Courier ▼	12pt ▼

1 Col ▲
2 Cols
3 Cols
4 Cols ▼

Courier 12pt   Doc 1 Pg 1 Ln 1" Pos 1"

EXERCISE DIRECTIONS:

1. Select Text Mode view.
2. Start with a clear screen.
3. Use the default margins.
4. Begin columns on Ln 2".
5. Create the article on the right using a two-column, *regular* newspaper-style format. Use the default distance between columns.
6. Double space the document.
7. Insert a vertical line (border) between columns.
8. Full justify document text.
9. Spell check.
10. Preview your document.
11. Print one copy.
12. Save the exercise; name it **PROCESS**.

continued . . .

The computer is an electronic device that can process vast amounts of facts and numbers and perform calculations at very high rates of speed. While a computer can accomplish many things, IT CANNOT THINK. A computer has to be "told" what to do with the information it receives. **Programs** are machine-language instructions which tell a computer what to do with information. Programs are developed by computer programmers.

Computers come in various sizes. Some computers are so large they fill an entire room, while others are so small, they can be held in your hand. No matter what their size, computers contain the same basic parts. Every computer has a way through which the operator can enter instructions and information. A keyboard is an "input" device which is common to all computers. The "storage" device (sometimes called memory) receives the information from the input device and holds it until it is needed. A "processing" device selects the instructions from the storage unit and processes the information as it has been directed. The "output" device translates the processed information into readable form. A typical output device would be a printer or a visual display.

TO CREATE TEXT COLUMNS (Newspaper)

Alt + F7

1. Place cursor where column is to begin

    or

    Select existing text to be included in columns.

2. Click on Layout .... 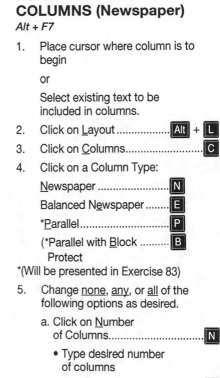 **Alt** + **L**

3. Click on Columns.......................... **C**

4. Click on a Column Type:

    Newspaper .... **N**

    Balanced Newspaper .... **E**

    *Parallel............................. **P**

    (*Parallel with Block .... **B**
    Protect

    *(Will be presented in Exercise 83)

5. Change none, any, or all of the following options as desired.

    a. Click on Number
    of Columns.............................. **N**

    • Type desired number
    of columns

    • ENTER.................................. ↵

b. Click on Distance
Between Columns .... **D**

    • Type desired distance

    • ENTER.................................. ↵

c. Click on Line Spacing
Between Rows......................... **S**

    • Type desired line spacing

    • ENTER.................................. ↵

d. Click on Column Borders .... **B**

    • Click on Border Style
    (Between Only)

    • ENTER.................................. ↵

6. Click on OK.................................. ↵

TO CREATE TEXT COLUMNS ON RIBBON

NOTE: Newspaper columns are the default for this procedure.

1. Place cursor where column is to begin

    or

    Select existing text to be included in columns.

2. Click on [**1 Col _**] on the ribbon.

3. Click on desired number of columns.

TO TURN OFF COLUMNS

Ctrl + F7

1. Place cursor where column is to be turned off.

2. Click on Layout .... **Alt** + **L**

3. Click on Columns......................... **C**

4. Click OFF .... **F**

TO MOVE CURSOR FROM COLUMN TO COLUMN

• Press
Ctrl + Home
→ or ← ....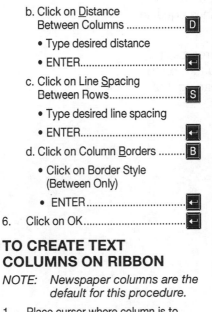**Ctrl** + **Home** **→** or **←**

TEXT COLUMNS: NEWSPAPER-STYLE

NOTES:

- In this exercise, you will create an article using a three-column *balanced newspaper column.* Balanced newspaper columns adjust on the page as you type so that each column is equal in length.

- The column heading should be centered before the column mode is turned on. If you turn on the column mode before you type the heading, the heading will center in the first column.

EXERCISE DIRECTIONS:

1. Select Text Mode view.
2. Start with a clear screen.
3. Use the default margins.
4. Begin the exercise on Ln 2"; center the heading.
5. Create the article on the right using a three-column balanced newspaper-style format. Use the default distance between columns.
6. Insert vertical lines (borders) between columns.
7. Spell check.
8. Preview your document.
9. Print one copy.
10. Save the exercise; name it **COOK.**

THE ART OF COOKING

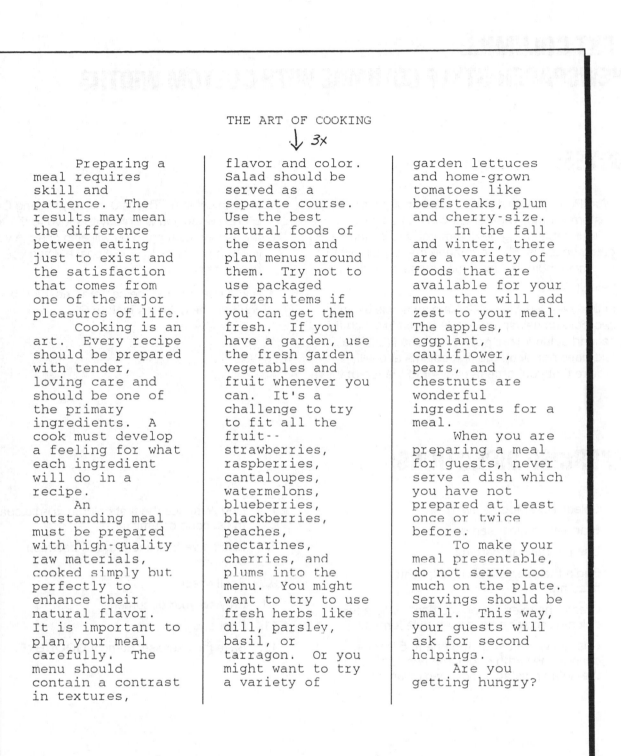

Preparing a meal requires skill and patience. The results may mean the difference between eating just to exist and the satisfaction that comes from one of the major pleasures of life.

Cooking is an art. Every recipe should be prepared with tender, loving care and should be one of the primary ingredients. A cook must develop a feeling for what each ingredient will do in a recipe.

An outstanding meal must be prepared with high-quality raw materials, cooked simply but perfectly to enhance their natural flavor. It is important to plan your meal carefully. The menu should contain a contrast in textures, flavor and color. Salad should be served as a separate course. Use the best natural foods of the season and plan menus around them. Try not to use packaged frozen items if you can get them fresh. If you have a garden, use the fresh garden vegetables and fruit whenever you can. It's a challenge to try to fit all the fruit-- strawberries, raspberries, cantaloupes, watermelons, blueberries, blackberries, peaches, nectarines, cherries, and plums into the menu. You might want to try to use fresh herbs like dill, parsley, basil, or tarragon. Or you might want to try a variety of garden lettuces and home-grown tomatoes like beefsteaks, plum and cherry-size.

In the fall and winter, there are a variety of foods that are available for your menu that will add zest to your meal. The apples, eggplant, cauliflower, pears, and chestnuts are wonderful ingredients for a meal.

When you are preparing a meal for guests, never serve a dish which you have not prepared at least once or twice before.

To make your meal presentable, do not serve too much on the plate. Servings should be small. This way, your guests will ask for second helpings.

Are you getting hungry?

TEXT COLUMNS:
NEWSPAPER-STYLE COLUMNS WITH CUSTOM WIDTHS

NOTES:

- WordPerfect allows you to create columns with custom widths. The default width of a two-column table using default margins is 3"; the gutter space is .5". To change the column width, you must indicate how wide you desire the column to be.

- In this exercise, you will create an article using a two-column newspaper-style format in which the second column is narrower than the first. The text does not fill up the first column and will require that you force the cursor to the top of the second column. This is done by pressing Ctrl + ENTER when you are ready to move to the top of the second column. You will also change your line spacing back to single space when you begin the second column.

- Remember to type the centered heading *before* you turn the columns feature ON.

EXERCISE DIRECTIONS:

1. Select Text Mode view.
2. Start with a clear screen.
3. Use the default margins.
4. Begin the exercise on Ln 2"; center the heading.
5. Create the exercise on the right using a two-column regular newspaper-style format.
6. Change width of column one to 5 inches; change the width of column two to 1". Use the default distance between columns.
7. Double space the first column; single space the second column.
8. Insert a vertical line (border) between columns.
9. Spell check.
10. Preview your document.
11. Print one copy.
12. Save the exercise; name it **GOODBYE.**

VACATION PLANNING

It can be very exciting to plan a vacation. There are a number of ways to go about it. Of course, you could have a travel agent make all the arrangements. But it is more exciting to investigate all the possibilities of travel.

First, you can check the hundreds of guidebooks which can be purchased at bookstores. Then, you can send away to the government tourist offices in the country you are planning to visit. They will send you lots of free literature about the country -- places to visit and a list of accommodations. The travel advertisements in your newspaper will tell you where the bargains are.

After you have planned your trip by looking through the guidebooks listed to the right, ask your travel agent to do the actual booking. Enjoy!

OFFICIAL AIRLINE GUIDE

RUSSELL'S NATIONAL MOTOR COACH GUIDE

STEAMSHIP GUIDE

HOTEL AND RESORT GUIDE

AUTO RENTAL GUIDE

RES- TAURANTS, INNS AND MUSEUMS GUIDE

SIGHT- SEEING GUIDE

CAMP- GROUND, FARM VACATIONS AND ADVENTURE TRAVEL GUIDE

TO CREATE COLUMNS WITH CUSTOM WIDTHS

1. Place cursor where column is to begin.
2. Click on Layout .... Alt + L
3. Click on Columns C
4. Click on Custom Widths .... W
5. ENTER .... ↵
6. Click on Width .... W
7. Type desired width.
8. ENTER, ENTER .... ↵, ↵
9. Highlight column 2 .... ↓
10. ENTER .... ↵
11. Repeat steps 6-8.

NOTE: Repeat entire procedure for additional columns.

12. Click on OK .... ↵

TEXT COLUMNS: PARALLEL COLUMNS

NOTES:

- WordPerfect's parallel column feature allows text to move across the columns.

- Parallel columns are particularly helpful when creating a list, a script, an itinerary, minutes of a meeting or any other document in which text is read horizontally.

- The procedure for creating parallel columns is the same as creating newspaper-style columns, except the "Column Type" must be changed to "Parallel."

- After text is entered in the first column, you must enter a hard page break (Ctrl + Enter) to force the cursor to move to the next column. After text is entered in the second column, a hard page break must be entered to force the cursor to the third column. A hard page break is also needed to move the cursor back to the first column.

- Text cannot be retrieved into parallel columns.

- In this exercise, you will create minutes of a meeting. The columns will be unequal —the first column will be narrower than the second.

- Be sure to type the centered heading before you turn on the column feature.

EXERCISE DIRECTIONS:

1. Select Text Mode view.
2. Start with a clear screen.
3. Use the default margins.
4. Begin the exercise on Ln 2"; center the headings.
5. Create the exercise on the right using a two-column parallel-style format.
6. Change the width of column one to 1.5"; change the width of column two to 4". Use the default distance between columns.
7. Spell check.
8. Preview your document.
9. Print one copy.
10. Save the exercise; name it **AGELESS**.

PERFECTION PLUS, INCORPORATED
MINUTES OF MEETING

March 29, 199-

Present   Robin Jones, Quincy Garin, Zachary Malavo,
                         Wendy Carley, Bill McKinley, Andrew Yang,
                         Shirley DeChan.

Research   Mr. Malvo announced the development of a
                         new product line. Several new chemical
                         formulas were developed for a cream which
                         will reduce skin wrinkling. The cream will
                         be called **Ageless**.

Publicity   To launch this new product, Ms. Carley
                         announced that promotions would be made at
                         all the high-end New York department
                         stores. Samples of the product will be
                         given away at demonstration counters.
                         Press releases will be sent to members of
                         the press.

Advertising   The advertising budget was estimated at
                         $5,223,000. Several advertising agencies
                         were asked to submit presentations, and a
                         decision will be made by the Advertising
                         Committee as to which agency will represent
                         this new line.

Sales   Mr. Garin, National Sales Manager,
                         projected that sales could reach
                         $10,000,000 the first year.

Adjournment   The meeting was adjourned at 4:00 p.m.
                         Another meeting has been scheduled for
                         Tuesday of next week to discuss future
                         research and marketing of this new product.

TEXT COLUMNS: PARALLEL COLUMNS

NOTES:

- In this exercise, you will create a name and address list using an equal parallel-column format.

EXERCISE DIRECTIONS:

1. Select Text Mode view.
2. Start with a clear screen.
3. Use the default margins.
4. Begin the exercise on Ln 2"; center the heading.
5. Create the exercise on the right using a three-column parallel-style format. Use the default column widths and distance between columns.

6. After the column feature is turned on, center (Shift + F6) the first column heading (NAME); then move the cursor to the second column (Ctrl + Enter) and center the second column heading (ADDRESS); move the cursor to the third column and center RESPONSIBILITY.
7. Spell check.
8. Preview your document.
9. Print one copy.
10. Save the exercise; name it **LIST**.

BUSINESS ASSOCIATION DIRECTORY

NAME	ADDRESS	RESPONSIBILITY
Adams, Brenda	765 West Avenue New York, NY 10098 212-555-5577	Convention
Appel, Peter	319 East 96 Street Brooklyn, NY 11214 718-555-5588	Publicity
Barnes, Desmond	10 West 66 Street New York, NY 10054 212-555-6666	Newsletter
Brady, Edward	21 Dolin Road Bronx, NY 10456 212-555-3333	Membership
Brown, Donna	2109 Broadway New York, NY 10199 212-555-2222	Political Action
Chou, David	76 River End Road Queens, NY 11312 718-555-0000	Convention/ Registration
Hussin, Ahmed	225 Racliff Street Bronx, NY 10456 212-555-1111	Membership
LeChamp, Renee	200 East 77 Street New York, NY 10023 212-555-8888	Newsletter
Sovino, Rosemarie	76 Kings Highway Brooklyn, NY 11223 718-555-2323	Publicity

TEXT COLUMNS: PARALLEL COLUMNS

NOTES:

- In this exercise, you will create an itinerary using an unequal parallel-column format.

- An itinerary is a travel schedule which includes departure and arrival dates and times, hotel/motel accommodations, and means of travel used. There are several acceptable formats for an itinerary. The example illustrated on the right is one of them.

EXERCISE DIRECTIONS:

1. Select Text Mode view.
2. Start with a clear screen.
3. Use the default margins.
4. Begin the exercise on Ln 2"; center the heading.
5. Create the exercise on the right using an unequal three-column parallel-style format. Use the default column widths and distance between columns.
6. Change the width of column one to 1"; change the width of column two to 1"; change the width of column three to 3". Use the default distance between columns.
7. Insert a hard space (HOME + Spacebar) between words that should be kept together.
8. Spell check.
9. Preview your document.
10. Print one copy.
11. Save the exercise; name it **ITINER**.

ITINERARY OF ANGELA BATTAGLIA
April 6-7, 199-

Monday, April 6	8:00 a.m.	Leave Newark International Airport, TWA, Flight 444.
	10:30 a.m.	Arrive Miami International Airport. Reservation at Maryatt Airport Hotel. Confirmation No. 444-444324-0.
	12:30 p.m.	Lunch with Dr. Andrew Zarou at Palm Restaurant in Maryatt Hotel. Dr. Zarou will meet you in restaurant.
	3:30 p.m.	Tour of computer facility at University of Miami.
	7:00 p.m.	Dinner with Dr. Lauren Namin, Director of Admissions. Dr. Namin will pick you up at your hotel.
Tuesday, April 7	10:00 a.m.	Conference at Seaview Hotel. Courtesy bus will pick you up outside your hotel at 9:15 a.m.
	12:30 p.m.	Lunch with Ms. Jackie Smith and Mr. Raymond Weill at Palm Court Restaurant at Seaview Hotel to discuss curriculum issues.
	3:00 p.m.	Presentation on "Using the Computer Across the Curriculum."
	7:00 p.m.	Leave Miami International Airport, TWA, Flight 55.
	9:45 p.m.	Arrive Newark International Airport. Limousine service home.

TABULAR COLUMNS

NOTES:

- Tabs may be used to align columns of information. However, since WordPerfect has a table feature which will organize information into columns and rows without using tabs or tab settings, using tab settings to align columns is not the most efficient way to tackle this task.

- Nonetheless, it is important for you to understand how tabs are set and the kinds of tab settings that are available since many tab types are used within the table feature. Tables will be covered beginning in Exercise 87.

- When you change tab settings in a document, changes take effect from that point forward.

- There are four different tab types:

  1. Left-aligned tab -   (the default) text moves to the right of the tab as you type.
     Example:
     xxxxxxxxx
     xxxxx
     xxxxxx

  2. Centered tab -   text centers at the tab stop.
     Example:
        xxxxxxx
          xxx
         xxxxx

  3. Right-aligned tab -   text moves to the *left* or backwards of the tab as you type.
     Example:
         xxxxxx
           xx
          xxxx

  4. Decimal-aligned tab-   text before the decimal point (or other designated alignment character) moves to the left of the tab. Text you type after the decimal point moves to the right of the tab. The decimals (or other align characters) stay aligned.

- Columns of text are generally horizontally centered between existing margins. To determine where to set your tabs so that they appear horizontally centered, it is necessary to create a "set-up" line. The "set-up" line is a blueprint for setting tab stops. Note the procedure:

  a.   Press Shift + F6 (center) and type the longest line of each column and the space between the columns. The recommended space between columns is as follows:

     2-column table = 10 spaces

     3-column table = 8 spaces

     4-column table = 6 spaces

  b.   Using the cursor arrow keys, move the cursor to the first character in each column of the "set-up" line and note the POS indicator. (You will set a tab stop at these positions.)

  c.   Delete the set-up line.

- Tabs are accessed by selecting "Tab Set" from the Layout main menu.

- To set new tabs, you must first access the "tab ruler" (Alt + L, B) and delete the existing default tab stops. Note the tab ruler illustrated below. The default tabs are left aligned (indicated by an "L") and are set .5" apart.

- Set new tabs according to how the text in the column is to be formatted (left aligned, right aligned, centered, decimal aligned).

- To set a left-aligned tab, move the cursor on the tab ruler to the desired tab setting and press "L."

Relative vs. Absolute Tabs

- When you set tabs, you can measure them from the left edge of the page (absolute tabs) or from the left margin (relative tabs). Default tab settings are *relative* to the left margin. However, to use the "set-up" line procedure outlined for setting tabs, you must use absolute tabs. Remember, when you choose absolute tabs, tabs are measured from the left edge of the page whether you change margins or not. The left edge of the page begins at zero (0) on the tab set ruler.

- In this exercise, you will format a tabular two-column document in which the first and second columns are left aligned.

```
 File   Edit   View   Layout   Tools   Font   Graphics   Window   Help
                                    Tab Set
      +0"      +1"      +2"      +3"      +4"      +5"      +6"
      L     L      L     L     L     L     L     L      L     L     L     L      L

  O Absolute     • Left     ┌Relative to Margin┐
  • Relative     O Right     Set Tab:  0"        Repeat Every:  0"
                 O Center
  □ Dot Leader   O Decimal   [Clear One]  [Clear All]   [ OK ]   [Cancel]

 Courier 12pt                              Doc 1 Pg 1 Ln 1" Pos 1"
```

Default tab set

EXERCISE DIRECTIONS:

1. Select Text Mode view.

2. Start with a clear screen.

3. Use the default margins.

4. Center title lines; return three times.

5. Set "absolute" tabs.

6. To determine where tab stops should be set, create the "set-up" line:

   a. center the longest line in each column, plus the intercolumn space.

   b. using the cursor arrow keys or clicking the mouse, move the cursor to the first character in each column and note their horizontal position on "Pos" indicator.

   c. delete the set-up line.

7. Clear all default tabs.

8. Set left-aligned tab for both columns at the noted horizontal positions.

9. Vertically center the exercise (center page top to bottom).

10. Preview your document.

11. Print one copy.

12. Save the exercise; name it **PRES.**

continued . . .

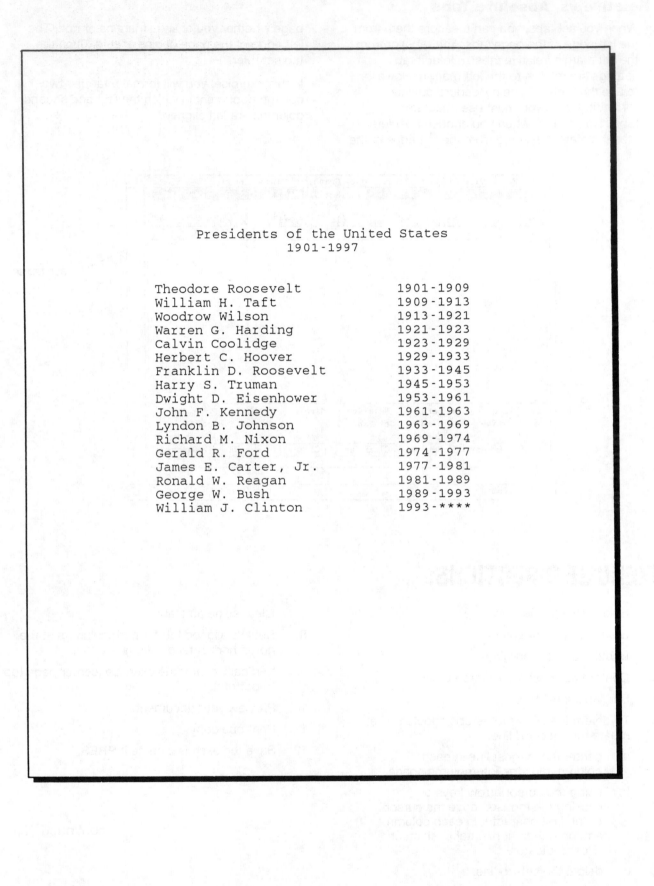

```
              Presidents of the United States
                        1901-1997

     Theodore Roosevelt           1901-1909
     William H. Taft              1909-1913
     Woodrow Wilson               1913-1921
     Warren G. Harding            1921-1923
     Calvin Coolidge              1923-1929
     Herbert C. Hoover            1929-1933
     Franklin D. Roosevelt        1933-1945
     Harry S. Truman              1945-1953
     Dwight D. Eisenhower         1953-1961
     John F. Kennedy              1961-1963
     Lyndon B. Johnson            1963-1969
     Richard M. Nixon             1969-1974
     Gerald R. Ford               1974-1977
     James E. Carter, Jr.         1977-1981
     Ronald W. Reagan             1981-1989
     George W. Bush               1989-1993
     William J. Clinton           1993-****
```

TO SET TAB STYLES

Shift + F8, L, T

1. Place cursor at location in document for tab change.

2. Click on <u>L</u>ayout .... [Alt] + [L]

3. Click on Ta<u>b</u> Set .... [B]

4. Click on how tabs are to be measured:

   - Absolute

   - Relative

5. Clear desired tab settings:

   - Move to desired setting and

     Click "Clear One"
     or press Del ....*Clear One* or [Del]
     to clear one

   or

   - Click on "Clear All" ....*Clear All* to remove all tabs

   or

   - Press Ctrl + End .... [Ctrl] + [End] to clear tabs to right of cursor.

6. Use cursor directional keys to move cursor to desired location, or use mouse to click on desired location on tab ruler to set tab.

7. Click on a Tab Type or press first letter of tab type:

   Left .... [L]

   <u>R</u>ight .... [R]

   <u>C</u>enter .... [C]

   De<u>c</u>imal .... [D]

   To include dot leaders between tabs:

   - Type a period (.) over the new or existing tab position. (The tab type will appear in reverse video.)

8. Repeat steps 6-7 for each desired tab set.

9. Click on OK and Close until you return to document .... [↵], [↵]

TABULAR COLUMNS: WITH DOT LEADERS

NOTES:

- In this exercise, you will format a tabular three-column document in which the first column has a left-aligned tab set, the second column has a decimal tab with a preceding dot leader, and the third column has a right-aligned tab set.

- A dot leader is a series of dots that connect one column to another to keep the reader's eye focused. You can turn on dot leaders and insert a row of dots when you press Tab. (See keystrokes in Exercise 86.)

- Use the method outlined in Exercise 86 to create a set-up line. To determine the placement of a

decimal tab, move your cursor to the location of the decimal and check the Pos indicator on the status line. For a right-aligned tab, move your cursor just past the last character in the second column and check the "Pos" indicator. On the tab ruler press "D" to indicate a decimal tab, "R" to indicate a right-aligned tab set, and press (.) on the "D" to set a preceding dot leader.

- After all tab settings are made, use the tab key to advance to each column. The dot leaders will automatically appear between the first and second columns.

EXERCISE DIRECTIONS:

1. Select Text Mode view.
2. Start with a clear screen.
3. Use the default margins.
4. Set "absolute" tabs.
5. Create a "set-up line":

   a. center the longest line in each column, plus the intercolumn space (leave 8 spaces between each column).

   b. Move the cursor to the first character in the first column and note its horizontal position; move the cursor to the decimal point and note its position; move the cursor to the last character in the second column and note its position.

   c. delete the "set-up" line.

6. Clear all default tabs.
7. Set a left-aligned tab for the left column, a decimal tab with a dot leader for the second column, and a right-aligned tab with a dot leader for the third column at the noted positions.
8. Vertically center the exercise (center page top to bottom).
9. Preview your document.
10. Print one copy.
11. Save the exercise; name it **WAGES.**

```
                    RAPID MESSENGER SERVICE
             EMPLOYEE HOURLY WAGES AND TOTAL EARNINGS
                            FOR 1994


Charles Palenlogis  . . .   $10.50   . . $24,500
Gina Lombardi   . . . . . .   7.80    . .  26,876
Robin M. Alter  . . . . . .   9.25    . . . 9,876
Jose Hernandez  . . . . . .   8.50    . .  18,450
Seung Kim   . . . . . . . .   7.50    . .  22,988
```

TABLES: CREATING A TABLE STRUCTURE

NOTES:

- The **Table** feature allows you to organize information into columns and rows without using tabs or tab settings.

- A table consists of rows, which run horizontally and are identified by number (1, 2, 3, etc.), and columns, which run vertically and are identified by letter (A, B, C, etc.). The rows and columns intersect to form empty boxes, called "cells." Note an example below of a table with 3 rows and three columns.

- Text and/or numbers are entered into the "cells" after you have defined the "structure" of your table—that is, how many columns and rows you will require for your table.

Creating the Table Structure

- The table structure is created by accessing Tables, Create from the Layout main menu.

- When the Create Table Dialog box appears, you must indicate how many columns and rows you plan to use in your table.

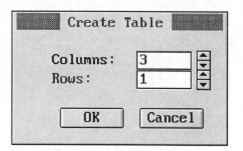

- WordPerfect automatically calculates the space between the document's left and right margins, and formats the column widths to fill all available space between those margins.

- WordPerfect allows you to create up to 32 columns and 32,765 rows. The exercises in this text will not require you to use anywhere near that capacity.

Moving the Cursor in a Table

- The cursor moves in a table the same way it moves in a document. You may use the mouse to click in the desired cell or you may use keystrokes to move around the cells (see keystrokes p. 250).

- If there is no text in a cell, the arrow keys move the cursor from cell to cell; otherwise, the arrow keys will move the cursor through text in the cell.

- Use the Tab key to move one cell to the right.

- When the cursor is in a table cell, the status line will indicate the cell location by displaying the cell's column letter and row number (example: A1).

Entering Text in a Table

- As you enter text in a table cell, the cell expands downward to accommodate the text. *Use the tab key to advance from one cell to the next. Do not press ENTER at the end of the row; use the tab key to advance to the next row.*

- Text may be aligned left (the default) aligned right, or center in an individual cell using the same alignment procedures learned previously. Aligning text in a column requires a different procedure and will be covered in the next exercise.

Editing a Table

- After the table is created, you may edit it to add or delete columns and rows, change format and fonts of table text, modify lines and borders, change column widths, etc. Editing a table will be covered in later lessons.

- While the table appears with grid lines, you may remove them later during the edit phase.

- In this exercise you will create a table which contains 2 columns and 9 rows. Be sure to center the title before using the table feature. In a later exercise, you will adjust the column widths and remove the grid lines to make this table more visually appealing.

EXERCISE DIRECTIONS:

1. Use Graphics Mode view.
2. Start with a clear screen.
3. Use the default margins.
4. Center the title lines; return three times.
5. Create the table shown on the right using 2 columns and 9 rows.
6. Center the first column heading within the cell (Shift + F6); press tab; center the second column heading within the cell.

NOTE: A column heading should be centered above column text. Notice that the column heading is centered within the cell (column) width specified by WordPerfect; it is not centered above column text. This will be adjusted in a later exercise when you modify column widths.

7. Enter the remaining table text.
8. Vertically center the exercise (center top to bottom).
9. Preview your document.
10. Print one copy.
11. Save the exercise; name it **RATING.**

TO MOVE BETWEEN CELLS:

To Move:	Press:
one cell down	`Alt` + `↓`
one cell left	`Shift` + `Tab`
one cell right	`Tab`
one cell up	`Alt` + `↑`
beginning of text in cell	`Ctrl` + `Home`, `↑`
last line of text in cell	`Ctrl` + `Home`, `↓`
first cell in column	`Ctrl` + `Home`, `Home`, `↑`
last cell in column	`Ctrl` + `Home`, `Home`, `↓`
first cell in row	`Ctrl` + `Home`, `Home`, `←`
last cell in row	`Ctrl` + `Home`, `End`
first cell in table	`Ctrl` + `Home`, `Home`, `Home`, `↑`
last cell in table	`Ctrl` + `Home`, `Home`, `Home`, `↓`
to a specific cell	`Ctrl` + `Home`, *cell name (A1,B2)*
to a specific column	`Ctrl` + `Home`, *column name*
to a specific row	`Ctrl` + `Home`, *row name*
to another table	`Ctrl` + `Home`, *table name*

TO CREATE A TABLE STRUCTURE

Alt + F7, T, C, then step 4

1. Position cursor at left margin where you want table to appear.
2. Click on Layout .... `Alt` + `L`
3. Click on Tables .... `T`
4. Click on Create .... `C`
5. Type desired number of columns.
6. ENTER .... `←`
7. Type desired number or rows.
8. ENTER .... `←`
9. Click on OK .... `←`
10. Click on Close .... `F7`

TO ENTER TEXT IN TABLES

1. Click in cell to receive text.
2. Type text.
3. Press tab
   to advance to cell to the right

   or

   use the following cursor movements:

NEC POWERMAKE PERSONAL COMPUTER
PERFORMANCE RATING

Performance	Score
CPU-intensive applications	Satisfactory
Disk-applications	Satisfactory
Multitasking performance	Excellent
File server performance	Satisfactory
Software compatibility	Excellent
Hardware compatibility	Excellent
Expandability	Good

TABLES: CREATING A TABLE STRUCTURE

NOTES:

- In this exercise you will create a table which contains 5 columns and 18 rows. Be sure to center the title before using the table feature. Note that "San Francisco" used two lines within the cell. In a later exercise, you will adjust the column widths so that the shorter columns have less space and the longer columns have more space, thereby allowing "San Francisco" to fit on one line.

EXERCISE DIRECTIONS:

1. Use Graphics Mode view.
2. Start with a clear screen.
3. Use the default margins.
4. Center the titles; return three times.
5. Create the table shown on the right using 5 columns and 18 rows.
6. Center the second, third and fourth column headings within each cell.
7. Enter the remaining table text.
8. Vertically center the exercise (center top to bottom).
9. Preview your document.
10. Print one copy.
11. Save the exercise; name it **ATBAT**.

THE WORLD SERIES
↓ 2×
WINNERS/LOSERS
1955-1970
↓ 3×

YEAR	WINNER	LEAGUE	LOSER	W-L
1955	Brooklyn	National	New York	4-3
1956	New York	American	Brooklyn	4-3
1957	Milwaukee	National	New York	4-3
1958	New York	American	Milwaukee	4-3
1959	Los Angeles	National	Chicago	4-2
1960	Pittsburgh	National	New York	4-3
1961	New York	American	Cincinnati	4-1
1962	New York	American	San Francisco	4-3
1963	Los Angeles	National	New York	4-0
1964	St. Louis	National	New York	4-3
1965	Los Angeles	National	Minnesota	4-3
1966	Baltimore	American	Los Angeles	4-0
1967	St. Louis	National	Boston	4-3
1968	Detroit	American	St. Louis	4-3
1969	New York	National	Baltimore	4-1
1970	Baltimore	American	Cincinnati	4-1

TABLES: ALIGNING TEXT

NOTES:

- In the previous two exercises, you centered text within an individual cell for the column headings. In addition to aligning text in an individual **cell**, WordPerfect allows you to specify a text alignment option for a **column**, for a **row** or for the entire table. You may align text left, center, right, left and right (full), or at a decimal either while creating the table or afterwards.

- Alignment options are made through the Table Edit Dialog box which appears when you create your initial table structure.

- To access this dialog box after the structure is created, select <u>T</u>able <u>E</u>dit from the <u>L</u>ayout main menu.

- To affect alignment in a column, click on "Column" in the Table Edit dialog box; then, click on a desired alignment option in the "Column Format" dialog box.

- In this exercise, you will *right*-align the text in column B while you are creating the table structure.

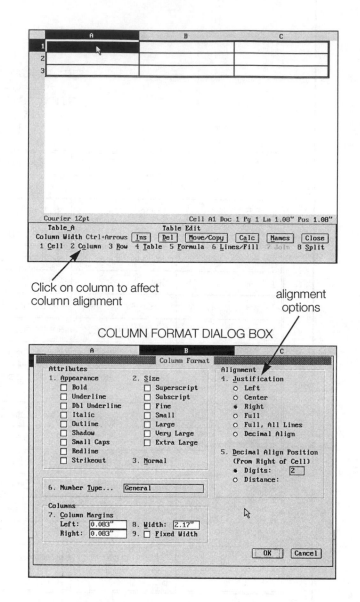

Click on column to affect column alignment

alignment options

COLUMN FORMAT DIALOG BOX

EXERCISE DIRECTIONS:

1. Use Graphics Mode view.
2. Start with a clear screen.
3. Use the default margins.
4. Center the title; return 3 times.
5. Create the table shown on the right using 2 columns and 9 rows and right-aligning text in column B.
6. Vertically center the exercise (center page top to bottom).
7. Preview your document.
8. Print one copy.
9. Save the exercise; name it **PLANET.**

PLANETS AND THEIR DISTANCE FROM THE SUN
(In Miles)

Mercury	36,000,000
Venus	67,230,000
Earth	92,960,000
Mars	141,700,000
Jupiter	483,700,000
Saturn	885,200,000
Uranus	1,781,000,000
Neptune	2,788,000,000
Pluto	3,660,000,000

TO ALIGN TEXT WITHIN CELLS, COLUMNS OR TABLE

While creating table

1. Click on Layout .... `Alt` + `L`
2. Click on Tables .... `T`
3. Click on Create .... `C`
4. Type desired number of columns.
5. ENTER .... `↵`
6. Type desired number of rows.
7. ENTER .... `↵`
8. Position cursor in cell, column or row to receive alignment change or anywhere in table (to affect change for entire table).

9. Click on location (radio button) to be affected:
   Cell .... `C`
   Column .... `O`
   Row .... `R`
   Table .... `T`
10. Click on a justification (alignment) option: .... `J`
   Left .... `L`
   Center .... `C`
   Right .... `R`
   Full .... `F`
   Full, All lines .... `A`
   Decimal align .... `D`

11. ENTER .... `↵`
12. Click on Close .... `F7`

After creating table

1. Position cursor in cell, column or row to receive alignment change or anywhere in table (to affect change for entire table. .... `Del`
2. Click on Layout .... `Alt` + `L`
3. Click on Tables .... `T`
4. Click on Edit .... `E`
5. Follow steps 9-12 above.

255

TABLES: ALIGNING TEXT

NOTES:

- In this exercise, you will decimal-align text in column B and right-align text in column C while creating the table structure. When selecting a decimal alignment option, you must indicate the position, either in decimal places, or a distance from the right of the cell where the decimal will be placed. The default is set to "2".

EXERCISE DIRECTIONS:

1. Use Graphics Mode view.
2. Start with a clear screen.
3. Use the default margins.
4. Center the title; return 3 times.
5. Create the table shown on the right using 3 columns and 5 rows. Decimal-align column B text and right-align column C text.
6. Vertically center the exercise (center page top to bottom).
7. Print one copy.
8. Save the exercise; name it **RMS.**

RAPID MESSENGER SERVICE
EMPLOYEE HOURLY WAGES AND TOTAL EARNINGS
FOR 1991

Charles Palenlogis	$10.50	$14,500
Gina Abrams	7.80	16,876
Robin M. Rahmin	9.25	8,876
George Torres	8.50	10,450
Hudson Giles	7.50	12,988

TABLES: TEXT ALIGNMENT

NOTES:

- Since columns A and D in this exercise contain text that is considerably shorter than the column headings, it would be visually more attractive to center the text in those columns.

- In this exercise, you will create the table structure, then edit it to center-align columns A and D.

EXERCISE DIRECTIONS:

1. Use Graphics Mode view.
2. Start with a clear screen.
3. Use the default margins.
4. Center the title; return two times; center the subtitle; return three times.
5. Create the table shown on the right. Determine the columns and rows needed.
6. Vertically center the exercise.
7. Preview your document.
8. Print one copy.
9. Save the exercise; name it **PURCHASE.**
10. Edit the table.
11. Center-align columns A and D.
12. Print one copy.
13. Close your file; save the changes.

MIDDLETOWN HIGH SCHOOL

SPRING SUPPLY ORDER
199-

CATALOG NUMBER	QUANTITY	DESCRIPTION	UNIT PRICE
23298	10 boxes	Staplers	4.24
3434D	12 boxes	Paper Clips	1.25
4D212	12 each	Blotters	5.00
56721	10 reams	Memo Pads	9.48
90-4P	12 boxes	Disks	7.88
T99-9	10 boxes	Markers	8.65
229-1	50 boxes	Chalk	1.10

TO ALIGN TEXT WITHIN CELLS, COLUMNS OR TABLES

After creating table

1. Position cursor in cell, column or row to receive alignment change or anywhere in table (to affect change for entire table).

2. Click on Layout .... `Alt` + `L`

3. Click on Tables .... `T`

4. Click on Edit .... `E`

5. Click on location (radio button) to be affected:

   Cell .... `C`

   Column .... `O`

   Row .... `R`

   Table .... `T`

6. Click on justification (alignment) option: .... `J`

   Left .... `L`

   Center .... `C`

   Right .... `R`

   Full .... `F`

   Full, All lines .... `A`

   Decimal align .... `D`

7. ENTER .... `↵`

8. Click on Close .... `F7`

TABLES: INSERTING TABS

NOTES:

- In this exercise, the text in column B and C is considerably shorter than the column headings. Like Exercise 92, it would be visually more attractive to center the text in those columns. However, since the text in column two contains decimals and the text in column C requires right justification, using the center alignment method learned earlier would produce the following result:

	A	B	C
1	NAME OF STOCK	PURCHASE PRICE	NO. SHARES PURCHASED
2	R & L	$ 60.00	100
3	TECH LABS	45.35	80
4	ASTEC IND.	14.85	250
5	X-MATION	2.50	800
6	IDM	50.00	8
7	NORDAK	101.44	1,000

- To properly center the text in column B at the decimal point, and center and right align column C text within the table cell in this exercise, it is necessary to set decimal and right alignment **tabs** in _each cell_ where this alignment is desired. Since setting a tab in each cell is time consuming, it would be more efficient to use a tabular column rather than a table with inserted tabs for a longer problem of this type. To illustrate inserting tabs, however, this short exercise is presented.

- To insert a tab within a table cell, you must press Control + A, Tab. You can then insert a specific tab type: left, right, center, or decimal.

EXERCISE DIRECTIONS:

1. Select Text Mode view.
2. Start with a clear screen.
3. Use the default margins.
4. Center all title lines; return three times.
5. Create the table shown on the right. Determine the column and rows needed.
6. Center (Shift + F6) "PURCHASE PRICE."
7. Set a decimal tab in each cell in column B; set a right-aligned tab in each cell in column C. Enter text as shown.
8. Vertically center the exercise.
9. Preview the exercise.
10. Print one copy.
11. Save the exercise; name it **STOCK.**

```
                    PORTFOLIO OF
                 REBECCA N. NARDINO
                       As Of
                   January 1994
```

NAME OF STOCK	PURCHASE PRICE	NO. SHARES PURCHASED
R & L	$ 60.00	100
TECH LABS	45.35	80
ASTEC IND.	14.85	250
X-MATION	2.50	800
IDM	50.00	8
NORDAK INDUSTRIES	101.44	1,000

TO INSERT TABS WITHIN A TABLE CELL

- Press Ctrl + A,
  then TAB.................... `Ctrl` + `A` , `Tab`

To Insert a:	Press:
left tab	`Home` , `Tab`
right tab	`Home` , `Alt` + `F6`
center tab	`Home` , `Shift` + `F6`
decimal tab	`Home` , `Ctrl` + `F6`

TABLES: INSERTING AND DELETING COLUMNS AND ROWS

NOTES:

- One or more rows and/or columns may be inserted or deleted from a table. When a column or row is deleted, the contents of that column or row is also deleted.

- Rows and columns may be inserted and deleted by accessing the Table Edit dialog box (Alt + L, T, E):

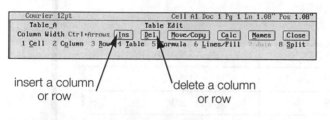

insert a column or row / delete a column or row

- To insert a column or row, click on "Ins"; the "Insert" dialog box will appear.

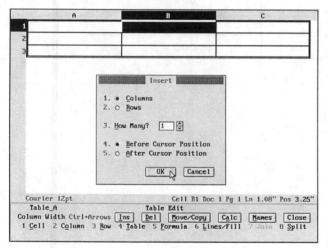

To delete a column or row, click on "Del"; the "Delete" dialog box will appear:

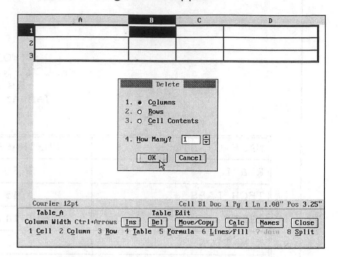

- It is within these dialog boxes that you indicate whether you wish to insert/delete columns or rows and how many. Follow keystrokes below carefully.

- In this exercise, you will insert one column and one row in a previously created table.

EXERCISE DIRECTIONS:

1. Select Text Mode view.
2. Open **RATING.**
3. Insert one row as shown.
4. Insert one column as shown.
5. Delete the last row (Expandability...).
6. Enter the new column/row text.
7. Print one copy.
8. Close your file; save the changes.

NEC POWERMAKE PERSONAL COMPUTER
PERFORMANCE RATING

insert column

insert w {

Performance	Score	Rater
CPU-intensive applications	Satisfactory	R. Alter
Disk-applications	Satisfactory	J. Sanchez
Multitasking performance	Excellent	M. Salazar
File server performance	Satisfactory	R. Alter
Communications	Excellent	J. Sanchez
Software compatibility	Excellent	R. Alter
Hardware compatibility	Excellent	M. Salazar
Expandability	Good	M. Salazar

{ *delete row*

TO INSERT ROWS/COLUMNS
Ctrl + Ins (insert row)

1. Open the file to be edited.
2. Click on Layout .... Alt + L
3. Click on Table .... T
4. Click on Edit................................. E
5. Click on Ins (insert)...................... I
6. Place cursor one *row above or below* or *one column* to the right or left of where insert should occur.
7. Click on insert option:
   Columns C
   Rows.................................. R
8. Click on How Many? .... H
9. Type number of columns or rows to be inserted.

To insert a column to the right of the last column:
   • Click on "After Cursor Position."
10. Click on OK .... ←
11. Click on Close F7

TO DELETE ROWS/COLUMNS
Ctrl + Del (delete row)

1. Open the file to be edited.
2. Click on Layout .... Alt + L
3. Click on Table .... T
4. Click on Edit................................. E
5. Click on Del (delete)...................... D
6. Place cursor in row or column to be deleted.
7. Click on delete option:
   Columns .... U
   Rows.................................. R
   Cell Contents.................... C
8. Click on How Many?.................... H
9. Type number of columns or rows to be deleted.
10. Click on OK .... ←
11. Click on Close F7

TABLES: INSERTING AND DELETING COLUMNS AND ROWS

NOTES:

- In this exercise, you will insert two rows and one column and delete one row.

- Note the illustration on the right. Once the new column is inserted (for social security numbers), column A becomes shorter and truncates the names. In the next exercise, you will learn to adjust column width for this document so that column A has more space and columns C and D have less space.

EXERCISE DIRECTIONS:

1. Select Text Mode view.
2. Open **RMS.**
3. Insert two rows as shown.
4. Insert one column as shown.
5. Enter the new column/row text.
6. Delete the second row (Gina Abrams information).
7. Print one copy.
8. Close the file; save the changes.

RAPID MESSENGER SERVICE
EMPLOYEE HOURLY WAGES AND TOTAL EARNINGS
FOR 1991

delete row

A	B	C	D
Charles Palenlogis	129-76-9999	$10.50	$14,500
~~Gina Abrams~~	~~222-22-9876~~	~~7.80~~	~~16,876~~
Robin M. Rahmin	555-99-2323	9.25	8,876
George Torres	210-34-7878	8.50	10,450
Hudson Giles	908-76-7654	7.50	12,988
Julie Marciano	138-90-8888	9.10	17,127
Calvin Verioski	333-98-1111	11.00	19,212

insert rows

insert column

TABLES: ADJUSTING COLUMN WIDTH; HORIZONTAL CENTERING OF TABLE

NOTES:

- WordPerfect sets column widths in a table to spread out evenly between the margins whether your table contains 2 or 10 columns.

- The column width of one or more columns in a table may be adjusted using the Table Editor. It allows you to shorten columns that have too much space and widen columns that require additional space.

- Two methods are available to adjust column width. You can use Ctrl + left arrow (to make column narrower) and Ctrl + right arrow (to make column wider) to adjust the widths one character at a time. Or, you can set the widths using a specific measurement in the Column Format dialog box.

- Using the Ctrl + arrow keys allows you to immediately see the width adjustments and their effect on the entire table. For ease of reading, leave at least .5" of space between columns. You can leave more space if you desire.

- After adjusting column widths, the new table defaults to the left margin. To return it to the center, you must specify "Center" as the "Table Position" in the Table Format Dialog box:

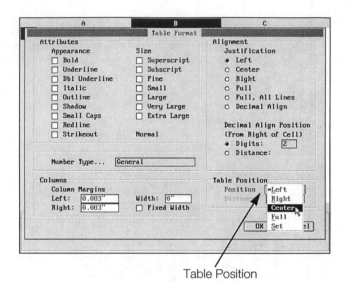

Table Position

- You may also position the table Right, Full or a Set position from the left margin.

- In this exercise, columns A and B require additional space and need to be widened, while columns C and D require less space and need to be shortened. You will make the necessary adjustments.

EXERCISE DIRECTIONS:

1. Select Graphics Mode view.
2. Start with a clear screen.
3. Open **RMS.**
4. Adjust column widths in all columns; leave approximately .5" between columns.
5. Reposition the table so it is centered horizontally.
6. Preview the exercise.
7. Print one copy.
8. Close the file; save the changes.

RAPID MESSENGER SERVICE
EMPLOYEE HOURLY WAGES AND TOTAL EARNINGS
FOR 1993

⟵⟶ ⟵⟶ ⟶ ⟵ ⟶ ⟵

Charles Palenlogis	129-76-9999		$10.50		$14,500
Robin M. Rahmin	555-99-2323		9.25		8,876
George Torres	210-34-7878		8.50		10,450
Hudson Giles	908-76-7654		7.50		12,988
Julie Marciano	138-90-8888		9.10		17,127
Calvin Verioski	333-98-1111		11.00		19,212

TO ADJUST COLUMN WIDTHS

procedure #1

1. Place cursor in the table.
2. Click on Layout .... Alt + L
3. Click on Table .... T
4. Click on Edit .... E

To make the column narrower:

5. Move cursor to column to be made narrower.
6. Press Ctrl + ← repeatedly until column is desired size.

To make the column wider:

7. Move cursor to column to be made wider.
8. Press Ctrl + → repeatedly until column is desired size.

procedure #2

1. Follow steps 1-4 above.
2. Place cursor in column to be changed.
3. Click on Column .... O
4. Click on Width .... W
5. Type desired width of column.
6. Click on OK .... ⏎

TO HORIZONTALLY POSITION TABLES

1. Follow steps 1-4 above (procedure 1)
2. Click on Table. .... T
3. Click on Table Position .... P
4. Click on desired position:
   Left L
   Center C
   Full .... F
   Set .... S
5. Click on OK .... ⏎
6. Click on Close F7 **267**

TABLES: ADJUSTING COLUMN WIDTH; HORIZONTAL CENTERING OF TABLE

NOTES:

- In this exercise you will adjust the column widths of two previously created documents. In the first document, use Ctrl + arrow keys to adjust column widths; in the second document, set the width of the column according to the directions in the exercise. You will re-position each table so they are centered horizontally on the page.

EXERCISE DIRECTIONS:

1. Select Graphics Mode view.
2. Start with a clear screen.
3. Open **ATBAT.**
4. Center-align columns A, C and E.
5. Adjust column widths in all columns; leave approximately .5" between columns.
6. Reposition the table so it is centered horizontally.
7. Preview the exercise.
8. Print one copy.
9. Close the file; save the changes.

10. Open **PLANET.**
11. Change column A width to 1"; change column B width to 1.75".

NOTE: Using the column widths indicated, you will be leaving approximately 1" between columns. This makes a two-column table more readable.

12. Reposition the table so it is centered horizontally.
13. Preview the exercise.
14. Print one copy.
15. Close your file; save the changes.

ATBAT (Before)

THE WORLD SERIES

WINNERS/LOSERS
1955-1970

YEAR	WINNER	LEAGUE	LOSER	W-L
1955	Brooklyn	National	New York	4-3
1956	New York	American	Brooklyn	4-3
1957	Milwaukee	National	New York	4-3
1958	New York	American	Milwaukee	4-3
1959	Los Angeles	National	Chicago	4-2
1960	Pittsburgh	National	New York	4-3
1961	New York	American	Cincinnati	4-1
1962	New York	American	San Francisco	4-3
1963	Los Angeles	National	New York	4-0
1964	St. Louis	National	New York	4-3
1965	Los Angeles	National	Minnesota	4-3
1966	Baltimore	American	Los Angeles	4-0
1967	St. Louis	National	Boston	4-3
1968	Detroit	American	St. Louis	4-3
1969	New York	National	Baltimore	4-1
1970	Baltimore	American	Cincinnati	4-1

ATBAT (After)

THE WORLD SERIES

WINNERS/LOSERS
1955-1970

YEAR	WINNER	LEAGUE	LOSER	W-L
1955	Brooklyn	National	New York	4-3
1956	New York	American	Brooklyn	4-3
1957	Milwaukee	National	New York	4-3
1958	New York	American	Milwaukee	4-3
1959	Los Angeles	National	Chicago	4-2
1960	Pittsburgh	National	New York	4-3
1961	New York	American	Cincinnati	4-1
1962	New York	American	San Francisco	4-3
1963	Los Angeles	National	New York	4-0
1964	St. Louis	National	New York	4-3
1965	Los Angeles	National	Minnesota	4-3
1966	Baltimore	American	Los Angeles	4-0
1967	St. Louis	National	Boston	4-3
1968	Detroit	American	St. Louis	4-3
1969	New York	National	Baltimore	4-1
1970	Baltimore	American	Cincinnati	4-1

PLANET (Before)

PLANETS AND THEIR DISTANCE FROM THE SUN
(In Miles)

Mercury	36,000,000
Venus	67,230,000
Earth	92,960,000
Mars	141,700,000
Jupiter	483,700,000
Saturn	885,200,000
Uranus	1,781,000,000
Neptune	2,788,000,000
Pluto	3,660,000,000

PLANET (After)

PLANETS AND THEIR DISTANCE FROM THE SUN
(In Miles)

Mercury	36,000,000
Venus	67,230,000
Earth	92,960,000
Mars	141,700,000
Jupiter	483,700,000
Saturn	885,200,000
Uranus	1,781,000,000
Neptune	2,788,000,000
Pluto	3,660,000,000

TABLES: LINES, BORDERS, FILLS

NOTES:

Lines and Borders

- A **border** is a line that surrounds either a cell or the table. A **line** divides the columns and rows to form the cells.

- By default, tables print with a double line around the outer edge (the table border) and single lines that divide columns and rows (table lines). Note the example below:

- WordPerfect allows you to change the type of border line used around a table and the type of line used between columns and rows (table lines).

- WordPerfect provides you with several line types: single, double, dashed, dotted, thick, extra thick or none. Note the table below which uses "thick" border lines and "dashed" table lines:

- You may also change the line type of individual lines in specific cells. Changing the line type of individual lines is an effective way to emphasize data within a cell. Note the table below in which the bottom and right lines of cell A1 are "thick" and the top, left and right lines of cell B2 are "double," while the bottom line of that cell is "thin/thick." All lines around cell C3 are "thick."

	A	B	C
1	bottom and right lines: thick		
2		top, left and right lines: double; bottom line: thin/thick	
3			all lines around this cell are thick

- There are many variations you can experiment with to emphasize data or make your table visually appealing. The table below was created with an "extra thick border" and no table lines. Using extra thick borders caused some of the text to be hidden. Note the effect:

cell A1	cell A2	cell A3
cell B1	cell B2	cell B3
cell C1	cell C2	cell C3

- To create the effect shown above without hiding text, enter one return before and after the table text, and center or move column so text aligning at the left margin will not be hidden by the border:

cell A1	cell A2	cell A3
cell B1	cell B2	cell B3
cell C1	cell C1	cell C3

- Or, you may choose to eliminate all the lines, making the table look like a tabular column:

NAME OF STOCK	PURCHASE PRICE	NO. SHARES PURCHASED
R & L	$ 60.00	100
TECH LABS	45.35	80
ASTEC IND.	14.85	250
X-MATION	2.50	800
IDM	50.00	8
NORDAK INDUSTRIES	101.44	1,000

- When you remove all lines, the table appears to be double spaced; it is not. While table lines are not visible, they are still part of the table structure. Since the table accommodates the lines, the text appears double spaced.

Fills (Shading)

- The "Fill" feature allows you to emphasize a cell, a row, a column, or a group of cells by shading it.

- "Gray" shading options are indicated as percents of black:

10% shaded fill	20% shaded fill	30% shaded fill
30% shaded fill	40% shaded fill	50% shaded fill

- While color shading options are available for *lines*, you need a color printer to output color.

- Line types and fills may be changed in the Table Edit dialog box by clicking on "Lines/Fill."

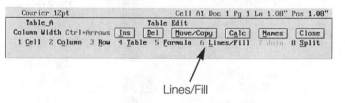

Lines/Fill

- Changes may be made during the table creation phrase or after creating the table. Note the keystroke procedures outlined on the next page.

EXERCISE DIRECTIONS:

1. Select Graphics Mode view.
2. Start with a clear screen.
3. Open **STOCK**.
4. Center align "NAME OF STOCK" within the cell.
5. Edit the table as follows:
   - Place a double line on the bottom and right of cells in the first row. (The top lines are already double because of the default double-line border.)
   - Use a 10% fill to shade the rows as shown.

6. Enter the new text below the table as indicated.
7. Preview the exercise.
8. Print one copy.
9. Close your file; save the changes.

continued . . .

TO CHANGE BORDERS AND LINES

For entire table

1. Place cursor in table.
2. Click on Layout .... `Alt` + `L`
3. Click on Table .... `T`
4. Click on Edit....................... `E`
5. Click on Lines/Fill.............. `L`
6. • Click on Default Line................ `D`
   to change *table lines*

   • Click on Line Style .... `L`

   • Highlight desired
   line style.................. `↑` `↓`

   • Click on Select .... `↵`

   • Click on
   Close twice................. `↵` , `↵`

   or

   • Click on Border/Fill .... `E`
   to change *border lines*

   • Click on Border Style............... `B`

   • Highlight desired border
   style arrow keys

   • Click on Select..................... `↵`

   • Click on OK............................. `↵`

   • Click on Close........................ `↵`

7. Press F7 to exit Table Edit
   and return
   to document screen .... `F7`

For Current Cell or Block of Cells:

1. Follow steps 1-4 above.
2. Place cursor in cell to be affected.

   or

   Highlight cell or block
   of cells to be
   affected...... `Alt` + `F4` `→` `←` `↑` `↓`
3. Click on Lines/Fill........................ `L`
4. Click on line to be affected

   Left................................. `L`

   Right .... `R`

   Top................................. `T`

   Bottom.............................. `B`

   Inside .... `I` (all cell sides)

   Outside .... `O` (all cell sides)

   NOTE: *When changing all sides of a*
   single cell, the "inside"
   option will have no effect.

5. Highlight desired
   line type .... `↑` `↓`
6. Click on Select............................ `↵`
7. Click on Close............................. `↵`
8. Press F7 to exit Table Edit and
   return to document screen.......... `F7`

TO USE FILLS (SHADING)

1. Follow steps 1-5 above ("for
   entire table").
2. Place cursor in first cell to
   be shaded

   or

   Highlight block of
   cells to be
   shaded...... `Alt` + `F4` `→` `←` `↑` `↓`
3. Click on Lines/Fill.................... `L`
4. Click on Fill............................. `F`
5. Click on Fill Style......................... `Y`
6. Highlight desired
   fill style................................. `↑` `↓`
7. Click on Select .... `↵`
8. Click on OK.............................. `↵`
9. Click on Close............................ `↵`

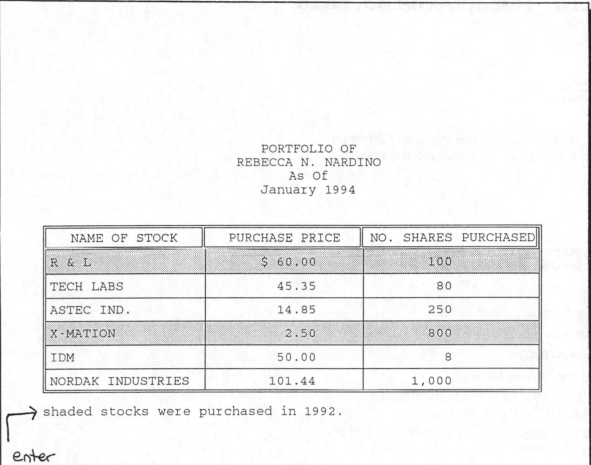

```
                    PORTFOLIO OF
                REBECCA N. NARDINO
                       As Of
                   January 1994
```

NAME OF STOCK	PURCHASE PRICE	NO. SHARES PURCHASED
R & L	$ 60.00	100
TECH LABS	45.35	80
ASTEC IND.	14.85	250
X-MATION	2.50	800
IDM	50.00	8
NORDAK INDUSTRIES	101.44	1,000

shaded stocks were purchased in 1992.

enter
new
text

TABLES: LINES, BORDERS, FILLS

NOTES:

- In this exercise, you will use the Lines/Fill feature to emphasize data of a table created previously.

EXERCISE DIRECTIONS:

1. Select Graphics Mode view.
2. Start with a clear screen.
3. Open **ATBAT.**
4. Edit the table as follows:
   - Use a 10% fill to shade the "National" LEAGUE rows as shown.
   - Use a thick line on the bottom and right of cells indicated.
   - Change the table border to a single line.
5. Preview the exercise.
6. Print one copy.
7. Close your file; save the changes.

THE WORLD SERIES

WINNERS/LOSERS
1955-1970

YEAR	WINNER	LEAGUE	LOSER	W-L
1955	Brooklyn	National	New York	4-3
1956	New York	American	Brooklyn	4-3
1957	Milwaukee	National	New York	4-3
1958	New York	American	Milwaukee	4-3
1959	Los Angeles	National	Chicago	4-2
1960	Pittsburgh	National	New York	4-3
1961	New York	American	Cincinnati	4-1
1962	New York	American	San Francisco	4-3
1963	Los Angeles	National	New York	4-0
1964	St. Louis	National	New York	4-3
1965	Los Angeles	National	Minnesota	4-3
1966	Baltimore	American	Los Angeles	4-0
1967	St. Louis	National	Boston	4-3
1968	Detroit	American	St. Louis	4-3
1969	New York	National	Baltimore	4-1
1970	Baltimore	American	Cincinnati	4-1

TABLES: LINES, BORDERS, FILLS

NOTES:

- In this exercise, you will create a table with 3 columns and 21 rows for an income statement. You will modify column width and use the Line/Fill feature to emphasize data.

- Remember, after you change column width, your table will left align horizontally. Reposition it so it is horizontally centered.

- An income statement shows the net income or loss earned by a business during a particular period.

EXERCISE DIRECTIONS:

1. Select Graphics Mode view.

2. Start with a clear screen.

3. Set .5" left and right margins.

4. Center all title lines; return three times.

5. Create the table shown on the right using 3 columns and 21 rows.

6. Change column A width to 4.5". (You will adjust columns B and C widths later.)

7. Right-align text in columns B and C.

8. Enter column text. Use Ctrl + A, Tab to tab text in the first column.

9. Edit the table as follows:

- Shorten columns B and C by 4 spaces.

- Reposition the table so it is centered horizontally.

- Create a dotted border around the table; remove the table lines.

- Use a 10% fill to shade the rows as shown.

- Use a double line on all sides of the cell for the Net Income amount as shown.

10. Vertically center the exercise.

11. Preview the exercise.

12. Print one copy.

13. Save the exercise; name it **IS**.

PAUL B'S CARD SHOP
INCOME STATEMENT
For the Month Ended April 30, 199-

Revenue:

Sales	25,700	
Less Sales Returns and Allowances	700	
Net Sales		25,000

Cost of Merchandise Sold:

Merchandise Inventory, April 1	50,250	
Purchases	9,250	
Merchandise Available for Sale	59,500	
Less Merchandise Inventory, April 30	40,000	
Cost of Merchandise Sold		19,500
Gross Profit On Sales		9,000

Operating Expenses:

Salaries	4,000	
Rent	1,666	
Taxes	400	
Utilities	345	
Advertising	500	
Depreciation on Equipment	210	
Insurance	65	
Total Operating Expenses		7,186

Net Income: 1,014

TABLES: FORMATTING WITHIN A DOCUMENT

NOTES:

- In this exercise, you will create a memorandum with an inserted table.

- When a table is inserted within a document, the table should appear indented on both sides of the paragraph margins. This gives the table more emphasis.

- Because tables fill the available space between margins, you will need to make your margins narrower before creating the table to "indent" it. After the table is complete, restore your margins to their original setting.

- While the table text appears to be double spaced in this exercise, it is not. Remember, table lines are still part of the table structure even though they have been removed. Since the table accommodates the lines, the text appears double spaced.

EXERCISE DIRECTIONS:

1. Select Graphics Mode view.
2. Start with a clear screen.
3. Use the default margins.
4. Create memo on the right as shown. Begin on Ln 2".
5. Change margins to 1.5" before creating the table.
6. Create a table using 2 columns and 10 rows.
7. Center each column heading within its cell; enter remaining table text.

8. Edit the table as follows:
   - Adjust column width: shorten column A by 3 spaces, and widen column B to fit Alan E. Ennis' title on one line.
   - Remove all table lines.
   - Reposition the table so it is horizontally centered.
9. Reset margins to the default.
10. Preview the exercise.
11. Print one copy.
12. Save the file; name it **OFFICER.**

TO: Management Vice Presidents

FROM: Carter Burlington

SUBJECT: Executive Officers of Technology, Inc.

DATE: Today's

The directors and executive officers of Technology, Inc. are
listed in the table below. Brief summaries of their business
experience are outlined in a report that will be forwarded to you
by the end of next week.

NAME	POSITION
Stephen Richardson	President and CEO
Alan E. Ennis	Vice Chair, Bd. of Directors
Nicholas Stannis	Executive VP and CFO
Pricilla Carroll	VP--Director of Sales
Judy M. Blane	VP--Director of Marketing
Gladys R. Grafe	Director
Kenneth Newman, Ph.D.	Director, Consultant
Donna Wolenski	Director
Norman Miller	Director

Mr. Richardson and Ms. Brown are also members of the Executive
Committee, while Mr. Miller and Ms. Blane are members of the
Audit Committee.

yo

TABLES: FORMATTING WITHIN A DOCUMENT

NOTES:

- In this exercise you will create a letter with an inserted table. All *column headings* are to be centered within the cell (Shift + F6); the *column text* that is shorter than the column headings are to be center-aligned in the column (use Table Edit).

- Type each multiple-line column heading in one cell. The cell will expand downward to accommodate the additional line.

- To make the table appear indented on both sides, you will need to make the document margins narrower before creating the table.

EXERCISE DIRECTIONS:

1. Select Graphics Mode view.
2. Start with a clear screen.
3. Set .5" left and right margins.
4. Create the full-block letter on the right. Begin on Ln 2".
5. Reset margins to 1" before creating table.
6. Create a table using 4 columns and 7 rows.
7. Center and bold each column heading within its cell. Enter remaining table text.
8. Edit the table as follows:
   - Adjust column widths: shorten columns B and D by 3 spaces; lengthen column A by 2 spaces.
   - Center-align text in columns B, C and D.
   - Create a dashed border around the table; remove the table lines.
   - Create a dashed bottom line below row one as shown (highlight row and change "bottom line" to dashed).
   - Use a 10% fill to shade row one as shown.
   - Reposition the table so it is horizontally centered.
9. Reset margins to .5" and complete the letter.
10. Spell check.
11. Preview the exercise.
12. Print one copy.
13. Save the file; name it **WORK.**

Today's date

Mr. Avram Issey
ABC Computer Company
785 Lighthouse Road
Portland, OR 98138

Dear Mr. Issey:

Listed below is our projected delivery schedule for the items you ordered.
We agreed that it normally takes approximately six weeks from the day of
purchase for you to receive your order. We are trying to make every effort
to deliver on time.

We want you to know when shipments will be arriving so you can have someone
there to accept them.

ITEM	YOUR ORDER NO.	EXPECTED DELIVERY DATE	QUANTITY SCHEDULED
Computer Paper	7651-988	Feb. 1	220
Computer Ribbons	2787-333	May 10	130
Printers	8861-123	May 15	89
Monitors	0098-234	May 16	10
Keyboards	3450-344	June 1	108
Disk Drives	0098-777	July 1	199

If there is a problem with any of the delivery dates, please phone me as
soon as possible. We will call you several days in advance if we expect a
problem with the delivery time.

Sincerely,

Jackson Kellogg
Distribution Manager

jk/

Lesson 11 / Summary Exercise A

EXERCISE DIRECTIONS:

1. Create the "SELECTED WORD PROCESSING TERMS" below using a parallel-column format.
2. Use the default margins.
3. Begin the exercise on 1".
4. Full-justify document text.
5. Preview the exercise.
6. Print one copy.
7. Save the exercise; name it **WP.**

```
AUTOMATIC RETURN
See "Wordwrap"
BLOCK
To highlight text that will be affected by the next action.
BOILERPLATE
Standardized or repetitive text which is saved for use in
assembling documents.
BOLD PRINT
Printing of characters to look larger and darker.
CENTERING
Automatic positioning of text between margins.
DECIMAL TAB
Automatic alignment of columns of decimal figures at the decimal
point.
DOCUMENT ASSEMBLY
Combining selections from recorded text to form a new document.
FORMAT
Layout of text on a page.  Includes page size, tab and margin
settings, line spacing, type size, and text alignment.  Once the
format is set, it may be saved and used at a later time.
HARD RETURN
Pressing the Enter key at the end of the line.
HEADERS/FOOTERS
Text placed at the top (header) or bottom (footer) of each page
in a document.
INDENT
Setting a temporary left or right margin where text will align.
MERGE
Combining a standard document with a variable document to create
new documents.
SAVE
The process of saving text on media for later retrieval.
SEARCH AND REPLACE
Searching for repeated occurrences of a character string and
replacing it with another character string within a document.
WORDWRAP
Automatic placement of text on to the next line (without pressing
the Enter key) when text reaches the right margin.  Also referred
to as SOFT RETURN and AUTOMATIC RETURN.
```

EXERCISE DIRECTIONS:

1. Create the memo below, inserting the table as shown.

2. Set left and right document margins to .5"; set 1" margins for the table.

3. Begin the exercise on Ln 2.5".

4. Remove table and border lines; use a dotted border around row #1 as shown.

5. Preview the exercise.

6. Print one copy.

7. Save the exercise; name it **COURSES.**

```
TO:        GUIDANCE PERSONNEL

FROM:      Cynthia Greenskill, Chairperson

RE:        Fall Computer Offerings

DATE:      Today's

Listed below is a tentative schedule of computer classes that our
department will be offering in the fall.  Please be sure to use the correct
code when registering students for the courses listed.
```

COURSE TITLE	COURSE CODE	TIME OF CLASS	INSTRUCTOR
Database	DB3	10:00 A. M.	Winston
Spreadsheets	SS101	9:20 A. M.	Rosen
Basic	BC1	11:00 A. M.	Grande
Desktop	DTP1	12:40 P. M.	Giordano
Word Processing	WP3	1:50 P. M.	Pilgrim

```
If you have any questions regarding the above, please call me.  Preliminary
scheduling will begin on Monday of next week.

cg/
```

LESSON 12 / EXERCISES 103-108
MATH

- Calculating in Columns
- Calculating in Tables
- Using Formulas
- Copying Formulas
- Using Functions

MATH: CALCULATING IN COLUMNS

NOTES:

- WordPerfect allows you to perform calculations in tabular columns or in tables. To perform complex calculations, use the Table Math feature. To perform simple calculations (like adding a column of numbers) you may use either the columnar math or table math feature. Table math will be covered in a later lesson.

- WordPerfect's columnar math feature allows you to calculate numbers in columns and rows. (Calculating rows in columnar columns will not be covered in this book. Refer to software documentation for instruction.)

- To use the math feature, numbers must be arranged in columns which were established with tab settings.

- The math feature is accessed by selecting Math from the Tools main menu.

- WordPerfect considers all alphabetic text entered in columns to be numeric. If some of your tabular columns are alphabetic text (like the exercise shown on p. 286), you must "define" them as such in the "math definitions dialog box" (illustrated below) before you turn on the math feature. The math definitions dialog box will appear after "define" is selected.

- Note that "Columns" are indicated by A, B, C, D, etc. Below the columns is the "Column Type" designation. Note that all columns are defaulted to "N" — indicating numeric columns.

- To tell WordPerfect that the first two columns in this exercise are text, you must set columns A and B to "Text" columns before turning on the math feature.

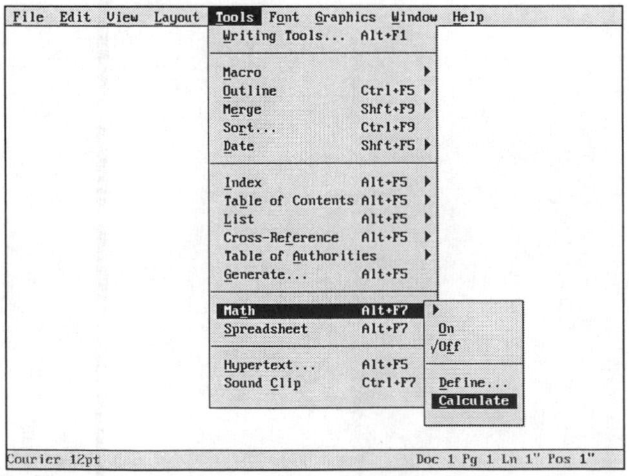

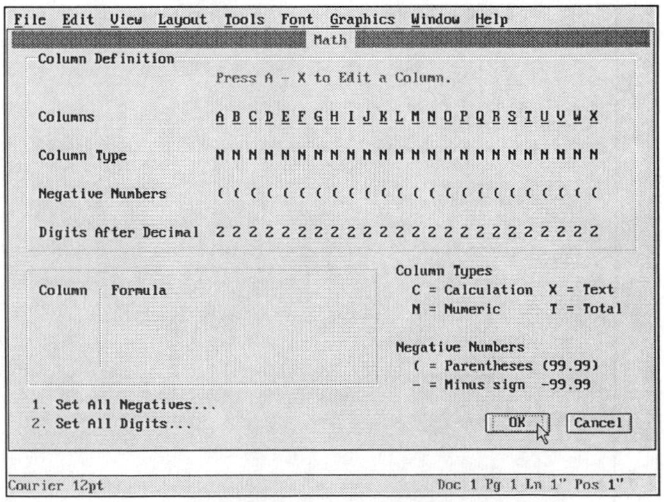

MATH DEFINITIONS DIALOG BOX

- After column types have been established in the math definitions dialog box and you have turned on the math feature, enter data into the columns *by tabbing to each column.* To calculate the column(s), tab to where the answer should appear and type a plus symbol (+). (The plus symbol will not appear on the screen.) Then, access the math feature, select "Calculate" and your answer will appear where you entered the plus (+) symbol.

```
 File  Edit  View  Layout  Tools  Font  Graphics  Window  Help
                          Writing Tools...  Alt+F1

                          Macro                    ▶
                          Outline          Ctrl+F5 ▶
                          Merge            Shft+F9 ▶
                          Sort...          Ctrl+F9
                          Date             Shft+F5 ▶

                          Index            Alt+F5  ▶
                          Table of Contents Alt+F5 ▶
                          List             Alt+F5  ▶
                          Cross-Reference  Alt+F5  ▶
                          Table of Authorities     ▶
                          Generate...      Alt+F5

                          Math             Alt+F7  ▶
                          Spreadsheet      Alt+F7  ▶   On
                                                       √Off
                          Hypertext...     Alt+F5
                          Sound Clip       Ctrl+F7      Define...
                                                        Calculate

 Courier 12pt                              Doc 1 Pg 1 Ln 1" Pos 1"
```

- The general procedures for calculating columns in this exercise are:
  1. Center the longest line in each column, plus the intercolumn space (reference line).
  2. Note where the columns begin. Set a left tab for the text columns; set a decimal tab at the decimal location for numeric columns.
  3. Delete the reference line.
  4. Define the columns.
  5. Turn on the math feature.
  6. Tab to each column and enter text/data. You will enter column headings after the math feature is turned off. Since all columns are left aligned, enter the headings at the same location above the column text.
  7. Tab to each column and enter text/data.
  8. Follow keystrokes to complete calculations.
  9. Turn off the math feature.

- In this exercise, you will create a five-column table with left-aligned column headings.

EXERCISE DIRECTIONS:

1. Select Text Mode view.
2. Start with a clear screen.
3. Use the default margins.
4. To establish tab settings, create a set-up line for the exercise shown on the right. Leave three spaces between each column.
5. Use "absolute" tabs.
6. Set left tabs for text columns and decimal tabs for numeric columns.
7. Access the math definitions dialog box; change the first two "Column Types" to "Text."
8. Enter text/data into the columns.
9. After turning off the math feature, enter column headings.
10. Total each money column.
11. Vertically center the exercise.
12. Preview the exercise.
13. Print one copy.
14. Save the exercise; name it **JUNE.**

continued . . .

```
                        MICRO ELECTRONICS
                   WEEKLY SALES BY SALESPERSON
                             JUNE


WEEK ENDING     TERRITORY     W. EMERY      A. RIVERA     J. THOMPSON

JUNE 5          EASTERN       $ 3,456.00    $ 2,345.22    $ 3,478.25
JUNE 12         WESTERN         2,455.23      5,321.95      5,190.75
JUNE 19         NORTHERN        2,100.77      4,165.20        900.87
JUNE 26         SOUTHERN        1,222.12      6,871.54        965.75

TOTALS
```

TO CALCULATE TOTAL IN COLUMNS:

Alt + F7

To define text columns:

1. Set tabs for all columns.
2. Click on Tools ....`Alt` + `T`
3. Click on Math ....`T`
4. Click on Define............................`D`
5. Click on Column letter to be defined ....**option**
6. Click on Column Type ....`T`
7. Click on Text................................`X`

8. Repeat steps 5-7 until all text columns are defined.
9. Click on OK twice..................`←`, `←`

To turn math ON:

11. Click on Tools ....`Alt` + `T`
12. Click on Math................................`T`
13. Click on On ....`O`

To calculate data:

14. TAB to each column and type data.
15. Tab to each bottom of numeric column to be calculated where answer should appear.

16. Type plus (+) ....`+`
17. Click on Tools ....`Alt` + `T`
18. Click on Math..............................`T`
19. Click on Calculate.....................`C` to display result.

To turn math OFF:

20. Click on Tools ....`Alt` + `T`
21. Click on Math..............................`T`
22. Click on Off ....`F`

MATH: CALCULATING IN COLUMNS

NOTES:

- In this exercise, you will create a four-column table with left-aligned column headings. While column B contains numbers (social security), it is considered a "text" column since the numbers will not be calculated.

EXERCISE DIRECTIONS:

1. Select Text Mode view.
2. Start with a clear screen.
3. Use the default margins.
4. To establish tab settings, create a set-up line for the exercise shown on the right. Leave three spaces between each column.
5. Use "absolute" tabs.
6. Set left tabs for text columns and decimal tabs for numeric columns.
7. Access the math definitions dialog box; change the first two "Column Types" to "Text."
8. Enter text/data into the columns.
9. After turning off the math feature, enter column headings.
10. Total each money column.
11. Vertically center the exercise.
12. Preview the exercise.
13. Print one copy.
14. Save the exercise; name it **WEEK**.

```
                   WEEKLY SALES AND SALARIES
                  FOR PART-TIME SALESPERSONS
                     Week of January 22


        NAME              SOC. SEC. #    SALES        SALARY

        Daniel Levin      129-38-9873   $1,234.00   $  685.00
        John Imperio      178-98-0000      865.99      290.00
        Rachael Simson    127-27-8888    2,775.45      888.35
        Corey Modeste     129-21-4443      553.12      578.55
        Patricia Nunez    127-32-2110      923.34      571.00
        Hubert Attale     210-32-2222      665.76      335.50

        TOTALS
```

MATH: CALCULATING IN TABLES; USING FORMULAS

NOTES:

- WordPerfect's Table Math feature allows you to perform calculations for addition, subtraction, multiplication and division, as well as calculate a subtotal, total and grand total within a table cell. Table Math also contains many features found in a spreadsheet program. The exercises in this lesson cover simple calculations for addition, subtraction, multiplication and division. Refer to software documentation for specialized calculations.

- To calculate within a table, a formula is inserted in the cell where the answer should appear. The formula tells WordPerfect what cells are to be calculated and what type of calculation is to be performed. Cells are identified by using their location (A1, B3, C4). The type of calculation is identified by one of the following symbols:

  - +　= addition

  - -　= subtraction

  - *　= multiplication

  - /　= division

- In addition to using symbols and cell locations to calculate, you can use *special symbols* to accomplish a quick calculation for subtotal, total and grand total:

  - + (subtotal)

  - = (total)

  - * (grand total)

  The *subtotal* special symbol adds numbers that are in the column above it; *total* calculates previous subtotals, and *grand total* calculates previous totals.

- Like columns, WordPerfect considers table cells to be numeric. When numbers in a cell are not to be calculated (like social security or employee numbers), you must change the cell type to "text."

- Note the example below of a table that used formulas and special symbols (for subtotal) to calculate answers:

	A	B	C	D
1	EMPLOYEE NAME	HRS. WORKED	HRLY RATE	TOTAL EARNINGS
2	Jensen	35	6.85	239.75
3	Robinson	26	7.91	205.4
4	Ling	15	8.16	122.4
5	Totals		76	22.91	567.55

BEFORE FORMATTING

- When the answers were calculated, (total earnings) the last digit for two of the answers did not appear. You can change the appearance of any numbers that have been entered as formulas. Since the numbers in columns C and D above are "currency," you can format them so they display two decimal places and a dollar sign to look like this:

EMPLOYEE NAME	HRS. WORKED	HRLY RATE	TOTAL EARNINGS
Jensen	35	$6.85	$239.75
Robinson	26	$7.91	$205.40
Ling	15	$8.16	$122.40
Totals	76	$22.91	$567.55

AFTER FORMATTING

- If you see ?? in a cell after you have entered a formula, WordPerfect is alerting you that there is a problem. Check the formula to see that you have used the correct cell locations, and re-enter it.

- When your cursor is sitting in a cell that contains a formula, the formula will appear in the lower left of your screen.

- Table math calculations are accomplished in the Table Edit dialog box. Note keystrokes p. 329.

- In this exercise, you will create a table and use the table math feature to perform multiplication and addition calculations.

EXERCISE DIRECTIONS:

1. Select Graphics Mode view.

2. Start with a clear screen.

3. Use the default margins.

4. Create the table shown on the next page using 4 columns and 6 rows.

6. Change column A width to 2". (You will adjust remaining columns later.)

7. Right-align columns B, C and D.

8. Enter column text. Center cell A1 title (DESCRIPTION).

9. Edit the table as follows:

   - Enter the formula B2*C2 in cell D2 to calculate the amount for Cans Tomato Paste.

   - Enter formulas to calculate AMOUNT for the remaining items.

   - Find totals for UNIT PRICE and AMOUNT.

   - Format columns C and D for currency.

   - Shorten column B by 7 spaces; column C by 4 spaces and column D by 4 spaces.

   - Use a 10% fill to shade the row as shown.

   - Use a thick line on the bottom and right of cells C6 and D6 as shown.

   - Reposition the table so it is centered horizontally.

10. Vertically center the exercise.

11. Preview the exercise.

12. Print one copy.

13. Save the exercise; name it **RECEIPT.**

continued . . .

	A	B	C	D
1	DESCRIPTION	QTY	UNIT PRICE	AMOUNT
2	Cans Tomato Paste	25	$0.25	
3	Cases Potato Chips	11	$8.45	
4	Cases Pop Corn	14	$3.15	
5	Turkeys	12	$7.12	
6	TOTALS			

TO CALCULATE IN TABLES
Using formulas

1. Create the table.
2. Click on Layout .... `Alt` + `L`
3. Click on Tables .... `T`
4. Click on Edit .... `E`
5. Place cursor in cell where answer should appear.
6. Click on Formula .... `F`
7. Type first cell location to be calculated.
   (e.g., A1).
8. Type calculation symbol:
   + (addition)
   - (subtraction)
   * (multiplication)
   / (division)

9. Type next cell location to be calculated.
10. ENTER .... `↵`
11. ENTER .... `↵`

Using special symbols
1. Follow steps 1-6 above.
2. Type special symbol:
   + (subtotal)
   = (total)
   * (grand total)
3. ENTER .... `↵`

TO FORMAT NUMBERS
1. Place cursor in table.
2. Click on Layout .... `Alt` + `L`
3. Click on Tables .... `T`
4. Click on Edit .... `E`
5. Place cursor in column where numbers are to be formatted.

6. Click on Column .... `O`
7. From the Column Format dialog box, Click on Number Type .... `T`
8. Click on a desired format:
   - General (the default) ...... `G`
   - Integer .... `I`
   - Fixed .... `F`
   - Percent .... `P`
   - Currency .... `C`
   - Accounting .... `A`
   - Commas .... `M`
   - Scientific .... `S`
   - Date .... `D`
   - Text .... `T`
9. Click on OK twice .... `↵` , `↵`

MATH: CALCULATING IN TABLES; COPYING FORMULAS

NOTES:

- In Exercise 105, you entered the same formula to calculate the AMOUNT column several times. WordPerfect's Move/Copy feature within Table Edit allows you to copy the formula you entered in one cell to another cell or to a group of cells.

- In this exercise, you will create a table and use the table math feature to perform subtraction and addition calculations. You will use the move/copy feature to copy the formula you enter in the "Difference" and "First Half Total" columns to calculate the remaining items in those columns.

EXERCISE DIRECTIONS:

1. Select Graphics Mode view.
2. Start with a clear screen.
3. Use the default margins.
4. Center all title lines; return three times.
5. Create the table shown on the right using 5 columns and 6 rows.
6. Enter column text as shown.
7. Center and bold column headings in row 1.
8. Edit the table as follows:

   - Enter the formula C2-B2 in cell D2 to calculate the difference between first and second quarter sales for disk drives.

   - Copy the formula down to calculate the difference for the other items.

   - Enter the formula B2+C2 in cell E2 to calculate the FIRST HALF TOTAL for disk drives.

   - Copy the formula down to calculate the FIRST HALF TOTAL for the other items.

   - Find TOTALS for columns B, C, D and E in row 6.

   - Format all money columns for currency.

   - Use a 10% fill to shade column D as shown.

   - Use a dotted line border around column E

9. Vertically center the exercise.
10. Preview the exercise.
11. Print one copy.
12. Save the exercise; name it **COMPARE.**

FIRST AND SECOND QUARTER
SALES COMPARISON
FOR SELECTED ITEMS
June 199-

	A	B	C	D	E
	ITEM	1ST. QTR. SALES	2ND. QTR. SALES	DIFFERENCE	FIRST HALF TOTAL
2	Disk Drives	$24,500.50	$28,456.00	C2-B2	B2+C2
3	Monitors	$34,234.12	$38,651.98	↓	↓
4	Keyboards	$44,500.22	$45,233.88		
5	Printers	$22,333.88	$63,999.12	↓	↓
6	TOTALS	+	+	+	+

TO COPY A FORMULA

1. Place cursor in cell that contains formula to be copied.
2. Click on Layout .... [Alt] + [L]
3. Click on Table .... [T]
4. Click on Edit .... [E]
5. Click on Move/Copy .... [M]
6. Click on Item to be moved/copied:
   - Row .... [R]
   - Column .... [O]
   - Cell.............................. [C]

7. Click on Copy .... [P]
8. Click on desired direction that formula will copied to:
   To Cell (a specific cell)....... [C]
   Down .... [D]
   Right .... [R]
9. Type number of times you want to copy the formula.
10. Click on OK twice .... [↵] , [↵]

MATH: CALCULATING IN TABLES; COPYING FORMULAS

NOTES:

- In this exercise, you will create a table and use the table math feature to perform multiplication and subtraction calculations for a payroll. You will use the move/copy feature to copy the formulas you enter in each column for the first employee to the other employees. The "taxes" were computed by multiplying the GROSS PAY by 20% (D2*.20).

EXERCISE DIRECTIONS:

1. Select Graphics Mode view.
2. Start with a clear screen.
3. Use the default margins.
4. Center all title lines; return three times.
5. Create the table shown on the right using 6 columns and 7 rows.
7. Enter column text as shown.
8. Center and bold column headings in row 1.
9. Edit the table as follows:
   - Enter the formulas as shown in the exercise to calculate each column.
   - Copy each formula down to the remaining employees in the column.
   - Right-align all money columns.
   - Center-align HOURS WORKED column.
   - Format all money columns for currency.

- Use a 10% fill to shade NET PAY column as shown.
- Use a thick border around row 1. (The border will hide the first line of the column heading. Make adjustments to the text to avoid this.)
- Use a dotted border for table lines.
- Use a single line table border.
- Reposition the table so it is centered horizontally.

10. Vertically center the exercise.
11. Preview the exercise.
12. Print one copy.
13. Save the exercise; name it **ABC.**

ABC PHARMACY
PART-TIME PAYROLL
WEEK ENDING June 199-

EMPLOYEE NAME	HOURLY RATE	HOURS WORKED	GROSS PAY	TAXES	NET PAY
HARRISON	$8.45	16	B2*C2	D2*.20	D2-E2
WILLIAMS	$7.35	18			
BHATT	$6.85	22			
BADAR	$8.65	30			
VALCOM	$5.55	28			
ARONSON	$7.35	14			

MATH: CALCULATING IN TABLES; USING FUNCTIONS

NOTES:

- In this exercise you are directed to find horizontal and vertical totals. The formula to find the total lodging expenses, for example, would be C2+C3+C4+C5+C6. WordPerfect provides over 100 specialized methods to do calculations automatically. These specialized methods are known as *functions*. We will concentrate on the most commonly used functions in this exercise. When you become more comfortable with this concept, you can experiment with the others.

- Rather than use the formula described above to find total lodging expenses for this exercise, you could use the "SUM function." The SUM function is used to add all values in a range or block of cells.

- Each function name is followed by a parenthesis. The function to find total lodging would be written like this: SUM(C2:C6). This tells WordPerfect to add cells C2 through C6.

- To find an average, you normally would have to add numbers to be averaged and then divide by the number of items. To find the average cost of lodging expenses, the formula would look like: C2+C3+C4+C5+C6/5. The function would be written like this: AVE(C2:C6). The other functions that will be used in this exercise include:

  COUNT – counts all cells in a range or block.

  MAX – indicates the highest value in a range or block.

  MIN – indicates the lowest value in a range or block.

- In this exercise, you will create a letter with an inserted table and use the table math feature and the SUM, AVERAGE, COUNT, MAX and MIN functions to perform the necessary calculations. You will use the move/copy feature to copy the formulas across the rows.

EXERCISE DIRECTIONS:

1. Select Graphics Mode view.
2. Start with a clear screen. Begin the exercise on Ln 1.5".
3. Use the default margins for the document; set 1.5" margins for the table.
4. Create the letter on the next page, inserting the table as shown.
5. Center column headings in row 1.
6. Enter the text as shown.
7. Edit the table as follows:

   - Adjust column widths as necessary to narrow money columns.
   - Right-align money amounts.
   - Enter the SUM function in cell C7 to find the TOTAL of LODGING expenses (cells c2:c6).
   - Enter the AVE (average) function in cell C8 to find the average LODGING costs.
   - Enter the COUNT function in cell C9 to find how many items are listed.

   NOTE: While you could simply count the items yourself, using the function here is for practice purposes. You would use this function to count numerous items in a list.

   - Enter the MAX function in cell C10 to find the maximum value in the list.
   - Enter the MIN function in cell C11 to find the minimum value in the list.
   - Copy the formulas for SUM, AVE, COUNT, MAX and MIN to the remaining items in the row.
   - Format all money columns for currency as shown.
   - Use a 10% fill to shade column F and row 7 as shown.
   - Use a thick top and bottom border line.
   - Remove all table lines.
   - Reposition the table so it is centered horizontally.

8. Preview the exercise.
9. Print one copy.
10. Save the exercise; name it **EXPENSES.**

Today's date ↵ 1.5"

Freed, Frank & Mulligan, Inc.
Attention Mr. Weston Freed
543 Main Street
Detroit, MI 48236

Ladies and Gentlemen:

We have reviewed Alison Jackson's expenses for September. We
find that all is in order. The following is a summary:

DATE	CITY/ STATE	LODGING	AUTO	FOOD
9/1	Miami, FL	$1,000.00	$195.00	$189.00
9/7	New York, NY	$450.00	$45.00	$215.00
9/14	Newton, MA	$189.00	$87.50	$105.65
9/21	Redding, PA	$175.00	$80.00	$125.50
9/28	Wayne, NJ	$250.00	$105.00	$85.00
TOTAL				
AVG				
COUNT				
MAX				
MIN				

We will file all the necessary end-of-quarter papers as we have
in the past. I think we should get an earlier start next year in
preparation of an audit. We should discuss how to proceed at our
next meeting.

Sincerely,

Matthew Tyler
Comptroller

mt/

TO USE FUNCTIONS

1. Click on Layout .... Alt + L
2. Click on Table .... T
3. Click on Edit .... E
4. Place cursor in cell where answer should appear.
5. Click on Formula .... F
6. Click on Functions F5
7. Highlight desired function .... ↑ ↓
8. ENTER .... ↵
9. Type range of cells to be affected ....(C5:C8).
10. ENTER .... ↵
11. Click on OK .... ↵
12. Click on Close .... F7 to return to document screen.

EXERCISE DIRECTIONS:

1. Select any desired view mode.
2. Start with a clear screen.
3. Use the default margins.
4. Create the exercise below using a tabular column format and any desired intercolumn space.
5. Total the "STAFF" and "SALES" COLUMNS.
6. Align column headings and column text as desired.
7. Vertically center the exercise.
8. Preview the exercise.
9. Print one copy.
10. Save the exercise; name it **BRANCH.**

BALIWANE SPORTSWEAR
New Branches/Locations/Gross Sales
As of January 31, 199 -

BRANCH	CITY	STATE	STAFF	SALES
Paramount	New York	NY	18	$350,000
Sunview	Hollywood	CA	12	125,000
Seaview	Portland	ME	8	100,000
Cornielle	Providence	RI	20	450,000
Astro Center	Houston	TX	19	99,000
Mountainaire	Troy	NY	6	95,000
5] TOTALS				

EXERCISE DIRECTIONS:

1. Start with a clear screen.
2. Open STOCK (shown in illustration A).
3. Make the necessary edits to STOCK so that it resembles illustration B.
4. Use the table math feature to find:
   - STOCK VALUE for all stocks listed.
   - TOTALS for NO. SHARES PURCHASED and STOCK VALUE.
   - AVERAGE PURCHASE PRICE.
5. Print one copy.
6. Close the file; save the changes.

ILLUSTRATION A

PORTFOLIO OF
REBECCA N. NARDINO
As Of
January 1994

NAME OF STOCK	PURCHASE PRICE	NO. SHARES PURCHASED
R & L	$ 60.00	100
TECH LABS	45.35	80
ASTEC IND.	14.85	250
X-MATION	2.50	800
IDM	50.00	8
NORDAK INDUSTRIES	101.44	1,000

shaded stocks were purchased in 1992.

ILLUSTRATION B

PORTFOLIO OF
REBECCA N. NARDINO
As Of
January 1994

NAME OF STOCK	PURCHASE PRICE	NO. SHARES PURCHASED	STOCK VALUE
R & L	$60.00	100	
TECH LABS	$45.35	80	
ASTEC IND.	$14.85	250	
X-MATION	$2.50	800	
IDM	$50.00	8	
NORDAK INDUSTRIES	$101.44	1,000	
TOTALS			
AVG. PUR. PRICE			

shaded stocks were purchased in 1992.

LESSON 13 / EXERCISES 109-129
ENHANCING A DOCUMENT

- Changing Typeface, Type Style, Type Size
- Using Graphics

- Using Lines
- Using Borders and Shading
- Using Watermarks

- Using Special WP Characters
- Using Line Draw

ENHANCING A DOCUMENT:
CHANGING TYPEFACE (FONT), TYPE STYLE AND TYPE SIZE

NOTES:

- In Exercises 23-25, you used bold, underline, italics, outline, and shadow type styles to emphasize text. WordPerfect allows you to further enhance your document by changing typefaces (font) and type size.

- A typeface is the design of a character. Each typeface has a distinctive character that will make your document attractive and able to communicate a particular message. A font is a set of characters available in a particular typeface, type style and sometimes type size. Therefore a font has two or three parts: the typeface is the design of the character (Roman, Helvetica, Courier, Dutch, New Century Schoolbook); the type style is how the character is emphasized (bold, underline, italic), and the type size is the way the character is measured. A font that might be available to you in WordPerfect is: *New Century Schoolbook Bold Italic*. Font is often used as another term for typeface.

- The typefaces that are available to you depend on the printer you are using. There are basically three types of typefaces: serif, sans serif, and script. Each design has a name and each is used to convey a different feeling. While there are hundreds of varieties of each, WordPerfect includes some typefaces that will work with most printers.

- A serif face has "serifs", curves or edges extending from the ends of the letter: **R**, while a sans serif face is straight-edged: **R**, and script looks like handwriting: $\mathscr{R}$.

- A serif typeface is generally used for long text because it is more readable. Sans serif is often used for headlines.

- WordPerfect will display typefaces on-screen in Graphics and Page Modes. Text mode does not display screen fonts as they will appear when printed.

- Typefaces are available in a variety of sizes. Type size is measured in points (there are 72 points to an inch). Use 10 or 12 point type size for document text and larger text for headings and headlines. WordPerfect can display and print point size only if that size is available for both the screen and printer font.

- You can change font and type size before or after typing text. Font and type size may be accessed on the Ribbon or by selecting "Font" on the Font main menu. Note ribbon below:

MAIN MENU

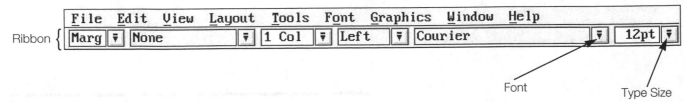

302

- You must have a mouse to use the ribbon to change font and type size. If you do not have a mouse or if you want to change font, type size, and apply an emphasis style (bold, italics, underline, etc.) at the same time, you should use the Font dialog box (which appears after Font is accessed from the main menu bar). Note Font dialog box below.

Using Relative Sizes

- The "Relative Size" option in the Font dialog box will change type to a "relative percentage" larger or smaller than the current font. For example, if you choose "Very Large", your text will change to 150% larger than the current font size. If the current font is 12 point, the very large option will change the font to 18 point (150% of 12 point). "Extra Large" will change your text to 200% larger than the current font. The advantage of this option is that if you change the current font, (from 12 point to 10 point), the text you specified as "Very Large" would automatically change to be 150% larger—to 15 point.

- In this exercise, you will change the typeface and type size of text in a document you created in a previous exercise.

```
 File   Edit   View   Layout   Tools   Font   Graphics   Window   Help
════════════════════════════════ Font ════════════════════════════════
 Type  Built-In                    QMS PS 810

 1. Font  Courier                            ▼   2. Size   12pt      ▼

 ┌─ 3. Appearance ──────────────────────────────┐  ┌─ 5. Position ──────┐
 │ ☐ Bold        ☐ Italics    ☐ Small Caps      │  │ ● Normal           │
 │ ☐ Underline   ☐ Outline    ☐ Redline         │  │ ○ Superscript      │
 │ ☐ Dbl Undline ☐ Shadow     ☐ Strikeout       │  │ ○ Subscript        │

 ┌─ 4. Relative Size ───────────────────────────┐  ┌─ 6. Underline ─────┐
 │ ● Normal      ○ Small     ○ Very Large       │  │ ☒ Spaces           │
 │ ○ Fine        ○ Large     ○ Extra Large      │  │ ☐ Tabs             │

 ┌─ Resulting Font ─────────────────────────────────────────────────────┐
 │                                                                      │
 │        The Quick Brown Fox Jumps Over The Lazy Dog                   │
 │                                                                      │
 │ Courier 12pt                                                         │
 └──────────────────────────────────────────────────────────────────────┘

 [ Setup... Shft+F1 ]   [ Normal ]   [ Color... ]        [ OK ]  [ Cancel ]

 Courier 12pt                              Doc 1 Pg 1 Ln 1" Pos 1"
```

Relative Size Options {

EXERCISE DIRECTIONS:

1. Select Graphics Mode view.

2. Start with a clear screen.

3. Open **RSVP.**

4. Make the typeface, type size and case changes indicated in the exercise shown on the right.

5. Center all 10-point text as shown.

6. Preview your document.

7. Print one copy.

8. Close the file; save the changes.

continued . . .

CELEBRATE
} serif 60 pt

ON THE HUDSON
} sans serif 35 pt

This New Year's Eve, there is no more elegant, more beautiful spot than the Hudson River Cafe. Dance with the Statue of Liberty in view to the sounds of our live band and DJ.

Enjoy a six-course Hudson Valley feast and a spectacular dessert to be remembered as the last memory of the year.
} Sans serif 10 pt

NEW YEAR'S EVE DINNER DANCE
} Sans serif 28 pt

Call for reservations 212-876-9888.
Our courteous staff will be glad to assist you at any time.
We are located at Four World Financial Center.
} Sans serif 10 pt

HUDSON RIVER CLUB
} Sans serif 28 pt

TO CHANGE TYPEFACE (FONT), TYPE SIZE and/or TYPE STYLE

Using DIALOG BOX
Ctrl + F8

1. Place cursor where font change will begin (before typing).

   or

   Block text to receive font change (after typing).

2. Click on F<u>o</u>nt ....

3. Click on F<u>o</u>nt .... O

4. Click on arrow list box to select typeface (font).

5. Highlight desired typeface.

6. ENTER .... ↵

   and/or

7. Click on arrow list box to select typesize.

8. Highlight desired type size or enter the desired type size in Size box.

9. ENTER .... ↵

   and/or

10. Click on desired check box(es) to select a type style(s) (bold, underline, etc.)

11. Click on OK .... ↵

To turn OFF type styles

12. Press Ctrl + N .... Ctrl + N

Using RIBBON (typeface and type size only)

1. Place cursor where font change will begin (before typing)

   or

   Block text to receive font change (after typing).

2. Click on arrow list box to select type face.

3. Highlight desired typeface.

4. ENTER .... ↵

5. Click on arrow list box to select type size.

6. Highlight desired type size.

7. ENTER .... ↵

ENHANCING A DOCUMENT:
CHANGING TYPEFACE (FONT), TYPE STYLE AND TYPE SIZE

NOTES:

- Since this is a formal announcement, note that the typeface chosen communicates a professional tone.

- In this exercise, you will change the typefaces and type sizes of text in the announcement you created earlier.

EXERCISE DIRECTIONS:

1. Select Graphics Mode view.
2. Start with a clear screen.
3. Open **CONGRATS.**
4. Change the left and right margins to 1.5".
5. Change the typeface, type size and type style (italics) indicated in the exercise.
6. Preview your document.
7. Print one copy.
8. Close the file; save the changes.

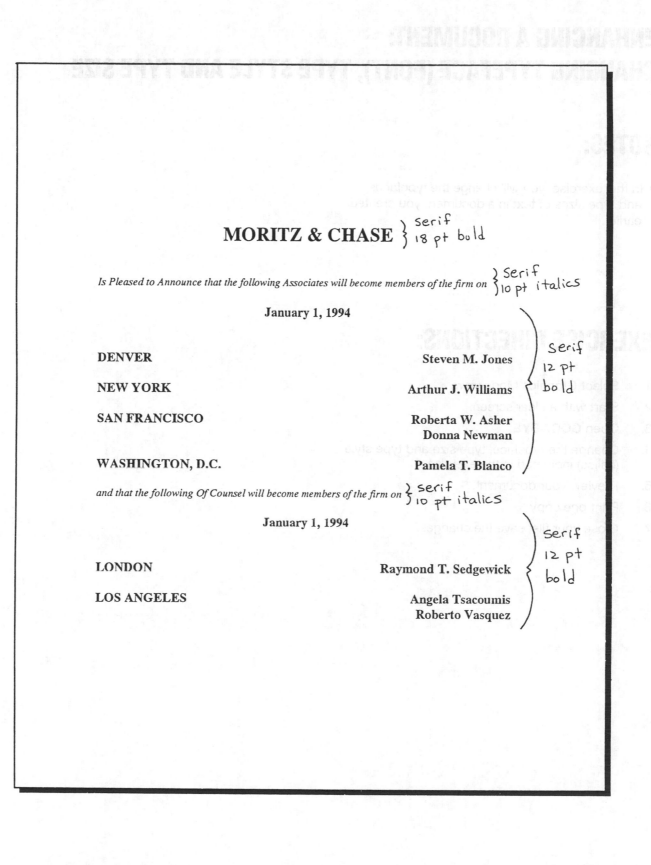

MORITZ & CHASE } serif
18 pt bold

Is Pleased to Announce that the following Associates will become members of the firm on } serif
10 pt italics

January 1, 1994

DENVER   **Steven M. Jones**

NEW YORK   **Arthur J. Williams**

SAN FRANCISCO   **Roberta W. Asher**
                              Donna Newman

WASHINGTON, D.C.   **Pamela T. Blanco**

serif
12 pt
bold

and that the following Of Counsel will become members of the firm on } serif
10 pt italics

January 1, 1994

LONDON   **Raymond T. Sedgewick**

LOS ANGELES   **Angela Tsacoumis**
                             Roberto Vasquez

serif
12 pt
bold

ENHANCING A DOCUMENT:
CHANGING TYPEFACE (FONT), TYPE STYLE AND TYPE SIZE

NOTES:

- In this exercise, you will change the typefaces and type sizes of text in a document you created earlier.

EXERCISE DIRECTIONS:

1.   Select Graphics Mode view.
2.   Start with a clear screen.
3.   Open **GOODBYE.**
4.   Change the typeface, type size and type style (italics) indicated in the exercise.
5.   Preview your document.
6.   Print one copy.
7.   Close your file; save the changes.

Serif
18
pt bold } **VACATION PLANNING**

*Set text to
San serif*)

Serif

It can be very exciting to plan a vacation. There are a number of ways to go about it. Of course, you could have a travel agent make all the arrangements. But it is more exciting to investigate all the possibilities of travel.

First, you can check the hundreds of guidebooks which can be purchased at bookstores. Then, you can send away to the government tourist offices in the country you are planning to visit. They will send you lots of free literature about the country -- places to visit and a list of accommodations. The travel advertisements in your newspaper will tell you where the bargains are.

After you have planned your trip by looking through the guidebooks listed to the right, ask your travel agent to do the actual booking. Enjoy! } *14 pt*

OFFICIAL
AIRLINE
GUIDE

RUSSELL'S)–*italics*
NATIONAL
MOTOR
COACH
GUIDE

STEAMSHIP
GUIDE

HOTEL AND
RESORT
GUIDE

AUTO
RENTAL
GUIDE

RES-
TAURANTS,
INNS AND
MUSEUMS
GUIDE

SIGHT-
SEEING
GUIDE

CAMP-
GROUND,
FARM
VACATIONS
AND
ADVENTURE
TRAVEL
GUIDE

ENHANCING A DOCUMENT: WORKING WITH GRAPHICS

NOTES:

- WordPerfect's graphics feature allows you to include pictures and images in a document. The ability to combine graphics and text will enable you to create newsletters, brochures, flyers, letterheads or other documents where pictures contribute to the effectiveness of the message.

- WordPerfect places each graphic image in a "box." WordPerfect uses a "Figure box" by default. A figure box is used to place images, diagrams or charts. When a figure box is used, a border appears around the graphic. You may choose from eight different types of graphic boxes. Other types will be covered in later exercises.

- There are two ways to add a graphic to a document. The first way is to create a Figure box and place the image into the box. The second way is to retrieve an image directly into the document. The second method does not immediately provide you with sizing and other options.

- WordPerfect contains 36 predesigned graphic image files which are often referred to as "clip art." Each file has its own name and is saved in the \WP60\GRAPHICS subdirectory of the WordPerfect main directory. The names of these files each contain the extension .WPG. The images are illustrated in Appendix A. You can, however, purchase disks with other graphics and import them into your documents.

- Graphics may be accessed by selecting "Retrieve Image" (this will not give you sizing and positioning options) or "Graphic Boxes" from the Graphics main menu.

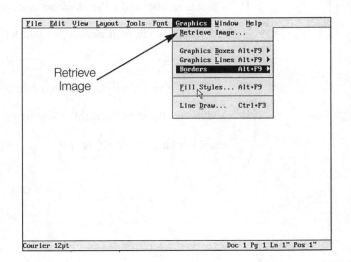

After selecting "Graphic Boxes," the following dialog box appears giving you sizing and other options.

```
File  Edit  View  Layout  Tools  Font  Graphics  Window  Help
┌──────────────────── Create Graphics Box ────────────────────┐
│                                                              │
│  1. Filename...                                              │
│                                                              │
│  2. Contents [None      ▼]   7. Attach To [Paragraph    ▼]  │
│                                                              │
│  3. Create Text...           8. Edit Position...            │
│                                 Horiz.  Right (Margin)      │
│  4. Create Caption...           Vert.   0"                  │
│                                                              │
│                              9. Edit Size...               │
│                                 Width   3.25"              │
│  5. Options                     Height  3.25" (Automatic)  │
│     Content Options...                                     │
│     Caption Options...       T. Text Flow Around Box       │
│                                 Text Flows [On Larger Side ▼]│
│  6. Edit Border/Fill...         □ Contour Text Flow        │
│                                                            │
│  Y. Based on Box Style...  Figure Box                      │
│  [Help]                                    [ OK ] [Cancel] │
└────────────────────────────────────────────────────────────┘
Courier 12pt                         Doc 1 Pg 1 Ln 1" Pos 1"
```

- When a graphic is imported, it is aligned at the right margin by default (note item 8 above: Edit Position option). However, you can change the horizontal/vertical alignment of the graphic. You can use the mouse to drag the graphic image anywhere on the page.

- A graphic is imported based on a size determined by WordPerfect. After a graphic is imported, you can reduce, enlarge, stretch, move or delete the graphic. The size of the image may be changed by specifying the dimensions in the dialog box (note item 9: Edit Size option) or by simply resizing the image to the desired size using the mouse.

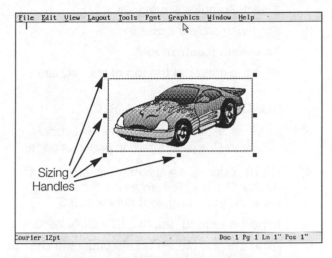

Sizing Handles

- To change the size of graphic, move or delete it, it must first be "selected" by clicking on the image. A "selected" image appears above. Note the "sizing handles" that appear once the graphic is "selected."

- To size a graphic using the mouse, place the mouse pointer on one of the handles, then click and hold the left mouse button as you drag the box to the desired size.

- To move a graphic using the mouse, place the mouse pointer in the center of the graphic, then click and hold the left mouse button as you drag the graphic. You may also move a graphic by specifying its horizontal and vertical position on the page. It is easier to use a mouse to position a graphic.

- To delete a graphic, select the graphic and press the Delete key.

- Graphics are visible only in Graphics Mode, Page Mode or Print Preview.

- In this exercise, you will create several "figure boxes," insert a graphic into each and align them left, right and center. You will also change their size, and move them to a new position on the page using the mouse.

continued . . .

EXERCISE DIRECTIONS:

1. Select Graphics Mode view.
2. Start with a clear screen.

   To create illustration A:

3. With the cursor at the top of your screen, import

   CONDUCT.WPG. (Alt + G, B, C).

   NOTE: *Make all changes in the Create Graphic Dialog Box (illustrated on previous page).*

4. Horizontally center the graphic; size it to 1" wide x 1" high. Return as many times as necessary to bring your cursor to 2.5".
5. Import a second graphic, DRAGON.WPG.
6. Align the graphic left on the page and change the size to 2" wide x 2" high. Return as many times as necessary to bring your cursor to 5".
7. Import a third graphic, HOTROD.WPG

8. Change the size to 3" wide x 3" high.
9. Save the exercise; name it **PICTURE.** Do not exit the document.

   To create illustration B:

10. "Select" the first graphic and delete it.
11. "Select" the second graphic and stretch it to extend between the left and right margins.
12. Select the third graphic and move it to the center below the dragon.
13. Preview your document.
14. Print one copy.
15. Close the file; save the changes.

TO IMPORT A GRAPHIC
Alt + F5

1. Place cursor where you want graphics box to appear.
2. Click on Graphics .... `Alt` + `G`
3. Click on Graphics Boxes .... `B`

   NOTE: *WordPerfect automatically numbers each graphics box.*

4. Click on Create .... `C`
5. Click on Filename .... `F`
6. Type name of graphic file.

   NOTE: *If filename is unknown, you can access File Manager (F5), and highlight file with a .WPG extension.*

7. Click on OK .... `←`

TO POSITION A GRAPHIC
(Set, Left, Right, Center, Full)

8. Click on Edit Position .... `E`
9. Click on Horizontal Position .... `H`
10. Select desired position:

    Set .... `S`

    Left .... `L`

    Right .... `R`

    Centered .... `C`

    Full .... `F`

TO SIZE A GRAPHIC

11. Click on Edit Size .... `S`
12. Click on Width .... `W`
    • Type desired width
    • ENTER .... `←`
    Click on Height .... `H`
    • Type desired height.
    • ENTER .... `←`
13. Click on OK .... `←`

TO DELETE A GRAPHIC

1. Select Graphic to be deleted. (click on graphic)
2. Press DEL .... `Del`

ILLUSTRATION A

ILLUSTRATION B

ENHANCING A DOCUMENT: WORKING WITH GRAPHICS

NOTES:

- In this exercise, you will combine text with a graphic to create a letterhead. To do this you will first create the graphic as described in Exercise 112 and position it in the center of the page. You will then type the text below it.

- After accessing the Create Graphics Box, it is important to note item 7: *Attach to*: **Paragraph.** This option allows you to specify the way you want the graphics box to be anchored. WordPerfect offers you three options:

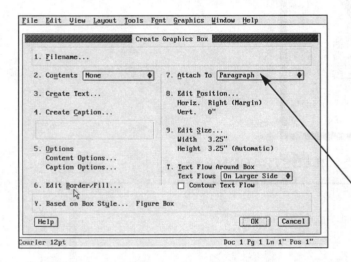

Attach to Paragraph

- If you leave the default setting (paragraph), the box stays with the paragraph surrounding it. If you move the text or paragraph, the box will move, too.

- To fix the graphic at a particular location on a page, you must change the setting to **"Page."** If you set a specific horizontal and vertical position for the graphics box, the attachment changes to "Fixed Page Position."

- To make the graphic part of text on a line, you must change the setting to **"Character."** The graphics box is treated as a character and wraps with the line of text to which the box is attached.

- In this exercise, you will use the default setting (Paragraph).

EXERCISE DIRECTIONS:

1. Select Graphics Mode view.

2. Start with a clear screen.

3. Set the top margin to .5".

4. With your cursor at the top of the screen, import and center HOTROD.WPG. Size the height of the graphic to 1.25".

5. Center the company name and address beginning on Ln 2".

6. Set the company name to sans serif 14 point. bold; set the address to sans serif 10 point.

7. Using your mouse, size the graphic to the same width as the company name.

8. Preview your work.

9. Print one copy.

10. Save the file; name it **AUTO.**

Central Motors Incorporated

777 Mercedes Drive
Los Angeles, CA 90210

ENHANCING A DOCUMENT: WORKING WITH GRAPHICS

NOTES:

- You must use the mouse to size and position the graphic between words in this exercise. If you do not have a mouse, positioning the graphic between the words as shown may be difficult. You will note that the "box" around the graphic has been removed.

- In this exercise, you will combine text with a graphic to create a letterhead. You will use your mouse to position the graphic, and you will remove the box around the graphic.

EXERCISE DIRECTIONS:

1. Select Graphics Mode view.
2. Start with a clear screen.
3. Set the top margin to .3".
4. With your cursor at the top of the page, type the address in sans serif 10 point. Return twice.
5. Type the company name in sans serif 14-point bold at the left margin (leave one space between each letter). Return twice.
6. Type the address and phone number information in sans serif 10 point.

7. With your cursor in an empty location on the page, retrieve GLOBE.WPG.
8. Using your mouse, size the graphic to approximately 1" x 1" and move it to the left of GLOBAL TRAVEL GROUP.
9. Remove the box around the graphic.
10. Preview your work.
11. Print one copy.
12. Save the file; name it **GLOBE.**

485 Madison Avenue
New York, NY 10034

GLOBAL
TRAVEL
GROUP

Phone: (212) 234-4566
Fax: (212) 345-9877

TO REMOVE BOX AROUND GRAPHIC

Alt + F9

1. Select graphic to be edited.
2. Click on Graphics .... Alt + G
3. Click on Graphics Boxes .... B
4. Click on Edit .... E
5. Click on Edit Border/Fill .... B
6. Click on Lines L
7. Click on Select All .... A
8. Double click on None
9. Click on Close twice .... ↵, ↵
10. Click on OK .... ↵

ENHANCING A DOCUMENT:
EDITING A GRAPHIC; SCALING AND ROTATING

NOTES:

Scaling a Graphic

- The scaling option allows you to expand or contract the graphic image horizontally or vertically (to have the image fill the box) by percentages. The default proportions for the image are 1.0 x 1.0. This equals 100%. If you wish to "stretch" the graphic to increase its height, you must enter a number greater than 1.0. If you wish to "shrink" the graphic to decrease its height, you must enter a number less than 1.0. The box will not change its size; only the image within the box will be rescaled. The examples in the right show an image in which the height and width have been scaled by various percentages.

- Scaling and Rotating a Graphic may be accessed by selecting Graphics Boxes, Edit from the Graphics main menu.

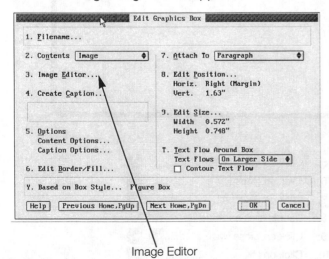

The following dialog box will appear:

Image Editor

- Changes may be made to the image by selecting "Image Editor" in the dialog box. The following screen will then appear (note the new button bar):

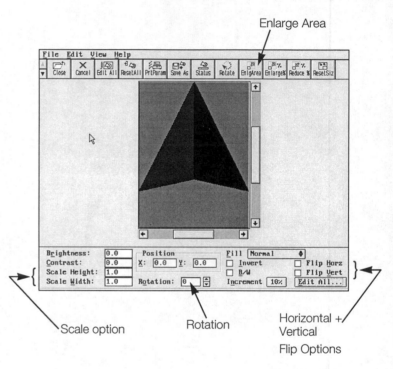

Enlarge Area

Scale option

Rotation

Horizontal + Vertical Flip Options

- To enlarge a specific portion of the graphics image, you may click on the EnlgArea button and drag the magnifying class icon to draw an outline around the area you want to enlarge; then release the mouse button. The Enlg Area button was used to enlarge the head of the parrot in the exercise illustration shown on the right.

- By clicking on the horizontal and vertical scroll bars, you can move the graphics image to the left, right, top or bottom of the box.

Rotating a Graphic

- The rotating option allows you to pivot the image by moving it clockwise or counter clockwise. Images may be rotated counter clockwise using the plus (+) key or clockwise using the minus (-) key. Or, they may be rotated by a specific amount of degrees (positive numbers only) by selecting "Rotation" in the dialog box and either entering the desired degrees or clicking on the up and down arrows next to the rotation text box.

- To create an interesting effect, you may also "flip" your image horizontally or vertically by clicking the Horizontal or Vertical Flip option in the dialog box. Note the examples below of an image that has been scaled, rotated and flipped:

Scale height 1.0
Scale width 1.0
(the Default)

Flip Horizontally

Scale height 2.3
Scale width 2.85
(Scroll bars used to move image in middle of box

Scale height 1.2
Scale width 0.8

Scale height 1.0
Scale width 2.0

Rotated 180°

continued . . .

EXERCISE DIRECTIONS:

1. Select Graphics Mode view.
2. Start with a clear screen.
3. Use the default margins.
4. Import PARROT.WPG and position it on the right (the default).
5. Import PARROT.WPG and position it on the left.
6. Edit the *left* image as follows:
   - Select Image Editor...
   - Using the Enlg Area button, enlarge the parrot's head to fill the box (or scale the height to 3.77 and the width to 3.77) and use the scroll arrows to show the parrot's head.
   - Return to the text screen.
   - Size the box to approximately 1" x 1"; select the image and drag the mouse to size the image.
   - Remove the box around the image.
   - Move the image to the top left corner of the page.
7. Save the image; name it **PAR1**.
8. Edit the right image as you did the left image, then:
   - Select Image Editor...
   - Flip the image horizontally.
   - Return to the text screen.
   - Move the image to the bottom right corner of the page.
9. Center the letterhead text using sans serif 14 point bold for the title and sans serif 10 point for the address and phone number.
10. Preview your document.
11. Print one copy.
12. Save the letterhead file; name it **POLLY**.

TO ROTATE/FLIP AN IMAGE
1. Click on Graphics .... `Alt` + `G`
2. Click on Graphic Boxes................ `B`
3. Click on Edit................................. `E`
4. Click on Edit Box .... `E`
5. Click on Image Editor .... `E`
6. Click on Rotation .... `O`
7. Type desired rotation percentage and/or
   - Click in Flip Horiz to flip horizontally.
   - Click in Flip Vert to flip vertically.
8. Press F7...................................... `F7`
   to close Image Editor.
9. Click on OK.................................. `↵`

TO SCALE AN IMAGE OR ENLARGE PART OF IMAGE
Alt + F9
1. Follow steps 1-5 above.
2. • Click on Scale Height .... `G`
   - Type scale height
   - Click on Scale Width .... `W`
   - Type scale width
   or
   - Click on *EnlgArea* button..... `EnlgArea`
   - Drag the magnifying glass icon to draw an outline around the area you want to enlarge; then release the mouse button.

3. Press F7 .... `F7`
   to close the Image Editor.
4. Click on OK.................................. `↵`

TO CHANGE SEVERAL EDIT OPTIONS AT ONE TIME
1. Follow steps 1-5 above.
2. Click on Edit All.......................... `E`
3. Make editing selections.
4. Press F7...................................... `F7`
   to close Image Editor.
5. Click on OK.................................. `↵`

POLLYWANNA CRACKER
Pet Supplies and Grooming

354 Northern Boulevard
Baldwin, NY 11571
516-555-5555

ENHANCING A DOCUMENT: EDITING A GRAPHIC; SIZING AND FLIPPING

NOTES:

- In this exercise, you will enhance an advertisement you created earlier by changing the fonts, and importing and editing a graphic. You will use this document in later exercises and make other enhancements. The possibilities are endless.

EXERCISE DIRECTIONS:

1. Select Graphics Mode view.
2. Start with a clear screen.
3. Open **PAPER.**
4. Import TREE.WPG four times. After each graphic is imported, size it to 1" x 1" and place each below the text side-by-side as shown.
5. Flip vertically the second and fourth image.

NOTE: Select the image first before you access Image Editor.

6. Change the heading to serif 14-point bold; change the paragraph text to serif 12-point bold; and change the centered text to a different 12-point serif bold (if available).
7. Preview your document. If the document is not centered on the page, insert returns to begin the exercise at 2.5".
8. Print one copy.
9. Save the exercise; name it **PAPER1.**

WATERSHED PAPER

Papers that perform. Consistently. Time after time. That's what you can always expect when you specify WATERSHED'S premium text, cover and writing finishes. And now you can see how brilliantly our papers perform with a variety of inks thanks to our new *Think Ink Guide.*

This invaluable tool features more than 400 visual references to help you make accurate color choices. And get the results you expect. You'll find printed examples of black, metallic and solid colors in halftones, line art and screen tints on every one of our four leading lines of paper:

ENVIRONMENT
CLASSIC LINEN
CREST LINEN
RAIN DROP

Discover for yourself how *WATERSHED PAPER* can be combined with a myriad of inks to expand your creativity.

For your copy of our new *Think Ink Guide,* just call the representatives listed on the enclosed brochure and ask for your guide.

ENHANCING A DOCUMENT:
TEXT FLOW OPTIONS; CREATING A CAPTION

NOTES:

- WordPerfect provides you with several options for wrapping text around the graphic. Note the text wrap options illustrated below and on next page:

This is practice text which will show you how text flows around a graphic. It is important for you to note the different text flow on options. Text can flow on the larger side, on the left side, on the right side, on both sides, on neither side, through the box, or as a contour text box in which the text flows around the graphic to form a silhouette. Each option can create an interest effect. When the contour text box is selected, the box or frame around the graphic does not appear. However, you might have to play with the graphic so that it doesn't break text in an awkward place. This happens frequently.

ON LARGER SIDE

This is practice text which will show you how text flows around a graphic. It is important for you to note the different text flow on options. Text can flow on the larger side, on the left side, on the right side, on both sides, on neither side, through the box, or as a contour text box in which the text flows around the graphic to form a silhouette. Each option can create an interest effect. When the contour text box is selected, the box or frame around the graphic does not appear. However, you might have to play with the graphic so that it doesn't break text in an awkward place. This happens frequently.

ON LEFT SIDE OF CENTERED IMAGE

 This is practice text which will show you how text flows around a graphic. It is important for you to note the different text flow on options. Text can flow on the larger side, on the left side, on the right side, on both sides, on neither side, through the box, or as a contour text box in which the text flows around the graphic to form a silhouette. Each option can create an interest effect. When the contour text box is selected, the box or frame around the graphic does not appear. However, you might have to play with the graphic so that it doesn't break text in an awkward place. This happens frequently.

ON RIGHT SIDE OF CENTERED IMAGE

This is practice text which will show you how text flows around a graphic. It is important for you to note the different text flow on options. Text can flow on the larger side, on the left side, side, on both neither side, box, or as a box in which flows around the side, on the on the right sides, on through the contour text the text graphic to form a silhouette. Each option can create an interest effect. When the contour text box is selected, the box or frame around the graphic does not appear. However, you might have to play with the graphic so that it doesn't break text in an awkward place. This happens frequently.

ON BOTH SIDES OF CENTERED IMAGE

This is practice text which will show you how text flows around a graphic. It is important for you to note the different text flow on options. Text can flow on the larger side, on the left side, on the right side, on both sides, on neither side, through the box, or as a contour text box in which the text flows around the graphic to form a silhouette. Each option can create an interest effect. When the contour text box is selected, the box or frame around the graphic does not appear. However, you might have to play with the graphic so that it doesn't break text in an awkward place. This happens frequently.

THROUGH BOX

```
This is practice text which will show you how
text flows around a graphic.  It is important
for you to note the different text flow on
options. Text can flow on the larger side, on
the left side, on the right side, on both
```

```
sides, on neither side, through the box, or as
a contour text box in which the text flows
around the graphic to form a silhouette. Each
option can create an interest effect.  When the
contour text box is selected, the box or frame
around the graphic does not appear. However,
you might have to play with the graphic so that
it doesn't break text in an awkward place. This
happens frequently.
```

ON NEITHER SIDE (OF CENTERED IMAGE)

```
This is practice text which will show you how
text flows around          a graphic.  It is
important for you            to note the different
text flow on                options. Text can flow
on the larger              side, on the
left side, on               the right side, on
both sides,               on neither side,
through                    the box, or as
a contour                   text box in which the
text flows around the graphic to form a
silhouette. Each option can create an interest
effect.  When the contour text box is selected,
the box or frame around the graphic does not
appear. However, you might have to play with the
graphic so that it doesn't break text in an
awkward place. This happens frequently.
```

CONTOUR TEXT BOX (ON BOTH SIDES)

- Text flow options are selected within the Create Graphics Boxes dialog box:

```
 File   Edit  View  Layout  Tools  Font  Graphics  Window  Help
┌──────────────────────────────────────────────────────────────┐
│▓▓▓▓▓▓▓▓▓▓▓▓▓▓▓▓▓▓▓▓▓ Create Graphics Box ▓▓▓▓▓▓▓▓▓▓▓▓▓▓▓▓▓▓▓▓▓│
│                                                                │
│  1. Filename...                                                │
│                                                                │
│  2. Contents [None            ⬍]   7. Attach To [Paragraph  ⬍] │
│                                                                │
│  3. Create Text...                 8. Edit Position...         │
│                                       Horiz.  Right (Margin)   │
│  4. Create Caption...                 Vert.   0"               │
│                                                                │
│  ┌──────────────────────────┐     9. Edit Size...             │
│  │                          │        Width   3.25"            │
│  └──────────────────────────┘        Height  3.25" (Automatic) │
│  5. Options                                                    │
│     Content Options...             T. Text Flow Around Box     │
│     Caption Options...                Text Flows [On Larger Side ⬍] │
│                                       ☐ Contour Text Flow      │
│  6. Edit Border/Fill...                                        │
│                                                                │
│  Y. Based on Box Style...  Figure Box                          │
│                                                                │
│  [Help]                               [ OK ]  [Cancel]         │
├──────────────────────────────────────────────────────────────┤
│ Courier 12pt                       Doc 1 Pg 1 Ln 1" Pos 1"     │
└──────────────────────────────────────────────────────────────┘
```

Create caption →

Text Flow Options }

- After importing the graphic in the Create Graphics Boxes dialog box (and sizing, and positioning the graphic, if desired), select "Text Flow Around Box" option, then "Text Flows." A list box will provide you with options. If you wish to contour text around a graphic (using any text flow you selected), click in the Contour Text Flow box. A Contour text flow will automatically eliminate the box around the graphic so that text can create a silhouette around the image.

- When text wrap is used, it is often necessary to adjust the graphic slightly to avoid awkward word breaks.

- A caption is text that appears below the graphic which sometimes explains or details the graphic image. When you select "Create Caption" from the Create Graphics dialog box (illustrated above), the screen will become blank for you to type the desired caption. The margins of the caption screen correspond to the margins of the box. The box number will appear in the caption screen automatically. To delete the box number, press backspace and then type your caption.

- In this exercise, you will create a two-column article and import several graphics using different text wrap options.

EXERCISE DIRECTIONS:

1. Select Graphics Mode view.

2. Start with a clear screen.

3. Use the default margins.

4. Begin the exercise on Ln 1.5".

5. Type the heading in sans serif 24 point bold. Return three times.

6. Create two columns.

7. Prepare the report illustrated on the right. Use sans serif 24 point bold for the heading, serif 11 point for the paragraph text, and sans serif 14-point bold for the subheadings.

8. Import PARROT.WPG. in the first column where shown.
   - Center and size it to .75" wide x .75" high.
   - Include a caption in sans serif 8-point bold italics that reads, "The Parrot."
   - Wrap text "On Both Sides."

9. Import HUMBIRD.WPG in the second column where shown.
   - Center and size it to .75" wide x .75" high.
   - Include a centered caption in sans serif 8-point bold italics that reads, "The Hummingbird."
   - Wrap text "On Neither Side."

10. Import PHEASANT.WPG.
    - Size it to 3" wide x 3" high.
    - Include a centered caption in sans serif 8-point bold italics that reads, "The Pheasant."
    - Use a "Contour Text Wrap."
    - Using the mouse, position the graphic between the columns as shown. Adjust the graphic as necessary to avoid awkward word breaks.

11. Preview your document.

12. Print one copy.

13. Save the file; name it **BIRDS**.

BIRDS

The Parrot/Parakeet

The parrot is a colorful bird that is found in warm, tropical regions. Because they can be affectionate and tame and taught to talk, they make popular pets. Parrots can be very noisy birds; they live in forested areas and mountains.

There are many different species of parrots. Half found in South parrots are have square are small and have pointed feathers.

the species are Central and America. True chubby and tails. Parakeets most of them tails and green

The Parrot

Parrots and Parakeets that are pets should be kept in cages large enough for them to exercise. They need water, fresh air and good food to grow and stay healthy. Don't become frustrated trying to teach your parrot to talk; words must be repeated many times for them to learn to repeat them.

The Hummingbird

The hummingbird is one of the smallest birds in the world. They live in the Western Hemisphere. They get their name from the sound that is made by the rapid flapping of their wings. Their wings can move 60-70 times per second.

The smallest hummingbird is brightly colored and is no larger than a bumblebee. Their long bills enable them to suck the flower nectar with

ease. They eat insects found inside flowers and on spider webs. The next

The Hummingbird

time you hear a humming sound, look quick; it might be a beautiful, brightly colored hummingbird!

The Pheasant

The pheasant is a medium to large bird related to the chicken. There are many different species of pheasants. They are found throughout the world but are primarily located in Southeast Asia, China, Japan and Russia.

Pheasants have short, stout bills and beautiful feathers on their long tail but can fly only short distances. Seeds, fruits, roots, greens, flowers, insects and small animals are food to the pheasant. People hunt pheasants for sport and for their tasty meat. Pheasant is considered a delicacy food in many parts of the world.

The Pheasant

TO IMPORT A GRAPHIC

1. Place cursor where you want graphics box to appear.
2. Click on Graphics .... Alt + G
3. Click on Graphics Boxes .... B

NOTE: WordPerfect automatically numbers each graphics box.

4. Click on Create C
5. Click on Filename .... F
6. Type name of graphic file.

NOTE: If filename is unknown, you can access File Manager (F5), and highlight file with a .WPG extension.

TO ADD A CAPTION

7. Click on Create Caption C
8. Press Backspace to delete "Figure #).
9. Type desired caption (in desired font and size).
10. Press F7 .... F7 to return to dialog box.

TO CHANGE TEXT FLOW

11. Click on Text Flows.
12. Click on a text flow option:

On Larger Side .... G

On Left Side L

On Right Side .... R

On Both Sides .... B

On Neither Side .... N

Through Box .... T

TO CONTOUR FLOW TEXT

Click on Contour Text Box.

ENHANCING A DOCUMENT: WATERMARKS

NOTES:

- A watermark is a lightened graphic image or text that prints in the background on a page. A watermark, like a header/footer, can appear on every page of your document or on selected pages.

- When the watermark screen appears, you can enter text or you can import a graphic image. You can apply typeface and type style changes to the text while you are in the watermark screen.

  However, you cannot change the size or position of the watermark graphic. By default, the

- watermark image is sized to the full page size and will be positioned between the margins. A box does not frame the image.

- When you return to your normal typing area, the watermark graphic or text will not be visible. You can view it through Print Preview.

- The watermark feature is accessed by selecting Header/Footer/Watermark on the Layout main menu.

EXERCISE DIRECTIONS:

1. Select Graphics Mode view.

2. Start with a clear screen.

3. Use the default margins.

4. Import SUMMRCNR.WPG as a watermark.

5. Create the invitation shown on the right. Use script 18-point and bold for "Cindy Davis."

6. Center the exercise top to bottom.

7. Preview your document.

8. Print one copy.

9. Save the exercise; name it **BEACH.**

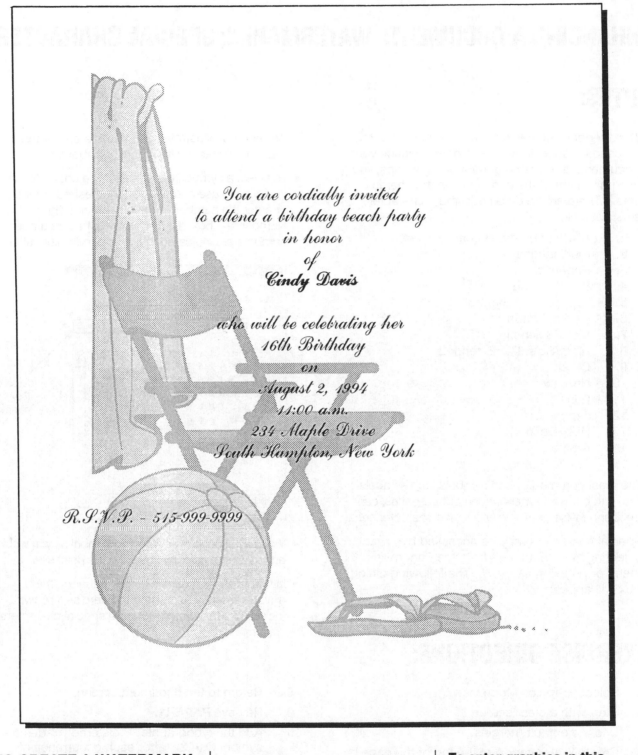

*You are cordially invited
to attend a birthday beach party
in honor
of
Cindy Davis*

*who will be celebrating her
16th Birthday
on
August 2, 1994
11:00 a.m.
234 Maple Drive
South Hampton, New York*

R.S.V.P. - 515-999-9999

TO CREATE A WATERMARK

Alt + F8

1. Click on Layout .... `Alt` + `L`
2. Click on Header/
    Footer/Watermark .... `H`
3. Click on Watermarks .... `W`
4. Click on Watermark A .... `A`

    or   or

    Click on Watermark B .... `B`
5. Click on a print page option:

    All Pages .... `A`
    Even Pages .... `V`
    Odd Pages .... `O`
6. Click on Create
    (Editing screen will appear).

To enter text in this screen:
    • Type text.

To enter graphics in this screen:

    • Click on Graphics .... `Alt` + `G`
    • Click on Graphics Boxes .... `B`
    • Click on Create .... `C`
    • Enter the graphic filename.
    • Click on OK .... `↵`
7. Press F7 .... `F7`
    to return to document.
8. Type document text as desired.

ENHANCING A DOCUMENT: WATERMARKS; SPECIAL CHARACTERS

NOTES:

- WordPerfect includes special characters that may be used for specific purposes or to enhance your document. If your printer supports graphics, you can print most of the characters in the character sets. There are 15 different symbol/character sets available:

  1. ASCII (the default character set)
  2. Multinational
  3. Phonetic
  4. Box Drawing
  5. Typographic Symbols
  6. Iconic Symbols
  7. Math/Scientific
  8. Math/Scientific Extended
  9. Greek
  10. Hebrew
  11. Cyrillic
  12. Japanese
  13. User-Defined
  14. Arabic
  15. Arabic Script

- The most commonly used symbols, and symbols that can be used for enhancement purposes, can be found in Typographic and Iconic character sets.

- Special characters may be accessed by selecting WP Characters from the Font main menu or pressing Ctrl + W. The following dialog box will appear:

- Appendix A illustrates all symbols/characters that are available within each symbol set.

- To select a symbol, either select the character set you wish to use and click on the desired symbol, or enter the number of the character in the Number text box. (Each character has a number; numbers are indicated in the appendix illustration).

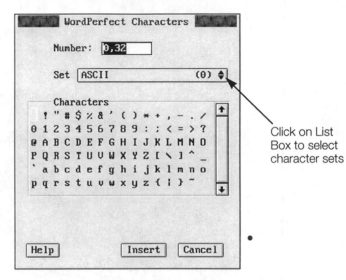

Click on List Box to select character sets

- You may change the size of the symbol as you would any other character by changing the point size.

- In this exercise, you will further enhance the advertisement you created in Exercise 116 by including a text watermark and special characters.

EXERCISE DIRECTIONS:

1. Select Graphics Mode view.
2. Start with a clear screen.
3. Use the default margins.
4. Create Watermark A at the top of the page by typing two lines of the word "WATERSHED" in sans serif 30 point bold. Use the iconic symbol shown (5,50) between each word.
6. Return to the document screen.
7. Create Watermark B at the bottom of the page (at Ln 9.3") as shown in sans serif 30 point bold. Use the iconic symbol shown (5,49) between each word.

8. Return to the document screen.
9. Retrieve **PAPER1.**
10. Add the typographic "registered" trademark symbol ® (**4,22**) after each occurrence of "WATERSHED PAPER."
11. Add the iconic check mark symbol (5,51) before each centered word.
12. Preview your document.
13. Print one copy.
14. Close your file; save the changes.

WATERSHED➤ WATERSHED➤
WATERSHED➤ WATERSHED➤

WATERSHED PAPER®

Papers that perform. Consistently. Time after time. That's what you can always expect when you specify WATERSHED'S premium text, cover and writing finishes. And now you can see how brilliantly our papers perform with a variety of inks thanks to our new *Think Ink Guide.*

This invaluable tool features more than 400 visual references to help you make accurate color choices. And get the results you expect. You'll find printed examples of black, metallic and solid colors in halftones, line art and screen tints on every one of our four leading lines of paper:

✓**ENVIRONMENT**

✓**CLASSIC LINEN**

✓**CREST LINEN**

✓**RAIN DROP**

Discover for yourself how *WATERSHED PAPER®* can be combined with a myriad of inks to expand your creativity.

For your copy of our new *Think Ink Guide,* just call the representatives listed on the enclosed brochure and ask for your guide.

WATERSHED➤ WATERSHED➤
WATERSHED➤ WATERSHED➤

TO INSERT SPECIAL CHARACTERS
Ctrl + W

1. Place cursor to the left of where you wish to insert character.

2. Press Ctrl + W, then skip to step 4.

   or

- Click on F**o**nt.................... `Alt` + `O`

3. Click on **W**P Characters............... `W`

4. Click on **S**et................................. `S`
   to display character set list.

5. Click on the desired character set.

6. Click on the desired symbol.

7. Click on Insert............................ `↵`

ENHANCING A DOCUMENT: WATERMARKS; SPECIAL CHARACTERS

NOTES:

- A watermark may be created before or after the document is on-screen.

- In this exercise, you will create a watermark and use special characters to enhance a memorandum you created earlier.

EXERCISE DIRECTIONS:

1. Select Graphics Mode view.

2. Start with a clear screen.

3. Open **MEMO.**

4. Import WATER4.WPG as a watermark.

5. Set all text to serif 12 point; set "MEMORANDUM" to 14 point.

6. Add the iconic clock symbol (5,31) before each bolded hotel (in the top list).

7. Preview your document.

8. Close the file; save the changes.

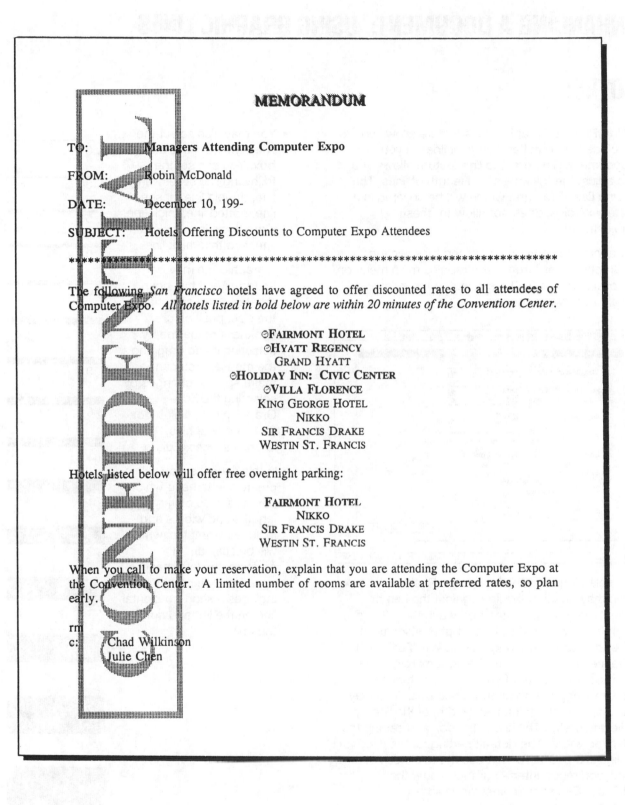

MEMORANDUM

TO: Managers Attending Computer Expo

FROM: Robin McDonald

DATE: December 10, 199-

SUBJECT: Hotels Offering Discounts to Computer Expo Attendees

****

The following *San Francisco* hotels have agreed to offer discounted rates to all attendees of Computer Expo. *All hotels listed in bold below are within 20 minutes of the Convention Center.*

FAIRMONT HOTEL
HYATT REGENCY
GRAND HYATT
HOLIDAY INN: CIVIC CENTER
VILLA FLORENCE
KING GEORGE HOTEL
NIKKO
SIR FRANCIS DRAKE
WESTIN ST. FRANCIS

Hotels listed below will offer free overnight parking:

FAIRMONT HOTEL
NIKKO
SIR FRANCIS DRAKE
WESTIN ST. FRANCIS

When you call to make your reservation, explain that you are attending the Computer Expo at the Convention Center. A limited number of rooms are available at preferred rates, so plan early.

rm

c: Chad Wilkinson
        Julie Chen

ENHANCING A DOCUMENT: USING GRAPHIC LINES

NOTES:

- WordPerfect's graphic lines feature allows you to include horizontal and vertical lines in your document. The graphic line feature allows you to adjust the thickness and length of lines. The "Line Draw" feature, which will be covered in a later exercise, does not allow for these adjustments.

- Graphic lines may be accessed by selecting "Graphic Lines" from the Graphics main menu or pressing Alt + F9. Once selected, the following dialog box will appear:

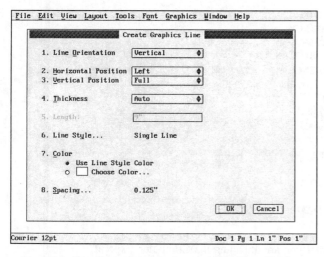

- By selecting from the Horizontal Position list box, you may position the line against the Left or Right margin, or Center it between the left and right margins, or start it at a Set Position from the left edge of the page, or have a "Full" line fill the area from the left to the right margin. You may set the length of your line by entering the desired length in the Length text box. You may also specify the thickness (width) of the line by clicking on the Thickness list box and setting the desired width. The default setting for the width of a line is 0.013". To increase the thickness of a line, you must enter a number higher than 0.013". See sample lines and width measurements on the right.

- You may also select the line style from this dialog box. You can set the following line styles: single line, double line, dashed line, dotted line, thick line, extra thick line, thick/thin line, and thin/thick line.

- A graphic line may be edited after it has been created. You can change the size, position or thickness of the line by selecting it and dragging the mouse. You can make specific changes by selecting the Edit Graphics Line dialog box (Click on Graphics, Graphics Lines, Edit.)

- In this exercise, you will create a letterhead which contains lines of varying lengths and widths and includes a graphic (which will be scaled). In addition, the letterhead contains footer text which includes a short horizontal line on the left and right of the text.

.013

.02

.03

.04

.05

.07

.08

.09

.1

.15

.2

.25

.3

.4

.5

EXERCISE DIRECTIONS:

1. Select Graphics Mode view.

2. Start with a clear screen.

3. Set the top and bottom margins to .5".

4. Create a horizontal line between the margins (full). Use the default thickness (.013).

5. Return twice.

6. Create a **left** horizontal line 1" in length, using the default width (.013").

7. Center text "The Lighthouse Inn" in serif 18-point bold. Insert any special character between each word.

8. Create a **right** horizontal line 1" in length using the default width (.013").

9. Return once.

10. Create a **left** horizontal line 1" in length, setting the width to 0.03". Create a right horizontal line using the same measurements.

11. Return twice.

12. Create a **left** horizontal line 1" in length, setting the width to .1".

13. Import and center LIGHTHS.WPG. Size the graphic to 3" wide x .5" high.

14. Using the Image Editor, scale the height of the graphic to 2.0" and the width to 5.0".

15. Create a **right** horizontal line 1" in length, setting the width to .1".

16. Return as many times as necessary to bring your cursor to 10.09".

17. Create a **left** horizontal line .5" in length, using the default width; center the footer text in sans serif 8 point. Use a special character between each word. Create a **right** horizontal line using the same measurements.

18. Preview your document.

19. Print one copy.

20. Save the exercise; name it **INN**.

continued . . .

The ☆ Lighthouse ☆ Inn

123 Wheel Avenue ☆ Ann Arbor ☆ Michigan ☆ 48187 ☆ 313 555-5555

TO CREATE HORIZONTAL LINES
Alt + F9, L

1. Click on Graphics .... Alt + G
2. Click on Graphics Lines L
3. Click on Create C
4. Select one or more of the following options:
   a. Click on Horizontal Position. .... H

Click on one:
   Set .... S
   • Type position
   • ENTER .... ↵
   Left L
   Right .... R
   Centered C
   Full .... F
   b. Click on Thickness .... T

   • Click on Set .... S
   • Type desired thickness
   c. Click on Length L
   • Type length
   d. Click on Line Style .... Y
   • double click on desired line style
5. Click on OK .... ↵

ENHANCING A DOCUMENT: USING GRAPHIC LINES

NOTES:

- WordPerfect allows you to create vertical lines of varying lengths and thickness.

- To create vertical graphic lines, you must access Graphics Lines from Graphics main menu as you did when you created horizontal lines. The adjustments are made in the Edit Graphic Lines dialog box:

```
File  Edit  View  Layout  Tools  Font  Graphics  Window  Help
┌──────────────────────────────────────────────────────────┐
│              ▓▓▓▓ Create Graphics Line ▓▓▓▓                │
│                                                          '│
│  1. Line Orientation    ┌Vertical      ⬍┐                 │
│                                                           │
│  2. Horizontal Position ┌Left          ⬍┐                 │
│  3. Vertical Position   ┌Full          ⬍┐                 │
│                                                           │
│  4. Thickness           ┌Auto          ⬍┐                 │
│                                                           │
│  5. Length:             ┌5"           ┐                   │
│                                                           │
│  6. Line Style...       Single Line                       │
│                                                           │
│  7. Color                                                 │
│      ● Use Line Style Color                               │
│      ○ □ Choose Color...                                  │
│                                                           │
│  8. Spacing...          0.125"                            │
│                                                           │
│                              ┌ OK ┐  ┌Cancel┐             │
└──────────────────────────────────────────────────────────┘
Courier 12pt                        Doc 1 Pg 1 Ln 1" Pos 1"
```

- To create a vertical line, you must first change the line orientation to "Vertical." The vertical line may be positioned slightly to the **L**eft of the margin or slightly to the **R**ight of the margin or centered between both margins. If you are creating a document containing columns, you may include vertical lines between specified columns. Or, you can use **S**et to enter a specific position from the left edge of the page. You may also adjust the Vertical Position of the line by indicating whether you want the line to start at the **T**op or **B**ottom margin, **C**enter it between the top and bottom margins, or Set the position of the line by indicating how far down from the top of the margin it should begin. If you want the line to extend from the top to the bottom margin, you may select the **F**ull page option. When you indicate that you would like a vertical line to start at the top or bottom margin, you can specify how long you would like the line to be. The length is calculated from the cursor to the specified margin.

- The line thickness is adjusted using the same measurements as the horizontal lines.

- In this exercise, you will enhance a menu you created earlier by creating a left and right vertical line which extends the full length of the page. Also included is a graphic which is scaled.

EXERCISE DIRECTIONS:

1. Select Graphics Mode view.
2. Start with a clear screen.
3. Open **FOOD**.
4. Set the top margin to .5"
5. With your cursor at the top of the screen, create a **left** vertical line extending the full length of the page, setting a .3" width.
6. Create a **right** vertical line extending the full length of the page, setting a .3" width.
7. Change the typeface, type style and type sizes of the text as follows:
   - "The Sherwood Forest Inn" to serif 36-point bold.
   - Address and phone number text to serif 10 point.
   - "BREAKFAST MENU" to sans serif 14 point bold.
   - Food item headings to serif 14 point.
   - Food items to serif 12 point.
   - "David Zeiss, Proprietor" to sans serif 12 point.
8. Insert 6 returns after the phone number.
9. Create a centered .02 horizontal graphic line below "BREAKFAST MENU," measuring 4.5" in length.
10. Import TREE.WPG. Size it to 1" x 1"; scale the height to 1.2" and the width to 1.7" and place it as shown.
11. Preview your document.
12. Print one copy.
13. Save the exercise; name it **FOOD1**.

The Sherwood Forest Inn

125 Pine Hill Road
Arlington, VA 22207
703-987-4443

BREAKFAST MENU

BEVERAGES

Herbal Tea...*$1.00*
Coffee...*$2.00*
Cappuccino...*$2.50*

FRUITS

Berry Refresher...*$3.00*
Sparkling Citrus Blend...*$3.00*
Baked Apples...*$3.50*

GRAINS

Fruity Oatmeal...*$3.50*
Bran Muffins...*$3.00*
Whole Wheat Zucchini Bread...*$3.00*
Four-Grain Pancakes...*$5.00*

EGGS

Baked Eggs with Creamed Spinach...*$6.50*
Poached Eggs with Hollandaise Sauce...*$6.00*
Scrambled Eggs...*$2.50*
Sweet Pepper and Onion Frittata...*$6.50*

David Zeiss, Proprietor

TO CREATE VERTICAL LINES
Alt + F9, L

1. Click on Graphics .... Alt + G
2. Click on Graphics Lines............... L
3. Click on Create C
4. Click on Line Orientation .... O
5. Select one or more of the following options:
   a. Select Vertical V
      OR

Click on Horizontal Position. .... H
Click on one:

Set... S
   • Type position
   • ENTER .... ↵
Left... L
Right .... R
Centered.................................... C
Between Columns .... B
b. Click on Thickness................... T

   • Click on Set......................... S
   • Type desired thickness
c. Click on Length......................... L
   • Type length
d. Click on Line Style .... Y
   • double click on desired line style
6. Click on OK................................. ↵

339

ENHANCING A DOCUMENT: USING TEXT BOXES

NOTES:

- In earlier exercises, you created a figure box for graphic images. The image was imported into the box. In this exercise, you will create a text box in which text will be inserted.

- Text boxes may be used for setting off special text from the rest of the document. The box may be horizontally positioned to the left, right or center of the document and may be positioned vertically on the page and sized as desired. These settings may be made on the Edit Graphics Dialog Box, the same dialog box used to create graphic images:

```
╔══════════ Edit Graphics Box ══════════╗
║                                        ║
║  1. Filename...                        ║
║                                        ║
║  2. Contents [None        ⬍]  7. Attach To [Paragraph      ⬍]
║                                        ║
║  3. Create Text...            8. Edit Position...
║                                  Horiz.  Right (Margin)
║  4. Create Caption...            Vert.   1.28"
║  ┌──────────────────────┐              ║
║  │                      │      9. Edit Size...
║  └──────────────────────┘         Width   1.79"
║  5. Options                       Height  1.01"
║     Content Options...                 ║
║     Caption Options...        T. Text Flow Around Box
║                                  Text Flows [On Larger Side ⬍]
║  6. Edit Border/Fill...           □ Contour Text Flow
║                                        ║
║  Y. Based on Box Style... Figure Box ◄─────
║  [Help] [Previous Home,PgUp] [Next Home,PgDn]    [OK] [Cancel]
╚════════════════════════════════════════╝
```

Change to "Text Box"

- WordPerfect automatically shades and includes a thick line above and below the box.

- To indicate that you are creating a text box, you must click on "Based on Box Style... and change the selection to "Text Box".

- The text box is similar to the figure box in that you can use the mouse to size and move the box when it is on-screen. In addition, you can rotate the box contents in 90°, 180° and 270° increments. In the illustration on the right, the word CHOCOLATE was rotated 90°.

- The text that will be used in the box can either be saved as a separate file and retrieved into the box or it can be typed into the box. Both procedures are outlined on the right.

- In this exercise, you will create an article, create two text boxes, one of which is rotated.

EXERCISE DIRECTIONS:

1. Select Graphics Mode view.

2. Start with a clear screen.

3. Use the default margins.

4. Create two-columns (newspaper style).

5. Type the text as shown; set it to serif 14 point.

6. Set line spacing to 1.3".

7. Create a text box; type the word CHOCOLATE (leave one space between each letter) in sans serif 48 point bold. Rotate the text box to 90°.

8. Size the text box so that the word appears as a strip (as shown) and place it at the left margin, approximately 2.5" from the top of the page. (The text will flow around the text box.)

9. Create another text box; center the text as shown in sans serif 14-point bold and place it at the right margin, approximately 2" from the top of the page.

NOTE: Since printers and typefaces available will vary, your text might run on to page 2. If this occurs, adjust your line spacing so that all text fits on one page.

10. Preview your document.

11. Print one copy.

12. Save the exercise; name it **COCOA**.

CHOCOLATE is probably the world's favorite food. You can drink it hot or cold, or eat it as a snack or as part of a meal. It is made into pies, cakes, cookies, candy, ice cream and even breakfast cereal. Chocolate comes in lacy Valentine boxes and in survival kits. It is nourishing, energy-giving and satisfying.

Chocolate came to us from Mexico, by way of Europe. When the Spanish explorer Cortez arrived at the court of Montezuma, the Aztec Emperor, he found him drinking a cold, bitter drink called Chocolatl. It was made from seeds of the cacao tree, ground in water and mixed with spices. Montezuma gave Cortez the recipe and some cacao and vanilla beans. Cortez took them back to Spain, where the Spanish king and queen quickly improved the drink by adding sugar and having it served hot. For about a hundred years, chocolate was exclusively a royal Spanish treat. But once the secret leaked out, the upper classes in most of the European capitals were soon sipping hot chocolate. From Amsterdam, the Dutch settlers brought chocolate to the American colonies, and in 1765 a man named Baker started a chocolate mill near Boston.

By this time, people had figured out how to make powdered cocoa by extracting some of the cocoa butter

---

THE CHOCOLATE FACTORY

SPECIALIZING IN CHOCOLATE CAKES, COOKIES, CANDY AND OTHER MOUTH-WATERING DELIGHTS.

754 Riverbend Drive
San Francisco, CA 94107

415-987-4333

HOURS: 9-7 DAILY.

---

and adding it to the ground beans to make solid chocolate.

A hundred years later a man in Switzerland found a way to make solid sweet milk chocolate, and a great candy business was born. Chocolate companies like Nestle and Hershey need a lot of cacao beans. About one-third of the supply, over 350 thousand tons, is imported each year from the African country of Ghana. Ghana is the world's largest supplier of cacao beans. For many years, chocolate was made by hand. Now, machines do most of the work.

THE CHOCOLATE FACTORY has been specializing in the finest chocolate products for over 50 years. Stop in and sample some of our outstanding chocolate delights.

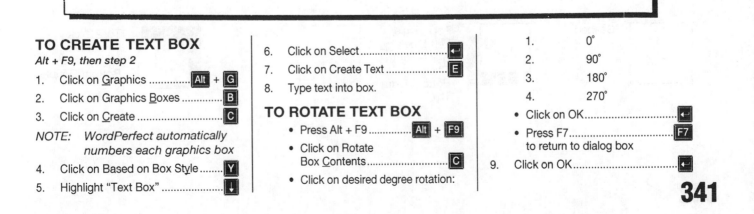

TO CREATE TEXT BOX
Alt + F9, then step 2
1. Click on Graphics .... Alt + G
2. Click on Graphics Boxes .... B
3. Click on Create C
NOTE: *WordPerfect automatically numbers each graphics box*
4. Click on Based on Box Style .... Y
5. Highlight "Text Box" .... ↓

6. Click on Select .... ↵
7. Click on Create Text .... E
8. Type text into box.

TO ROTATE TEXT BOX
• Press Alt + F9 .... Alt + F9
• Click on Rotate Box Contents C
• Click on desired degree rotation:

1. 0°
2. 90°
3. 180°
4. 270°
• Click on OK .... ↵
• Press F7 .... F7
  to return to dialog box
9. Click on OK .... ↵

341

ENHANCING A DOCUMENT: USING BORDERS AND FILLS

NOTES:

- WordPerfect's border feature allows you to place a border around a paragraph, a page or text that is formatted in columns.

- To place a border around a paragraph, position your cursor anywhere in the paragraph and follow the keystrokes outlined. The border will appear around the paragraph you specified and all paragraphs that follow. If, however, you want the border to appear around one paragraph only, select the paragraph to have a border and follow the keystrokes outlined.

- When a border is applied to a paragraph, the border will automatically extend between the left and right margins. A paragraph which contains a border may look like a text box. Remember, however, a text box can be sized; a paragraph with a border cannot!

- The default border style is a single border on all four sides. You can customize your border by choosing a separate style for individual lines, create a drop shadow effect to the border, or indicate square or rounded corners. This may be accomplished by selecting any one of the following other border styles for any side of your graphics box through the Borders Style dialog box:

- However, WordPerfect also allows you to change the border style and/or fills (shading) of the graphic or text boxes you create.

- You may change the border style or fill while in the process of creating the graphic or text box by selecting Edit Border/Fill from the Edit Graphics dialog box (Alt + G, B) shown below:

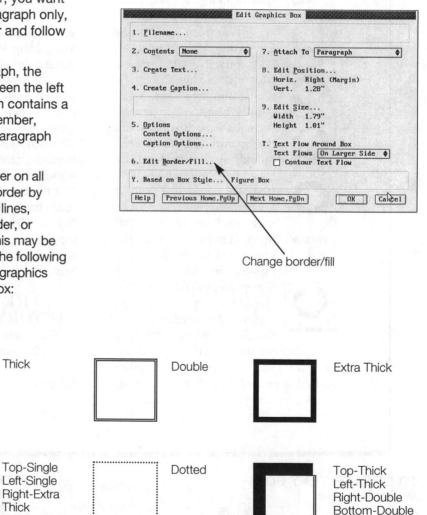

Change border/fill

☐ Single (the default)	☐ Thick	☐ Double	☐ Extra Thick
☐ Dashed	☐ Top-Single Left-Single Right-Extra Thick Bottom-Extra Thick	☐ Dotted	☐ Top-Thick Left-Thick Right-Double Bottom-Double

- If the graphic or text box has already been created, you may edit the border style and/or fill by selecting Borders or Fill Styles from the Graphics main menu.

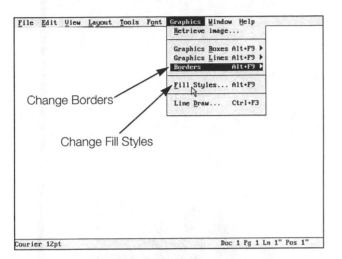

Change Borders

Change Fill Styles

- Through the Fills Style dialog box, you may shade your graphics box by selecting the percentage of black you wish to create. Note the examples below:

- In order to edit a graphic or text box that has already been created, you must first select the graphic (or text box) and then access the options through the menus.

- When a graphic image is used in a shaded box, some printers will shade inside the image while some printers leave a white inside image.

- The quality of shading will vary depending on the type of printer used.

- In this exercise, you will import the same graphic four times and give each a different border and fill in each of them. You will also place a dotted border around the title.

Single Border
25% Shading

Double Border
50% Shading

Dashed Border
75% Shading

Dotted Border
100% Shading

EXERCISE DIRECTIONS:

1. Select Graphics Mode view.

2. Start with a clear screen.

3. Create each graphic, including the caption, indicated on the next page. Use PENPUSH.WPG as your image. Change the borders and fills as directed in each caption.

4. Position images 1 and 3 left and images 2 and 4 right; size each graphic to 2" wide x 2" tall.

5. Preview your exercise.

6. Print one copy.

7. Save the exercise; name it **BORDERS**.

continued . . .

Double Line Border;
10% Fill

Dashed Border; 20% Fill

Dotted Border; 40% Fill

Extra Thick Border; 60%
Fill

TO PLACE BORDER AROUND PARAGRAPH, COLUMN OR PAGE

Alt + F9

1. Position cursor in paragraph to receive border

   or

   Select text in paragraph you want to receive border.

2. Click on <u>G</u>raphics .... `Alt` + `G`
3. Click on B<u>o</u>rders .... `O`
4. Click on type of border you want to add:

   - <u>P</u>aragraph .... `P`
   - Pa<u>g</u>e .... `G`
   - <u>C</u>olumn .... `C`

TO CHANGE BORDER STYLE

a. Click on <u>B</u>order Style............... `B`

b. Highlight desired border style .... `↑` `↓`

c. Click on Select........................... `↵`

TO CHANGE FILL STYLE

a. Click on <u>F</u>ill Style .... `F`

b. Highlight desired fill percent...................... `↑` `↓`

c. Click on Select........................... `↵`

d. Click on Close........................... `↵`

TO CUSTOMIZE BORDER STYLE

a. Click on <u>C</u>ustomize................... `C`

b. Click on <u>L</u>ines .... `L`

c. Click on line to customize:

   - Select <u>A</u>ll .... `A`
   - <u>L</u>eft Line .... `L`
   - <u>R</u>ight Line................... `R`
   - <u>T</u>op Line...................... `T`
   - <u>B</u>ottom Line .... `B`

d. Highlight desired line style .. `↑` `↓`

e. Click on Select........................... `↵`

f. Click on Close........................... `↵`

g. Click on Close........................... `↵`

5. Click on OK................................. `↵`

TO CHANGE BORDER STYLE/FILL OF GRAPHIC OR TEXT BOX

1. Click on <u>G</u>raphics .... `Alt` + `G`
2. Click on Graphic <u>B</u>oxes............... `B`
3. Click on <u>C</u>reate .... `C`

   After importing desired graphic or creating desired text box:

4. Click on Edit <u>B</u>order/Fill .... `B`
5. Follow steps b-g left for "Customize Border Style" and/or steps a-d left for "Change Fill Style."
6. Click on OK................................. `↵`

ENHANCING A DOCUMENT: USING BORDERS AND FILLS

NOTES:

- In this exercise, you will import a graphic and place a double line border around it. In addition, you will create a border around paragraphs of text and around the entire page. To create the "drop shadow" effect around the page, you will create extra thick right and bottom lines.

EXERCISE DIRECTIONS:

1. Select Graphic Mode view.
2. Start with a clear screen.
3. Open **RSVP**.
4. Reveal your codes and delete the Center Page Top to Bottom Code.
5. Insert 9 returns at the top of the page.
6. Import SKIPPER.WPG; center and size it to 1.5" wide x 1.5" high.
7. Select the first two paragraphs indicated, and place a border around them with a 10% fill.
8. Select the second paragraph indicated and place a border around it with a 10% fill.
9. Place a border around the entire page. Create an extra thick right and bottom line to create the drop shadow effect.
10. Preview your document.
11. Print one copy.
12. Save the file; name it **RSVP2**.

CELEBRATE

ON THE HUDSON

This New Year's Eve, there is no more elegant, more beautiful spot than the Hudson River Cafe. Dance with the Statue of Liberty in view to the sounds of our live band and DJ.

Enjoy a six-course Hudson Valley feast and a spectacular dessert to be remembered as the last memory of the year.

NEW YEAR'S EVE DINNER DANCE

Call for reservations 212-876-9888.
Our courteous staff will be glad to assist you at any time.
We are located at Four World Financial Center.

HUDSON RIVER CLUB

ENHANCING A DOCUMENT:
USING BORDERS, FILLS AND TEXT BOXES

NOTES:

- In this exercise, you will create a fax cover sheet using a text box and place a border and shade "To/From/Number of Pages/Remarks" information. You will also include a page border.

EXERCISE DIRECTIONS:

1. Select Graphics Mode view.

2. Start with a clear screen.

3. Use the default margins.

4. Create a watermark that reads, FAX♦FAX♦FAX in sans serif 60-point bold using a special character between words as shown.

5. Center "TO" at Ln 5" in sans serif 18-point bold. Return four times.

6. Center the remaining headings using sans serif 18-point bold and return four times between each as shown.

7. Center the address and phone information at Ln 9.83" in sans serif 10-point bold.

8. Create a page border.

9. Create a centered text box and center "GLOBAL TRAVEL GROUP" within it in sans serif 12-point bold. Size it to 1.3" wide x 1.3" high. Create a left, right, top and bottom "thick" line on the box.

10. Using the mouse, position the box about one inch above "TO."

11. Import GLOBE.WPG. Size it to .5" wide x .5" high and place it above the text box. Remove the border lines.

12. Create a border around TO/FROM/NUMBER OF PAGES/REMARKS and use a 20% fill.

13. Preview your document.

14. Print one copy.

15. Save the exercise; name it **FAX**.

FAX✦FAX✦FAX

GLOBAL TRAVEL GROUP

TO

FROM

NUMBER OF PAGES

REMARKS

485 Madison Avenue✦New York, NY✦10034✦Phone: (212) 234-4566✦ Fax: (212)345-9877

ENHANCING A DOCUMENT: CREATING A NEWSLETTER

NOTES:

- A newsletter is a document used by an organization to communicate information about an event, news of general interest, or information regarding new products.

- Newsletters consist of several parts:

    NAMEPLATE – may include the name of the newsletter, the organization publishing the newsletter, the logo (a symbol or distinctive type style used to represents the organization).

    DATELINE – includes the volume number, issue number and the date.

    HEADLINE – title preceding each article.

    BODY TEXT – the text of the article.

- To draw the reader's attention to emphasize a major point in an article, a "pull quote" may be used. A pull quote is set off in larger point size and a different type style than the body text. Note example on the right.

- In this exercise, you will create the three-column newsletter shown. The pull quote is created as a text box and placed as desired.

EXERCISE DIRECTIONS:

1. Select Text Mode view.

2. Start with a clear screen.

3. Enter the following pull quote into a text box:

    "If we continue to ignore the need for wildlife conservation, today's endangered species will soon become extinct."

4. Save the file; name it **QUOTE**.

5. Start with a clear screen.

6. Set left, right, top and bottom margins to .5".

7. Center the nameplate as shown. Set "Save the" to sans serif 14-point bold. Set the first and last "S" in "Species" to serif 48-point bold cap. Set the remaining characters in the word to serif 30-point bold. Use any desired special character set to 30-point bold before and after the word "Species."

8. Change the font to sans serif 10-point bold italic.

9. Return twice.

10. Create a .1" "full" horizontal line between the margins. Return once.

11. Enter dateline information as shown (left-align "Volume 1," center "Quarterly Newsletter of the Wildlife Society" and right-align "Summer 1994").

12. Create a horizontal line between the margins using the default thickness. Return three times.

13. Create three columns.

14. Type the newsletter as shown; note the following:

    - Center the headlines; set them to sans serif 14-point bold.

    - Set all paragraph text to serif 12 point.

    - Full justify all paragraph text.

    - Create a dashed box around "Save the Species...." and center each line within the column as shown.

    - Import the text box, **QUOTE**. Use the mouse to size it to approximately 2.5" wide x 1.75" high, and place as shown.

    - Import PHEASANT.WPG. Use the mouse to size it to approximately 1.5" wide x 1" high; use a contour text wrap and place it as shown. Create a centered caption in sans serif 10-point bold that reads, "KEEP ME FLYING."

    - Set "In the next issue:" information to 14-point, italic.

15. Spell check.

16. Preview your document.

17. Print one copy.

18. Save the file; name it **SPECIES**.

Save The

⋆SPECIES⋆

Volume 1   *Quarterly Newsletter of the Wildlife Society*   Summer 1994

What is Wildlife Conservation?

Wildlife Conservation includes all human efforts to preserve wild animals and plants and save them from extinction. Our organization supports the protection and wise management of wild species and their environment. The greatest danger to wildlife results from human activities; your contributions aid us in funding demonstrations and activities which help educate others about the dangers of these activities and help preserve the existence of disappearing species. Send contributions to:

Save the Species
1356 Pacific Road
San Francisco, CA 90456

If we continue to ignore the need for wildlife conservation, today's endangered species will soon become extinct. Extinction is particularly dangerous due to the economic, scientific and survival value of wildlife. Wild species of animals and plants provide many substances which are valuable to the economies of different countries, both as food products and as

products for trade. The study of wildlife provides important knowledge about life processes which has led to the discovery of medical and scientific products. Additionally, the existence of many species of wildlife maintains the balance of living systems on the earth. The loss of certain species will affect the existence of others that depend on it perhaps for food. Volunteer for *Save the Species* and help us convince Washington that it is vital to protect the existence of endangered species through legislation!

Endangered Species of the Season: The California Condor

The California condor, a vulture, is the largest flying land bird in North America and makes its home in Southern California. Black feathers cover most of the bird's body except for the white area on the underside of the condor's wings. The neck and head have no

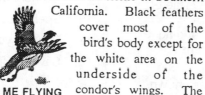

KEEP ME FLYING

feathers and are a red-orange color. The condor is a unique bird because it does not build a nest, but lays its eggs in caves, holes, or among rocks. It is also a particularly strong flier; it can soar and glide in the air for long distances, flapping its wings an average of only once an hour. It is a carnivore and eats the remains of dead animals.

By the end of the 1980s, only 30 condors remained in the United States. The diminished number of condors is a result of hunting. The growth of urban areas in Southern California also poses a threat to the natural habitat of the bird. *Save the Species* urges you to write to your Congressperson and local government officials to inform them of your support of more land for sanctuaries to help keep the condor alive.

In the next issue: What is happening to the Killer Whale and its cousin, The Dolphin.

> **"If we continue to ignore the need for wildlife conservation, today's endangered species will soon become extinct."**

ENHANCING A DOCUMENT: CREATING A NEWSLETTER

NOTES:

- In this exercise, you will create another newsletter using the techniques you learned in earlier exercises.

EXERCISE DIRECTIONS:

1. Select Text Mode view.

2. Start with a clear screen.

3. Enter the following text into a text box in sans serif 10-point bold italics:

   Travel Trivia: Q: What city is said to take its name from a Huron word meaning "Meeting Place of the Waters?" A: Toronto.

4. Save the file; name it **TRIVIA**.

5. Start with a clear screen.

6. Select Graphics Mode view.

7. Type the nameplate as shown using serif 30-point bold for "American," 60-point bold for the "T" in "Traveler," and 48-point bold for the remaining letters in the word.

8. Change the font to sans serif 10 point.

9. Return twice.

10. Create a .1" thick "full" horizontal line, and place it above the "R" in "Traveler" as shown.

11. Create a 0.13 thick "full" horizontal line between the margins. Return once.

12. Enter the dateline information as shown; (left-align "Volume 3, Number 3," center "A Publication of Carls Travel Network," and right-align "Summer 1994. " Return three times .

13. Import GLOBE.WPG. Size it to approximately 1" x 1" and place it as shown.

14. Create three columns; insert vertical lines between each column.

15. Type the newsletter as shown; note the following:

    - Center the headlines; set them to sans serif 14-point bold.

    - Set all paragraph text to serif 12 point. Set initial capitals for each paragraph to serif 18-point bold.

    - Set "The Greek Islands" to serif 14-point bold; set Greek Island text to sans serif 10-point.

    - Import the text box, **TRIVIA**. Use the mouse to size it to approximately 1.75" wide x 2.5" high, and place it as shown.

    - Import SKIPPER.WPG. Use the mouse to size it to approximately .5" wide x 2" high; use a contour text wrap, and place it as shown.

    - Shade the indicated text using the following paragraph border settings:

      Border Style: None

      Fill Style: 20% shaded fill

    - Create a page border around the entire document.

16. Spell check.

17. Preview your document.

18. Save the file; name it **JOURNEY**.

AMERICAN
TRAVELER

Volume 3, Number 3   A Publication of Carls Travel Network   Summer 1994

SMOKERS MEET NEW RESTRICTIONS DURING TRAVEL

Travelers should be aware of increased constraints on the ability to smoke in public places. About five years ago, smoking was prohibited on all domestic airline flights. The Dallas-Fort Worth Airport recently declared the entire

TRAVEL TRIVIA:

Q: What city is said to take its name from a Huron word meaning "Meeting Place of the Waters?"

A: Toronto.

passenger terminal off limits to smokers. Those wishing to smoke will now have to leave the airport premises to do so.

Perhaps more far reaching is the law passed in Los Angeles which makes cigarette smoking illegal in restaurants. Violators face a $50 fine for the first offense, $100 fine for the second offense within a year, and $250 fine for every offense after that. Be cautious when traveling not to violate unexpected smoking laws!

CRUISING ON THE RHINE

Strasbourg, the capital of French Alsace, is a wonderful city to begin or end a cruise. Its pink sandstone Cathedral and a well-preserved old town are enchanting attractions for vacationing tourists. The cost of a three-day cruise including two evening meals, two breakfasts, two luncheons and coffee and cakes will be approximately $567 a person. The view from the middle of the river is more dramatic than the glimpses of the same

scenery that a passenger sees on the train ride along the river bank from Cologne to Frankfurt. For further information, contact your local travel agent and request the RHINE RIVER CRUISES PACKAGE or the SILLIA TOURS PACKAGE.

TRAVEL HIGHLIGHT OF THE SEASON THE GREEK ISLANDS

There are over 3,000 islands which comprise "The Greek Islands." However, only 170 of these islands are inhabited, each with its own character and terrain. This summer, Sunshine Travel Network is offering special fares on cruises to many of these charming islands. A four-day cruise to Rhodes, Heraklion, Santorini, and Piraeus costs $799 per person. This package is definitely the buy of the season!

ENHANCING A DOCUMENT: USING LINE DRAW

NOTES:

- WordPerfect's Line Draw feature allows you to use the four cursor arrow keys to draw charts, boxes, graphs, or do line drawings around existing text.

- If you make an error, you can erase it by selecting the erase feature and retracing your lines.

- If you wish to draw lines around text, first type the text, then turn on the Line Draw feature. However, if you wish to add text to a Line Draw box, use TYPEOVER. (Press "Ins" key once.)

- The Line Draw feature gives you three options to select a draw character: option 1 - a single line, option 2 - a double line, option 3 - defaults to an asterisk but can be changed, using option 4, to a shaded line or any character you wish.

- Sometimes it becomes necessary to suspend the Line Draw feature temporarily so that you can move the cursor to another location without drawing. You can do this by accessing the Line Draw feature and selecting "Move."

- You can use the Line Draw feature with the REPEAT KEY function. Therefore, if you wanted

to draw a line 35 characters long, you would depress Ctrl + R and indicate 35 before you drew the line.

- You cannot use Line Draw with a proportionally spaced font. You must use a monospaced font (such as Courier) to use this feature.

- Some printers do not support the Line Draw feature.

- You may wish to combine Graphics Lines, Text Boxes and Line Draw features. The Line Draw feature does not enable you to vary the thickness of the lines or move them as you can with the Graphics Line feature. Select the feature(s) that best accomplishes your task.

- To exit Line Draw, press F7.

- Line Draw cannot be used with centered text; use it on left-justified text only.

- In this exercise, you will create an organizational chart using the Line Draw feature. An organizational chart lists the hierarchy or ranking/reporting order of people in an organization.

EXERCISE DIRECTIONS:

1. Select Graphics Mode view.

2. Start with a clear screen.

3. Use the default margins.

4. Begin the exercise on Ln 2".

5. Center the heading using serif 14-point bold.

6. Using the Line Draw feature, create the organizational chart on the right. HINT: Center the words "House of Representatives," note the "Pos" indicator, delete the center command and space it

back to the correct "Pos." Then draw the box around it. Draw all other boxes, then insert the words within them. REMINDER: When inserting words within a box, be sure the TYPEOVER mode is on.

Use your judgement for establishing box sizes.

7. Print one copy.

8. Save the exercise; name it **RANK**.

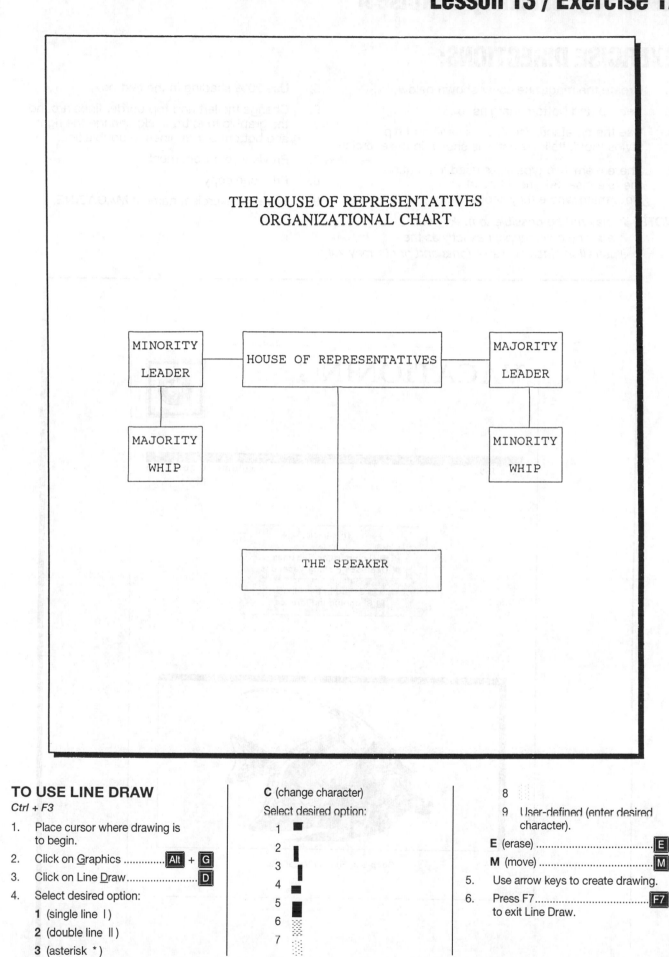

THE HOUSE OF REPRESENTATIVES
ORGANIZATIONAL CHART

MINORITY LEADER — HOUSE OF REPRESENTATIVES — MAJORITY LEADER

MAJORITY WHIP

MINORITY WHIP

THE SPEAKER

TO USE LINE DRAW
Ctrl + F3

1. Place cursor where drawing is to begin.
2. Click on Graphics .... Alt + G
3. Click on Line Draw...................... D
4. Select desired option:

    1 (single line │)

    2 (double line ‖)

    3 (asterisk *)

C (change character)
Select desired option:

1

2

3

4

5

6

7

8

9 User-defined (enter desired character).

E (erase) .... E

M (move) .... M

5. Use arrow keys to create drawing.

6. Press F7................................... F7
    to exit Line Draw.

355

EXERCISE DIRECTIONS:

1. Create the magazine cover shown below.

2. Set top and bottom margins to .5".

3. Use the typefaces (serif, sans serif) and type styles (bold, italic) exactly as shown in the exercise.

4. There were two type sizes used in creating the exercise: 36 and 14 point. Determine where they should be used.

NOTE: It may not be possible to make your magazine cover appear exactly as the illustration since available fonts and prints may vary.

5. Use 20% shading in the text box.

6. Change the left and top border lines around the graphic to extra thick; change the right and bottom border lines to double line.

7. Preview your document.

8. Print one copy.

9. Save the exercise; name it **MAGAZINE**.

EXERCISE DIRECTIONS:

1. Create the alumni newsletter shown below.

2. Set top and bottom margins to .5".

3. Use the typefaces (serif, sans serif) and type styles (bold, italics) exactly as shown in the exercise.

4. There were six type sizes used in creating the exercise: 48, 30, 24, 18, 12, 10 and 8 point. Determine where they should be used.

NOTE: It may not be possible to make your newsletter appear exactly as the illustration since available fonts and printers vary.

5. Use 10% shading in the text box.

6. Spell check.

7. Preview your document.

8. Print one copy.

9. Save the exercise; name it **ALUMNI**.

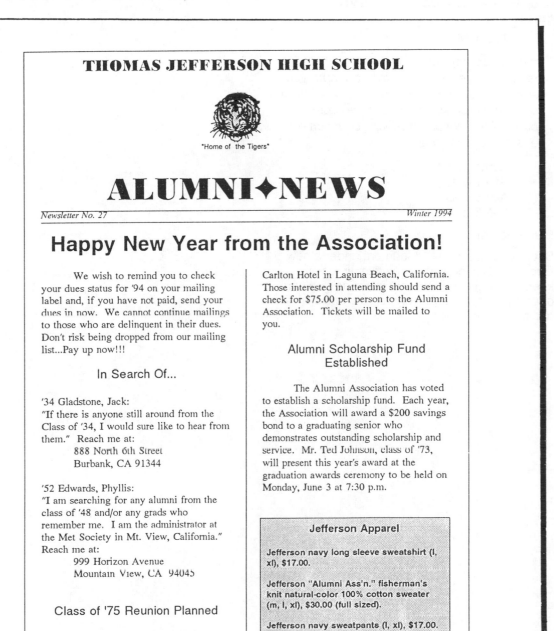

THOMAS JEFFERSON HIGH SCHOOL

"Home of the Tigers"

ALUMNI◆NEWS

Newsletter No. 27   *Winter 1994*

Happy New Year from the Association!

We wish to remind you to check your dues status for '94 on your mailing label and, if you have not paid, send your dues in now. We cannot continue mailings to those who are delinquent in their dues. Don't risk being dropped from our mailing list...Pay up now!!!

In Search Of...

'34 Gladstone, Jack:
"If there is anyone still around from the Class of '34, I would sure like to hear from them." Reach me at:
888 North 6th Street
Burbank, CA 91344

'52 Edwards, Phyllis:
"I am searching for any alumni from the class of '48 and/or any grads who remember me. I am the administrator at the Met Society in Mt. View, California." Reach me at:
999 Horizon Avenue
Mountain View, CA 94045

Class of '75 Reunion Planned

Mr. Robert Wascher, 1975 Class President, is organizing a reunion for the graduating class of 1975. The reunion will be held on September 29, 1995 at the Ritz-

Carlton Hotel in Laguna Beach, California. Those interested in attending should send a check for $75.00 per person to the Alumni Association. Tickets will be mailed to you.

Alumni Scholarship Fund Established

The Alumni Association has voted to establish a scholarship fund. Each year, the Association will award a $200 savings bond to a graduating senior who demonstrates outstanding scholarship and service. Mr. Ted Johnson, class of '73, will present this year's award at the graduation awards ceremony to be held on Monday, June 3 at 7:30 p.m.

Jefferson Apparel

Jefferson navy long sleeve sweatshirt (l, xl), $17.00.

Jefferson "Alumni Ass'n." fisherman's knit natural-color 100% cotton sweater (m, l, xl), $30.00 (full sized).

Jefferson navy sweatpants (l, xl), $17.00.

Make checks payable to "Jefferson Alumni Association"

DO-IT YOURSELF, EXTRA-CREDIT PROJECTS:

EXERCISE DIRECTIONS:

1. Using the enhancement techniques you have learned in Lesson 13 and your own creativity, open the following documents and enhance them:

    RESUME

    NOTE: *It is not appropriate to include graphics in a resume. Use typeface, type style and type size enhancements. You might also want to use a page border or lines to separate parts of the document.Keep you resume design conservative.*

    COMPANY
    BULLETS
    AGELESS
    ITINER

2. Print one copy of each.

3. Save each enhanced document under a new filename. (Saving with a new filename will keep the original document intact so you can open the original again and create another design.)

LESSON 14 / EXERCISES 130-135
SORTING / FILE MANAGER

- **Basic Sorting**
- **Using File Manager Options:**
  - **- Deleting Files**
  - **- Renaming Files**
  - **- Copying Files**
  - **- Word/Name Searching**

BASIC SORTING: BY LINE

NOTES:

- WordPerfect's Sort feature allows you to arrange text alphabetically or numerically by line, by paragraph, by record within a merge data file or table, or within parallel columns.

- When sorting by line, text or numbers may be arranged in ascending order (from A to Z) or 1 to 25) or descending order (Z to A or 21 to 1). *By default, WordPerfect sorts by line in ascending order.*

- A line sort should be used to arrange lists or columns of text and/or numbers.

- Before you perform a sort, you must be sure your data is set up properly. A line record must end with a hard or soft return and records should have one tab per column. You can, however, type a list at the left edge of the screen and sort it.

- To begin the sort, place your cursor in the first column to be sorted and follow the keystroke procedures on the next page.

- Sort may be accessed by selecting Sort from the Tools main menu or by clicking on Sort on the TOOLS button bar. The following Sort (Source and Destination) dialog box appears.

The *From* (Source) text box requires you to indicate the name of the file you wish to sort. Since your file is already on the screen, click on OK or press ENTER to accept the default (Document on Screen).

The *To* (Destination) text box requires you to indicate the name of the file where you wish to save the sorted text.   If you want the sorted text to be saved to another file, click on File (or press L) and enter the file name. If you want the sorted text to appear on the screen, click on OK or press ENTER to accept the default (Document on Screen).

Caution: It is important to save your document before you begin a sort. If your sort produces unexpected results, you can close your file without saving it, open the file again, and repeat the sort process.

```
┌──────────── Sort (Source and Destination) ────────────┐
│                                                        │
│  ┌ From (Source) ──────────────────────────────────┐  │
│  │  1. ☒ Document on Screen                         │  │
│  │  2. ☐ File: [_____▼]  │  │
│  └──────────────────────────────────────────────────┘  │
│  ┌ To (Destination) ───────────────────────────────┐  │
│  │  3. ☒ Document on Screen                         │  │
│  │  4. ☐ File: [_____▼]  │  │
│  └──────────────────────────────────────────────────┘  │
│  [ File List... F5 ]  [ QuickList... F6 ]   [ OK ] [ Cancel ] │
└────────────────────────────────────────────────────────┘
```

- After indicating the source and destination files, the dialog box shown below will appear.

  The *Record Type* text box requires you to indicate the type of sort you are performing: line, paragraph, or merge data file.

  The *Sort Keys* selection enables you to give WordPerfect information about how you want the material sorted: the type of sort, the field to use and the word to use.

  - "Key" refers to the item (field and word in the field). Key one (the default) is the primary sort item. Key two is the secondary sort item.

  - Type" refers to the kind of data to be sorted: Alpha(betic) or Num(eric).

- "Ord" refers whether you want the sort in ascending (↑) or descending (↓) order.

- "Field" refers to a column of text. In tabulated data, the first field is the left margin, the second field is the first tab stop, the third field is the second tab stop, etc.

- "Word" refers to what word in the field (column) you wish to sort on — first (1) second (2), third (3), last (-1), second from last (-2), etc.

- To activate the sort, select "Perform Action" or press ENTER.

- In this exercise, you will sort the names in ascending order (alphabetically A-Z). Be sure to set tabs for each column.

```
C:\PAT\FORM.FF                                    Doc 1 Pg 1 Ln 1" Pos 1"
▓▓▓▓▓▓▓▓▓▓▓▓▓▓▓▓▓▓▓▓▓▓▓▓▓▓▓▓ Sort ▓▓▓▓▓▓▓▓▓▓▓▓▓▓▓▓▓▓▓▓▓▓▓▓▓▓
1. Record Type  │Line              ⬍│
                                    ┌─Key Type  Ord Field      Word─┐
2. Sort Keys (Sort Priority)   Add  │ 1  Alpha   ↑    1          1  │▲│
                               Edit │                               │ │
                               Delete│                              │ │
                               Insert│                              │▼│
                                    └───────────────────────────────┘
3. Select Records: │                                              │
4. ☐ Select Without Sorting
5. ☐ Sort Uppercase First   │Perform Action│  │View│  │Close│  │Cancel│
```

EXERCISE DIRECTIONS:

1. Select Text Mode view.

2. Start with a clear screen.

3. Use the default margins.

4. Create the exercise shown on the next page using tabular columns. (Use absolute tabs.)

5. Center the exercise vertically.

6. Save the exercise; name it **SORT**. *DO NOT EXIT THE DOCUMENT.*

7. Sort the first word in the name column alphabetically (ascending order).

8. Save the sorted text to a new file; name it **SORT1**.

9. Sort the second column alphabetically.

10. Save the sorted text to a new file; name it **SORT2**.

11. Print SORT1 and SORT2 from the File Manager screen (F5).

continued . . .

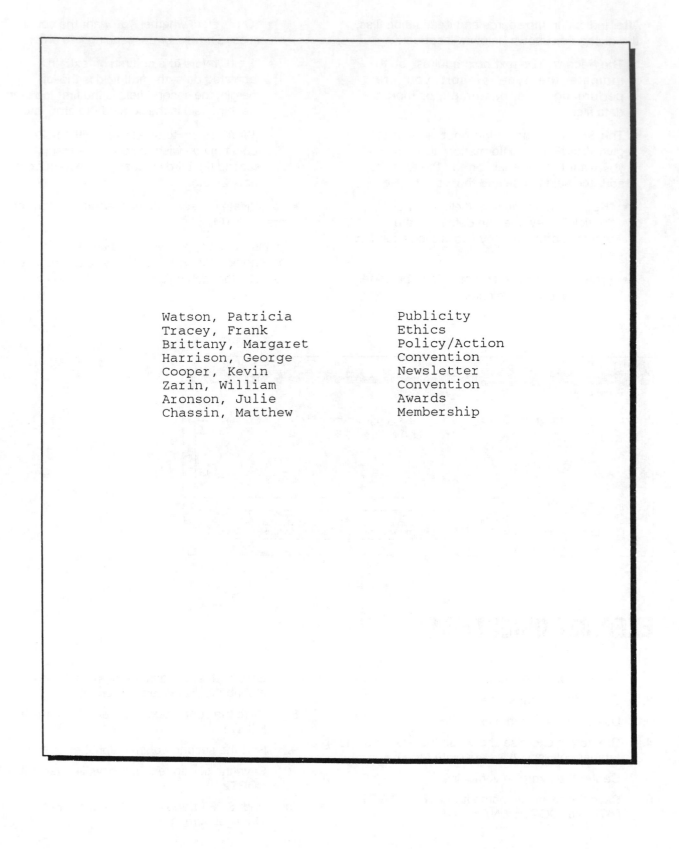

```
Watson, Patricia          Publicity
Tracey, Frank             Ethics
Brittany, Margaret        Policy/Action
Harrison, George          Convention
Cooper, Kevin             Newsletter
Zarin, William            Convention
Aronson, Julie            Awards
Chassin, Matthew          Membership
```

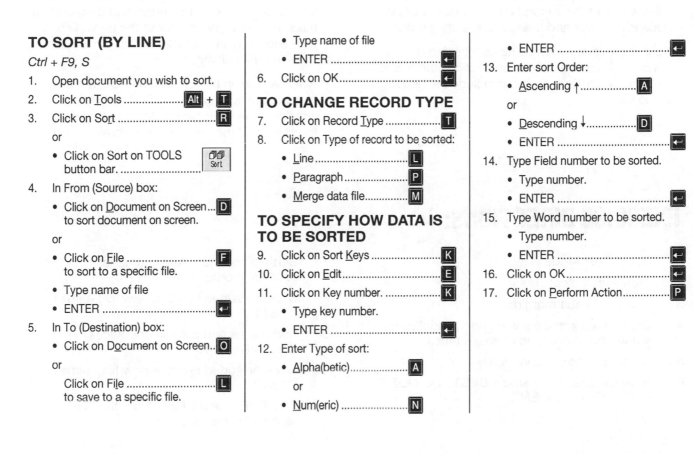

TO SORT (BY LINE)

Ctrl + F9, S

1. Open document you wish to sort.
2. Click on Tools .... `Alt` + `T`
3. Click on Sort .... `R`

   or

   - Click on Sort on TOOLS button bar. .... `[Sort]`

4. In From (Source) box:

   - Click on Document on Screen... `D`
     to sort document on screen.

   or

   - Click on File .... `F`
     to sort to a specific file.
   - Type name of file
   - ENTER .... `↵`

5. In To (Destination) box:

   - Click on Document on Screen.. `O`

   or

   Click on File .... `L`
   to save to a specific file.

- Type name of file
- ENTER .... `↵`

6. Click on OK.................................. `↵`

TO CHANGE RECORD TYPE

7. Click on Record Type .... `T`
8. Click on Type of record to be sorted:

   - Line .... `L`
   - Paragraph .... `P`
   - Merge data file.............. `M`

TO SPECIFY HOW DATA IS TO BE SORTED

9. Click on Sort Keys .... `K`
10. Click on Edit................................ `E`
11. Click on Key number. .... `K`

    - Type key number.
    - ENTER .... `↵`

12. Enter Type of sort:

    - Alpha(betic).................... `A`

      or

    - Num(eric) .... `N`

- ENTER .... `↵`

13. Enter sort Order:

    - Ascending ↑.................. `A`

    or

    - Descending ↓................ `D`
    - ENTER .... `↵`

14. Type Field number to be sorted.

    - Type number.
    - ENTER .... `↵`

15. Type Word number to be sorted.

    - Type number.
    - ENTER .... `↵`

16. Click on OK................................ `↵`
17. Click on Perform Action.............. `P`

BASIC SORTING: BY LINE

NOTES:

- In this exercise, you will create a two-column table and sort the second column numerically in ascending order and then in descending order.

- Note that this exercise contains a centered heading. If you sorted the second column of this exercise, WordPerfect would include the heading in the sort.

- To sort columns containing other text, you must first block the text to be sorted and then perform the sort. Place your cursor at the beginning of the second column, block the text (Alt + F4); then sort the column.

- When you are in the Sort Dialog Box, remember that you are sorting "Field 3." WordPerfect considers the left margin field one; the first tab, field two; and the third tab, field three.

EXERCISE DIRECTIONS:

1. Select Text Mode view.
2. Start with a clear screen.
3. Use the default margins.
4. Create the exercise shown on the right using tabular columns. (Use absolute tabs.)
5. Center the exercise vertically.
6. Save the exercise; name it **DEBT**. *DO NOT EXIT THE DOCUMENT.*
7. Sort the second column numerically in ascending order.
8. Save the sorted text to a new file; name it **DEBT1**.
9. Sort the second column numerically in descending order.
10. Save the sorted text to a new file; name it **DEBT2**.
11. Print DEBT1 and DEBT2 from the File Manager screen (F5).

```
              OUTSTANDING ACCOUNTS
                    OCTOBER

ABC Carpets                        4,4456.87
R & R Jewelers                       786.77
Alison's Sweet Shoppe                234.56
Harrison Taylor, Ltd.              2,192.33
P & A Brands, Inc.                   456.99
Jolson Brothers                    1,443.98
```

TO BLOCK SORT

1. Place cursor on first line to be sorted.
2. Highlight text to be sorted........ `Alt` + `F4`, `↑` `←` `↓` `→`
3. Click on Tools .... `Alt` + `T`
4. Click on Sort .... `R`
5. Follow steps 4-16 on page 405.

BASIC SORTING: BY LINE

NOTES:

- In the previous exercises, you sorted one column of records alphabetically or numerically in ascending or descending order. In other words, you sorted on one "key" field.

- It is possible to sort one column of records (Key 1 field) and then sub-sort another column (Key 2 field) within the first column.

- In this exercise, for example, you are directed to create a membership list. Suppose you wanted to sort the records by "CITY" and then sub-sort the records by "LAST" name. The Key 1 field would be "CITY" and the Key 2 field would be "LAST." The Sort Dialog box appears below. Note the Key 1 entries: since "CITY" is the fifth column (the left margin is considered the first column), the Field number to be sorted is "5", and since there is only one word in the field, the Word to be sorted is "1".

- In order to make entries for "Key 2" you must select "Add" to include another sort line.

- Note the Key 2 entries: since "LAST" is the third column, the field number to be sorted is "3", and since there is only one word in the field, the Word to be sorted is "1". Since sort and sub-sort will be alphabetical, the *Type* is entered as "Alpha" in both cases.

- In this exercise, you will perform several sorts and sub-sorts. Remember, since there is other text in the exercise beside the columns (the title lines and column headings), be sure to block highlight the text to be sorted before starting the sort procedure. DO NOT INCLUDE TITLES AND COLUMN HEADINGS WHEN HIGHLIGHTING THE COLUMNS.

EXERCISE DIRECTIONS:

1. Select Text Mode view.

2. Start with a clear screen.

3. Set left and right margins to "0".

4. Create the exercise on the right using tabular columns. Left-align column headings. Leave two spaces between columns.

5. Center the exercise vertically.

6. Save the exercise; name it **JOIN**. *DO NOT EXIT THE DOCUMENT.*

7. Sort the records in alphabetical order by LAST name.

8. Save the sorted text to a new file; name it **JOIN1**.

9. Sort the records in numerical order by ZIP.

10. Save the sorted text to a new file; name it **JOIN2**.

11. Sort the records in numerical order by PHONE.

12. Save the sorted text to a new file; name it **JOIN3**.

13. Sort the records in alphabetical order by CITY and sub-sort in alphabetical order by LAST name.

14. Save the sorted text to a new file; name it **JOIN4**.

15. Sort the records in numerical order by ZIP and sub-sort in alphabetical order by LAST name.

16. Save the sorted text to a new file; name it **JOIN5**.

17. Print one copy of **JOIN1, JOIN2, JOIN3, JOIN4**, and **JOIN5** from the File Manager screen.

```
                    ASTOR ASSOCIATION MEMBERSHIP LIST
                              SPRING 1994

FIRST      LAST      ADDRESS          CITY        ZIP     PHONE

Leah       Davis     54 Wilmer St.    Brooklyn    11234   718-555-7765
Pamela     Johns     234 Davis Dr.    Bronx       10434   212-555-8887
Roy        Porter    500 E. 78 St.    Manhattan   10023   212-555-4343
Edwin      Case      2 Imperial Way   Queens      11434   718-555-9898
David      Asher     61 Chambers St.  Manhattan   10003   212-555-6666
Janice     Paoli     150 Broadway     Manhattan   10011   212-555-8456
Michael    Griffin   2345 Albee St.   Bronx       10456   212-555-3426
Rose       Casen     710 Linden St.   Brooklyn    11234   718-555-2222
Miles      Brown     1640 Ocean Ave.  Brooklyn    11234   718-555-0000
Sharon     Walker    376 Jewel Ave.   Queens      11414   718-555-7676
Robert     Payne     34 W. 68 St.     Manhattan   10011   212-555-5271
Natasha    Alesi     545 Prince St.   Manhattan   10032   212-555-6545
```

BASIC SORTING: TABLES

NOTES:

- WordPerfect can sort data that has been arranged within tables using the Table feature.

- Note the dialog box below. If your cursor is inside a table when you access the Sort feature, WordPerfect automatically enters "Table" as the Record Type. Note, too, that the default in "Key 1" is set for an alpha, ascending sort on "Cell 1". Cell 1 is Column A. Unless you change the settings, the first word in the first line of each cell in Column A will be used as the basis for the sort.

- If there is other text in the table exercise beside the columns (title lines and column headings), be sure to block highlight the text to be sorted before starting the sort procedure.

- In this exercise, you will sort column C (Cell 3) in alphabetical order and save the file. You will then sort column D (cell 4) in descending order and save the file.

CATALOG NUMBER	QUANTITY	DESCRIPTION	UNIT PRICE
23298	10 boxes	Staplers	4.24
3434D	12 boxes	Paper Clips	1.25
4D212	12 each	Blotters	5.00
56721	10 reams	Memo Pads	9.48
90-4P	12 boxes	Disks	7.88
T99-9	10 boxes	Markers	8.65
229-1	50 boxes	Chalk	1.10

Courier 12pt   Cell A1 Doc 2 Pg 1 Ln 1.12" Pos 0.433"

Sort

1. Record Type [Table   ⬍]

2. Sort Keys (Sort Priority)   Key Type   Ord   Cell   Line   Word
                                Add   1   Alpha ↑   1   1   1
                                Edit
                                Delete
                                Insert

3. Select Records: [   ]
4. ☐ Select Without Sorting
5. ☐ Sort Uppercase First   [Perform Action] [View] [Close] [Cancel]

EXERCISE DIRECTIONS:

1. Select Text Mode view.
2. Start with a clear screen.
3. Open **PURCHASE**.
4. Sort the records in alphabetical order by **DESCRIPTION**.
5. Save the sorted text to a new file; name it **PURSORT1**.

6. Sort the records in descending order by UNIT PRICE.
7. Save the sorted text to a new file; name it **PURSORT2**.
8. Print one copy of **PURSORT1** and **PURSORT2** from the File Manager screen (F5).

continued . . .

MIDDLETOWN HIGH SCHOOL

SPRING SUPPLY ORDER
199-

CATALOG NUMBER	QUANTITY	DESCRIPTION	UNIT PRICE
23298	10 boxes	Staplers	4.24
3434D	12 boxes	Paper Clips	1.25
4D212	12 each	Blotters	5.00
56721	10 reams	Memo Pads	9.48
90-4P	12 boxes	Disks	7.88
T99-9	10 boxes	Markers	8.65
229-1	50 boxes	Chalk	1.10

TO SORT A TABLE

Ctrl + F9, S

1. Open table you wish to sort.
2. Place cursor inside the table.
3. Highlight text to be sorted....... Alt + F4 , ↑ ← ↓ →
4. Click on Tools .... Alt + T
5. Click on Sort .... R

    or

    • Click on Sort on TOOLS button bar .... [Sort]

6. In From (Source) box:
    • Click on Document on Screen.. D to sort document on screen

    or

    • Click on File .... F to sort to a specific file.
    • Type name of file.
    • ENTER .... ↵

7. In To (Destination) box:
    • Click on Document on Screen.. O

    or

    Click on File .... L to save to a specific file.
    • Type name of file
    • ENTER .... ↵

8. Click on OK .... ↵

TO SPECIFY HOW DATA IS TO BE SORTED

9. Click on Sort Keys .... K
10. Click on Key number.
    • Type key number.
    • ENTER .... ↵
11. Enter Type of sort:
    • Alpha(betic) .... A

    or

    • Num(eric) .... N
    • ENTER .... ↵

12. Enter sort Order:
    • Ascending ↑ .... A

    or

    • Descending ↓ .... D
    • ENTER .... ↵
13. Type Cell number to be sorted.
    • Type cell location.

    NOTE: Cell 1 is Column A.

    • ENTER .... ↵
14. Type Line to be sorted.
    • Type line number.
    • ENTER............................... ↵.
15. Type Word number to be sorted.
    • Type number.
    • ENTER .... ↵
16. Click on OK .... ↵
17. Click on Perform Action .... P

FILE MANAGER: DELETING, RENAMING, COPYING FILES

NOTES:

- By accessing File Manager (F5), you can:

  – open a file (*Open into New Document*)

  – retrieve a file (*Retrieve into Current Document*)

  – view a file without opening it (*Look*)

  – copy a file (*Copy*)

  – move or rename a file (*Move/Rename*)

  – delete a file (*Delete*)

  – print a file (*Print*)

  – print a list of files in List Files (*Print List*)

  – sort files on File Manager screen by filename, extension, date/time or size (*Sort by*)

  – change the subdirectory displayed on the screen or create new subdirectories (*Change Default Dir*)

  – search for a word or phrase in all files in a subdirectory (*Find*)

  – search to find a single filename or directory quickly (*Search*)

  – search the directory for a particular file (*Name Search*)

- File Manager is accessed by pressing F5, ENTER. This will display all the files in the default directory. If you wish to see files in another directory, press F5 and enter the directory name, and then press ENTER.

```
╔══════════════════ File Manager ══════════════════╗
║ Directory:  C:\WP60\*.*                    06-09-93  02:46a
║ ┌─Sort by: Filename──────────────┐↑ ┌──────────────────────┐
║ │  .    Current    <Dir>         │  │ 1. Open into New Document │
║ │  ..   Parent     <Dir>         │  │ 2. Retrieve into Current Doc │
║ │  GRAPHICS.       <Dir> 06-06-93 11:12p │ 3. Look... │
║ │  LEARN   .       <Dir> 06-06-93 11:12p │ │
║ │  MACROS  .       <Dir> 06-06-93 11:11p │ 4. Copy... │
║ │  CHARACTR.DOC  124,378 05-03-93 06:00a │ 5. Move/Rename... │
║ │  CHARMAP .TST   69,953 05-03-93 06:00a │ 6. Delete │
║ │  CV      .EXE  208,129 05-03-93 06:00a │ 7. Print... │
║ │  CV{DLG} .FIL   19,012 05-03-93 06:00a │ 8. Print List │
║ │  CV{HLP} .FIL   74,078 05-03-93 06:00a │ │
║ │  CVDA12X .CVX   48,089 05-03-93 06:00a │ 9. Sort by... │
║ │  CVDASC  .CVX   15,562 05-03-93 06:00a │ H. Change Default Dir... │
║ │  CVDBMP  .CVX    8,664 05-03-93 06:00a │ U. Current Dir... F5 │
║ │  CVDCGM  .CVX   50,391 05-03-93 06:00a │ F. Find... │
║ │  CVDCOM  .CVX    2,201 05-03-93 06:00a │ E. Search... F2 │
║ │  CVDDXF  .CVX   52,604 05-03-93 06:00a │ N. Name Search │
║ │  CVDEPS  .CVX    4,328 05-03-93 06:00a │ │
║ │  CVDGIF  .CVX    7,857 05-03-93 06:00a │ * (Un)mark │
║ │  CVDHPGL .CVX   30,196 05-03-93 06:00a │↓ Home,* (Un)mark All │
║ │─Files:    135─────Marked:      0─│  │
║   Free:   2,027,520  Used:   11,819,713 │ [Setup... Shft+F1] [Close] │
╚═══════════════════════════════════════════════════╝
```

- In Lesson 2, you learned to print many files at one time by "marking" them with an asterisk (*). You can delete or copy many files at one time using this same procedure.

- Using the "Rename" option, you can move the file to another directory or subdirectory by specifying a different path and keeping the same filename. Or, you can give the file a new name and keep the file in the current directory.

- To prevent loss of data, it is recommended that backup files be made. The "Copy" option may be used for this purpose. If you are saving your

data on a hard drive or a network, you can use "Copy" to copy your data to an external disk by indicating the drive where the disk is residing. After highlighting the file on the File Manager screen to be copied and selecting "Copy", a dialog box will appear asking you to indicate where to copy the highlighted file. Type "A" (the drive where the external disk resides) and press ENTER.

- In this exercise, you will use File Manager to delete single files and groups of files, and rename files.

```
┌──────────────────────── File Manager ────────────────────────┐
│ Directory:  C:\WP60\LEARN\*.*                08-23-93  10:26p │
│ ┌Sort by: Extension───────────────────┐▲                       │
│ │  .    Current    <Dir>              │   Open into New Document │
│ │  ..   Parent     <Dir>              │   Retrieve into Current Doc │
│ │ LESSON02.    1,593  05-03-93 06:00a │   Look...                │
│ │ LESSON03.    1,399  05-03-93 06:00a │                          │
│ │ LESSON04.    1,384  05-03-93 06:00a │   Copy...                │
│ │ LESSON05.    1,758  05-03-93 06:00a │   Move/Rename...         │
│ │ LESSON06.    2,469  05-03-93 06:00a │   Delete                 │
│ │ LESSON07.    6,071  05-03-93 06:00a │   Print...               │
│ │ LESSON08.    6,142  05-03-93 06:00a │   Print List             │
│ │ LESSON10.   16,413  05-03-93 06:00a │                          │
│ │ LESSON11.    4,307  05-03-93 06:00a │   Sort by...             │
│ │ LESSON12.    9,041  05-03-93 06:00a │   Change Default Dir...  │
│ │ LESSON13.    9,246  05-03-93 06:00a │   Current Dir... F5      │
│ │ LESSON14.    9,259  05-03-93 06:00a │   Find...                │
│ │ LES ─────────────────── Copy ──────────────────────────      │
│ │ LES                                                          │
│ │ LES  Copy Highlighted File to: [a:_                        ] │
│ │ LES                                                          │
│ │ LES  [Directory Tree... F8]  [QuickList... F6]  [OK] [Cancel]│
│ │ F                                                            │
│ │ Free:  11,325,440  Used:     317,263   [Setup... Shft+F1] [Close] │
└───────────────────────────────────────────────────────────────┘
```

EXERCISE DIRECTIONS:

1. Access File Manager (F5).
2. Mark the files indicated on the right for deletion.
3. Delete the files.
4. Rename the files indicated on the right.

continued . . .

DELETE THE FOLLOWING:	RENAME THE FOLLOWING:	
Congrats	Wages	- Money
Company	Week	- 7Days
Tryagain	Work	- Toil
Try	Document	- Voucher
Voyage		
Upndown		

TO DELETE/RENAME/COPY A FILE

F5, ENTER

1. Click on File .... Alt + F
2. Click on File Manager .... F

   or

   • Click on File Mgr in the WPMAIN button bar ....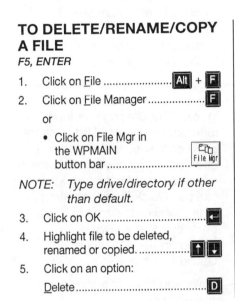

   NOTE: *Type drive/directory if other than default.*

3. Click on OK .... ⏎
4. Highlight file to be deleted, renamed or copied. .... ↑ ↓
5. Click on an option:

   Delete .... D

   • Press Y to confirm

   Move/Rename............................. M

   • Type NEW document name.

   • ENTER .... ⏎

   Copy.. C

   • Type drive/letter, colon (A:) where file will be copied.

   • ENTER .... ⏎

6. Press F7 to return to document.

TO DELETE/COPY A GROUP OF FILES (MARK FILES)

1. Follow steps 1-3 left.
2. Press Shift + 8 to insert asterisk next to each file to be deleted.
3. To delete or copy a group of files:

   • Click on Delete.......................... D

   • Click on Yes............................. Y

   • Click on Yes............................. Y

   OR

   • Click on Copy C

   • Click on Yes............................. Y

   • Type drive/directory where files are to be copied.

FILE MANAGER: SEARCHING FILES

NOTES:

- The "Find" selection in File Manager allows you to search all files in a subdirectory *for a particular word or phrase*. This is particularly helpful if you forget the name of a file but remember some of its contents, or if you are gathering information about a particular topic and want a listing of all files containing that topic. When the search is complete, a new File Manager screen is displayed with only those files which contain the particular word that was searched for.

- When the Find option is selected, the following Find dialog box appears. Note the explanation of each option:

Name — allows you to search the current directory for **filenames** that meet certain conditions. WordPerfect searches the entire displayed list of file names.

Document Summary — allows you to search document summary screens associated with a particular file. (Document Summary may be accessed by selecting Summary from the File main menu [Alt + F, U]. This feature allows you to further identify your document by inserting a non-printing comment in a document.)

First Page — allows you to search only the first page of each document.

Entire Document — allows you to search the entire document.

Conditions — allows you to add a condition when searching for a word. For example, you might want to indicate that you are searching for files containing the word "computer" but only if the word "OCR" is in that file.

QuickFinder — allows you to search a word that was saved in a QuickFinder File Index. The QuickFinder Index is a full-text, alphabetical list of every word contained in the files and directories you specify. Once you create a QuickFinder index, you can use QuickFinder to search the index for words, word patterns or phrases. See software documentation to create a QuickFinder Index.

Undo — allows you to clear a previously entered condition.

- The Search option is used to search for the name of a file in a subdirectory. You may have forgotten how you named the file, but remember the first three letters. Using the Search option, you can enter the first three letters or a filename and WordPerfect will display on the bottom left of the screen the number of files found with that search string. With Name Search, you can highlight a filename by typing that name.

- In this exercise you will search for files containing specified words and quickly locate a file using the Search option.

```
┌──────────────────────── File Manager ────────────────────────┐
│ Directory:  C:\WP60\LEARN\*.*              08-23-93   10:28p  │
│ ┌─Sort by: Extension──────────────┐  ┌────────── Find ──────  │
│ │ .    Current    <Dir>           │↑ │                    Doc │
│ │ ..   Parent     <Dir>           │  │  1. Name...            │
│ │ LESSON02.    1,593  05-03-93 06:00a │                       │
│ │ LESSON03.    1,399  05-03-93 06:00a │  2. Document Summary...│
│ │ LESSON04.    1,384  05-03-93 06:00a │                       │
│ │ LESSON05.    1,758  05-03-93 06:00a ·│  3. First Page...     │
│ │ LESSON06.    2,469  05-03-93 06:00a │                       │
│ │ LESSON07.    6,071  05-03-93 06:00a │  4. Entire Document...│
│ │ LESSON08.    6,142  05-03-93 06:00a │                       │
│ │ LESSON10.   16,413  05-03-93 06:00a │  5. Conditions...     │
│ │ LESSON11.    4,307  05-03-93 06:00a │                       │
│ │ LESSON12.    9,041  05-03-93 06:00a │  6. QuickFinder...    │
│ │ LESSON13.    9,246  05-03-93 06:00a │                       │
│ │ LESSON14.    9,259  05-03-93 06:00a │  7. Undo              │
│ │ LESSON15.   10,476  05-03-93 06:00a │                       │
│ │ LESSON16.   11,824  05-03-93 06:00a │                       │
│ │ LESSON17.   15,905  05-03-93 06:00a │           ┌────────┐  │
│ │ LESSON18.   17,537  05-03-93 06:00a │           │ Cancel │  │
│ │ LESSON19.    3,595  05-03-93 06:00a │↓          └────────┘  │
│ ├─────────────────────────────────┤  Home,* (Un)mark All     │
│   Files:    32      Marked:     0                             │
│   Free:  11,325,440  Used:  317,263  [Setup... Shft+F1] [Close]│
└───────────────────────────────────────────────────────────────┘
```

EXERCISE DIRECTIONS:

1. Access File Manager.

2. Using the Find option, search the Entire Document on your data disk for those which contain the word "computer." Make note of them.

3. Search all files for those which contain the word "Trinitron." Make note of them.

4. Search all files for a letter addressed to Ms. Elizabeth DeKan. Make note of it.

5. Using the Search option, find the file STOCK.

TO SEARCH FOR A WORD IN A FILE

OR

A FILE IN THE FILE MANAGER DIRECTORY

1. Click on File .... `Alt` + `F`

2. Click on File Manager .... `F`

   or

   • Click on *File Mgr* in the WPMAIN button bar .... `File Mgr`

NOTE: Type drive/directory if other than default.

3. Click on OK .... `←`

4. Click on an option:

Find .... `F`

• Click on a Find option:

Name .... `N`

   • Type word pattern

   • ENTER .... `←`

Document Summary .... `D`

   • Type word pattern

   • ENTER .... `←`

First Page .... `P`

   • Type word pattern

   • ENTER .... `←`

Entire Document .... `E`

   • Type word pattern

   • ENTER .... `←`

Conditions .... `C`

   • Select options

   • Type conditions

   • ENTER .... `←`

Quickfinder .... `Q`

Undo .... `U`

5. Click on OK .... `←`

To search for a file in the directory

Search .... `E`

   • Type filename or first several letters of filename.

   • ENTER .... `←`

6. Press F7 to return to File Manager .... `F7`

WORDPERFECT CLIPART GRAPHICS

BORDER4.WPG

ECOLOGO.WPG

GRIZZLY.WPG

INDANCE.WPG

MEDICAL1.WPG

FACTORY.WPG

JEEP.WPG

BORDER7.WPG

HOTAIR.WPG

MTNCLIMB.WPG

FISHTROP.WPG

HOTROD.WPG

JOCKEY.WPG

OVERHD1.WPG

CONDUCT.WPG

LIGHTS.WPG

HUMBIRD.WPG

DRAGON.WPG

GLOBE.WPG

PHEASANT.WPG

PARROT.WPG

SKIER.WPG

TREE.WPG

WINRACE.WPG

SKIPPER.WPG

PENPUSH.WPG

SUMMRCNR.WPG

WATER4.WPG

WIZARD.WPG

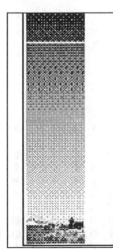

PLAN2.WPG

TIGERHD.WPG

WATER7.WPG

WSKIER.WPG

WINDMILL.WPG

WORDPERFECT SPECIAL CHARACTERS

ASCII -- (0)

```
    0                   1                   2
    0 1 2 3 4 5 6 7 8 9 0 1 2 3 4 5 6 7 8 9 0 1 2 3 4 5 6 7 8 9
  0
 30           ! " # $ % & ' ( ) * + , - . / 0 1 2 3 4 5 6 7 8 9 : ;
 60   < = > ? @ A B C D E F G H I J K L M N O P Q R S T U V W X Y
 90   Z [ \ ] ^ _ ` a b c d e f g h i j k l m n o p q r s t u v w
120   x y z { | } ~
```

Multinational -- (1)

```
    0                   1                   2
    0 1 2 3 4 5 6 7 8 9 0 1 2 3 4 5 6 7 8 9 0 1 2 3 4 5 6 7 8 9
  0
 30   Ä ä À à Å å Æ æ Ç ç É é È è Ë ë Ê ê Í í Î î Ï ï Ĭ ĭ ß K Ĳ ĳ Á Ñ á ñ Â å
 60   Ô ô Ö ö Ò ò Ú ú Ç ú Ù ù Ü ü Ù ù Ý ý Ã ã Đ ð Ø ø Õ õ Ę ę Ğ ğ Đ đ Ø ø
 90   Ă ă Ą ą Ą ą Ć ć Č č Ç ç Č č Ç ç Ċ ċ Đ đ IJ ij Ĵ ĵ Ķ ķ Ĺ ĺ Ľ ľ Ļ ļ
120   Ģ ģ Ĝ ĝ Ġ ġ Ĥ ĥ Ħ ħ İ ı IJ ij Ĵ ĵ Ķ ķ Ŗ ŗ Ř ř Ŗ ŗ Ŝ ŝ Ś ś Š š Ż ż
150   Ĺ ĺ Ł ł Ń ń Ň ň Ņ ņ Ő ő Ő ő Ő ő IJ ij Œ œ Ŕ ŕ Ř ř Ŗ ŗ Ŗ ŗ Ş ş Š š Ż ż Ż ż
180   Ŝ ŝ Ţ ţ Ţ ţ Ţ ţ Ŭ ŭ Ų ų Ů ů Ű ű Ũ ũ Ơ ơ Ư ư Ŵ ŵ Ẃ ẃ Ý ý Ŷ ŷ
210   Ŋ ŋ Đ đ Ŧ ŧ Ŀ ŀ Ŧ ŧ
240   Ő ő
```

Phonetic -- (2)

```
    0                   1                   2
    0 1 2 3 4 5 6 7 8 9 0 1 2 3 4 5 6 7 8 9 0 1 2 3 4 5 6 7 8 9
  0
 30
 60
 90
120
```

Box Drawing -- (3)

```
    0                   1                   2
    0 1 2 3 4 5 6 7 8 9 0 1 2 3 4 5 6 7 8 9 0 1 2 3 4 5 6 7 8 9
  0
 30
 60
```

Typographic Symbols -- (4)

```
    0                   1                   2
    0 1 2 3 4 5 6 7 8 9 0 1 2 3 4 5 6 7 8 9 0 1 2 3 4 5 6 7 8 9
  0
 30
 60
 90
```

Iconic Symbols -- (5)

```
    0                   1                   2
    0 1 2 3 4 5 6 7 8 9 0 1 2 3 4 5 6 7 8 9 0 1 2 3 4 5 6 7 8 9
  0
 30
 60
 90
120
150
180
210
240
```

Math/Scientific -- (6)

	0	1	2	3	4	5	6	7	8	9
0	¬	±	≤	≥	∝	Å	/	∖	+	∣
30	▼	·	∙	,	°	∘	μ	÷	×	∫
60	←	↶	↕	⊥	□	■	◇	◆	[	]
90			∀							
120										
150										
180			ℰ	ℱ	ℂ	I	N	R		
210	⧫	ℰ	ℱ	ℂ	I	N	R			

Math/Scientific Ext. -- (7)

	0	1	2	3	4	5	6	7	8	9
0	⌈	⌉	∣	_	√	‾	Σ	Π	∐	
30		}	}							
60		∪	∩							
90		→	←							
120										
150	∧	⋀	∨	⋁	⊗	⊗	⊕	⊕	⊙	⊙
180	⊖	⊖	⊕	⊕						
210	≂	≃	≃	≃	·	≡				

Greek -- (8)

	0	1	2	3	4	5	6	7	8	9
0	Α	α	Β	β	Β	ϐ	Γ	γ	Δ	δ
30	Ο	ο	Π	π	Ρ	ρ	Σ	σ	Σ	ς
60	Ϊ	ϊ	Ϋ	ό	ύ	Ϋ	ϋ	Ω	ώ	
90										
120										
150										
180										
210						F	Ϙ	Ϡ		

Hebrew -- (9)

	0	1	2	3	4	5	6	7	8	9
0	א	ב	ג	ד	ה	ו	ז	ח	ט	י
30										
60										
90										

Cyrillic -- (10)

	0	1	2	3	4	5	6	7	8	9
0	А	а	Б	б	В	в	Г	г	Д	д
30	О	о	П	п	Р	р	С	с	Т	т
60	Э	э	Ю	ю	Я	я	Ѕ	ѕ	Ѓ	ѓ
90										
120										
150			Ѳ	ѳ						
180										
210										
240										

APPENDIX B

Proofreaders' Marks

Symbol	Meaning	Edited	Corrected
	Transpose	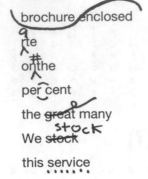brochure enclosed	enclosed brochure
	Insert	rte	rate
	insert space	on the	on the
	Close	per cent	percent
	Delete	the ~~great~~ many	the many
	Change word	stock We stock	We stock
stet or…	Do not delete	this service	this service will
⑤ or .⑤]	Indent number of spaces or inches shown	⑤ Each year we	Each year we
→ or →]	Move to the right or tab	→ it is	it is
← [←	Move to the left	← We should	We should
/	Change capital left to lowercase	in your Company	in your company
≡	Change lowercase letter to capital	if he comes	If he comes
▬▬	Change to all capitals	Business	BUSINESS
ss	Use single spacing	ss { I think he will be there.	I think he will be there
ds	Use double spacing	ds { She will not go if you go also	She will not go if you go also.
▬	Underscore	This is <u>not</u> correct	This is <u>not</u> correct
▬▬	Double Underscore	This is <u>not</u> correct	This is <u>not</u> correct
∿∿∿	Use bold	This is not correct	This is **not** correct
◯	Spell out	Send ③ people	Send three people
◯→	Move as shown	Try to find the document word in the long.	Try to find the word in the long document
¶	New paragraph	This note was past due as of last week. We know this to be true.	The note was past due as of last week. We know this to be true.
] [	Center	] Meeting Agenda [	Meeting Agenda
< >	Use thesaurus to replace word	The meeting was <noisy>	The meeting was boisterous

382

APPENDIX C

QUICK REFERENCE TO WORDPERFECT KEYSTROKES

FEATURE	MENU	KEYBOARD	QUICK KEYS
APPEND	Edit, Append	Alt + E	Alt + F4, Highlight, Ctrl + F4, A
BOLD	Font, Bold	Alt + O	F6
BOOKMARK	Edit, Bookmark	Alt + E	Shift + F12
BUTTON BAR	View	Alt + V	—
BUTTON BAR SETUP	View, Button Bar Setup	Alt + V	—
CENTER	Layout, Alignment	Alt + L	Shift + F6
CENTER PAGE	Layout, Page	Alt + L	Shift + F8, P
CLOSE	File, Close	Alt + F	F7, Y, N
CHANGE VIEW MODE	View	Alt + V	Ctrl + F3
COLUMNS	Layout, Columns	Alt + L	Alt + F7
CONVERT CASE	Edit, Convert Case	Alt + E	Shift + F3
COPY	Edit, Copy	Alt + E	—
CUT	Edit, Cut	Alt + E	Block Text, Ctrl + X
DATE CODE	Tools, Date, Code	Alt + T	Shift + F5
DATE TEXT	Tools, Date, Text	Alt + T	Shift + F5
DECIMAL TABS		Ctrl + F6	
DELETE	Edit, Cut and Paste	Alt + E	—
DOUBLE INDENT	Layout, Alignment	Alt + L	Shift + F4
END FIELD code	—	—	F9
END RECORD code	—	—	Shift + F9
ENDNOTE	Layout, Endnote	Alt + L	Ctrl + F7
ENVELOPES	Layout, Envelope	Alt + L	Alt + F12
ESCAPE	—	—	Esc
EXIT	File, Exit WP	Alt + F	F7, N, Y
FILE MANAGER	File, File Manager	Alt + F	F5
FLUSH RIGHT	Layout, Alignment	Alt + L	Alt + F6
FONT	Font, Font	Alt + O	Ctrl + F8
FOOTNOTE	Layout, Footnote	Alt + L	Ctrl + F7
GO TO	Edit, Go to	Alt + E	Ctrl + Home
GRAMMATIK	Tools, Writing Tools	Alt + T	Alt + F1
GRAPHICS	Graphics, Graphics Boxes	Alt + G	Alt + F9
HANGING INDENT	Layout, Alignment	Alt + L	—
HARD PAGE BREAK	—	—	Ctrl + Return
HARD SPACE	—	—	Home + Spacebar

HEADERS/FOOTERS	Layout, Header/Footer/Watermark	Alt + L	Shift + F8
HELP	Help	Alt + H	F1
HIDE RULER/BUTTON BAR			
HYPHENATION	Layout, Line	Alt + L	Shift + F8
INDENT	Layout, Alignment	Alt + L	F4
ITALICS	Font, Italic	Alt + O	Ctrl + I
JUSTIFY	Layout, Justification	Alt + L	Shift + F8, L, J
Right	—	—	R
Center	—	—	C
Full	—	—	F
Left	—	—	L
LABELS	Layout, Page	Alt + L	Shift + F8, P, L
LINES (GRAPHIC)	Graphics, Graphics Lines	Alt + G	Alt + F9
LINE DRAW	Graphics, Line Draw	Alt + G	Ctrl + F3
LINE SPACING	Layout, Line	Alt + L	Shift + F8, L, S
MACRO			
Record	Tools, Macro	Alt + T	Ctrl + F10
Play	Tools, Macro	Alt + T	Alt + F10
MARGINS	Layout, Margins	Alt + L	Shift + F8
MATH	Tools, Math	Alt + T	Alt + F7, M
MERGE	Tools, Merge	Alt + T	Shift + F9, Ctrl + F9
MOVE (CUT AND PASTE)	Edit, Cut and Paste	Alt + E	Block Text, Ctrl + Del
NEW DOCUMENT	File, New	Alt + F	—
OPEN DOCUMENT	File, Open	Alt + F	Shift + F10
OUTLINE	Tools, Outline	Alt + T	Ctrl + F5
NUMBER OF COPIES	File, Print	Alt + F	Shift + F7, N
PAGE NUMBER	Layout, Page	Alt + L	Shift + F8
PAPER SIZE/TYPE	Layout, Page	Alt + L	Shift + F8
PASTE	Edit , Paste	Alt + E	Ctrl + V
PRINT	File, Print/Fax	Alt + F	Shift + F7
PRINT PREVIEW	File, Print Preview	Alt + F	Shift + F7
REPLACE	Edit, Replace	Alt + E	Alt + F2
RETRIEVE	File, Retrieve	Alt + F	Shift + F10, Retrieve
REVEAL CODES	View, Reveal Codes	Alt + V	Alt + F3
SAVE			
And Continue	File, Save	Alt + F	Ctrl + F12
And Clear	File, Close	Alt + F	F7, Y, N

And Exit	File, Exit	Alt + F	F7, Y, Y
SAVE AS	File, Save As	Alt + F	F10
SEARCH	Edit, Search	Alt + E	F2
SELECT TEXT	Edit, Select	Alt + E	Alt + F4
SORT	Tools, Sort	Alt + T	Ctrl + F9, S
SPELL	Tools, Writing Tools	Alt + T	Alt + F1
SUPER/SUBSCRIPT	Font, Font	Alt + O	Ctrl + F8, P
TAB SET	Layout, Tab Set	Alt + L	Shift + F8, L
TABLES	Layout, Tables	Alt + L	Alt + F7
THESAURUS	Tools, Writing Tools	Alt + T	Alt + F1
TYPEOVER	—	—	Ins
UNDELETE	Edit, Undelete	Alt + E	Esc
UNDERLINE	Font, Underline	Alt + O	F8
UNDO	Edit, Undo	Alt + E	Ctrl + Z
WATERMARK	Layout, Header/Footer /Watermark	Alt + L	Shift + F8, H
WIDOW/ORPHAN	Layout, Other	Alt + L	Shift + F8
WP CHARACTERS	Font, WP Characters	Alt + O	Ctrl + W
ZOOM	View, Zoom	Alt + V	—

APPENDIX D

INDEX OF WORDPERFECT FUNCTIONS

386

SUPPORT MATERIALS
FOR LEARNING WORDPERFECT 6

Solutions/Data Disk

Provides the data for each exercise in this book as well as the solution as it should appear on your screen. Reduces keyboarding time and enables the trainer to skip different exercises. Check formatting codes and check printer capabilities.

3 1/2 Disk   Cat. No. 5W36...**$7.50 each**
Cat. No. SW36SL...**$65 site license**

Transparencies for Training

Selected transparencies of screens, menus and dialog boxes. Call outs define and explain as you teach.

20 Transparencies   Cat. No. T26 ....**$50**

Test yourself on WordPerfect 6

Can you turn *this...*   **into** *this?*

Designed to measure your software skills with a suggested time frame and point scale to determine your competency level.

Includes booklet and 3 1/2 disk   Cat. No. T-WP60.......................**$14.95**

DDC PUBLISHING (800)528-3897 FAX (800)528-3862